2nd edition

Teaching Assistant's

HANDBOOK

NVQ & SVQ Levels 2 & 3

Teena Kamen

HODDER
EDUCATION
AN HACHETTE UK COMPANY

To my son, Tom Jennings
With love and affection

Orders: please contact Bookpoint Ltd, 130 Milton Park, Abingdon, Oxon OX14 4SB.
Telephone: (44) 01235 827720. Fax: (44) 01235 400454. Lines are open from 9.00–5.00,
Monday to Saturday, with a 24-hour message answering service. You can also order
through our website www.hoddereducation.co.uk.

British Library Cataloguing in Publication Data
A catalogue record for this title is available from the British Library.

ISBN: 978 0 340 95938 1

First Published 2008
Impression number   10 9 8 7 6 5 4
Year   2012 2011 2010 2009

Hachette UK's policy is to use papers that are natural, renewable and recyclable
products and made from wood grown in sustainable forests. The logging and
manufacturing processes are expected to conform to the environmental regulations of
the country of origin.

Cover photos © Digital Vision/Getty Images, Purestock and Digital Vision
Typeset by Pantek Arts Ltd, Maidstone, Kent
Printed in Italy for Hodder Education, an Hachette UK Company, 338 Euston Road,
London NW1 3BH

Contents

Acknowledgements   iv

Introduction   v

How to use this book   vi

Principles and values   vii

1   Supporting learning activities   1

2   Safeguarding children   17

3   Supporting children's development   49

4   Promoting positive pupil behaviour   86

5   Promoting positive working relationships   111

6   Developing professional practice   138

7   Promoting children's well-being and resilience   161

8   Supporting children's play   181

9   Supporting curriculum delivery   197

10 Supporting literacy and numeracy activities   222

11 Supporting pupils with additional needs   255

12 Supporting the wider work of the school   283

Appendix: Record of key tasks   298

Glossary   303

Bibliography   305

Index   309

Acknowledgements

Many thanks to the pupils and staff at Rood End Primary School and Withymoor Primary School where I gained much of my experience of working with children.

Thanks also to the students and staff at Birmingham College of Food, Tourism & Creative Studies and Sandwell College of Further & Higher Education where I developed my skills of designing and implementing learning/assessment materials for students on early years care and education courses.

Special thanks to Karl Doughty, Chris Helm, Terry James and Pauline White for their technical (and emotional!) support during the writing of this book.

The author and the publishers would like to thank the following for permission to reproduce material in this book:

p.3, 132, 141, 219, 233, 248, 286 educationphotos.co.uk/Walmsley; p.90 Jacky Chapman/Alamy; p.166 CW Images/Alamy; p.186 Sally and Richard Greenhill/Alamy; p.234 Jacky Chapman/Photofusion; p.237 Sally and Richard Greenhill; p.249 John Birdsall; p.264 Paula Solloway/Photofusion; p.289 Sally Greenhill.

Every effort has been made to trace and acknowledge ownership of copyright. The publishers will be glad to make suitable arrangements with any copyright holders whom it has not been possible to contact.

Introduction

Teaching Assistant's Handbook, 2nd edition is a comprehensive and practical guide to supporting the development and learning of pupils in a variety of education settings including primary, secondary and special schools as well as extended schools.

The book covers practical considerations such as:

- ☆ Supporting the teacher in delivering learning activities
- ☆ Maintaining pupils' safety and security
- ☆ Behaviour management
- ☆ Preparing and maintaining classroom resources
- ☆ Record-keeping
- ☆ Using ICT to support learning
- ☆ Developing effective practice.

The book clearly links theory and practice by exploring different theoretical aspects of children's development (e.g. social, physical, intellectual, communication and emotional) and relating these to providing practical support for teaching and learning in schools. The book explains complex theoretical issues in ways which can be easily understood, but is sufficiently challenging to assist students in developing a sound knowledge-base to complement their practical skills.

There is particular emphasis on the role of the teaching assistant in supporting learning activities, including detailed information on helping pupils to develop literacy and numeracy skills as well as supporting pupils with special educational needs.

This book is for students (and their tutors/assessors) on teaching assistant courses and provides the background knowledge relevant to the requirements of supporting teaching and learning in primary, secondary and special schools.

How to use this book

This book contains the knowledge requirements for a range of topics related to supporting the development and learning of pupils. The book includes practical ideas for linking knowledge and understanding with performance criteria to meet the National Occupational Standards (NOS) in *Supporting Teaching and Learning in Schools* for Levels 2 and 3, and is suitable for students on a wide range of teaching assistant courses including:

- ✰ NVQ/SVQ Levels 2 and 3 in Supporting Teaching and Learning in Schools
- ✰ CACHE Levels 2 and 3 Certificate for Teaching Assistants
- ✰ NCFE Levels 2 and 3 Certificate for Teaching Assistants
- ✰ Edexcel Levels 2 and 3 BTEC Certificate for Teaching Assistants
- ✰ ABC Levels 2 and 3 Certificate for Teaching Assistants
- ✰ OCR Levels 2 and 3 Certificate for Teaching Assistants.

The book may also be of interest to experienced teaching assistants who are updating their current practice as part of their Continuing Professional Development.

The headings in each section are related to NOS Levels 2 and 3 for ease of reference (see the specifications at: www.ukstandards.org/Admin/DB/0090/S64STL%20full%20suite.pdf).

Read the relevant chapter for the topic you are currently studying and do the activities as specified. The **key tasks** can be done in any order, as appropriate to your college and/or school requirements, and can contribute to your formal assessment, e.g. as part of your portfolio of evidence. However, it is suggested that you read Chapter 3: **Supporting children's development** *before* you start planning and implementing your own learning activities for pupils. *Do* remember to follow your school/college guidelines.

You need to complete only the key tasks relevant to the units you are studying and/or your role and responsibilities in school. The appendix at the back of the book will help you to keep a record of the key tasks as you complete them.

Principles and values

All work with children should be underpinned by the principles and values as stated in the National Occupational Standards in Children's Care, Learning and Development.

Principles:

1. The welfare of the child is paramount.
2. Practitioners contribute to children's care, education and learning, and this is reflected in every aspect of practice and service provision.
3. Practitioners work with parents and families who are partners in the care, development and learning of their children and are the child's first and most enduring educators.

Values:

1. The needs, rights and views of the child are at the centre of all practice and provision.
2. Individuality, difference and diversity are equally valued and celebrated.
3. Equality of opportunity and anti-discriminatory practice are actively promoted.
4. Children's health and well-being are actively promoted.
5. Children's personal and physical safety is safeguarded whilst allowing for risk and challenge as appropriate to the capabilities of the child.
6. Self-esteem, resilience and positive self-image are recognised as essential to every child's development.
7. Confidentiality and agreements about confidential information are respected as appropriate unless a child's protection and well-being are at stake.
8. Professional knowledge, skills and values are shared appropriately in order to enrich the experience of children more widely.
9. Best practice requires reflection and a continuous search for improvement.

(NDNA, 2004)

1 Supporting learning activities

Key points:

* ✱ Roles and responsibilities within the school
* ✱ The supporting role of the teaching assistant
* ✱ The responsibilities of the teaching assistant
* ✱ Supporting the teacher in the planning of learning activities
* ✱ Supporting the teacher in the delivery of learning activities
* ✱ Supporting the teacher in the evaluation of learning activities
* ✱ Providing information on pupil progress and responses.

Roles and responsibilities within the school

The teaching assistant and the teacher need to be aware of their different roles. The teacher's role is to plan lessons, direct and assess pupils' learning. The teaching assistant's role is to assist the teacher by supporting pupils during the teaching of the curriculum. The teaching assistant works with the teacher to support pupils' learning within the whole class or works on their own to support the learning of an individual pupil or small group of pupils. Remember, the teaching assistant always works under the direction of the class or subject teacher.

> EXERCISE: Briefly describe the role of the teaching assistant in relation to the teacher.

The roles and responsibilities of others within the school

The headteacher is responsible for all the pupils in the school while each class or subject teacher is responsible for all the pupils in their own class. The teacher is responsible for the learning of all pupils including those with special educational needs and Individual Education Plans or Behaviour Support Plans.

The headteacher and the senior management team (e.g. deputy/assistant headteacher(s), special educational needs co-ordinator (SENCO), Key Stage co-ordinators) are responsible for the creation and maintenance of the learning environment throughout the school as a whole. The class or subject teacher is responsible for the preparation and maintenance of an appropriate learning environment within their own classroom and/or subject area. Working as part of a team, the teacher decides how best to use the resources allocated to the class, which include adult resources such as teaching assistants, nursery nurses and parent helpers as well as the necessary equipment and materials for learning activities. The teacher should ensure that these adults are used to their full potential in order to respond appropriately to the needs of all pupils in the class. As a teaching assistant you must help with the preparation and organisation of the learning environment as directed by the teacher.

> EXERCISE: Briefly outline the role and responsibilities of: the headteacher; deputy/assistant headteacher(s); SENCO; key stage co-ordinators; subject co-ordinators; class/subject teachers.

The supporting role of the teaching assistant

Adults who work in classrooms alongside teachers have various job titles including: learning support assistant; classroom assistant; special needs assistant; and non-teaching assistant. Teaching assistant is now the preferred term for adults (in paid employment) whose main role is to assist the teacher in a primary, secondary or special school.

To function effectively you need to be clear about your role as a teaching assistant. Your role will depend on the school and your experience/qualifications. There may be different requirements between teaching assistants even within the same school. A teaching assistant may have a *general* role working with different classes in a year group/Key Stage or *specific* responsibilities for a pupil, subject area or age group.

> EXERCISE: Make a list of the things expected from you as part of your role in supporting an individual pupil or group of pupils.

Effectively managed, skilled teaching assistants make a valuable contribution to pupil achievement within the learning environment. Teaching assistants may be needed to attend to a pupil's care needs; or they may have a more educational role working with a pupil or group of pupils under the guidance of the class or subject teacher; or they may be involved in implementing a programme devised by a specialist, such as a speech and language therapist.

The term 'teaching assistant' indicates their central role of supporting the teacher. Teachers are responsible for planning and directing pupils' learning. Teaching assistants give *support* to class or subject teachers by *assisting* with the teaching of pupils in a whole class, in small groups or with individuals, but *always* under a teacher's direction.

Teaching assistant supporting pupils

In order to provide effective support, teaching assistants need to know: teacher and school expectations for pupils' progress; learning objectives for pupils; behaviour expectations; inclusion of pupils with special educational needs. Teaching assistants working with specific pupils need information regarding their special educational needs and provision including details of any statement of special educational needs, Individual Education Plans (IEPs) and/or Behaviour Support Plans.

Supporting the pupil

Teaching assistants support the individual pupil by:

- ✰ understanding the pupil's learning support needs
- ✰ listening to the pupil
- ✰ enabling the pupil to access the curriculum
- ✰ respecting and valuing the pupil
- ✰ gaining the pupil's trust and confidence
- ✰ responding appropriately to the pupil's physical needs
- ✰ encouraging independence
- ✰ promoting acceptance by the rest of the class
- ✰ using plenty of praise and rewards.

Supporting the teacher

Teaching assistants support the class or subject teacher by:

- ✰ working in partnership to prepare and maintain the learning environment
- ✰ helping to monitor and evaluate pupil progress
- ✰ providing feedback about pupils' learning and behaviour
- ✰ helping with classroom resources and pupil records.

Supporting the school

Teaching assistants support the school by:

- ✰ working with other members of staff as part of a team
- ✰ attending staff meetings
- ✰ working in partnership with parents
- ✰ making contributions to assessments and reviews

- ☆ knowing and following relevant school policies and procedures
- ☆ recognising and using personal strengths and abilities
- ☆ developing skills through in-service training and other courses.

Supporting the curriculum

Teaching assistants also provide support for the curriculum under the direction and guidance of the class or subject teacher. This involves an awareness and understanding of:

- ☆ theories concerning how pupils think and learn
- ☆ the sequences of expected development
- ☆ factors affecting pupils' learning progress in learning difficulties
- ☆ national curriculum documents
- ☆ the national literacy strategy
- ☆ the national numeracy strategy
- ☆ the planning process.

The responsibilities of the teaching assistant

You need to understand clearly what your responsibilities are as a teaching assistant. Your responsibilities should be set out in your job description if you are already employed as a teaching assistant. (As a student you should have guidelines from your college.)

When you know what your responsibilities are, you will be clear about what is required from you. You should not be required to perform duties or activities that you are not qualified or not allowed to do, for example, give first-aid or administer medicines. However, do not refuse to do a task just because it is not in your job description – sometimes it may be necessary for everyone to help out. (There is more on understanding your responsibilities and those of others in Chapter 6.)

General tasks

Here are some of the general tasks you may be expected to do as a teaching assistant:

- ☆ Set out or put away equipment
- ☆ Help younger pupils, or older pupils who have physical disabilities get ready for a PE lesson
- ☆ Check pupils' work
- ☆ Encourage pupils to correct their own mistakes
- ☆ Supervise practical work activities
- ☆ Keep an individual pupil and/or group on task
- ☆ Assist the pupil(s) to catch up on any missed work
- ☆ Check equipment for safety.

Job Description for a Teaching Assistant

Job title: Teaching Assistant   **Grade:** NVQ Level 2
School: Evergreen Primary School
Responsible to: Key Stage 2 Co-ordinator (Line manager)
Liaises with: Year 4 class teacher
Support teachers (for pupils with special educational needs)
Special Educational Needs Co-ordinator (SENCO)

Main Purpose of Job

As a teaching assistant you will be a member of the Key Stage 2 (KS2) team, under the direct leadership of the KS2 Co-ordinator and supervision of the Year 4 class teacher. Under the class teacher's direction you will support the education and personal/social development of the children through the provision of support in the classroom and establishing a positive relationship with pupils.

Duties and Responsibilities

Support for pupils:

- To help pupils access the subject matter provided by the class teacher
- To supervise individuals/groups of pupils during specified learning activities, as directed by the class teacher, e.g. supervising a group of pupils using computers
- To assist in preparing and maintaining an effective learning environment for pupils
- To provide support for pupils' independent learning
- To ensure the safety of pupils and to assist in their general welfare
- To facilitate pupils' physical, social, emotional and educational development
- To promote and reinforce the self-esteem of all pupils
- To encourage acceptance and inclusion of pupils with special educational needs
- To assist with sick children and deal with minor cuts and grazes
- To develop positive working relationships with the pupils in order to assist pupil progress and attainment.

Support for the teacher:

- To assist the class teacher in the implementation of set tasks for an individual/small group of pupils, including clearing up the classroom before and after activities
- To assist in the production of teaching aids and preparation of work for pupils as required, e.g. charts, displays, work cards and worksheets
- To assist in the monitoring/recording of pupil progress as required by the school
- To support the teacher in providing for the safe supervision of pupils in the classroom
- To provide general classroom help, including preparation of rooms, materials and equipment, e.g. changing/mixing paint, cutting card/paper, setting up PE equipment, covering books/work cards, sharpening pencils, putting away materials/equipment correctly, checking materials, displaying work, duplicating written materials, recording radio/television programmes, cataloguing and processing books/resources
- To assist with classroom administration, e.g. collecting dinner money, lost property.

Support for the school:

- To be aware of the school's policies and procedures
- To understand own role and responsibilities in relation to the school's policies
- To maintain confidentiality in accordance with the school policy
- To attend review meetings for Year 4 pupils with special educational needs
- To attend staff meetings and training sessions as appropriate
- To acquire the full range of skills and knowledge needed to satisfy job requirements.

Support for the curriculum:

- To assist in the delivery of the *Primary Framework for literacy and mathematics* with individuals and small groups of pupils
- To assist with the planning and implementation of learning activities
- To assist with other curriculum duties as appropriate to own role and responsibilities.

Arrangements for Appraisal of Performance

An annual appraisal will provide the opportunity for discussion about own performance and professional development with the line manager.

Specific tasks

Teaching assistants also have specific tasks that the class or subject teacher asks them to do. For example, supporting pupils' learning during a lesson or activity by:

☆ repeating instructions given by the teacher
☆ taking notes for a pupil while the teacher is talking
☆ transcribing a pupil's dictation
☆ clarifying meaning and/or ideas
☆ explaining difficult words to a pupil
☆ promoting the use of dictionaries
☆ reading and clarifying textbook/worksheet activities for a pupil
☆ reading a story to an individual pupil or small group
☆ listening to pupils read
☆ playing a game with an individual pupil or small group
☆ directing computer-assisted learning programmes
☆ assisting pupils with special equipment (e.g. hearing aid or a Dictaphone)
☆ making worksheets and other resources as directed by the teacher
☆ observing/recording pupil progress during an activity
☆ providing any other appropriate assistance during an activity
☆ reporting problems and successes to the teacher
☆ contributing to planning and review meetings about pupils.

> EXERCISE:
> 1. Think about your current role and responsibilities. List examples of your own general and specific tasks.
> 2. If you are already employed as a teaching assistant, include your job description in your portfolio of evidence.

Supporting the teacher in the planning of learning activities

As appropriate to your particular role, you will need to support the teacher in planning, delivering and evaluating learning activities according to the relevant curriculum framework(s) as appropriate to the ages, needs and abilities of the pupils you work with and the requirements of your school. This includes preparing, implementing and monitoring curriculum plans according to the curriculum frameworks for education for your home country: England, Northern Ireland, Scotland or Wales (see Chapter 9).

Planning learning activities

Effective planning is based on pupils' individual needs, abilities and interests, hence the importance of accurate pupil observations and assessments (see sections on observing and assessing development in Chapter 3 and making assessments in Chapter 9). These needs should be integrated into the learning activities for the pupils you work with. These learning activities must be related to the relevant curriculum requirements applicable to the pupils in your own country and workplace (see section on curriculum frameworks in Chapter 9).

Planning learning activities involves a continuous cycle of: identifying learning needs; preparing, organising and implementing learning activities; observing and recording pupil responses; evaluating learning activities; identifying future learning needs.

The planning process involves:

1. Identification of individual learning needs.
2. Specification of intended learning outcomes for the pupil(s).
3. Preparation for the learning activity.
4. Selection of resources for the learning activity.
5. Organisation of the learning activity.
6. Identification of staff roles.
7. Implementation of the learning activity.
8. Observation and recording of pupil responses including achievements/difficulties.
9. Evaluation of the learning activity.
10. Identification of future learning needs.

You will need to follow the agreed plans for all learning activities. When providing support for learning activities, you may be working with several plans:

☆ An overall curriculum plan (usually linked to a topic or theme) demonstrating how the teacher intends to extend pupils' learning within the National Curriculum, the National Literacy Strategy and the National Numeracy Strategy frameworks.

☆ Lesson or activity plans with detailed information about the learning activities including specific learning objectives, resources/staff required and support strategies.

☆ A timetable for the school day outlining when and where the learning activities will take place and including routines that have to be done at specific times, e.g. registration, break/playtime, lunchtime, assembly, home time.

☆ Structured learning programmes for individual pupils, such as particular activities to encourage the development of pupils with special educational needs including Individual Education Plans and individual Behaviour Support Plans.

The teaching assistant's role in planning learning activities

Advanced planning and the detailed preparation of work are central to the effective delivery of the curriculum and to providing appropriate support for teaching and learning. Teachers should involve teaching assistants in the planning and preparation of their work by having regular planning meetings about once a term or every half-term.

In addition, each day the teacher and the teaching assistant should discuss:

- ☆ the teacher's lesson plans
- ☆ the objectives of the learning activities
- ☆ the teaching assistant's contribution to learning activities
- ☆ the type and level of support for the pupils
- ☆ the specific strategies for supporting learning activities.

These regular planning meetings and discussions will help to avoid confusion as both the teacher and the teaching assistant will then be clear about the exact tasks to be performed and the level of support to be provided. Short discussions after lessons are also helpful as teaching assistants can provide feedback to the teacher about the progress of pupils during group or individual learning activities. This feedback can make a valuable contribution to the teacher's assessment of pupils and help with the future planning of learning activities.

As directed by the teacher, you will need to plan, implement and evaluate the learning activities of the pupil or pupils you work with in the school. When planning and/or implementing learning activities, your overall aims should be to:

- ☆ support all the pupils you work with as directed by the teacher
- ☆ ensure each pupil has full access to the curriculum
- ☆ encourage participation by all pupils
- ☆ meet pupils' individual learning needs
- ☆ build on pupils' existing knowledge and skills
- ☆ enable all pupils to achieve their full learning potential.

Some classrooms have a teaching assistant folder that is kept on the teacher's desk or teaching base. The teacher may write notes for the teaching assistant in an exercise book or there may be separate teaching assistant plans for each lesson or learning activity. These teaching assistant plans may include space for you to record what you actually did and what happened to the pupils.

EXERCISE:
Give examples of how you plan activities.

Supporting the teacher in the delivery of learning activities

The teaching assistant supports the delivery of learning activities as directed by the teacher. To provide effective support the teaching assistant must know and understand the objectives of the learning activities and the strategies to support pupils' learning.

As a teaching assistant, you should be aware of your experience and expertise in relation to supporting learning activities and how this relates to the planned activities. You should ensure that you are adequately prepared for your contribution to the learning activities such as understanding the relevant subject knowledge and support strategies as well as obtaining appropriate resources. This may mean discussing development opportunities to improve your skills in areas where you currently lack experience or expertise (see Chapter 6).

When supporting learning activities you should remember these important points:

1. **Develop an effective partnership with the class teacher:** know and understand your exact role; know and understand the teacher's role; contribute to the planning of learning activities; use the same strategies as the teacher to support learning; share the same goals as the teacher for pupils' learning; establish good communication with the teacher.

2. **Follow agreed class rules and class routines:** how the pupils enter and exit the classroom; classroom organisation; the storage and use of materials and equipment; discipline – approaches to pupil behaviour; rewards and sanctions; marking work.

3. **Understand the teaching methods for learning activities:** class teaching; question time; group work; individual tasks.

4. **Provide effective support during learning activities:** understand requirements of the lesson; know the intended learning outcomes for pupils; prepare and organise resources as directed by the teacher; know the group, e.g. their character, ability, strengths, individual needs, etc; know what support individuals within the group may need; use appropriate support strategies; give the teacher feedback on the pupils' responses including their achievements and any difficulties experienced during the learning activity.

(Balshaw and Farrell, 2002)

The teaching assistant's role in delivering learning activities

Your role will depend on the school and your own experience and/or qualifications. As a teaching assistant you may have a general role working with different classes in a year group/Key Stage or specific responsibilities for a pupil, subject area or age group. When working with a specific pupil or pupils you should have information regarding their special educational needs and any special provision including details of statements of special educational needs, Individual Education Plans and/or Behaviour Support Plans. You may be involved in implementing a structured programme designed by a specialist such as a speech and language therapist (see Chapter 11).

When delivering learning activities you should ensure that you make accurate and detailed records of what has been planned and delivered in order to: clarify the aims and learning objectives of activity plans; avoid contradictory strategies/unnecessary duplication of work; use the time available more effectively; evaluate the success of plans/activities; provide continuity and progression for future planning.

Preparing for learning activities

The teacher's short-term plans (e.g. individual lesson plans and/or activity plans) should include information about your role in delivering learning activities. These plans should include the learning objectives and the teacher's expectations of what the learning outcomes for the pupils might be. Use your personal timetable, the class timetable and the available systems of communication within the school to help you know and understand what you have to do before you deliver the learning activity; where, when and with whom the learning activity will take place; and why the learning activity is being implemented.

You need the relevant lesson plans at least the day before so that you have time to prepare what you need for the learning activities. This preparation may involve: finding resources; doing some photocopying; checking equipment and its availability; reading up on a subject; finding artefacts or reference books for the pupils; and asking the teacher for further information.

You need time and the opportunity to discuss the teacher's plans beforehand. If you do not understand any aspect of the learning activities you are expected to support, then you must ask the teacher for further information. You will not be able to provide effective support for the pupils unless you are absolutely clear about the requirements of each learning activity (Watkinson, 2003).

Your role in delivering learning activities involves assisting the teacher by:

- ✮ preparing the learning environment to meet the individual learning needs of each pupil in the class
- ✮ providing appropriate learning activities for individuals and groups of pupils
- ✮ selecting and using appropriate learning materials
- ✮ supervising an individual or small group of pupils
- ✮ maintaining pupil safety during the learning activity
- ✮ interacting with the pupils in ways that focus their attention on the learning potential of the learning materials, e.g. asking questions such as 'What happens if you do…?'
- ✮ using praise and encouragement to help pupils participate fully in learning activities
- ✮ observing pupil responses during the learning activity (see below).

EXERCISE:
Describe your role in delivering learning activities.

Organising learning resources

The learning resources in the school should support learning activities across the full range of the curriculum. A wide variety of learning resources will help to maintain interest in the subject area and help to support individual learning needs. The school should decide on spending priorities when allocating resources as some areas of the curriculum may require more substantial or expensive learning materials than others. Careful criteria should be set for selecting and using learning resources, for example: health and safety; ages/ability levels of the pupils; quality and durability; versatility and value for money; special educational needs (e.g. specialist or modified learning materials); equal opportunities (e.g. resources reflecting positive images of cultural diversity, gender roles and people with disabilities).

The organisation of learning resources is also an important consideration. For example, to encourage independent learning, classroom resources should be organised in ways that allow pupils to locate the learning resources they need and to put them away afterwards. Learning resources should be clearly labelled and stored where they are accessible to the pupils. Learning resources must be regularly maintained, cleaned and checked for damage. Items that are incomplete, unhygienic or past repair should be appropriately discarded. (There is more detailed information about resources in Chapter 12.)

Providing support for learning activities

When supporting learning activities you will need to: deliver learning activities as directed by the teacher; use appropriate resources and support strategies for each pupil's needs and abilities; adapt learning activities to meet the learning objectives; assist each pupil at an appropriate level; and promote independent learning (see below).

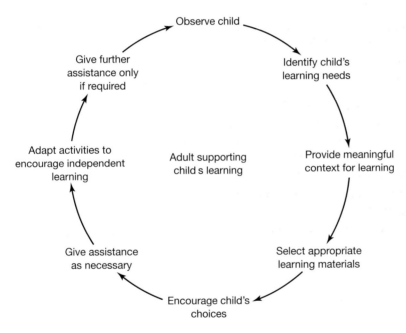

Supporting children's learning

The strategies to support learning should ensure that each pupil participates fully in every lesson. As a teaching assistant you should:

- ☆ ensure that pupils in your group(s) concentrate and behave responsibly
- ☆ ensure that pupils understand and follow the teacher's instructions
- ☆ remind pupils of teaching points made by the teacher
- ☆ translate or explain words and phrases used by the teacher
- ☆ use the correct language and vocabulary for the learning activity
- ☆ question pupils and encourage their participation

- ☆ organise and participate in appropriate play activities or games
- ☆ help pupils to use equipment and resources relevant to the learning activity
- ☆ use visual or practical aids, or a computer with suitable software, especially when supporting pupils with special educational needs
- ☆ look for and note any common problems that pupils have, or mistakes that they make, so that the teacher can address these in future learning activities.

Promoting independent learning

You need to arrange with the teacher the strategies and resources to be used to promote independent learning. To promote independent learning you can: encourage and support pupils in making decisions about their own learning; provide appropriate levels of assistance for individual pupils; use technology to enable pupils to work more independently; provide challenges to promote independent learning; encourage pupils to review their own learning strategies, achievements and future learning needs. All pupils should be encouraged to develop independent learning in preparation for the next Key Stage, college, work and adult life.

Younger pupils should be encouraged to develop these independent learning skills:

- ☆ Take turns to speak and listen
- ☆ Respond appropriately to other pupils and adults
- ☆ Know, understand and apply class/school rules
- ☆ Ask an appropriate adult for help
- ☆ Make choices about books
- ☆ Listen carefully and follow verbal instructions
- ☆ Use pre-selected learning materials for independent learning
- ☆ Select resources independently
- ☆ Follow simple written instructions
- ☆ Work with a partner to check or review work
- ☆ Use spelling aids, e.g. individual wordbooks, topic word banks and simple dictionaries
- ☆ Use the school library with support
- ☆ Access information from pictures, artefacts, simple charts and diagrams with support.

Older pupils should be encouraged to continue using the skills listed above and also to develop these independent learning skills:

- ☆ Start work independently
- ☆ Interpret written instructions independently
- ☆ Work co-operatively with other pupils
- ☆ Manage own reading book and help keep reading record up to date

- ✰ Put name on any loose paperwork
- ✰ Put correct date on all work
- ✰ Aim to complete all tasks set in a given time
- ✰ Carefully organise and keep own work
- ✰ Be able to make notes during lessons
- ✰ Use the school library independently
- ✰ Use computers independently
- ✰ Access information from artefacts, simple charts, diagrams and text with increasing independence
- ✰ Use information from various sources and include references.

EXERCISE:
1. What strategies have you used to support pupils' learning?
2. Give examples of how you have promoted independent learning, e.g. using ICT skills.

Pupil responses and preferences

Pupil responses should also be considered when providing support for learning activities. Take notice of non-verbal responses and preferences demonstrated by the pupils; these are just as important as what the pupil says. You should be sensitive to pupil needs and desires. Despite careful planning, you may find that when you are delivering a learning activity it is not appropriate for all the pupils you are working with. You will need to monitor pupils' responses to learning activities and take appropriate action to modify or adapt activities to achieve the intended learning objectives or provide additional activities to extend their learning.

You can use pupils' positive or negative responses to modify or extend activities to meet each pupil's needs more effectively. For example, if the learning objectives prove too easy or too difficult, you may have to set new goals. By breaking down learning activities into smaller tasks, you may help individual pupils to achieve success more quickly. You may need to provide an alternative version of the activity or you might be able to present the learning materials in different ways or offer a greater/lesser level of assistance.

You may need to modify or adapt activities for the following reasons: the pupil lacks concentration; the pupil is bored or uninterested; the pupil finds the activity too difficult or too easy; the pupil is upset or unwell (if so, you may need to abandon/postpone the activity). In modifying plans you are continuing a cycle of planning and implementing activities. Remember to give the pupils encouragement and positive feedback to reinforce and sustain their interest and efforts in the learning process. (See section on the importance of praise and encouragement in Chapter 5.)

Dealing with problems and difficulties

Regular observations and evaluations of learning activities are helpful in identifying any potential problems pupils may have in their development, learning or behaviour. By carefully observing pupils during learning activities you can identify: the ways in which individual pupils learn; how pupils interact with each other, e.g. behaviour and social skills; any difficulties pupils may have during the learning activity, e.g. following instructions, performing the necessary skills or understanding concepts.

A continuous record of a pupil's learning difficulties can help identify specific problems. Working with parents, colleagues and specialist advisors (if necessary) the teacher can then plan a suitable programme to enable the pupil to overcome these difficulties. Observations can provide a check that the pupil's learning is progressing in the expected ways.

You will need to be able to resolve any difficulties you may have in supporting the learning activities as planned, for example: modifying or adapting an inappropriate activity; coping with insufficient materials or equipment breakdown (see Chapter 12); dealing with unco-operative or disruptive pupils (see Chapter 4). You must report any problems you are unable to resolve to the teacher.

Supporting the teacher in the evaluation of learning activities

After you have planned and/or delivered a learning activity, you will need to evaluate it. Some evaluation also occurs during the learning activity, providing continuous assessment of a pupil's performance. It is important to evaluate the learning activity so that you can: identify whether the learning activity has been successful, e.g. the aims and learning objectives or outcomes have been met; consider the ways in which the learning activity might be modified/adapted to meet the individual learning needs of the pupil or pupils; provide information on learner responses and whether a particular learning activity has been successful to the teacher, SENCO or other professionals.

Evaluating learning activities

When involved in evaluating learning activities for an individual pupil or group of pupils, remember these important points:

- ✮ How do the pupil or pupils respond to the learning activity?
- ✮ Do you need to adapt the original plan, e.g. change the resources or the timing of the learning activity?
- ✮ Did the pupil(s) achieve the intended learning objectives?
- ✮ How effective was the preparation and delivery of the learning activity?
- ✮ Make a note of pupil achievements and/or any difficulties.
- ✮ Record these using methods as appropriate to your role.
- ✮ Report achievements, difficulties or concerns to the teacher.
- ✮ Have you identified any future learning needs for the pupil(s) as a result of pupil responses during this learning activity?

☆ Are there any possible modifications you could make for future learning activities?

☆ Discuss your ideas with the teacher.

Providing information on pupil progress and responses

You will need to keep accurate records of pupil progress and responses to learning activities in order to feed back information to the teacher and other relevant people. You can record significant aspects of pupil participation and progress during the learning activity (if possible) or shortly afterwards so that you remember important points.

After the activity, use all the available relevant information to evaluate the effectiveness of your planning and implementation of the activity, e.g. information from parents, colleagues and other professionals. You must provide feedback about the pupils' learning achievements to the teacher. Any suggested changes to future activity plans should be agreed with the teacher and other relevant staff.

You can provide information on pupil progress and responses by considering these questions:

1. Did the pupil(s) achieve the objectives/outcomes set? If not, why not?
2. If the pupil(s) has achieved the objectives, what effect has it had (e.g. on behaviour, learning or any special need)?
3. Were the objectives too easy or too hard for the pupil(s)?
4. How did any staff involvement affect pupil achievement?
5. Was the lesson or activity plan successful? If not, why not?

 KEY TASK

1. Describe **two** learning activities you have helped to plan, deliver and evaluate. Include: a brief description of each learning activity; the objectives of each learning activity; a list of materials and/or equipment used; your contribution to the learning activities; the type and level of support for the pupils; the specific strategies for supporting learning activities; and an evaluation of each learning activity.

2. Include copies of planning and evaluation sheets.

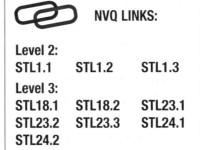

NVQ LINKS:

Level 2:
STL1.1   STL1.2   STL1.3

Level 3:
STL18.1   STL18.2   STL23.1
STL23.2   STL23.3   STL24.1
STL24.2

Further reading

Balshaw, M. and Farrell, P. (2002) *Teaching assistants: practical strategies for effective classroom support.* David Fulton Publishers.

DfES (2000) *Working with teaching assistants: a good practice guide.* DfES.

Kerry, T. (2001) *Working with support staff: their roles and effective management in schools.* Pearson Education.

Wyse, D. and Hawtin, A. (1999) *Children: a multi-professional perspective.* Hodder Arnold. [Covers child development and learning from birth to 18 years.]

2 Safeguarding children

Key points:

* Preparing and maintaining a safe learning environment
* Statutory and regulatory health and safety requirements
* Safety checks in the learning environment
* Maintaining child safety during play and learning activities
* Dealing with accidents, emergencies and illness
* Following the procedures for storing and administering medicines
* Supporting the safeguarding of children from abuse
* The teaching assistant's responsibilities for child protection
* Responding to a child's disclosure of abuse
* Helping children to protect themselves from abuse.

Preparing and maintaining a safe learning environment

You will need to know, understand and follow the legal and organisational requirements of the school for establishing and maintaining the health, safety and security of yourself and others at all times as well as the procedures for reporting any concerns or problems to the appropriate person. You will also need to use safe working practices in all that you do, which includes ensuring that someone in authority (e.g. the class teacher and/or your line manager) knows where you are at all times in case of an emergency. You should also know the local and national requirements regarding health, hygiene, safety and supervision in the school, including access to premises; storerooms and storage areas; and the health and safety requirements for the materials and equipment being used.

Statutory and regulatory health and safety requirements

You need to be aware of the statutory and regulatory health and safety requirements for pupils, staff, families and visitors in the school. Health and safety legislation places overall responsibility for health and safety with the employer. However, as an employee working within a school, you also have responsibilities with regard to maintaining health and safety. All employees have the following responsibilities under the *Health and Safety at Work Act 1974*:

* To take reasonable care for the health and safety of themselves and of any person who might be affected by their acts or omissions at work
* To co-operate with the relevant authorities (e.g. Ofsted) in meeting statutory requirements
* To not interfere with or misuse anything provided in the interests of health, safety and welfare
* To make themselves aware of all safety rules, procedures and safe working practices applicable to their posts. (When in doubt they must seek immediate clarification from the delegated person responsible for health and safety in the setting)
* To ensure that tools and equipment are in good condition and report any defects to the delegated person
* To use protective clothing and safety equipment provided and to ensure that these are kept in good condition
* To ensure that any accidents, whether or not an injury occurs, are reported to the delegated person
* To report potential hazards or any possible deficiencies in health and safety arrangements to the delegated person.

The Workplace (Health, Safety and Welfare) Regulations 1992 clarify and consolidate existing legislation. They also establish a consistent set of standards for the majority of workplaces. The regulations expand on the responsibilities placed on employers (and others in control of premises) by the Health and Safety at Work Act 1974 including: health and safety in the workplace; welfare facilities for people at work; maintenance of the workplace.

The workplace and equipment need to be maintained in an efficient state, in working order, and in good repair. Buildings, including mobile or temporary rooms, should be in a good state of repair and services should be in efficient working order. In general, indoor workplaces should be reasonably comfortable, reasonably clean, properly illuminated and adequately spacious.

The environmental requirements of the regulations apply to the workplace, but existing education standards for children's working space, temperature, ventilation and so on may be more appropriate for education settings. *The Education (School Premises) Regulations 1999* provide the statutory requirements for the minimum standards of both new and existing schools. The regulations include a general requirement that all parts of the school's premises must be reasonably maintained to ensure the health, safety and welfare of all users. These regulations also include the specific requirements for acoustics, ancillary facilities, drainage, heating, lighting, medical accommodation, playing fields, washrooms, staff accommodation, structural matters, ventilation, water supply and weather protection.

The Management of Health and Safety at Work Regulations 1999 require a risk assessment of facilities, a safety policy regarding these risks and appropriate health and safety training. You should be able to recognise any risks within the learning environment and take the appropriate action to minimise them, e.g. reporting potential health and safety hazards to the relevant person. (See section on risk assessment below.)

Regulations for manual handling

The Manual Handling Operations Regulations 1992, as amended in 2002, apply to manual handling activities such as lifting, lowering, pushing, pulling and carrying. The load being handled may be a box, trolley, person or animal. The regulations require employers to:

* **avoid** the need for hazardous manual handling, so far as is reasonably practicable
* **assess** the risk of injury from any hazardous manual handling that cannot be avoided
* **reduce** the risk of injury from hazardous manual handling, so far as is reasonably practicable.

The regulations require employees to: follow appropriate systems of work laid down for their safety; make proper use of equipment provided for their safety; co-operate with their employer on health and safety matters; inform the employer if they identify hazardous handling activities; take care to ensure their activities do not put others at risk (HSE, 2004).

You should be aware of the risks associated with lifting and carrying children, e.g. possible back injuries. Ensure that you follow your school's procedures for lifting and carrying pupils.

The Health and Safety Executive (HSE) provides guidance on manual handling (see Further reading at the end of this chapter). (See also section below on risk assessment applicable to the learning environment.)

Safety checks in the learning environment

You need to know the location of safety equipment in the different areas of the learning environment. You must be clear about the safety arrangements for the areas and pupils you work with including: the position of fire exits, extinguishers, fire blanket, first-aid boxes; your role during a fire drill; what to do in case of fire or other emergency, especially the procedures for pupils with physical disabilities or sensory impairments; escape routes and alternatives if blocked by fire, etc.

All equipment in the school should be safe and approved for safety, e.g. BSI Kitemark, European standards markings, BEAB mark of safety. You should know the operating procedures and safety requirements of the school before using any equipment. Operating instructions should be available and in many cases an experienced/knowledgeable member of staff may show you how to use the equipment beforehand. If not, it is essential to ask, especially when dealing with electrical equipment for safety reasons and because of the possibility of damaging expensive equipment – you do not want to cause hundreds or even thousands of pounds worth of damage to a computer or photocopier! You should follow any instructions carefully. Allow yourself plenty of time to do this thoroughly. Five minutes before you need to show the group/class a video is not the time to start learning how to use the school's video player for the first time! As with all learning activities you must plan ahead.

You should check equipment that you use regularly to ensure that it is safe and in proper working order – for example, check the television, video or computer is in working order before you or the pupils need it so that you can sort out any problems in advance. If there is a fault and the equipment is not functioning properly or not at all, you need to know the school procedures for dealing with faults – for example, which can be dealt with by you and which require reporting to the appropriate person. It is also important to check classroom equipment and materials regularly for damage and to report any damage to the appropriate person such as the class or subject teacher. Serious damage will have to be repaired by a professional (e.g. a technician or the school caretaker) or the item will have to be replaced.

Storage areas should be kept tidy, with sufficient space for the materials and equipment being stored there. Storage facilities should be easily accessible and where appropriate, lockable. Potentially hazardous materials must be stored away from pupils and locked away. Storage space should be organised so that heavy equipment is stored at a low level. Lightweight equipment may be stored above head level if space is limited. One of your responsibilities as a teaching assistant may be to ensure that all equipment and surfaces are safe, hygienic and usable. If working with pupils who have been using messy materials such as glue or paint, you will need to wipe tables or easels clean after use and clean any brushes ready for the next time. Any major cleaning tasks that are not part of your responsibilities should be referred to the class or subject teacher for attention. It is also important to ensure proper hygiene and correct use of equipment – for example, using fresh ingredients when doing cooking activities and ensuring pupils wash their hands before and after or following the correct procedures during science experiments.

Toy safety

Every year in the UK over 35,000 children under the age of 15 years are treated in hospital following an accident involving a toy (CAPT, 2004b). It is essential to provide pupils with toys and play equipment that are appropriate for their age and level of development. Most toys will have a suggested age range. It is a legal requirement for all toys sold in the European Union to carry a CE mark but this does not necessarily guarantee safety or quality. When selecting toys for children always look for one of these safety marks – **European Standard BS EN 71** indicates the toy has been tested to the agreed safety standards, or the **Lion Mark** indicates the toy has been made to the highest standards of safety and quality.

Play areas and playgrounds

There is a duty under Sections 3 and 4 of the *Health and Safety at Work Act 1974* to ensure the health and safety of users of playground equipment as far as is reasonably practicable (RoSPA, 2004a). Evidence of good practice in ensuring the health and safety of users includes compliance with the relevant safety standards, for example, EN 1176 for children's playground equipment and EN

1177 for playground surfaces. Safety checks for indoor play areas and outdoor play areas/playgrounds include: inspecting the play area/playground equipment on a regular basis; reporting any faults to the appropriate person promptly; ensuring that pupils do not use the faulty equipment until mended or replaced; getting the necessary repairs done as quickly as possible; having an annual inspection by an independent specialist. (See section below on maintaining child safety during play and learning activities.)

Ten important safety points to remember

Remember the following important safety points when establishing a healthy, safe and secure learning environment:

1. All equipment and materials must be appropriate to the ages/levels of development of the pupils, for example, small items are potential choking hazards for young children.

2. Pupils must listen carefully and follow instructions on the use of equipment and materials during activities, e.g. handling fragile or breakable objects with care.

3. Pupils must be told never to put anything in their mouths during learning activities unless instructed to do so by the adult in charge, e.g. they may be allowed to sample food during a cooking or tasting activity.

4. Safety goggles to British Standard BS2092 (that can also be worn with spectacles) should be worn by pupils engaged in potentially hazardous activities such as sawing, hammering and science experiments involving chemicals.

5. Pupils should not touch electrical equipment, especially with wet hands.

6. When pupils are doing cooking activities ensure that ingredients are fresh and in good condition; dried ingredients are stored in airtight containers; cooking utensils and table surfaces are scrupulously clean; all hands are washed beforehand.

7. Check whether any pupil is prevented from taking part in an activity due to cultural or religious dietary prohibitions; ensure that individual children are not allergic to any of the ingredients or materials.

8. Long hair should be tied back during construction, cooking, PE and science activities.

9. Pupils should be taught how to use, arrange and store PE apparatus correctly and safely as appropriate to their age and level of development.

10. Pupils should report all accidents to the teacher or teaching assistant.

EXERCISE: List ten important safety points to remember when organising classroom resources.

Toilet and wash areas

It is important that toilet and wash facilities are maintained in a clean and orderly condition with adequate lighting and ventilation. For children over two years old there should be one toilet and hand basin for every ten children. There should be separate toilet facilities for pupils and staff. There should be an adequate supply of drinking water that is easily accessible to pupils. The school should ensure that toilet facilities are maintained to high standards of hygiene. There should be adequate supplies of toilet paper, soap, warm water and disposable paper towels and/or access to hot air driers. The cleaning routines for toilets and washbasins should be regular and thorough to maintain high standards of hygiene. To minimise the spread of infection, the school should advise parents whose children have diarrhoea that the children should stay away from the setting until they no longer have symptoms. Your role might involve checking pupil toilet areas to see that they are used correctly and that pupils wash their hands after using the toilet or before handling food. You may be required to assist very young pupils (or pupils with physical disabilities) with their toileting needs. You should know the school's procedures for dealing with pupils who wet or soil themselves, including the location of appropriate spare clothing.

You may need to provide reassurance and support for a girl who starts menstruation but does not have any sanitary protection. (Girls as young as eight or nine can start their first period while at the setting.) You should know the school's procedures for dealing with this situation, including accessing emergency supplies of sanitary protection and its disposal. If you are a male teaching assistant then you must know who to go to for help if this situation occurs.

If you experience any concerns or problems with pupils when carrying out hygiene routines, you should report these to the class teacher. This includes reporting any hazard or unsafe situation you discover when using the school's toilet or wash facilities.

EXERCISE:
1. What are your school's procedures for checking toilet and wash areas?
2. What are your responsibilities for checking these areas?

The movement and activity of pupils

Schools cater for the arrival and departure of children, families, workers and visitors either as pedestrians or in vehicles including delivery vans and taxis for pupils with special needs. Traffic routes should be properly organised so that both pedestrians and vehicles can move safely in and around the school. Particular care should be taken of everyone using or having access to the premises, especially young children and people with disabilities. The school may have to cope with the large-scale movement of pupils and staff during busy periods – for example, the start and end of lessons. Care should be taken to avoid accidents such as slips, trips or falls, particularly in main corridors and staircases. Floor surfaces should be appropriate for their use and free from hazards or obstructions that might cause people to trip or fall. Particular attention should be given to: holes, bumps and uneven surfaces; wear and tear on carpeted areas; procedures for dealing with spillages; snow and ice on external pathways; precautionary measures prior to repairs, e.g. barriers, alternative routes.

Security arrangements for pupil arrival and departure

You must know and follow the school's policy and procedures for gaining access to the premises, e.g. entry systems, visitors' book, identity tags for visitors in the school. Security arrangements should include a registration system, e.g. a record of the time of arrival and departure of pupils and staff; a visitors' book to record the names of visitors, who they are/who they work for, time of arrival, who they are visiting, car registration if applicable, and time of departure. Anyone visiting the school for the first time should provide proof of identity. Pupils should never be left unattended with an adult who is not a member of staff.

A pupil must not be allowed to leave the school with an adult who does not usually collect the pupil without prior permission. You should also know and follow your school's policy and procedures for uncollected pupils or late arrival of parent or carer to collect younger pupils.

Risk assessment applicable to the learning environment

You must know and understand the importance of pupils being given opportunities to play and learn within an environment that will not harm their health and safety. However, pupils still need to be provided with activities and experiences that have levels of challenge and risk that will help them to develop confidence and independence. You need to be able to identify potential hazards (e.g. activities likely to cause harm) and assess possible risks (e.g. the seriousness of the hazards and their potential to cause actual harm).

1. The purpose of risk assessment is to: undertake a systematic review of the potential for harm; evaluate the likelihood of harm occurring; decide whether the existing control measures are adequate; decide whether more needs to be done.
2. The sequence for risk assessment is: classify the activity; identify potential hazard(s); evaluate possible risks; evaluate control measures; specify any further action.
3. Once the risk assessment has been carried out the hierarchy for control measures is: eliminate hazard; reduce hazard; isolate hazard; control hazard.
4. Once the risk assessment and control measures have been completed, no further action needs to be taken unless there is a significant change in that area.

(RoSPA, 2004b)

Remember that despite the school's procedures to maintain children's safety, there may still be times when accidents or injuries occur. Ensure that you know how to deal with accidents and injuries as well as the arrangements for first-aid. (See section below on dealing with accidents, emergencies and illness.)

KEY TASK

1. Find out about the statutory and regulatory requirements that apply to your school.
2. Find out about your school's policy and procedures for health and safety.
3. Outline the procedures for risk assessment and dealing with hazards in your school.

NVQ LINKS:

Level 2:
STL3.1   STL13.1   STL13.2

Level 3:
STL3.1   STL31.1   STL31.2
STL31.3   STL45.3   STL46.1

4. What are your responsibilities for dealing with the following types of possible hazards that can occur in the school: unsafe buildings, fixtures and fittings; unsafe equipment including play and learning resources; hazardous substances, e.g. cleaning materials; hygiene hazards in toilet or kitchen areas; security hazards, e.g. inadequate boundaries, unauthorised visitors?

Maintaining child safety during play and learning activities

You are responsible for the health and safety arrangements of the pupils (and others) under your supervision. This includes exercising effective supervision over those for whom you are responsible, including pupils, students, parent helpers and volunteers. You must be aware of and implement safe working practices and set a good example. You should provide written instructions, warning notices and signs as appropriate. You must provide appropriate protective clothing and safety equipment as necessary and ensure that these are used as required, e.g. safety goggles. You should provide for adequate instruction, information and training in safe working methods and recommend suitable safety training where appropriate.

You also need to encourage pupils to be aware of their own safety, other people's safety and their own personal responsibilities for maintaining health and safety in the school. The school should ensure that pupils (and where appropriate their parents) are aware of their responsibilities through direct instruction, notices and the school handbook. As appropriate to their ages and abilities, all pupils should be expected to: exercise personal responsibility for the safety of themselves and other pupils; observe standards of dress consistent with safety and/or hygiene (this precludes unsuitable footwear, knives and other items considered dangerous); observe all the safety rules of the school, in particular the instructions of adults in the event of a fire or other emergency; use and not wilfully misuse, neglect or interfere with items provided for safety purposes, such as fire alarms and fire extinguishers.

You must know and follow the school's policies and procedures for maintaining pupil safety at all times, especially during play and learning activities including outings. It is important to provide challenging and exciting play opportunities and learning activities that encourage pupils to develop and explore whilst maintaining their physical safety and emotional welfare. Accidents are common in children because they are developing and learning rapidly and it can be difficult for adults to keep up with their changing developmental abilities. Accidents also occur because children are naturally curious and want to explore their environment and in doing so may expose themselves to danger. The school should provide play and learning activities that encourage pupil curiosity and exploration whilst protecting them from unnecessary harm. Pupils also need to learn how to deal with risk so that they can keep themselves safe as they grow up. Bumps, bruises, minor cuts and scrapes are all part of play and learning but there is no need for pupils to suffer serious injuries. To avoid accidents the school should provide adult care and supervision as well as ensuring safe play equipment design and appropriate modifications to the learning environment (CAPT, 2004a).

The design, location and maintenance of play areas are important to maintaining pupil safety during play and learning activities. For example:

- ☆ The layout must ensure that activities in one area do not interfere with other areas
- ☆ Play areas for younger pupils should be separated from that for older pupils
- ☆ Paths must be safely situated away from equipment areas, especially swings
- ☆ Clear sight lines in the play area make it easier to supervise pupils
- ☆ Secure fencing is required if there are roads, rivers or ponds close to the play area
- ☆ Safe access for pupils with disabilities should be considered
- ☆ Lighting must be adequate for safety and supervision
- ☆ Repair and replace old or worn play equipment
- ☆ Ensure all play equipment is suitable for the age of the pupils using it
- ☆ Use impact-absorbing surfaces such as rubber, bark chips and other materials.

(CAPT, 2004c)

Making sure that pupils are aware of safe behaviour when using play equipment can also help to maintain their safety and protect them from unnecessary accidents. Examples of safe behaviour include: no walking in front of swings or other moving equipment; no pushing or shoving; being aware of younger pupils and those with disabilities; removing scarves or other things that could get caught in equipment; taking extra care when using high play equipment such as climbing frames (CAPT, 2004c).

KEY TASK

Outline your school's policies and procedures relating to health and safety and maintaining pupil safety during play and learning activities.

 NVQ LINKS:

Level 2:

STL3.1	STL10.5	STL13.1
STL13.2		

Level 3:

STL3.1	STL31.1	STL31.2
STL31.3	STL45.2	STL45.3
STL46.1	STL46.2	STL54.4
STL59.1	STL59.2	

Dealing with accidents, emergencies and illness

To help the teacher prepare and maintain a healthy, safe and secure learning environment you must know and follow the correct procedures for accidents, injuries, illnesses and other emergencies in the school. This involves: following emergency evacuation procedures; following procedures for missing pupils; dealing with accidents and injuries; following first-aid arrangements; recognising and dealing with common childhood illnesses; following the procedures for storing and administering medicines; supporting pupils with special medical needs.

Following emergency evacuation procedures in the school

You need to know about the fire and emergency evacuation procedures for the school. The purpose of fire and emergency evacuation procedures is to prevent panic and to ensure the safe, orderly and efficient evacuation of all occupants of the school using all the exit facilities available and to help individuals to react rationally when confronted with a fire or other emergency, either at the school or elsewhere. **In the event of a fire or other emergency (such as a bomb scare) all staff should know and understand that their first consideration must be the evacuation of all the pupils to a place of safety.** The sequence for fire and emergency evacuation procedures should be as follows: sound the fire alarm; evacuate the building; call the fire brigade; assemble at the designated assembly point; take a roll call using registers if possible.

The fire alarm signals the need to evacuate the building. You should give calm, clear and correct instructions to the people involved in the emergency as appropriate to your role in implementing emergency procedures within the school. You will need to make sure that any pupils for whom you are responsible leave the building in the appropriate manner, e.g. walking, no running or talking.

This will help to maintain calm and minimise panic as the pupils focus on following the appropriate evacuation procedures. All rooms must have evacuation instructions, including exit routes, prominently displayed.

You also need to know what to do if there is a bomb scare or an intruder in the school. Evacuation procedures would usually be the same as for a fire. You should report any problems with emergency procedures to the relevant colleague, e.g. the class teacher. Visitors to the school should normally be asked to sign in (and out) so that the people responsible for health and safety know who is in the building (and where) in case of emergencies.

If you work with pupils with special needs, you must know how to assist them in the event of an emergency – for example, a pupil with physical disabilities may need to leave the building via a special route or require access to a lift. You should check with the class teacher or SENCO about the exact procedures to follow. You should know where the fire alarm points and fire exits are, the location of fire extinguishers and fire blankets and how to use them. There may be different types of extinguishers for use with different hazardous substances, e.g. in kitchens water must not be used to put out oil or electrical fires as this can make the situation worse. Carbon dioxide extinguishers will be located in the necessary places.

> **EXERCISE:**
> 1. Find out about your school's emergency evacuation procedures.
> 2. Briefly outline the school's procedures in the event of a fire or other emergency evacuation, including your specific role.

Following procedures for missing pupils

A register of pupils attending each class in the school should be taken at the start of each session. A register should also be taken for pupils participating in outings/visits away from the school and a duplicate left with the headteacher. Pupils should be made aware (or reminded) of the boundaries of the school at each session. Pupils should be appropriately supervised at all times. However, despite these safeguards pupils may still go missing from the school.

You need to be aware of the school's procedures for dealing with missing pupils. These procedures may include: contacting the class teacher or headteacher immediately; calling the register to check which pupil is missing; searching classrooms, play areas and school grounds to ensure the pupil has not hidden or been locked in anywhere within the school; the headteacher contacting the police and the parent/carers.

If a pupil is found to be missing while on an outing the teaching assistant should: contact the class teacher immediately; check the register again; keep the rest of the group together while searching the area; contact the class teacher again (who will contact the headteacher, the police and the pupil's parents/carers).

Dealing with accidents and injuries

When responding to accidents or injuries that occur within the school, you should remain calm and follow the relevant procedures. You must immediately call for qualified assistance (e.g. the designated first-aider or the emergency services) and take appropriate action in line with your role and responsibilities within the school. If you are a *designated* first-aider then you can administer first-aid; if not, you can comfort the injured person by your physical presence and by talking to them until the arrival of a designated first-aider, doctor, paramedic or ambulance staff. You will then help to establish and maintain the privacy and safety of the area where the accident or injury occurred and provide support for any other people involved. When qualified assistance arrives you should give them clear and accurate information about what happened. Afterwards, you will need to follow the school's procedures for recording accidents and injuries. This will normally involve recording the incident in a special book. Serious accidents are usually recorded on an official form. Accuracy in recording accidents and injuries is essential because the information may be needed for further action by senior staff or other professionals. Certain types of accidents and injuries must be reported to an official authority under the **Reporting of Injuries, Diseases and Dangerous Occurrences Regulations 1985** – for example, local authority and school playgrounds must report to the Health and Safety Executive.

You must follow basic good hygiene procedures and take the usual precautions for avoiding cross infection. You should use protective disposable gloves and be careful when dealing with spillages of blood or other body fluids, including the disposal of dressings, etc. You should be aware of issues concerning the spread of hepatitis, HIV and AIDS.

Following first-aid arrangements

You must know and understand the first-aid arrangements that apply in the school, including the location of first-aid equipment/facilities and the designated first-aider(s). A designated first-aider must complete a training course approved by the Health and Safety Executive. Remember that even if you have done first-aid as part of your teaching assistant training, your first-aid certificate should be updated every three years.

First-aid notices should be clearly displayed in all rooms; make sure you read this information. First-aid information is usually included in induction programmes to ensure that new staff and pupils know about the school's first-aid arrangements. Detailed information on the school's first-aid policy and procedures will also be in the staff handbook.

Accident/Incident Report Form

Date: Time:

Location of accident/incident:

Address:

Person reporting the accident/incident:

Address:

Details of the accident/incident: (Continue on reverse and additional sheets if necessary)

Action taken: (Continue on reverse and additional sheets if necessary)

Witnesses or others informed of accident/incident: (Continue on reverse and additional sheets if necessary)

1. Name:

Address:

2. Name:

Address:

Any further action required: (Continue on reverse and additional sheets if necessary)

Signed: Date of report:

Number of additional sheets:

Accident/incident report form

The aims of first-aid

1. *To preserve life* by providing emergency resuscitation; controlling bleeding; treating burns; and treating shock.
2. *To prevent the worsening of any injuries* by covering wounds; immobilising fractures; and placing the casualty in the correct and comfortable position.
3. *To promote recovery* by providing reassurance; giving any other treatment needed; relieving pain; handling gently; moving as little as possible; and protecting from the cold.

The priorities of first-aid

* ☆ **A** is for Airway: establish an open airway by tilting the forehead back so that the child can breathe easily.
* ☆ **B** is for Breathing: check that the child is breathing by listening, looking and feeling for breath.
* ☆ **C** is for Circulation: apply simple visual checks that the child's blood is circulating adequately, by watching for improved colour, for coughing or eye movement.

First-aid equipment

First-aid equipment must be clearly labelled and easily accessible. All first-aid containers must be marked with a white cross on a green background. There should be at least one fully stocked first-aid container for each building within the setting, with extra first-aid containers available on split-sites/levels, distant playing fields/playgrounds and any other high-risk areas (e.g. kitchens) and for outings or educational visits. Here are some suggestions for the contents of a **first-aid kit**: a first-aid manual or first-aid leaflet; assorted bandages, including a wrapped triangular bandage, a one-inch and a two-inch strip for holding dressings and compresses in place; medium and large individually wrapped sterile un-medicated wound dressings; two sterile eye pads; safety pins; adhesive tape; sterile gauze; a pair of sharp scissors; tweezers; child thermometer; disposable gloves.

> EXERCISE: Find out about your school's policy and procedures for dealing with accidents and injuries including the provision of first-aid.

Recognising and dealing with common childhood illnesses and allergies

Babies and young children should be vaccinated against diseases including diphtheria, measles, meningitis, mumps, polio, rubella, tetanus and whooping cough. The first immunisations start when a baby is two months old. The child's parents will usually receive appointments by post to attend their local clinic or GP surgery. You need to be aware of the range of common illnesses that may affect children. These include: allergies, asthma, bronchitis, chicken pox, colds, diabetes, diarrhoea, earache, flu, glandular fever, headache, measles, meningitis, mumps, sore throat, and worms.

Recognising signs and symptoms

By knowing the usual behaviour and appearance of the pupils you work with, you will be able to recognise any significant changes that might indicate possible illness. You need to be able to recognise the differences between pupils who are: pretending to be ill; feeling 'under the weather'; or experiencing a health problem. The signs of possible illness in children include:

☆ Changes in facial colour, e.g. becoming pale or very red

☆ Changes in temperature, e.g. becoming very hot or cold, becoming clammy or shivering (a fever usually indicates that the child has an infection)

☆ Changes in behaviour, e.g. not wanting to play when they would usually be very keen

☆ Being upset or generally distressed

☆ Having reduced concentration levels or even falling asleep

☆ Scratching excessively (check the setting's policy regarding head lice)

☆ Complaining of persistent pain, e.g. headache or stomach-ache

☆ Coughing or sneezing excessively

☆ Diarrhoea and/or vomiting

☆ Displaying a rash (this could indicate an infection or allergic reaction). Make sure you are aware of any children who may have severe allergic reactions – see section on supporting pupils with special medical needs.

(Watkinson, 2003)

Responding to signs and symptoms

You should know what to do if pupils come to the setting when they are unwell. The most common childhood illness is the common cold. A young child may have as many as five to six colds a year. Pupils do not need to be kept away from school because of a cold unless their symptoms are very bad. Make sure that a box of tissues is available for pupils to use and that used tissues are disposed of properly to avoid the spread of germs. Colds and flu are caused by viruses and so cannot be helped by antibiotics. However, cold and flu viruses can weaken the body and lead to a secondary bacterial infection such as tonsillitis, otitis media (middle ear infection), sinusitis, bronchitis and pneumonia. These bacterial infections require antibiotic treatment. You also need to know what to do if a pupil becomes ill while at the setting. You should seek medical advice if you have concerns about any of the following:

☆ The child's high temperature lasts for more than 24 hours.

☆ The child has a persistent cough with green or yellow catarrh (possible bronchitis or pneumonia).

☆ The child has pain above the eyes or in the face (possible sinusitis).

☆ The child has a severe sore throat (possible tonsillitis).

☆ The child has a bad earache (possible ear infection).

Seek medical advice **immediately** if:

- ☆ You think the child may have meningitis.
- ☆ The child has breathing difficulties.
- ☆ The child's asthma deteriorates.
- ☆ The child has a convulsion.
- ☆ The child has very poor fluid intake or cannot swallow liquids.
- ☆ A baby persistently refuses to take feeds.
- ☆ The child has been to a country where there is a risk of malaria, in the last 12 months.

Recording and reporting signs of illness

Ensure that you know what to do when pupils are sick – for example, where or to whom to send sick pupils. You may need to stay with a sick pupil while someone else summons assistance. If you have any concerns regarding the health of the pupils you work with, you should always inform the class teacher. You need to be able to recognise any changes to a pupil's behaviour or appearance that may indicate a possible health problem and report these appropriately. Whatever the illness, you should know where and when to seek assistance. You should also know what types of written records are required and to whom you should report any concerns regarding any pupil's health. Check whether you are allowed to contact parents/carers directly regarding a sick pupil or whether this is the responsibility of someone else, e.g. the class teacher or headteacher.

Following the procedures for storing and administering medicines

Parents are responsible for their own children's medication. Children under the age of 16 should not be given medication without their parent's written consent. The headteacher usually decides whether the school can assist a pupil who needs medication during the school day. The school will have a form for the parent to sign if their child requires medication while at school. Many pupils with long-term medical needs will not require medication while at the school. If they do, pupils can usually administer it themselves depending on their age, level of development, medical needs and type of medication. The school's policy should encourage self-administration where appropriate and provide suitable facilities for pupils to do so in safety and privacy. (See section below on supporting pupils with special medical needs.)

Teaching assistants have no legal duty to administer medication or to supervise a pupil taking it. This is a voluntary role similar to that of being a designated first-aider (see above). The headteacher, parents and relevant health professionals should support teaching assistants who volunteer to administer medication by providing information, training, and reassurance about their legal liability. Arrangements should be made for when the teaching assistant responsible for providing assistance is absent or not available.

The health and safety of pupils and staff must be considered at all times. Safety procedures must be in place regarding the safe storage, handling, and disposal of medicines. Some medication (e.g. reliever inhaler for asthma or adrenalin device for severe anaphylaxis) must be quickly available in an emergency and should not

ILLNESS	INCUBATION PERIOD	INFECTIOUS PERIOD	HOW TO RECOGNISE IT	WHAT TO DO
	(The time between catching an illness and becoming unwell)	(When your child can give the illness to someone else)		
CHICKENPOX	11–21 days	From the day before the rash appears until all the spots are dry.	Begins with feeling unwell, a rash and maybe a slight temperature. Spots are red and become fluid-filled blisters within a day or so. Appear first on the chest and back, then spread, and eventually dry into scabs, which drop off. Unless spots are badly infected, they dont usally leave a scar.	No need to see your GP unless you're unsure whether it's chickenpox, or your child is very unwell and/or distressed. Give plenty to drink. Paracetamol will help bring down a temperature. Baths, loose, comfortable clothes and calamine lotion can all ease the itchiness. You should also inform the school/nursery in case other children are at risk. Keep your child away from anyone who is, or who is trying to become, pregnant. If your child was with anyone pregnant just before he or she became unwell, let that woman know about the chickenpox (and tell her to see her GP). Sometimes chickenpox in pregnancy can cause miscarriage or the baby may be born with chickenpox.
MEASLES	7–12 days	From a few days before until 4 days after the appearance of the rash.	Begins like a bad cold and cough with sore, watery eyes. Child becomes gradually more unwell, with a temperature. Rash appears after third or fourth day. Spots are red and slightly raised; may be blotchy, but are not itchy. Begins behind the ears, and spreads to the face and neck and then the rest of the body. Children can become very unwell, with cough and high temperature. The illness usually lasts about a week.	See your GP. If your child is unwell give him or her rest and plenty to drink. To ease the cough. Paracetamol will ease discomfort and lower the temperature. Vaseline around the lips protects the skin. Wash crustiness from eyelids with warm water.
MUMPS	14–21 days	From a few days before becoming unwell until swelling goes down. Maybe 10 days in all.	At first, your child may be mildly unwell with a bit of fever, and may complain of pain around the ear or feel uncomfortable when chewing. Swelling then starts under the jaw up to the ear. Swelling often starts on one side, followed (though not always) by the other. Your child's face is back to normal size in about a week. It's rare for mumps to affect boys' testes (balls). This happens rather more often in adult men with mumps. For both boys and men, the risk of any permanent damage to the testes is very low.	Your child may not feel especially ill and may not want to be in bed. Baby or junior paracetamol will ease pain in the swollen glands. Check correct dosage on pack. Give plenty to drink, but not fruit juice. This makes the saliva flow, which can hurt. No need to see your GP unless your child has stomach ache and is being sick, or develops a rash of small red/purple spots or bruises.
PARVOVIRUS B19 (ALSO CALLED FIFTH DISEASE OR SLAPPED CHEEK DISEASE)	Variable 1–20 days	It is most infectious in the days before the rash appears.	Begins with a fever and nasal discharge. A bright red rash similar to a slap appears on the cheeks. Over the next 2–4 days, a lacy type of rash spreads to the trunk and limbs.	Although this is most common in children, it can occur in adults. In the majority of cases it has no serious consequences, but it may cause complications for people with chronic anaemic conditions (e.g. sickle cell disease). Rarely, in pregnant women who are not immune to the disease, the infection may result in stillbirth or affect the baby in the womb. Pregnant women who come into contact with the infection or develop a rash should see their GP as soon as possible.
RUBELLA (GERMAN MEASLES)	14–21 days	One week before and at least 4 days after the rash first appears.	Can be difficult to diagnose with certainty. Starts like a mild cold. The rash appears in a day or two, first on the face, then spreading. Spots are flat. On a light skin, they are pale pink. Glands in the back of the neck may be swollen. Your child won't usually feel unwell.	Give plenty to drink. Keep your child away from anybody you know who's up to 4 months pregnant (or trying to get pregnant). If your child was with anyone pregnant before you knew about the illness, let her know. If an unimmunised pregnant woman catches German measles in the first 4 months of pregnancy, there is a risk of damage to her baby. Any pregnant woman who has had contact with German measles should see her GP. The GP can check whether or not she is immune and, if not, whether there is any sign of her developing the illness.
WHOOPING COUGH	7–14 days	From the first signs of the illness until about 6 weeks after coughing starts. If an antibiotic is given, the infectious period is up to 5 days after beginning the course of treatment.	Begins like a cold and cough. The cough gradually gets worse. After about 2 weeks, coughing bouts start. These are exhausting and make it difficult to breathe. Your child may choke and vomit. Sometimes, but not always, there's a whooping noise as the child draws in breath after coughing. It takes some weeks before the coughing fits start to die down.	If your child has a cough that gets worse rather than better and starts to have longer fits of coughing more and more often, see your doctor. It's important for the sake of other children to know whether or not it's whooping cough. Talk to your GP about how best to look after your child and avoid contact with babies, who are most at risk from serious complications.

Childhood illnesses

be locked away. The relevant staff members and the pupils concerned must know where this medication is stored.

Supporting pupils with special medical needs

All schools will have pupils with medical needs at some time. Some medical needs are short-term, e.g. a pupil finishing a course of antibiotics or recovering from an accident/surgery. Some pupils may have long-term medical needs due to a particular medical condition or chronic illness. The majority of pupils with long-term medical needs will be able to attend a mainstream setting regularly and can participate in the usual setting activities with the appropriate support from the staff. The medical conditions in children that cause most concern in schools are asthma, diabetes, epilepsy and severe allergic reaction (anaphylaxis).

Asthma

About 1 in 10 children in the UK have asthma. People with asthma have airways that narrow as a reaction to a variety of triggers such as animal fur, grass pollen, house dust mites and viral infections. Stress or exercise can also bring on an asthma attack in a susceptible person. A person with asthma can usually relieve the symptoms of an asthma attack with an inhaler.

It is essential that children with asthma have immediate access to their reliever inhalers in the event of an asthma attack in the setting. Children with asthma should be encouraged from an early age to take charge of their own inhaler and know how to use it. Children who can use their inhalers themselves should be permitted to carry these with them at all times. When a child is too young or immature to be personally responsible for their inhaler, then staff must ensure that the inhaler is kept in a safe but accessible place with the child's name clearly written on it. The symptoms of an **asthma attack** are: excessive coughing; wheezing; difficulty breathing, especially breathing out; possible anxiety and distress; lips and skin turning blue (in severe attacks). A child having an asthma attack should be prompted to use their inhaler if they are not using it already. It is good practice to provide comfort and reassurance (to alleviate possible anxiety and distress) while encouraging the child to breathe slowly and deeply. The child should sit rather than lie down. Medical advice must be sought and/or an ambulance called if: the medication has no effect after 5–10 minutes; the child seems very distressed; the child is unable to talk; or the child is becoming exhausted (DfES/DH, 2005). For more detailed information see the **Asthma UK** website at **www.asthma.org.uk**.

Diabetes

Approximately 1 in 550 children have diabetes. Diabetes is a medical condition where the person's normal hormonal mechanisms do not control their blood sugar level properly. Children with diabetes usually need to have daily insulin injections, monitor their blood sugar glucose and eat regularly. Diabetes in most children is controlled by twice daily injections of insulin and it is not likely that these will need to be administered during school hours. If children do need insulin while at the setting then an appropriate, private area should be provided for this. Most children with diabetes can administer their own insulin injections but younger children will require adult supervision. Children with diabetes need to check that their blood sugar levels remain stable by using a testing machine at regular intervals. They may need to check their levels during lunch time or more frequently if their insulin requires adjustment. The majority of children are able to do this themselves and just need an appropriate place to carry out the checks. Children with diabetes must be allowed to eat regularly throughout the day. This might include eating snacks during lesson time or before physical play activities or PE lessons. Blood sugar levels may fall to too low a level if a child misses a snack or meal or after strenuous physical activity, resulting in a hypoglycaemia episode (hypo). A hypo left untreated can lead to a diabetic coma. The symptoms of a **hypo** include: drowsiness; glazed eyes; hunger; irritability; lack of concentration; pallor; shaking; and sweating. If a child experiences a hypo it is important that a fast-acting sugar is given immediately, e.g. glucose tablets, glucose-rich gel, sugary drink or a chocolate bar. A slower acting starchy food should be given once the child has recovered, e.g. a sandwich or two biscuits and a glass of milk. If the child's recovery takes longer than 10–15 minutes, or if there are any concerns about the child's condition, then an ambulance should be called (DfES/DH, 2005). For more detailed information see the **Diabetes UK** website at **www.diabetes.org.uk**.

Epilepsy

Approximately 1 in 200 children have epilepsy and about 80% of these attend mainstream settings. People with epilepsy have recurrent seizures (commonly called fits). The nature, frequency and severity of seizures will vary between individuals. The majority of seizures can be controlled by medication. Seizures may be *partial*, when the person's consciousness is affected but not necessarily lost, or *generalised*, where the person does lose consciousness.

Most children with epilepsy have symptoms that are well-controlled by medication and seizures are therefore unlikely to occur in the setting. The vast majority of children with epilepsy experience seizures for no apparent reason. However, susceptible children may have seizures triggered by tiredness and/or stress; flashing or flickering lights; computer games and graphics; and some geometric shapes or patterns. The symptoms of **epileptic seizures** include: having convulsions; losing consciousness; experiencing strange sensations; exhibiting unusual behaviour (e.g. plucking at clothes or repetitive movements).

Once a seizure has started nothing should be done to stop or change its course except when medication is given by appropriately trained staff. The child should not be moved unless they are in a dangerous place, but something soft may be placed under their head. No attempt should be made to restrain the child or to put anything into their mouth. The child's airway must be maintained at all times. When the convulsion has finished the child should be put in the recovery position. Someone should stay with the child until they have recovered and become re-orientated. If the seizure lasts longer than usual or one seizure follows another without the child regaining consciousness or where there are any concerns about the pupil's condition, then an ambulance should be called (DfES/DH, 2005). For more detailed information see the **National Society for Epilepsy** website at **www.epilepsynse.org.uk**.

Severe allergic reaction (anaphylaxis)

Children with severe allergies learn from an early age what they can and cannot eat or drink.

The most common cause for severe allergies is food, especially nuts, fish or dairy products. Wasp and bee stings can also cause severe allergic reactions. Anaphylaxis is a very severe allergic reaction that requires urgent medical treatment. In its most severe form (anaphylactic shock) the condition is potentially life-threatening, but can be treated with medication. This may include antihistamine, adrenaline inhaler or adrenaline injection depending on the severity of the allergic reaction. Anaphylactic shock is rare in children under 13 years old.

People with severe allergic reactions usually have a device for injecting adrenaline that looks like a fountain pen and is pre-loaded with the exact dose of adrenaline required. The needle is not exposed and the injection is easy to administer, usually into the fleshy part of the thigh.

A child may be responsible for keeping the necessary medication with them at all times. The safety of all children should be taken into account and it might be more appropriate to store the medication in a safe but instantly accessible place, especially if working with younger children. All staff should be aware of any children with this condition and know who is responsible for administering the emergency treatment. Responsibility for giving the injection should be on a voluntary basis and should never be done by a person without appropriate training from a health professional. An allergic reaction will usually occur within a few seconds or minutes of exposure to an allergen. The symptoms of a **severe allergic reaction** include: metallic taste or itching in the mouth; flushed complexion; abdominal cramps and nausea; swelling of the face, throat, tongue and lips; difficulty swallowing; wheezing or difficulty breathing; rise in heart rate; collapse or unconsciousness. An ambulance should be called immediately, especially if there are concerns about the severity of the allergic reaction or if the pupil does not respond to the medication (DfES/DH, 2005). For more detailed information see **The Anaphylaxis Campaign** website at www.anaphylaxis.org.uk.

> EXERCISE: List the main symptoms for the following: asthma attack; diabetic hypo; epileptic seizure; severe allergic reaction.

HIV and AIDS

HIV (human immunodeficiency virus) is a virus that damages the body's immune system. The immune system fights the virus and if the body's defences are severely weakened this can lead to AIDS (acquired immune deficiency syndrome). AIDS is the collective name of different diseases that can cause serious illness or death in both adults and children. HIV is very fragile and cannot be easily transmitted. For example, it cannot survive in very hot water, in bleach or in detergent. HIV is transmitted in three ways: through unprotected vaginal or anal intercourse; by infected blood entering the blood stream (e.g. from a blood transfusion or from needle stick injuries); from a woman with HIV to her baby either during pregnancy, during delivery or from breastfeeding. There is no evidence that HIV can be caught from social contact. HIV cannot be spread by: hugs and kisses; coughs and sneezes; shared toilet seat; shared drinking fountain; showers and swimming pools; sweat, tears and saliva; animals and pets. Details of the HIV status of any pupil must not be passed on without the parents' or child's permission. This means that in most schools, staff will not know if a pupil is HIV positive. It is therefore essential that health and safety procedures for cleaning up blood and blood-stained body fluids are rigorously adhered to, and that disposable gloves are worn when treating bleeding children (ATL, 2002). For more detailed information see **The Terrence Higgins Trust** website at **www.tht.org.uk**.

Strategies for supporting pupils with long-term medical needs

The school will need additional procedures to maintain the health and safety of pupils with long-term medical needs; these may include an individual health care plan (see below). The school has a responsibility to ensure that all relevant staff are aware of pupils with long-term medical needs and are trained to provide additional support if necessary. Staff providing support for pupils with long-term medical needs must know and understand: the nature of the pupil's medical condition; when and where the pupil may need additional support; the likelihood of an emergency arising (especially if it is potentially life threatening); and what action to take if an emergency occurs.

The headteacher and other staff must treat medical information in a sensitive and **confidential** manner. The headteacher should agree with the pupil (if appropriate) and their parents, which staff members should have access to records and other information about the pupil's medical needs in order to provide a good support system. However, where medical information is not given to staff they should not usually be held responsible if they provide incorrect medical assistance in an emergency but otherwise acted in good faith.

Health care plans in schools

Some pupils with long-term medical needs may require a health care plan to provide staff with the necessary information to support the pupil and to ensure the pupil's safety. A health care plan for a pupil with special medical needs is used to identify the level of support the pupil requires in the school. The health care plan is a written agreement between the school and parents that specifies the assistance that the school can provide for the pupil. The plan should be reviewed at least once a year or more if the pupil's medical needs change. A written health care plan should be drawn up in consultation with the pupil (if appropriate), their parents and the relevant health professionals. The amount of detail contained in a health care plan will depend on the particular needs of the individual pupil. The plan should include: details of the pupil's medical condition; any special requirements, e.g. dietary needs; medication and its possible side effects; how staff can support the pupil in school; and what to do and who to contact in an emergency (DfES/DH, 2005).

KEY TASK

1. Find out about your school's procedures for: dealing with accidents and injuries; providing first-aid; dealing with common childhood illnesses; storing and administering medicines; supporting pupils with long-term medical needs.

2. Describe your role and responsibilities in the event of an accident, injury, illness and other emergencies.

 NVQ LINKS:

Level 2: STL3.2

Level 3: STL3.2
        STL43
        [single element unit]

Supporting the safeguarding of children from abuse

All schools should establish and maintain a safe environment for pupils and deal with circumstances where there are child welfare concerns. Through their child protection policies and procedures for safeguarding children, schools have an important role in the detection and prevention of child abuse and neglect.

What is child abuse?

The Children Act 1989 defines child abuse as a person's actions that cause a child to suffer **significant harm** to their health, development or well-being. Significant harm can be caused by: punishing a child too much; hitting or shaking a child; constantly criticising, threatening or rejecting a child; sexually interfering with or assaulting a child; neglecting a child, e.g. not giving them enough to eat or not ensuring their safety. The Department of Health (DH) defines child abuse as the abuse or neglect of a child by inflicting harm or by failing to prevent harm. Children may be abused by someone known to them, e.g. a parent, sibling, babysitter, carer or other familiar adult. It is very rare for a child to be abused by a stranger (DH, 2003).

Types of child abuse

- **Physical abuse** involves causing deliberate physical harm to a child and may include: burning, drowning, hitting, poisoning, scalding, shaking, suffocating or throwing. Physical abuse also includes deliberately causing, or fabricating the symptoms of, ill health in a child (e.g. Munchausen's Syndrome by Proxy).

- **Emotional abuse** involves the persistent psychological mistreatment of a child and may include: making the child feel inadequate, unloved or worthless; imposing inappropriate developmental expectations on the child; threatening, taunting or humiliating the child; exploiting or corrupting the child.

- **Sexual abuse** involves coercing or encouraging a child to engage in sexual activities to which the child does not or cannot consent because of their age or level of understanding. These sexual activities may involve physical contact such as penetrative and/or oral sex or encouraging the child to watch the adult masturbate or to look at pornographic material.

- **Neglect** involves the persistent failure to meet a child's essential basic needs for food, clothing, shelter, loving care or medical attention. Neglect may also include when a child is put at risk by being left alone without proper adult supervision.

(DH, 2003)

Identifying signs of possible abuse

As a teaching assistant, you need to be aware of the signs and indicators of possible child abuse and neglect and to whom you should report any concerns or suspicions. You may have contact with pupils on a daily basis and so have an essential role to play in recognising indications of possible abuse or neglect, such as outward signs of physical abuse, uncharacteristic behaviour patterns or failure to develop in the expected ways.

Indications of possible **physical abuse** include:

- ✩ Recurrent unexplained injuries or burns
- ✩ Refusal to discuss injuries
- ✩ Improbable explanations for injuries
- ✩ Watchful, cautious attitude towards adults
- ✩ Reluctance to play and be spontaneous
- ✩ Shrinking from physical contact
- ✩ Avoidance of activities involving removal of clothes, e.g. swimming
- ✩ Aggressive or bullying behaviour
- ✩ Being bullied
- ✩ Lack of concentration
- ✩ Difficulty in trusting people and making friends.

Indications of possible **emotional abuse** include:

- ✩ Delayed speech development
- ✩ Very passive and lacking in spontaneity
- ✩ Social isolation, e.g. finding it hard to play with other children
- ✩ Unable to engage in imaginative play
- ✩ Low self-esteem
- ✩ Easily distracted
- ✩ Fear of new situations

☆ Self-damaging behaviour, e.g. head-banging, pulling out hair

☆ Self-absorbing behaviour, e.g. obsessive rocking, thumb-sucking

☆ Eating problems, e.g. overeating or lack of appetite

☆ Withdrawn behaviour and depression.

Indications of possible **sexual abuse** include:

☆ Sudden behaviour changes when abuse begins

☆ Low self-esteem

☆ Using sexual words in play activities uncharacteristic for age/level of development

☆ Withdrawn or secretive behaviour

☆ Starting to wet or soil themselves

☆ Demonstrating inappropriate seductive or flirtatious behaviour

☆ Frequent public masturbation

☆ Frightened of physical contact

☆ Depression resulting in self-harm (or an overdose)

☆ Bruises, scratches, burns or bite marks on the body.

Indications of possible **neglect** include:

☆ Slow physical development

☆ Constant hunger and/or tiredness

☆ Poor personal hygiene and appearance

☆ Frequent lateness or absenteeism

☆ Undiagnosed/untreated medical conditions

☆ Social isolation, e.g. poor social skills

☆ Compulsive stealing or begging.

(Indications of possible bullying are dealt with in Chapter 4.)

The law regarding child protection

Information on protecting and safeguarding children can be found in the guidance document *Working Together to Safeguard Children: a guide to inter-agency working to safeguard and promote the welfare of children (2006)*. See full text at: **www.everychildmatters.gov.uk**.

This revised guidance replaces *Working Together to Safeguard Children*, published in 1999. *Working Together to Safeguard Children 2006* incorporates changes in safeguarding policy and practice since 1999. In response to the statutory inquiry into the death of Victoria Climbié (2003) and the first joint Chief Inspectors' report on safeguarding children (2002), the government produced *Every Child Matters* (see above) and set out better provisions to safeguard children in the *Children Act 2004* including: the creation of children's trusts under the duty to co-operate; the setting up of Local Safeguarding Children Boards (LSCBs), and the duty on all agencies to make arrangements to safeguard and promote the welfare of children (HM Government, 2006).

Working Together to Safeguard Children 2006 sets out how agencies and professionals should work together to promote the welfare of children and to protect children from abuse and neglect. The document applies to those working in education, health and social services as well as the police and the probation service. It is relevant to those working with children and their families in the statutory, independent and voluntary sectors. The document sets out:

- ✯ A summary of the nature and impact of child abuse and neglect.
- ✯ How to operate best practice in child protection procedures.
- ✯ The roles and responsibilities of different agencies and practitioners.
- ✯ The role of Local Safeguarding Children Boards.
- ✯ The processes to be followed when there are concerns about a child.
- ✯ The action to be taken to safeguard and promote the welfare of children experiencing, or at risk of, significant harm.
- ✯ The important principles to be followed when working with children and families.
- ✯ Training requirements for effective child protection.

The Framework for the Assessment of Children in Need and their Families (2000) provides a systemic framework to help professionals identify children in need and assess the best approach to help children in need and their families. *What to do if you're worried a child is being abused (2003)* is a guide for professionals working with children explaining the processes and systems contained in *Working Together to Safeguard Children* and *Framework for Assessment of Children in Need and their Families.*

As a further safeguard to children's welfare, *The Protection of Children Act 1999* requires childcare organisations (including any organisation concerned with the supervision of children) not to offer employment involving regular contact with children, either paid or unpaid, to any person listed as unsuitable to work with children on the Department of Health list and the Department for Education and Employment's List 99. The Criminal Records Bureau acts as a central access point for criminal records checks for all those applying to work with children and young people.

The school's child protection policy and procedures

The school's child protection policy should include information on the roles and responsibilities of staff members and the procedures for dealing with child protection issues. For example:

1. All staff members should attend child protection training.
2. The school will comply with the Local Safeguarding Children Board procedures.
3. If any member of staff is concerned about a child they must inform a senior colleague. The member of staff must record information regarding such concerns on the same day. This record must give a clear, precise and factual account of their observation.
4. Confidentiality is crucial and incidents should be discussed only with the relevant person, e.g. senior colleague or external agency.

5. The headteacher will decide whether the concerns should be referred to external agencies, e.g. social services and/or the police.
6. The school should work co-operatively with parents unless this is inconsistent with the need to ensure the child's safety.
7. If a referral is made to social services, the headteacher will ensure that a report of the concerns is sent to the social worker dealing with the case within 48 hours.
8. Particular attention will be paid to the attendance and development of any child identified as 'at risk' or who has been placed on the Child Protection Register.

As teaching assistants have close contact with children, they should be aware of the signs of possible abuse or neglect and know what to do if they have concerns about a child's welfare (see below). The school should have clear procedures, in line with the LSCB procedures, on the situations in which teaching assistants should consult senior colleagues and external agencies (e.g. social services and the police) when they have concerns about the welfare of a child.

EXERCISE: Find out about your school's child protection policy and procedures.

The teaching assistant's responsibilities for child protection

All adults who work with children have a duty to safeguard and promote the welfare of children. As a teaching assistant, you need to be aware of: the signs of possible abuse, neglect and bullying; to whom you should report any concerns or suspicions; the school's child protection policy and procedures; the school's anti-bullying policy; the school's procedures for actively preventing all forms of bullying among pupils; the school's procedure to be followed if a staff member is accused of abuse. You may be involved in child protection in the following ways:

✴ You may have concerns about a pupil and refer those concerns to a senior colleague in the school (who will then refer matters to social services and/or the police as appropriate).
✴ You may be the senior practitioner who is responsible for referring concerns about a child's welfare to social services or the police.
✴ You may be approached by social services and asked to provide information about a child or to be involved in an assessment or to attend a child protection conference. This may happen regardless of who made the referral to social services.
✴ You may be asked to carry out a specific type of assessment, or provide help or a specific service to the child as part of an agreed plan and contribute to the reviewing of the child's progress (including attending child protection conferences).

(DH, 2003)

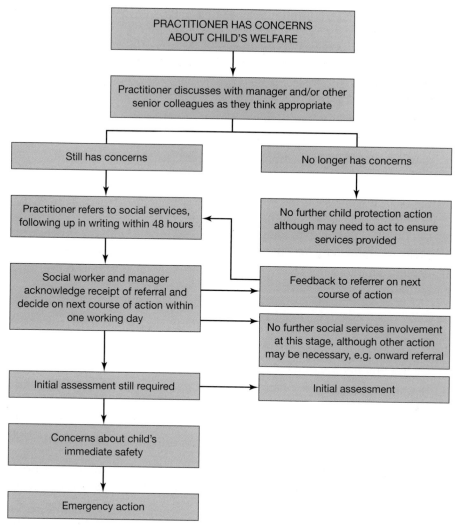

The processes for safeguarding children

Teaching assistants working closely with pupils in schools are well placed to identify the early signs of abuse, neglect or bullying. In addition, many pupils may view the school as neutral territory where they may feel more able to talk with an adult they trust about what is happening to them. If you have concerns that a pupil in your school may be experiencing possible abuse or neglect, you **must** report these concerns promptly to the relevant person, e.g. class teacher, headteacher or teacher responsible for child protection issues.

Responding to a child's disclosure of abuse

A pupil may make a personal disclosure to a member of staff relating to an experience in which the pupil may have been significantly harmed. A pupil may make a disclosure to you at an inappropriate place or time. If this happens, you should talk again individually to the pupil before the end of the day. You may be able to discuss the issue with a senior colleague without giving the name of the pupil. If not, you should follow the school's confidentiality policy and child protection procedures. If a pupil makes a personal disclosure that s/he has been abused in some way, you should:

- ☆ listen to what the child has to say
- ☆ accept what the child is saying
- ☆ allow the child to talk openly
- ☆ listen to the child rather than ask direct questions
- ☆ not criticise the alleged perpetrator of the abuse
- ☆ reassure the child that what has happened is not his or her fault
- ☆ stress to the child that it was the right thing to tell someone
- ☆ reassure the child but not make promises that you might not be able to keep
- ☆ not promise the child to keep the disclosed information confidential (as it might be necessary for the matter to be referred to social services)
- ☆ explain simply to the child what has to be done next and who has to be told.

After a pupil has made a disclosure to you:

1. Make brief notes as soon as possible after the conversation
2. Do not destroy the original notes, as the courts may need these
3. Record the date, time, place and any noticeable non-verbal behaviour as well as the words used by the child
4. Draw a diagram to indicate the position of any bruising or other injury
5. Record only statements and observations rather than interpretations or assumptions.

Dealing with a disclosure from a pupil or being involved in a child protection case can be a very distressing and stressful experience. You may require support for yourself and should discuss with a senior colleague how to access support when dealing with a case of child abuse or neglect.

Allegations of abuse against staff or volunteers

If a pupil, or parent, makes a complaint of abuse against a member of staff or volunteer, the person receiving the complaint must take it seriously and follow the relevant procedures in line with LSCB procedures. Professionals who are independent of the school should investigate all allegations of abuse against staff or volunteers.

If you have reason to suspect that a pupil may have been abused by another member of staff, either in the school or elsewhere, you must immediately inform a senior colleague. You should make a record of the concerns including a note of anyone else who witnessed the incident or allegation. The headteacher will not investigate the incident themselves but will assess whether it is necessary to refer the matter to social services.

If the headteacher decides that the allegation warrants further action through child protection procedures, a referral will be made direct to social services. If the allegation constitutes a serious criminal offence it will be necessary to contact social services and the police before informing the member of staff. If it is decided that it is not necessary to refer the matter to social services then the headteacher will consider whether there needs to be an internal investigation. If the complaint is about the headteacher, then the LSCB should be contacted for information on the necessary procedures to be followed.

EXERCISE: Find out about your school's procedures for dealing with allegations of abuse against staff or volunteers.

The confidentiality of information relating to abuse

Child protection raises issues of confidentiality that must be clearly understood by everyone within the school. You must be absolutely clear about the boundaries of your legal and professional role and responsibilities with regard to the confidentiality of information relating to abuse. A clear and explicit confidentiality policy that staff, pupils and parents can all understand should ensure good practice throughout the school.

Teaching assistants have a legal duty of confidence with regard to the personal information they hold about pupils and their families. Any information you receive about pupils (and their families) in the course of your work should be shared only within appropriate professional contexts. All information, including child protection records, should be kept securely. The law allows the disclosure of confidential personal information in order to safeguard a child or children. Usually, personal information should be disclosed to a third party (e.g. social services) only after obtaining the consent of the person to whom the information relates. In some child protection matters it may not be possible or desirable to obtain such consent. The Data Protection Act 1998 allows disclosure without consent in some circumstances, e.g. to detect or prevent a crime, to apprehend or prosecute an offender.

The safety and well-being of pupils must always be your first consideration. You cannot offer or guarantee absolute confidentiality, especially if there are concerns that a pupil is experiencing, or is at risk of, significant harm. You have a responsibility to share relevant information about the protection of children with other professionals, particularly the investigative agencies, e.g. social services and the police. If a pupil confides in you and requests that the information is kept secret, it is important that you explain to the pupil in a sensitive manner that you have a responsibility to refer cases of alleged abuse to the appropriate agencies for the pupil's sake. Within that context, the pupil should, however, be assured that the matter will be disclosed only to people who need to know about it.

As a teaching assistant you should understand the following:

- ✫ be absolutely clear about your school's child protection policy
- ✫ know and understand your exact role and responsibilities with regard to confidentiality and child protection issues
- ✫ if a pupil asks to speak to you in confidence, they should always be told beforehand that unconditional confidentiality may not always be possible if someone is in danger of abuse

- ☆ if confidentiality is to be breached, the pupil needs to know who will be told, why and what the outcome is likely to be and how they will be supported
- ☆ know when and who to contact if further advice, support or counselling is needed
- ☆ ensure all pupils and their parents/carers are aware of the school's confidentiality policy and how it works in practice
- ☆ make sure pupils are informed of sources of confidential help, e.g. ChildLine.

 KEY TASK

1. What are your responsibilities for reporting information on possible abuse to a senior colleague?
2. How and to whom should you pass on information from a pupil's personal disclosure of abuse? For example, your role and responsibilities for providing information on the disclosure to a senior colleague.
3. Find out about your school's policy and procedures with regard to the confidentiality of information in child protection matters.

 NVQ LINKS:

Level 2 and Level 3: STL3.3

Helping children to protect themselves from abuse

An effective child protection policy will promote a caring and supportive environment in the school and create an atmosphere in which pupils feel that they are secure, valued, listened to and taken seriously. The school's child protection policy should support children's learning and development in ways that foster their security, confidence and independence.

Child protection not only involves the detection of abuse and neglect but also the *prevention* of abuse by helping pupils to protect themselves. As part of this preventive role you should work with the class teacher to help pupils to: understand what is and is not acceptable behaviour towards them; stay safe from harm; speak up if they have worries and concerns; develop awareness and resilience; prepare for their future responsibilities as adults, citizens and parents. Being actively involved in prevention helps pupils to keep safe both now and in the future. Pupils need to know how to take responsibility for themselves and to understand the consequences of their actions. Pupils should know and understand: that they all deserve care and respect; their rights and how to assert them; how to do things safely and how to minimise risk; how to deal with abusive or potentially abusive situations; and when and how to ask for help and support.

Helping pupils to keep themselves safe

Critical thinking and decision-making are also essential for helping pupils to keep themselves safe. You can help them to develop these skills by encouraging them to participate in decision-making within the school and providing opportunities for co-operation. You should also encourage pupils to trust their own feelings and good judgement in difficult situations. By learning to trust their inner feelings, they can avoid many potentially risky situations. Use role-play to help them think about what they should do if their friends want them to do something they dislike or feel uncomfortable about, e.g. going to a party, getting drunk, having sex, shoplifting, taking drugs, etc. Peer pressure can be very strong; encourage pupils to decide and set limits about what they will and will not do so that they know how to cope before the situation arises. Make sure that pupils understand the dangers of situations that may put their personal safety at risk, such as being left at home alone; playing in deserted or dark places; being out on their own; getting lost, e.g. on outings; walking home alone, especially in the dark; talking to strangers; accepting lifts from strangers including hitchhiking.

As pupils get older they need opportunities to explore their environment and to develop their independence. To do this safely they will need to know and understand about acceptable risk-taking. Risk-taking can be explored through stories (e.g. *Jack and the Beanstalk*) and television programmes. Pupils can think about and discuss the risks taken by their favourite characters. Encourage them to identify some of the risks they take in their own lives and look at ways they can minimise risk. Puppets and role-play can be used to help them deal with potentially risky situations. Ensure pupils know and understand **The Keepsafe Code** (see www.kidscape.org.uk).

Helping pupils to access appropriate support when necessary

Pupils need to know where to go for help and support in difficult situations. They should be encouraged to identify people in the school and the local community who help them to keep safe, e.g. worries about bullying or problems at home may be discussed with a member of school staff; if they get lost they can ask a police officer for assistance. Encourage pupils to think of a trusted adult (e.g. parents, other relative, best friend, teacher, teaching assistant) they could talk to about a difficult situation, e.g. abuse, bullying, negative peer pressure, etc. Ensure that they understand that if they go to an adult for help, especially within the school, they will be believed and supported. Provide them with information about other sources of help and support, e.g. ChildLine, The Samaritans, etc.

 KEY TASK

Think about the ways your setting helps children and young people to protect themselves.

 NVQ LINKS:

Level 3: STL46.3

Further reading

Dare, A. and O'Donovan, M. (2000) *Good practice in child safety.* Nelson Thornes.

DfEE (1998a) *Guidance on first-aid for schools: a good practice guide.* DfEE.

DfEE (1998b) *Health and safety of pupils on educational visits: a good practice guide.* DfEE.

DfES/DH (2005) *Managing medicines in schools and early years settings.* DfES/Department of Health.

Gamlin, L. (2005) *The allergy bible.* 2nd edition. Quadrille Publishing Ltd.

Department of Health (2003) *What to do if you're worried a child is being abused.* DH. (Free copies of this booklet are available via the DH website: www.dh.gov.uk.)

HSE (2004) *Getting to grips with manual handling: a short guide.* Leaflet INDG143 (rev2). HSE Books.

HSE (2005) *COSHH: a brief guide to the regulations: what you need to know about the Control of Substances Hazardous to Health Regulations 2002.* Leaflet INDG136 (rev3). HSE Books.

HSE (2006) *Five steps to risk assessment.* INDG163 (rev2). HSE Books.

HSE (2006) *Health and safety law: what you should know.* Leaflet (ISBN: 0 7176 1702 5). HSE Books. Available free at: http://www.hse.gov.uk/pubns/law.pdf.

Lindon, J. (2003) *Child protection.* 2nd edition. Hodder Arnold.

St. John Ambulance, St. Andrew's Ambulance Association and British Red Cross (2006) *First-aid manual.* Dorling Kindersley.

[Note: DfES publications are available free from: www.teachernet.gov.uk and single copies of the above HSE leaflets are also available free from: www.hse.gov.uk.]

3 Supporting children's development

Key points:

- ✳ Observing and assessing development
- ✳ The basic principles of child observation
- ✳ Observation methods
- ✳ Recording observations and assessments
- ✳ Planning provision to promote development
- ✳ The planning cycle
- ✳ Implementing and evaluating plans to promote development
- ✳ Understanding children's development
- ✳ The sequence of children's development
- ✳ Promoting children's social, physical, intellectual, communication and emotional development.

Observing and assessing development

Accurate observations and assessments are essential to effective educational practice. Careful observations enable you and the teacher to make objective assessments relating to each pupil's behaviour patterns, learning styles, levels of development, existing skills, curriculum strengths and weaknesses, current learning needs and learning achievements. Assessment of this information can help highlight and celebrate pupils' strengths as well as identify any gaps in their learning. This information can form the basis for the ongoing planning of appropriate learning activities; it may also be a useful starting point for future learning goals or objectives.

Why do you need to observe pupils?

There are many reasons why it is important to observe pupils. For example:

- ☆ To understand the wide range of skills in all areas of their development
- ☆ To know and understand the sequence of children's development
- ☆ To use this knowledge to link theory with your own practice in the school

✮ To assess children's development and existing skills or behaviour

✮ To plan activities appropriate to children's individual learning needs.

Thinking about observing by Jackie Harding and Liz Meldon-Smith (2001)

EXERCISE: Write a short account explaining why it is important to observe and assess pupils' development.

Where and what should you observe?

You will usually be observing activities which are part of the pupil's usual routine. You can observe pupils' development, learning and behaviour in a variety of situations. For example, you might observe the following:

✮ A child talking with another child or adult

✮ An adult working with a small group of children

✮ A child or a small group of children playing indoors or outdoors, or participating in a small or large group discussion, e.g. circle time

✮ An adult reading/telling a story to a child or group of children

☆ A child or group of children participating in a creative, literacy, mathematics or science activity, e.g. doing painting, writing, numeracy work or carrying out an experiment.

The basic principles of child observation

Some important points have already been mentioned with regard to observing children's development, learning and behaviour. You also need to consider the following:

1. **Confidentiality** must be kept at all times. You *must* have the teacher's and/or the parents' permission before making formal observations of pupils.

2. **Be objective.** Record only what you actually see or hear not what you think or feel. For example, the statement *'The child cried'* is objective, but to say *'The child is sad'* is subjective, as you do not know what the child is feeling; children can cry for a variety of reasons, e.g. to draw attention to themselves or to show discomfort.

3. **Remember equal opportunities.** Consider children's cultural backgrounds, e.g. children may be very competent at communicating in their community language, but may have more difficulty in expressing themselves in English; this does *not* mean they are behind in their language development. Consider how any special needs may affect children's development, learning and/or behaviour.

4. **Be positive!** Focus on the children's strengths not just on any learning or behavioural difficulties they may have. Look at what children *can* do in terms of their development and/or learning and use this as the foundation for providing future activities.

5. **Use a holistic approach.** Remember to look at the 'whole' child. You need to look at *all* areas of children's development in relation to the particular aspect of development or learning you are focusing on. For example, when observing children's drawing or painting skills, as well as looking at their intellectual development you will need to consider: their physical development (fine motor skills when using a pencil or paintbrush); their language development and communication skills (vocabulary and structure of language used to describe their drawing or painting if appropriate); their social and emotional development (interaction with others and behaviour during the drawing or painting activity).

6. **Consider the children's feelings.** Depending on the children's ages, needs and abilities, you should discuss the observation with the children to be observed and respond appropriately to their views.

7. **Minimise distractions.** Observe children without intruding or causing unnecessary stress. Try to keep your distance where possible, but be close enough to hear the children's language. Try not to interact with the children (unless it is a participant observation – see below), but if they do address you, be polite and respond positively, e.g. explain to the children simply what you are doing and keep your answers short.

8. **Practise.** The best way to develop your skills at observing children's development, learning and behaviour is to do observations on a regular basis.

The teacher and your college tutor/assessor will give you guidelines for the methods most appropriate to your role as a teaching assistant in your particular school. Your observations and assessments must be in line with the school's policy for record-keeping and relevant to the routines and activities of the pupils you work with. You must follow the school's policy regarding **confidentiality** at all times and be able to implement data protection procedures as appropriate to your role and responsibilities. (See sections on confidentiality matters in Chapter 5 and maintaining pupil records in Chapter 12.)

The school should obtain permission from the parents or carers of the pupils being observed, e.g. a letter requesting permission to do regular observations and assessments could be sent out for the parents to sign giving their consent. If you are a student, before doing any portfolio activities for your NVQ assessment involving observations of children, you MUST negotiate with the class teacher when it will be possible for you to carry out your observations and have written permission to do so.

Observation methods

When observing pupils you need to use an appropriate method of observation as directed by the teacher. When assisting the teacher in observing and reporting on a pupil's development ensure that you consider all relevant aspects of development, for example: Social; Physical; Intellectual; Communication; Emotional.

You may observe an individual pupil or group of pupils on several occasions on different days of the week and at different times of the day. Use developmental charts for the pupil's age group to identify areas of development where the pupil is making progress, as well as those where the pupil is under-achieving. For example, a pupil with limited speech may still be developing positive social relationships with other children by using non-verbal communication during play activities.

Observations and assessments should cover all relevant aspects of pupil development including: physical skills; language and communication skills; social and emotional behaviour during different learning activities.

The class teacher will give you guidelines for the methods most appropriate to your role as a teaching assistant in your particular school. The methods for observations and assessments depend on school policies and any legal requirements. Your observations and assessments must always be in line with the school policy for record-keeping and relevant to the learning activities of the pupils you work with. You must follow the school policy regarding confidentiality at all times (see section on confidentiality matters in Chapter 5).

You may be able to assist the class or form teacher to compile a portfolio of relevant information about each pupil. A portfolio could include: observations; examples of the pupil's work; photographs of the pupil during learning activities; checklists of the pupil's progress. Assessment of this information can help highlight and celebrate the pupil's strengths as well as identify any gaps in their learning. This information can form the basis for the ongoing planning of appropriate learning activities and can be a useful starting point for future learning goals/objectives. (Information about formative and summative assessments can be found in Chapter 9.)

Tick chart: *Group observations of children at snack/meal time*

Self-help skills	Children's names			
	Shafik	Sukhvinder	Ruth	Tom
goes to the toilet				
washes hands				
dries hands				
chooses own snack/meal				
uses fingers				
uses spoon				
uses fork				
uses knife				
holds cup with 2 hands				
holds cup with 1 hand				

KEY: ✓ = competent at skill. \ = attempts skill/needs adult direction. ✗ = no attempt/requires assistance.

Pie chart: *Time sample observation of child's play activities*

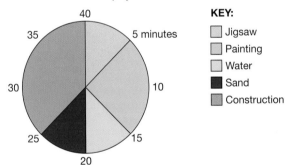

KEY:
- Jigsaw
- Painting
- Water
- Sand
- Construction

Bar graph: *Time sample observation of child's social play*

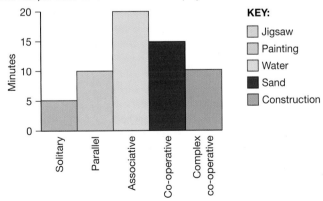

KEY:
- Jigsaw
- Painting
- Water
- Sand
- Construction

Examples of observation charts

Recording observations and assessments

You should record your observations and assessments using an agreed format. This might be a: written descriptive account; structured profile (with specified headings for each section); or a pre-coded system of recording. Once you have recorded your observation of the pupil (or group of pupils), you need to make an **assessment** of this information in relation to:

✶ the aims of the observation, e.g. why you were doing this observation

✶ what you observed about the pupil's development, learning and/or behaviour in *this* particular activity

✶ how this compares to the expected level of development for a pupil of this age

✶ any factors which may have affected the pupil's ability to learn and/or behave, e.g. the immediate environment, significant events, illness, pupil's cultural background, special needs.

Your assessment may include charts, diagrams and other representations of the data you collected from your observation (see examples of observation charts above). Your college tutor or assessor should give you guidelines on how to present your observations. Otherwise you might find this suggested format useful:

Suggested format for presenting observations

Date of observation:

Method:

Start time:

Finish time:

Number of pupils/staff:

Permission for observation:

Type of school and age range: *e.g. nursery, primary, secondary or special school*

Immediate context/background information: *including the activity and its location*

Description of pupil or pupils: *including age(s) in years and months*

Aims: *why are you doing this particular observation?*

Observation: *the observation may be a written report, a pie chart or bar graph, tick chart*

Assessment: *include the following:*

● *Did you achieve your aims?*

● *Your assessment of the pupil s development, learning and/or behaviour, looking at all aspects of the pupil's development but with particular emphasis on the focus area (e.g. literacy or numeracy skills).*

● *References to support your comments.*

Personal learning: *what you gained from doing this observation, e.g. what you have learned about this aspect of child development and using this particular method of observing pupils, e.g. was this the most appropriate method of observation for this type of activity?*

Recommendations:

- *On how to encourage/extend the pupil's development, learning and/or behaviour in the focus area, e.g. suggestions for activities to develop the pupil's literacy or numeracy skills.*
- *For any aspect of the pupil's development, learning and/or behaviour which you think requires further observation and assessment.*

References/bibliography: *list details of all the books used to complete your assessment.*

 KEY TASK

1. Observe a pupil during a learning activity.
2. Include the following information in your assessment:
   - The type of learning activity observed (e.g. curriculum subject/area of learning).
   - The intended learning goals/objectives for the pupil.
   - The actual development and learning skills demonstrated by the pupil.
   - The pupil's communication skills and behaviour during the activity.
   - Suggestions for extending the pupil's development and learning in this area.
3. Use relevant sections from this chapter (and other education books) to help you with your assessment. Remember your setting's guidelines for pupil observations.

 NVQ LINKS:

Level 2:

STL2.1	STL2.2	STL2.3
STL2.4	STL9.1	STL9.2

Level 3:

STL18.1	STL27.3	STL29.1

Planning provision to promote development

As directed by the teacher you may be involved in planning provision for the pupils you work with based on assessments of their developmental progress. You should recognise that developmental progress depends on each pupil's level of maturation and their prior experiences (see section below on understanding children's development). You should take these into account and have realistic expectations when planning activities to promote pupils' development. This includes regularly reviewing and updating plans for individual pupils and ensuring that plans balance the needs of individual pupils and the group as appropriate to your school. You should know and understand that pupils develop at widely different rates but in broadly the same sequence. When planning provision to promote pupils' development you need to recognise that children's development is holistic even though it is divided into different areas, e.g. **SPICE**: Social; Physical; Intellectual; Communication and language; Emotional. You should remember to look at the 'whole' child. You need to look at *all* areas of children's development in relation to the particular aspect of development or learning you are focusing on when planning provision to promote pupils' development. (More detailed information can be found in the section on understanding children's development below.)

The planning cycle

Following observations and assessments of a pupil's development, learning and/or behaviour, the recommendations can provide the basis for planning appropriate activities to encourage and extend the pupil's skills in specific areas. Effective planning is based on individual needs, abilities and interests, hence the importance of accurate and reliable child observations and assessments. You will also support the teacher in planning provision based on the requirements for the relevant curriculum frameworks.

When planning learning activities, your overall aims should be to: support the development and learning of *all* the pupils you work with; ensure every pupil

Planning children's activities by Jackie Harding and Liz Meldon-Smith (2001)

has full access to the appropriate curriculum; meet pupils' individual developmental and learning needs; build on each pupil's existing knowledge, understanding and skills. (For detailed information on planning learning activities see Chapters 1 and 9.)

EXERCISE: Describe how *you* plan provision to promote pupils' development in your school. Include examples of any planning sheets you use.

Implementing and evaluating plans to promote development

Good preparation and organisation are essential when implementing plans to promote pupils' development including: having ready any instructions and/or questions for the pupil or group of pupils, e.g. prompt cards, worksheet, work card or written on the board; ensuring there are sufficient materials and equipment including any specialist equipment; setting out the materials and equipment on the table ready or letting the pupils get the resources out for themselves depending on their ages and abilities. Implementing an activity may involve: giving out any instructions to the pupils; showing pupils what to do, e.g. demonstrate a new technique; keeping an individual pupil and/or group of pupils on task; clarifying meaning and/or ideas; explaining any difficult words to the pupils; assisting pupils with any special equipment, e.g. hearing aid or a Dictaphone; providing any other appropriate assistance; encouraging the pupils to tidy up afterwards as appropriate to their ages and abilities; remembering to maintain pupil safety at all times.

After you have planned and/or implemented an activity you will need to evaluate it. Some evaluation also occurs during the activity, providing continuous assessment of a pupil's performance. It is important to evaluate the activity so that you can: assess whether the activity has been successful, e.g. the aims and objectives have been met; identify possible ways in which the activity might be modified/adapted to meet the individual needs of the pupil or pupils; provide accurate information for the teacher, SENCO or other professionals about the success of a particular activity. The teacher or your college tutor/assessor should give you guidelines on how to present your activity plans. If not, you might find this suggested format useful:

Suggested format for activity plans:

Title: *brief description of the activity*

Date: *the date of the activity*

Plan duration: *how long will the activity last?*

Aim and rationale: *the main purpose of the activity including how it will encourage development, learning and/or behaviour. The rationale should outline why this particular activity has been selected (e.g. identified particular pupil's need through observation; links to topics/themes within the class or school). How does the activity link with curriculum requirements?*

Staff and school: *the roles and number of staff involved in the activity, plus the type of school and the age range of the pupils.*

Details of pupil or pupils: *activity plans involving an individual pupil or small group of pupils should specify first name, age in years and months, plus any relevant special needs; activity plans involving larger groups should specify the age range and ability levels.*

Learning objectives for the pupil or pupils: *indicate what the pupil or pupils could gain from participating in the activity in each developmental area: SPICE.*

Preparation: *what do you need to prepare in advance (e.g. selecting or making appropriate materials; checking availability of equipment)? Think about the instructions and/or questions for the pupil or pupils; will these be spoken and/or written down, e.g. on a worksheet/card or on the board? Do you need prompt cards for instructions or questions?*

Resources: *what materials and equipment will you need? Where will you get them from? Are there any special requirements? Remember equal opportunities, including special needs. How will you set out the necessary resources (e.g. setting out on the table or the pupils getting out materials and equipment for themselves)?*

Organisation: *where will you implement the activity? How will you organise the activity? How will you give out any instructions the pupils need? Will you work with pupils one at a time or as a group? Are there any particular safety requirements? How will you organise any tidying up after the activity? Will the pupils be encouraged to help tidy up?*

Implementation: *describe what happened when you implemented the activity with the pupil or pupils. Include any alterations to the original plan, e.g. changes in timing or resources.*

Equal opportunities: *indicate any multicultural aspects to the activity and any additional considerations for pupils with special needs.*

Review and evaluation: *review and evaluate the following:*

- *The aims and learning objectives*
- *The effectiveness of your preparation, organisation and implementation*
- *What you learned about children's development and learning*
- *What you learned about planning activities*
- *Possible modifications for future similar activities.*

References and/or bibliography: *the review and evaluation may include references appropriate to children's development, learning and behaviour. Include a bibliography of any books used as references or for ideas when planning the activity.*

 KEY TASK

Use your suggestions from your observation of a pupil during a learning activity (see page 55) to plan an activity to extend the pupil's skills in a specific area. After discussing your plan with the class teacher, implement and then evaluate the activity.

NVQ LINKS:

Level 2:
STL1.1   STL1.2   STL1.3
STL2.4   STL10.1

Level 3:
STL18.1   STL23.1   STL23.2
STL23.3   STL24.1   STL24.2
STL27.1   STL27.2   STL27.3
STL29.2

Understanding children's development

The most essential aspect of supporting pupils' development involves your role and responsibilities for providing routines and activities that will help to meet *all* the children's developmental needs: **SPICE** – Social; Physical; Intellectual; Communication and language; Emotional. To do this you need to know and understand children's development.

The sequence of children's development

It is more accurate to think in terms of a sequence of children's development rather than stages of development. This is because stages refer to development that occurs at *fixed ages* while sequence indicates development that follows the same basic pattern *but not necessarily at fixed ages.* You should really use the term 'sequence' when referring to all aspects of children's development. However, the work of people such as Mary Sheridan provides a useful guide to the milestones of *expected* development, that is, the usual pattern of children's development or norm. As well as their chronological age, children's development is affected by many other factors, e.g. maturation, social interaction, play opportunities, early learning experiences, special needs. The developmental charts in this chapter *do* indicate specific ages, but only to provide a framework to help you understand children's development. Always remember that all children are unique individuals and develop at their own rate.

Promoting children's social development

Promoting children's social development involves helping children to develop social skills such as: **socialisation** (how children relate socially and emotionally to other people); developing **independence** (including self-help skills, e.g. feeding, toileting, dressing); understanding **moral concepts** (the difference between right and wrong); developing acceptable **behaviour** patterns; developing positive **relationships**; understanding the **needs and rights of others**. (For detailed information on children's behaviour see Chapter 4 and see Chapter 7 for more information on children's social development.)

The sequence of children s social development: 0 to 16 years

Age 0 to 3 months

- *Cries to communicate needs to others; stops crying to listen to others.*
- *Responds to smiles from others; responds positively to others, e.g. family members and even friendly strangers unless very upset (when only main caregiver will do!).*
- *Considers others only in relation to satisfying own needs for food, drink, warmth, sleep, comfort and reassurance.*

Age 3 to 9 months

- *Responds positively to others, especially to familiar people such as family members; by 9 months is very wary of strangers.*

- *Communicates with others by making noises and participating in 'conversation-like' exchanges; responds to own name.*
- *Begins to see self as separate from others.*

Age 9 to 18 months

- *Responds to simple instructions (if wants to!).*
- *Communicates using (limited) range of recognisable words.*
- *Shows egocentric behaviour, e.g. expects to be considered first; all toys belong to them.*
- *Is unintentionally aggressive to other children.*

Age 18 months to 2 years

- *Responds positively to others, e.g. plays alongside other children and enjoys games with known adults.*
- *Communicates more effectively with others; responds to simple instructions.*
- *Wants to help adults and enjoys imitating their activities.*
- *May be interested in older children and their activities; imitates these activities.*
- *May unintentionally disrupt the play of others, e.g. takes toys away to play with by self.*
- *Becomes very independent, e.g. wants to do things by self.*
- *Still demonstrates egocentric behaviour; wants own way and says 'No!' a lot.*

Age 2 to 3 years

- *Continues to enjoy the company of others.*
- *Wants to please and seeks approval from adults.*
- *Is still very egocentric and very protective of own possessions; unable to share with other children although may give toy to another child if adult requests it, to please the adult.*
- *May find group experiences difficult due to this egocentric behaviour.*
- *Uses language more effectively to communicate with others.*

Age 3 to 5 years

- *Enjoys the company of others; learns to play with other children, not just alongside them.*
- *Uses language to communicate more and more effectively with others.*
- *Develops self-help skills (e.g. dressing self, going to the toilet) as becomes more competent and confident in own abilities.*
- *Still wants to please and seeks approval from adults.*
- *Observes closely how others behave and imitates them.*
- *Still fairly egocentric; may get angry with other children if disrupt play activities or snatch play items required for own play; expects adults to take their side in any dispute.*
- *Gradually is able to share group possessions at playgroup or nursery.*

Age 5 to 7 years

- *Enjoys the company of other children; may have special friend(s).*
- *Uses language even more effectively to communicate, share ideas, engage in more complex play activities.*
- *Appears confident and competent in own abilities.*
- *Co-operates with others, takes turns and begins to follow rules in games.*
- *Seeks adult approval; will even blame others for own mistakes to escape disapproval.*
- *Observes how others behave and will imitate them; has a particular role model.*
- *May copy unwanted behaviour, e.g. swearing, biting or kicking to gain adult attention.*

Age 7 to 12 years

- *Continues to enjoy the company of other children; wants to belong to a group; usually has at least one special friend.*
- *Uses language to communicate very effectively, but may use it in negative ways, e.g. name-calling or telling tales, as well as positively to share ideas and participate in complex play activities often based on television characters or computer games.*
- *Is able to play on own; appreciates own space away from others on occasion.*
- *Becomes less concerned with adult approval and more concerned with peer approval.*
- *Is able to participate in games with rules and other co-operative activities.*

Age 12 to 16 years

- *Continues to enjoy the company of other children/young people; individual friendships are still important; belonging to group or gang becomes increasingly important but can also be a major source of anxiety or conflict.*
- *The desire for peer approval can overtake the need for adult approval and may cause challenges to adult authority at home, school or in the play setting, particularly in the teenage years.*
- *Participates in team games/sports or other group activities including clubs and hobbies; can follow complex rules and co-operate fully but may be very competitive.*
- *Strongly influenced by a variety of role models, especially those in the media, e.g. sports celebrities and film/pop stars.*
- *Is able to communicate very effectively and uses language much more to resolve any difficulties in social interactions.*
- *Can be very supportive towards others, e.g. people with special needs or those experiencing difficulties at home, school, in the play setting or the wider community.*

KEY TASK

1. Observe a group of pupils during a play activity or playing a game. Focus on one pupil's social development.

2. In your assessment comment on: the pupil's level of social interaction; the pupil's use of language and communication skills; the pupil's behaviour during the activity; the role of the adult in promoting the pupil's social development; suggestions for further activities to encourage or extend the pupil's social development including appropriate resources.

NVQ LINKS:

Level 2:
STL2.2   STL9.1   STL9.2
STL10.1

Level 3:
STL18.1   STL27.3   STL29.1

Five ways to promote children's social development

As a teaching assistant, you should support the teacher in providing appropriate routines and activities to encourage and extend the children's social skills. You can help to promote children's social development by:

1. **Setting goals and boundaries** to encourage socially acceptable behaviour as appropriate to the children's ages and levels of development. Using appropriate praise and rewards can help.

2. **Encouraging the children's self-help skills**. Be patient and provide time for the child to do things independently, e.g. choosing play activities and selecting own materials; helping to tidy up; dressing independently during dressing-up.

3. **Providing opportunities for the children to participate in social play**, e.g. encourage children to join in team games, sports and other co-operative activities.

4. **Using books, stories, puppets and play people** to help the children understand ideas about fairness, jealousy and growing up, dealing with conflict situations.

5. **Encouraging the children to take turns**, e.g. sharing toys and other play equipment. Emphasising co-operation and sharing rather than competition.

KEY TASK

1. Plan a play activity which encourages or extends a pupil's social development. For example, encouraging the pupil to use a variety of social skills such as: demonstrating positive behaviour; being independent (e.g. using self-help skills or making choices); using effective communication skills; sharing resources; understanding the needs and feelings of others. Use the assessment from your observation of a pupil's social development from page 62 as the basis for your planning.

> **NVQ LINKS:**
>
> **Level 2:**
> STL1.2   STL1.3   STL2.4
> STL10.1   STL12.2
>
> **Level 3:**
> STL18.1   STL18.2   STL 23.1
> STL23.2   STL23.3   STL 24.1
> STL24.2   STL27.1   STL27.2
> STL27.3   STL29.2   STL37.1
> STL38.2

2. Consider how you could meet the needs of a pupil or pupils with behavioural difficulties with this activity (see Chapter 11).

3. If possible, ask the class teacher for permission to implement the activity. Evaluate the activity afterwards.

Promoting children's physical development

Physical development involves children's increasing ability to perform more complex physical activities: **gross motor skills** involving whole body movements, e.g. walking, running, climbing, hopping, jumping, skipping, cycling, swimming and ball games; **fine motor skills** involving whole hand movements, wrist action or delicate procedures using the fingers, e.g. drawing, painting, writing, model-making, playing with wooden/plastic bricks or construction kits, cutting with scissors, doing/undoing buttons, shoelaces and other fastenings; and **co-ordination** involving hand–eye co-ordination (e.g. drawing, painting, using scissors, writing and threading beads), whole body co-ordination (e.g. crawling, walking, cycling, swimming and playing football or netball) and balance (e.g. hopping and gymnastics).

As directed by the teacher you should help to provide appropriate play opportunities for children and young people to develop their physical skills (see Chapter 8). Remember that some children may be limited in their physical abilities due to physical disability, sensory impairment or other special needs (see Chapter 11).

The sequence of children's physical development: 0 to 16 years

Age 0 to 3 months

- *Sleeps much of the time and grows fast.*
- *Tries to lift head.*
- *Starts to kick legs with movements gradually becoming smoother.*
- *Starts to wave arms about.*
- *Begins to hold objects when placed in hand, e.g. an appropriate size/shaped rattle.*
- *Grasp reflex diminishes as hand and eye co-ordination begins to develop.*
- *Enjoys finger play, e.g. simple finger rhymes.*
- *Becomes more alert when awake.*
- *Learns to roll from side on to back.*
- *Sees best at distance of 25cm then gradually starts watching objects further away.*
- *Needs opportunities to play and exercise, e.g. soft toys, cloth books and playmat with different textures and sounds.*

Age 3 to 9 months

- *Establishes head control; moves head round to follow people and objects.*
- *Begins to sit with support; from about 6 months sits unsupported.*
- *Rolls over.*
- *May begin to crawl, stand and cruise while holding on to furniture (from about 6 months).*
- *Learns to pull self up to sitting position.*
- *Begins to use palmar grasp and transfers objects from one hand to the other.*
- *Develops pincer grasp using thumb and index finger from about 6 months.*
- *Continues to enjoy finger rhymes.*
- *Drops things deliberately and searches for hidden/dropped objects (from about 8 months).*
- *Puts objects into containers and takes them out.*
- *Enjoys water play in the bath.*
- *Needs opportunities for play and exercise including soft toys, board books, bricks, containers, activity centres, etc.*

Age 9 to 18 months

- *Is now very mobile, e.g. crawls, bottom-shuffles, cruises, walks.*
- *Starts to go upstairs (with supervision) but has difficulty coming down.*
- *Needs safe environment in which to explore as becomes increasingly mobile, e.g. remember safety gates on stairs, etc.*
- *Throws toys deliberately.*
- *Watches ball rolling towards self and tries to push it back.*
- *Has mature pincer grasp and can scribble with crayons.*
- *Points to objects using index finger.*
- *Places one (or more) bricks on top of each other to make a small tower.*
- *Holds a cup and tries to feed self.*

▶

- *Continues to enjoy finger rhymes plus simple action songs.*
- *Needs space, materials and opportunities to play alongside other children.*

Age 18 months to 2 years

- *Starts using potty but has difficulty keeping dry.*
- *Can feed self.*
- *Walks well and tries to run but has difficulty stopping.*
- *Comes downstairs on front with help.*
- *Learns to push a pedal-less tricycle or sit-and-ride toy with feet.*
- *Tries to throw ball but has difficulty catching.*
- *Bends down to pick things up.*
- *Uses several bricks to make a tower.*
- *As fine motor skills improve, continues to scribble and can do very simple jigsaw puzzles.*
- *Enjoys action songs and rhymes.*
- *Needs space, materials and opportunities to play alongside other children.*

Age 2 to 3 years

- *Uses potty and stays dry more reliably.*
- *Comes downstairs in upright position one stair at a time.*
- *Starts to climb well on play apparatus.*
- *Kicks a ball, learns to jump and may learn to somersault.*
- *Learns to pedal a tricycle.*
- *Can undress self; tries to dress self but needs help, especially with socks and fastenings.*
- *Fine motor skills improving: has increased control of crayons and paintbrush; tries to use scissors.*
- *Enjoys construction activities and can build more complex structures.*
- *Continues to enjoy action songs and rhymes.*
- *Needs space, materials and opportunities to play alongside and with other children.*

Age 3 to 5 years

- *Usually clean and dry but may have occasional 'accidents'.*
- *Able to run well – and stop!*
- *Competent at gross motor skills such as jumping, riding a tricycle, climbing play apparatus, using a swing.*
- *Throws and catches a ball but is still inaccurate.*
- *Fine motor skills continue to improve, e.g. can use scissors.*
- *Continues to enjoy action songs plus simple singing and dancing games.*
- *Needs space, materials and opportunities to play co-operatively with other children.*

Age 5 to 7 years

- *Clean and dry but may still have occasional 'accidents' if absorbed in an activity or upset.*

- *Can dress/undress self but may still need help with intricate fastenings and shoelaces.*
- *Has improved gross motor skills and co-ordination so is more proficient at running, jumping, climbing and balancing.*
- *Has some difficulty with hopping and skipping.*
- *Has improved ball skills but still learning to use a bat.*
- *May learn to ride a bicycle (with stabilisers).*
- *Enjoys swimming activities.*
- *Fine motor skills continue to improve: has better pencil/crayon control; is more competent at handling materials and making things.*
- *Continues to enjoy action songs plus singing and dancing games.*
- *Needs space, materials and opportunities to play co-operatively with other children.*

Age 7 to 12 years

- *Can dress/undress self including fastenings and shoelaces.*
- *Grows taller and thinner; starts losing baby teeth.*
- *Improved gross motor skills and co-ordination lead to proficiency in climbing, running, jumping, balancing, hopping and skipping.*
- *Can hit a ball with a bat.*
- *Learns to ride a bicycle (without stabilisers).*
- *Learns to swim (if taught properly).*
- *As fine motor skills improve, handwriting becomes easier and more legible.*
- *Can do more complex construction activities.*
- *Continues to enjoy singing and dancing games.*
- *Needs space, materials and opportunities to play co-operatively with other children.*

Age 12 to 16 years

- *Can dress/undress self including intricate fastenings and shoelaces.*
- *Grows taller and thinner; continues losing baby teeth.*
- *Physical changes of puberty.*
- *Improved gross motor skills and co-ordination lead to proficiency in climbing, running, jumping, balancing, hopping, skipping and swimming.*
- *Enjoys team games and sports.*
- *Rides a bicycle with competence and confidence.*
- *Improved fine motor skills make handwriting easier and more legible.*
- *Can do more complex construction activities.*
- *Continues to enjoy singing and dancing but often prefers performing set dance routines rather than participating in dancing games.*
- *Needs space, materials and opportunities to play co-operatively with other children.*

KEY TASK

1. Observe a pupil involved in a physical activity, e.g. using play equipment or PE apparatus. Focus on the physical skills demonstrated by the pupil.

2. In your assessment comment on: the pupil's gross motor skills; the pupil's fine motor skills; the pupil's co-ordination skills; the role of the adult in promoting the pupil's physical development; suggestions for further activities to encourage or extend the pupil's physical development.

NVQ LINKS:

Level 2:
STL2.1   STL2.2   STL2.3
STL2.4   STL9.1   STL9.2

Level 3:
STL18.1   STL27.3   STL29.1

Five ways to promote children's physical development

As a teaching assistant, you should support the teacher in promoting children's physical development and physical well-being. You can help to promote children's physical development by:

1. **Providing play opportunities for children to explore and experiment** with their gross motor skills both indoors and outdoors, with and without play apparatus or other equipment. Help children to practise fine motor skills (e.g. bricks, jigsaws, play dough, sand, construction kits, drawing) and to develop body awareness through action songs such as 'Head, shoulders, knees and toes'.

2. **Maintaining the children's safety** by supervising the children at all times and checking any equipment used meets required safety standards and is positioned on an appropriate surface. Ensure the children know how to use any equipment correctly and safely.

3. **Selecting activities, tools and materials** that are appropriate to the ages and levels of development of the children to help the children practise their physical skills. Encourage children to persevere with tackling new skills that are particularly difficult and praise the children as they become competent in each physical skill.

4. **Using everyday routines** to develop the children's fine motor skills, e.g. getting dressed, dealing with fastenings and shoelaces, using a cup, using a spoon, fork or knife, helping prepare or serve food, setting the table, washing up (remember safety!).

5. **Allowing the children to be as independent as possible** when developing their physical skills including adapting activities and/or using specialist equipment for children with special needs to enable their participation in physical activities as appropriate.

KEY TASK

1. Plan an activity which encourages or extends a pupil's physical skills such as gross motor skills, fine motor skills and/or co-ordination skills. Use the assessment information from your observation of a pupil's physical development from page 67 as the basis for your planning.

2. Consider how you could meet the needs of pupils with physical disabilities with this activity (see Chapter 11).

NVQ LINKS:

Level 2:

STL1.1	STL1.2	STL1.3
STL2.1	STL2.4	STL10.4
STL12.2		

Level 3:

STL18.1	STL18.2	STL23.1
STL23.2	STL23.3	STL24.1
STL24.2	STL27.1	STL27.2
STL27.3	STL29.2	STL38.2

3. If possible, ask the class teacher for permission to implement the activity. Evaluate the activity afterwards.

Promoting children's intellectual development

Intellectual or cognitive development involves the processes of gaining, storing, recalling and using information. To develop as healthy, considerate and intelligent human beings, all children require intellectual stimulation as well as physical care and emotional security. Children are constantly thinking and learning, gathering new information and formulating new ideas about themselves, other people and the world around them.

The inter-related components of intellectual development are: **thinking**, the intellectual process of using information to find solutions (e.g. problem-solving in mathematics; investigating and hypothesising in science; identifying and solving design needs in technology); **perception**, which involves the ability to identify the differences between objects or sounds (e.g. *auditory perception* – differentiating between sounds; *visual perception* – differentiating between objects or the distance between objects); **language**, the essential component of intellectual development as it enables pupils to make sense of the world around them, access new experiences, store new information and communicate more effectively with others (e.g. ask appropriate questions; verbalise their thoughts; express their opinions and ideas); **problem-solving**, which involves using the intellectual processes of *logic* and *reasoning* to make personal judgements or make connections between existing information and new information (e.g. making mathematical calculations and scientific predictions); **concepts** such as *concrete concepts* like colour, number and shape recognition and *abstract concepts* like telling the time; **memory**, which involves the ability to recall or retrieve information stored in the mind (e.g. *recalling information* about past experiences, events, actions or feelings; *recognising information* and making connections with previous experiences; *predicting*, i.e. using past information to anticipate future events); **concentration**, which involves the ability to pay attention to the situation or task in hand which is necessary for the development of other intellectual processes such as developing language skills and understanding concepts; and **creativity**, which is the use of the imagination and involves the ability to invent ideas or form images of things which are not actually there or do not exist (e.g. creative skills used in play, art, design, technology, music, dance, drama, story-writing and poetry). (There is detailed information about supporting children's thinking and learning in Chapter 9.)

The sequence of children's intellectual development: 0 to 16 years

Age 0 to 3 months

- *Recognises parents; concentrates on familiar voices rather than unfamiliar ones.*
- *Aware of different smells.*
- *Explores by putting objects in mouth.*
- *Observes objects that move; responds to bright colours and bold images.*
- *Stores and recalls information through images.*
- *Sees everything in relation to self (is egocentric).*

Age 3 to 9 months

- *Knows individuals and recognises familiar faces.*
- *Recognises certain sounds and objects.*
- *Shows interest in everything, especially toys and books.*
- *Concentrates on well-defined objects and follows direction of moving object.*
- *Anticipates familiar actions and enjoys games such as 'peep-po'.*
- *Searches for hidden or dropped objects (from about 8 months).*
- *Observes what happens at home and when out and about.*
- *Explores immediate environment once mobile.*
- *Processes information through images.*
- *Enjoys water play in the bath.*
- *Sees everything in relation to self (is still egocentric).*

Age 9 to 18 months

- *Explores immediate environment using senses, especially sight and touch; has no sense of danger.*
- *Concentrates more, due to curiosity and increased physical skills, but still has short attention span.*
- *Follows one-step instructions and/or gestured commands.*
- *Observes other people closely and tries to imitate their actions.*
- *Uses 'trial and error' methods when playing with bricks, containers.*
- *Searches for hidden or dropped objects (aware of object permanence).*
- *Learns that objects can be grouped together.*
- *Continues to store and recall information through images.*
- *Is still egocentric.*

▶

Age 18 months to 2 years

- *Recognises objects from pictures and books.*
- *Points to desired objects; selects named objects.*
- *Matches basic colours; starts to match shapes.*
- *Does very simple puzzles.*
- *Follows one-step instructions.*
- *Concentrates for longer, e.g. searching for hidden object, but attention span still quite short.*
- *Shows lots of curiosity and continues exploring using senses and 'trial and error' methods.*
- *Processes information through images and increasingly through language too.*
- *Shows preferences and starts to make choices.*
- *Is still egocentric.*

Age 2 to 3 years

- *Identifies facial features and main body parts.*
- *Continues to imitate other children and adults.*
- *Follows two-step instructions.*
- *Matches more colours and shapes including puzzles and other matching activities.*
- *Points to named object in pictures and books.*
- *Develops understanding of big and small.*
- *Begins to understand concept of time at basic level, e.g. before/after, today/tomorrow.*
- *Enjoys imaginative play; able to use symbols in play, e.g. pretend a doll is a real baby.*
- *Concentrates on intricate tasks such as creative activities or construction, but may still have short attention span, especially if not really interested in the activity.*
- *Is very pre-occupied with own activities; still egocentric.*
- *Shows some awareness of right and wrong.*
- *Processes information through language rather than images.*

Age 3 to 5 years

- *Learns about basic concepts through play.*
- *Experiments with colour, shape and texture.*
- *Recalls a simple sequence of events.*
- *Follows two- or three-step instructions including positional ones, e.g. 'Please put your ball in the box under the table'.*
- *Continues to enjoy imaginative and creative play.*
- *Interested in more complex construction activities.*
- *Concentrates on more complex activities as attention span increases.*

▶

- *Plays co-operatively with other children; able to accept and share ideas in group activities.*
- *Shows some awareness of right and wrong, the needs of others.*
- *Holds strong opinions about likes and dislikes.*
- *Processes information using language.*

Age 5 to 7 years

- *Is very curious and asks lots of questions.*
- *Continues to enjoy imaginative and creative play activities.*
- *Continues to enjoy construction activities; spatial awareness increases.*
- *Knows, matches and names colours and shapes.*
- *Follows three-step instructions.*
- *Develops interest in reading for themselves.*
- *Enjoys jigsaw puzzles and games.*
- *Concentrates for longer, e.g. television programmes, longer stories and can recall details.*
- *Shows awareness of right and wrong, the needs of others.*
- *Begins to see other people's points of view.*
- *Stores and recalls more complex information using language.*

Age 7 to 12 years

- *Learns to read more complex texts and continues to develop writing skills.*
- *Enjoys number work, but may still need real objects to help mathematical processes.*
- *Enjoys experimenting with materials and exploring the environment.*
- *Develops creative abilities as co-ordination improves, e.g. more detailed drawings.*
- *Begins to know the difference between real and imaginary, but still enjoys imaginative play, e.g. acting out ideas, pretending to be characters from television or films.*
- *Interested in more complex construction activities.*
- *Has longer attention span; does not like to be disturbed during play activities.*
- *Follows increasingly complex instructions.*
- *Enjoys board games and other games with rules; also computer games.*
- *Develops a competitive streak.*
- *Has increased awareness of right and wrong, the needs of others.*
- *Sees other people's points of view.*
- *Seeks information from various sources, e.g. encyclopaedia, Internet.*
- *Processes expanding knowledge and information through language.*

Age 12 to 16 years

- *Reads more complex texts with improved comprehension and extends writing skills.*
- *Develops understanding of abstract mathematical/scientific processes, e.g. algebra, physics.*
- *Continues to enjoy experiments and exploration of the wider environment.*
- *Develops more creative abilities, e.g. very detailed drawings and stories.*
- *Knows the difference between real and imaginary.*
- *Has increased concentration levels.*
- *Continues to follow more complex instructions.*
- *Continues to enjoy board games and computer games which require strategy skills.*
- *Has a competitive streak and may have particular interests which allow them to show off their intellectual abilities, e.g. chess, computer clubs.*
- *Has well-defined understanding of right and wrong; can consider the needs of others.*
- *Sees other people's point of view.*
- *Continues to seek information from various sources, e.g. encyclopaedia, Internet.*
- *Continues to process increasing knowledge and information through language.*

⬤ KEY TASK

1. Observe a pupil during a learning activity. Focus on the pupil's intellectual development.

2. In your assessment, comment on: the pupil's imaginative and creative skills; the pupil's level of concentration; any problem-solving skills used by the pupil; the pupil's use of language and communication skills; the role of the adult in promoting the pupil's intellectual development; and suggestions for further activities to encourage or extend the pupil's intellectual development including appropriate resources.

 NVQ LINKS:

Level 2:
STL2.1   STL2.2   STL2.3
STL2.4   STL9.1   STL9.2

Level 3:
STL18.1   STL27.3   STL29.1

Five ways to promote children's intellectual development

As a teaching assistant, you should support the teacher in providing learning opportunities to encourage children's intellectual skills. You can help to promote children's intellectual development by:

1. **Providing opportunities and materials to increase the children's curiosity**, e.g. books, games, posters, pictures, play equipment and toys. Encourage children to observe details in the environment, e.g. colours, shapes, smells, textures. Talk about weather conditions. Take the children on outings. Do gardening and/or keep pets.

2. **Participating in the children's activities to extend their development and learning** by asking questions, providing answers and demonstrating possible ways to use play equipment and other learning resources. Demonstrate how things work or fit together when the children are not sure what to do. Make sure your help is wanted (and necessary). Use verbal prompts where possible to encourage children to solve the problem for themselves.

3. **Providing gradually more challenging play and learning activities** but do not push the children too hard by providing activities which are obviously too complex; instead of extending the children's abilities this will only put them off due to the frustration of not being able to do the activity. Provide repetition by encouraging the children to play with toys and games more than once; each time they play, they will discover different things about these activities. Encourage acceptable risk-taking during play opportunities.

4. **Helping the children to develop their concentration and memory skills by**: ensuring the children are looking and listening attentively when giving new information; explaining how new information is connected to the children's existing experiences and knowledge (e.g. by linking activities with a common theme); dividing complex activities into smaller tasks to make it easier for children to concentrate; using memory games to encourage/extend concentration levels; singing songs and rhymes, e.g. following a number sequence in songs like Five brown teddies, Ten green bottles, When I was one I was just begun…

5. **Encouraging the children to use their senses to experiment with different materials and to explore their environment**, e.g. doing arts and crafts; playing with sand, water, clay, dough, wood; playing with manufactured materials such as plastic construction kits; modelling with safe household junk materials; cooking activities; singing rhymes and songs; clapping games; outings to the local park; matching games, jigsaws and lotto.

KEY TASK

1. Plan a learning activity which encourages or extends a pupil's intellectual development such as: imaginative and creative skills; concentration and memory skills; problem-solving skills; language and communication skills. Use the assessment information from your observation of a child's intellectual development from page 72 as the basis for your planning.

2. Consider how you could meet the needs of pupils with learning difficulties and children with exceptional abilities with this activity (see Chapter 11).

3. If possible, ask the class teacher for permission to implement the activity. Evaluate the activity afterwards.

 NVQ LINKS:

Level 2:
STL1.1   STL1.2   STL1.3   STL2.2   STL2.3   STL2.4   STL10.1
STL10.2   STL10.3   STL10.5   STL12.2
and depending on the learning activity:
STL7.2   STL8.2 (ICT activity)   STL6.1 (literacy activity)
STL6.2 (numeracy activity)

Level 3:
STL18.1   STL18.2   STL23.1   STL23.2   STL23.3   STL24.1   STL24.2
STL27.1   STL27.2   STL27.3   STL29.2   STL38.2
and depending on the learning activity:
STL8.2 (ICT activity)   STL25.1   STL25.2   STL25.3 (literacy activity)
STL26.1   STL26.2 (numeracy activity)

Promoting children's communication skills and language development

Language is a key factor in all children's development as it provides them with the skills they need to communicate with others, relate to others, explore the environment, understand concepts, formulate ideas and express feelings. The word 'language' is often used to describe the process of speaking and listening, but it is much more than verbal communication.

The human ability to utilise language depends on the use of a *recognised system of symbols* and a common understanding of what those symbols mean. Obviously there are many different systems of symbols, as indicated by the many different languages and alphabet systems used by people throughout the world. At first, very young children are not able to use a complex system of symbols; it takes time to learn the system of their particular community language. Children (and adults) use a variety of ways to communicate. These *modes of language* are essential to being able to communicate effectively with others and to being fully involved in a wide range of social interactions. The different modes of language can be described as: **non-verbal communication**; **thinking**; **listening**; **speaking**; **reading**; and **writing**. Each mode of language involves a variety of communication skills which are inter-related; some of the skills are required in more than one mode, e.g. reading and writing both involve the processing of oral language in a written form.

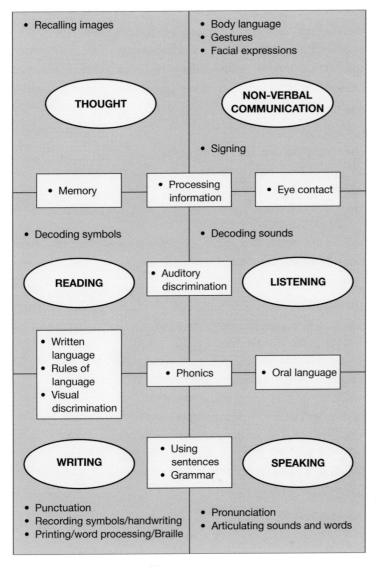

Inter-related components of the modes of language

You should provide opportunities for children to develop the necessary communication skills to become competent at using these different modes of language. Opportunities for talk are especially helpful in promoting language development and the use of communication skills. When working with children you must be aware of and provide for appropriate play opportunities and learning activities to enable the children to develop effective communication skills. (See section on developing speaking and listening skills in Chapter 10.) Remember that some children may be limited in their ability to use some modes of language due to sensory impairment or other special needs (see Chapter 11).

The sequence of children's language development: 0 to 16 years

Age 0 to 3 months

- *Recognises familiar voices; stops crying when hears them.*
- *Aware of other sounds; turns head towards sounds.*
- *Responds to smiles; moves whole body in response to sound/to attract attention.*
- *Pauses to listen to others; makes noises as well as crying, e.g. burbling.*

Age 3 to 9 months

- *Responds with smiles.*
- *Recognises family names, but cannot say them.*
- *Enjoys looking at pictures and books.*
- *Even more responsive to voices and music.*
- *Participates in simple games, e.g. 'peep-po'; tries to imitate sounds, e.g. during rhymes.*
- *Starts babbling, uses single-syllable sounds, e.g. 'daa', 'baa' and 'maa'.*
- *From about 7 months uses two-syllable sounds, e.g. 'daada', 'baaba', 'maama'.*
- *Shouts to attract attention.*

Age 9 to 18 months

- *Continues to imitate sounds; starts jargoning, e.g. joins up syllables so more like 'sentences' such as 'Maama-baaba-daa'.*
- *Learns to say first real words, usually the names of animals and everyday things.*
- *Uses gestures to emphasise word meanings.*
- *Uses vocabulary of between 3 and 20 words.*
- *Participates in simple finger rhymes; continues to enjoy books.*
- *Over-extends words, that is, uses same word to identify similar objects, e.g. all round objects are called 'ball'.*

Age 18 months to 2 years

- *Uses language to gain information, e.g. starts asking 'What dat?'*
- *Repeats words said by adults.*
- *Acquires 1–3 words per month; by 2 years has vocabulary of about 200 words.*
- *Participates in action songs and nursery rhymes; continues to enjoy books and stories.*
- *Uses telegraphic speech, e.g. speaks in 2–3-word sentences such as 'Daddy go' or 'Milk all gone'.*

▶

Age 2 to 3 years

- *Has vocabulary of about 300 words.*
- *Uses more adult forms of speech, e.g. sentences now include words like 'that', 'this', 'here', 'there', 'then', 'but', 'and'.*
- *Can name main body parts.*
- *Uses adjectives, e.g. big, small, tall; words referring to relationships, e.g. I, my, you, yours.*
- *Asks questions to gain more information.*
- *Sings songs and rhymes; continues to participate in action songs and enjoy books/stories.*
- *Can deliver simple messages.*

Age 3 to 5 years

- *Has vocabulary of between 900 and 1500 words.*
- *Asks lots of questions.*
- *Uses language to ask for assistance.*
- *Talks constantly to people knows well.*
- *Gives very simple accounts of past events.*
- *Can say names of colours.*
- *Begins to vocalise ideas.*
- *Continues to enjoy books, stories, songs and rhymes.*
- *Listens to and can follow simple instructions; can deliver verbal messages.*

Age 5 to 7 years

- *May use vocabulary of about 1500 to 4000 words.*
- *Uses more complex sentence structures.*
- *Asks even more questions using what, when, who, where, how and especially why!*
- *Develops early reading and writing skills.*
- *Continues to enjoy books, stories and poetry; by age 7 can recall the story so far if book read a chapter at a time.*
- *Shows interest in more complex books and stories; continues to enjoy songs and rhymes.*
- *Gives more detailed accounts of past events.*
- *Vocalises ideas and feelings.*
- *Can listen to and follow more detailed instructions; can deliver more complex verbal messages.*

Age 7 to 12 years

- *Has extensive vocabulary of between 4000 and 10,000 words.*
- *Uses more complex sentence structures.*
- *Develops more complex reading skills including improved comprehension.*

- *Develops more complex writing skills including more accurate spelling, punctuation and joined-up writing.*
- *Continues to enjoy books, stories and poetry.*
- *Gives very detailed accounts of past events and can anticipate future events.*
- *Vocalises ideas and feelings in more depth.*
- *Listens to and follows more complex instructions.*
- *Appreciates jokes due to more sophisticated language knowledge.*
- *Uses literacy skills to communicate and to access information, e.g. story and letter writing, use of dictionaries, encyclopaedia, computers, Internet, e-mail.*

Age 12 to 16 years

- *Has an extensive and varied vocabulary of between 10,000 and 20,000 words.*
- *Uses appropriate language styles for different occasions, e.g. standard English for formal situations.*
- *Has more complex reading skills including detailed comprehension skills, e.g. comments on structure and themes of a book or other piece of writing.*
- *Has more complex writing skills including accurate spelling and punctuation; neat and legible joined-up writing.*
- *Can use different writing styles including word-processing on a computer.*
- *Continues to enjoy more complex texts including fiction, poetry and factual books.*
- *Gives very detailed accounts of past events using varied expression and vocabulary.*
- *Can anticipate future events and give detailed reasons for possible outcomes.*
- *Vocalises ideas and feelings in greater depth including justifying own views and opinions.*
- *Listens to and follows complex sets of instructions.*
- *Appreciates complex jokes and word play.*
- *Continues to use literacy skills to communicate and to access information, e.g. taking notes, writing essays and letters; using dictionaries/thesaurus, encyclopaedia; computers, Internet, e-mail.*

 KEY TASK

1. Observe a pupil involved in a conversation, discussion or circle time. Focus on the language development and communication skills demonstrated by the pupil.

2. In your assessment, comment on: the verbal and/or non-verbal communication used by the pupil; the complexity of any language used by the pupil; the level of social interaction; the role of the adult in promoting the pupil's language development; suggestions for further activities to encourage or extend the pupil's language development.

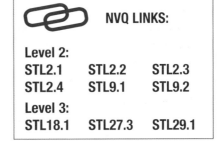

NVQ LINKS:

Level 2:
STL2.1 STL2.2 STL2.3
STL2.4 STL9.1 STL9.2
Level 3:
STL18.1 STL27.3 STL29.1

Five ways to promote children's language development

The teaching assistant plays a vital role in encouraging and extending children's language development and communication skills. You can help to promote children's language development by:

1. **Talking to the children about anything and everything!** Show the children what you are talking about, e.g. use real objects/situations, pictures, books, and other visual or audio aids.

2. **Using straightforward sentences** with words appropriate to the children's levels of understanding and development; avoid over-simplifying language; do not use 'baby talk' – children need to hear adult speech to learn language. Use repetition to introduce or reinforce new vocabulary and ideas. Do not make the children repeat things back over and over; this is boring and frustrating.

3. **Copying the children's sounds and words** including any extensions or corrections to positively reinforce and extend the children's vocabulary, sentence structures, etc. For example: if a child says 'ball', you could reply 'Yes, that is Tom's red ball'; or if a child says 'moo!' you could reply 'Yes, the cow goes moo!'

4. **Remembering turn-taking in language exchanges**. Ask questions to stimulate the children's responses and to encourage or extend their speech. Look at the children when you are talking with them. Remember to be at the children's level, e.g. sitting on a low chair or even on the floor; do not tower over them.

5. **Sharing books, stories and rhymes** with children including babies.

 KEY TASK

1. Plan an activity which encourages or extends a pupil's language and communication skills. Include a variety of communication techniques such as: active listening (e.g. listening carefully and focusing on what the pupil has to say); leaving time for the pupil to respond/talk; careful

phrasing of adult questions and responses. Use the assessment information from your observation of a pupil's language and communication skills from page 78 as the basis for your planning.

2. Consider how you could meet the needs of pupils with communication difficulties with this activity (see Chapter 11).

3. Consider how you could meet the needs of bilingual children with this activity (see Chapter 10).

4. If possible, ask the class teacher for permission to implement the activity. Evaluate the activity afterwards.

NVQ LINKS:

Level 2:

STL1.1	STL1.2	STL1.3
STL2.3	STL2.4	STL4.1
STL4.3	STL10.1	STL11.2
STL12.2		

Level 3:

STL18.1	STL18.2	STL20.2
STL23.1	STL23.2	STL23.3
STL24.1	STL24.2	STL25.3
STL27.1	STL27.2	STL27.3
STL29.2	STL35.2	STL38.2

Promoting children's emotional development

Emotional development can be defined as the development of personality and temperament. This includes how each child develops as a unique individual; sees and feels about themselves; *thinks* other people see them; expresses their individual needs, desires and feelings; relates to others; and interacts with their environment. As a teaching assistant, you need to know and understand the process of children's personality development in order to provide appropriate assistance and guidance. Children inherit their particular temperaments which are then influenced by the environment they are raised in. Babies develop an awareness of others in relation to themselves, e.g. people who fulfil their needs for food and drink, warmth and shelter, sleep, physical comfort and entertainment. Babies develop strong **attachments** to the people they see most often and who satisfy the above needs. One attachment is usually stronger than the others and this is usually the baby's mother, but the attachment can be to another family member or anyone outside the immediate family who spends a significant amount of time with the young child, such as a grandparent or nanny. The security of these early attachments is essential to babies and young children because they provide a firm foundation for promoting **emotional well-being, positive relationships with other people** and **confidence in exploring the environment**. These early attachments enable children to feel secure about their relationships and to develop trust in others. **Security** and **trust** are important elements in young children's ability to separate from their parents and carers in order to develop their own independence and ideas. (For detailed information on children's well-being and resilience see Chapter 7.)

The sequence of children's emotional development: 0 to 16 years

Age 0 to 3 months

- *Becomes very attached to parent/carer (usually the mother).*
- *Experiences extreme emotions, e.g. very scared, very happy or very angry; these moods change in an instant.*
- *Requires the security and reassurance of familiar routines.*
- *May be upset by unfamiliar methods of handling and care.*

Age 3 to 9 months

- *Has strong attachment to parent/carer (usually the mother).*
- *Develops other attachments to people sees regularly.*
- *By 6 or 7 months shows clear preferences for familiar adults as can differentiate between individuals.*
- *Demonstrates strong emotions through body language, gestures and facial expressions.*
- *Dislikes anger in others and becomes distressed by it.*
- *Has clear likes and dislikes, e.g. will push away food, drink or toys does not want.*

Age 9 to 18 months

- *Likes to get own way; gets very angry when adult says 'No!'.*
- *Has emotional outbursts ('temper tantrums') when does not get own way or is otherwise frustrated, e.g. unable to do activity because of physical limitations.*
- *Shows fear in new situations, e.g. attending parent/toddler group, visiting somewhere new such as the farm or nature centre.*
- *Relies on parent/carer for reassurance and support in new situations.*
- *Is upset by the distress of other children (even if they caused it).*
- *Seeks reassurance and contact with familiar adults throughout waking hours.*

Age 18 months to 2 years

- *Begins to disengage from secure attachment, e.g. wants to do things by self – 'Me do it!'.*
- *Still emotionally dependent on familiar adult(s) but this leads to conflict as need for independence grows.*
- *Has mood swings, e.g. clingy one moment, then fiercely independent the next.*
- *Becomes very frustrated when unable/not allowed to do a particular activity which leads to frequent but short-lived emotional outbursts ('temper tantrums').*
- *Explores environment; even new situations are less frightening as long as parent/carer is present.*

Age 2 to 3 years

- *May still rely on parent/carer for reassurance in new situations or when with strangers.*
- *Still experiences emotional outbursts as independence grows and frustration at own limitations continues, e.g. aggressive towards toys that cannot get to work.*

- Begins to understand the feelings of others but own feelings are still the most important.
- Has very limited understanding of other people's pain, e.g. if hits another child.
- Feels curious about their environment but has no sense of danger, e.g. that they or other people can be hurt by their actions.

Age 3 to 5 years

- Less reliant on parent/carer for reassurance in new situations.
- May be jealous of adult attention given to younger sibling or other children in a group.
- Argues with other children but is quick to forgive and forget.
- Has limited awareness of the feelings and needs of others.
- May be quite caring towards others who are distressed.
- Begins to use language to express feelings and wishes.
- Still has emotional outbursts, especially when tired, stressed or frustrated.

Age 5 to 7 years

- Becomes more aware of the feelings and needs of others.
- Tries to comfort others who are upset, hurt or unwell.
- May occasionally be aggressive as still learning to deal with negative emotions.
- Uses language to express feelings and wishes.
- Uses imaginative play to express worries and fears over past or future experiences, e.g. hospital visits, family disputes, domestic upheaval.
- Has occasional emotional outbursts when tired, stressed or frustrated.
- Argues with other children but may take longer to forgive and forget.
- Confidence in self can be shaken by 'failure'.
- May have an 'imaginary friend'.

Age 7 to 12 years

- Becomes less egocentric as understands feelings, needs and rights of others.
- Still wants things that belong solely to them, e.g. very possessive of own toys, puts own name on everything they possess!
- Becomes more aware of own achievements in relation to others but this can lead to a sense of failure if feels does not measure up; hates to lose.
- May be very competitive; rivalry may lead to aggressive behaviour.
- Argues with other children but may take even longer to forgive and forget.
- Has increased awareness of the wider environment, e.g. the weather, plants, animals, and people in other countries.

Age 12 to 16 years

- *Sensitive to own feelings and those of others, with a growing understanding of the possible causes for why people feel and act as they do.*
- *Emotional changes due to puberty.*
- *Understands issues relating to fairness and justice.*
- *Can anticipate people's reactions and consider the consequences of own actions.*
- *Is increasingly able to see different viewpoints in order to resolve difficulties in relationships.*
- *Has confidence in own skills and ideas; is more able to be assertive rather than aggressive or passive.*
- *May have very strong opinions or beliefs, leading to arguments with adults and peers; may hold grudges and find it difficult to forgive or forget.*
- *Has more understanding of complex issues concerning the wider environment, e.g. ethics, philosophy, religion, politics.*

⊙ KEY TASK

1. Observe a pupil during an imaginative play or creative activity. Focus on the pupil's emotional development.

2. In your assessment, comment on: the pupil's imaginative and creative skills; the pupil's ability to make choices or decisions; the pupil's use of language to express needs and/or feelings; the role of the adult in promoting the pupil's emotional development; suggestions for further activities to encourage or extend the pupil's emotional development including appropriate resources.

 NVQ LINKS:

Level 2:
STL2.2   STL2.3   STL2.4
STL9.1   STL9.2

Level 3:
STL18.1   STL27.3   STL29.1

Five ways to promote children's emotional development

As a teaching assistant, you should support the teacher in providing appropriate routines and activities to promote children's emotional development. You can help to promote children's emotional development by:

1. **Using praise and encouragement** to help the pupils focus on what they are good at. Treat every pupil in the school as an individual. Each pupil has unique abilities and needs. Help pupils to maximise their individual potential.

2. **Taking an interest in the pupils' efforts as well as achievements**. Remember the way pupils participate in activities is more important than the end results, e.g. sharing resources, helping others and contributing ideas. Encourage the pupils to measure any achievements by comparing these to their own efforts. Foster co-operation between pupils rather than competition.

3. **Giving pupils opportunities to make decisions and choices**. Letting pupils participate in decision-making, even in a small way, helps them to feel positive and important; it also prepares them for making appropriate judgements and sensible decisions later on.

4. **Promoting equal opportunities by providing positive images of children and adults** through: sharing books and stories about real-life situations showing children (and adults) that the pupils can identify with; providing opportunities for imaginative play that encourage the pupils to explore different roles in positive ways, e.g. dressing-up clothes, cooking utensils, dolls and puppets.

5. **Being consistent about rules and discipline**. All pupils need consistency and a clearly structured framework for behaviour so that they know what is expected of them. Remember to label the behaviour not the pupils as this is less damaging to their emotional well-being, e.g. 'That was an unkind thing to say' rather than 'You are unkind'.

● KEY TASK

1. Plan an activity which encourages or extends a pupil's emotional development. For example, encouraging the pupil to use a variety of emotional abilities such as: imaginative and/or creative skills to express feelings; ability to make choices or decisions; language and communication skills to express needs and/or feelings; understanding the needs and feelings of others. Use the assessment information from your observation of a pupil's emotional development from page 83 as the basis for your planning.

	NVQ LINKS:	
Level 2:		
STL1.1	STL1.2	STL1.3
STL2.2	STL2.4	STL10.1
STL10.2	STL10.3	STL12.2
Level 3:		
STL18.1	STL18.2	STL23.1
STL23.2	STL23.3	STL24.1
STL24.2	STL27.1	STL27.2
STL27.3	STL29.2	STL38.2

2. Consider how you could meet the needs of pupils with emotional difficulties with this activity (see Chapter 11).

3. If possible, ask the class teacher for permission to implement the activity. Evaluate the activity afterwards.

Further reading

Harding, J. and Meldon-Smith, L. (2001) *How to make observations and assessments.* 2nd edition. Hodder Arnold.

Kamen, T. (2000) *Psychology for childhood studies.* Hodder Arnold.

Lindon, J. (2005) *Understanding child development: linking theory and practice.* Hodder Arnold.

Lindon, J. (2007) *Understanding children and young people: development from 5–18 years.* Hodder Arnold.

Meggitt, C. (2006) *Child development: an illustrated guide.* 2nd edition. Heinemann Educational Publishers.

Sheridan, M. (1997) *From birth to five years: children's developmental progress.* 4th revised edition. Routledge.

Wyse, D. and Hawtin, A. (1999) *Children: a multi-professional perspective.* Hodder Arnold. [Covers child development and learning from birth to 18 years.]

4 Promoting positive pupil behaviour

Key points:

* Promoting positive behaviour
* Implementing the school behaviour management policy
* The teaching assistant's role in managing pupil behaviour
* Factors affecting pupil behaviour
* Reporting concerns about pupil behaviour
* Supporting behaviour management strategies
* School code of conduct for pupils
* Setting goals and boundaries
* Rewards and sanctions
* Managing pupils' challenging behaviour
* Dealing with bullying.

Promoting positive behaviour

Creating an environment that promotes positive behaviour helps to shape the school's ethos and reflect the setting's values. Positive behaviour is an essential building block for creating a welcoming and pleasant learning environment in which all members of the school feel respected, safe and secure. Identifying and implementing appropriate behaviour policies, procedures and strategies helps to establish pupil and parent confidence in the school. An effective behaviour policy also helps to attract and retain good-quality and well-motivated staff.

When helping teachers to create an environment that promotes positive behaviour, you should remember that pupils are more likely to behave in positive ways if they are: in a welcoming and stimulating learning environment; engaged in interesting and challenging learning activities that are appropriate to their ages and levels of development; given clear and realistic guidelines on behaviour; and can work with adults who have positive expectations for pupil behaviour.

Pupil behaviour can be defined as a pupil's actions and reactions or a pupil's treatment of others. Behaviour involves children *learning to* *conform* to parental expectations for behaviour, school expectations for behaviour and society's expectations for behaviour.

Parental expectations for behaviour

Parents have expectations for their children's behaviour based on: the media; cultural or religious beliefs; individual variations in child-rearing practices; adherence to traditional child-rearing practices; comparisons to other children (of relatives, friends and neighbours); perceptions of their own childhood and *their* parents' attitudes to behaviour.

Many parents may have idealised or unrealistic expectations concerning their children's behaviour because some childcare/education books and the media promote unrealistic age-related expectations so that many children do not seem to 'measure up' to what the experts say. Smaller families (often with few or no relatives nearby) mean many parents lack first-hand experience of caring for children *before* they have their own children and may feel less confident about their parenting skills. Parents of children with special needs may be unsure of what to expect from their children in terms of behaviour; they may over-compensate for their child's special needs by being over-protective or by letting the child get away with behaviour that would not be appropriate in a child of similar age/level of development.

In the past, children did not dare challenge parental authority for fear of physical punishment. Today some parents still feel that if they were brought up this way, then this is how they expect their children to behave. In the 21st century, society recognises the rights of the child and has the expectation that all parents should be more caring and responsive to their children's needs by using positive methods such as praise, encouragement, negotiation and rewards to achieve appropriate behaviour.

Children learn what their parents consider to be appropriate behaviour and will bring these expectations to the setting. Children also observe their parents' behaviour that may be:

- ☆ **assertive:** sensitive to their own *and* other people's needs
- ☆ **passive:** too sensitive to other people's needs so *ignores own needs*
- ☆ **aggressive:** obsessed with own needs so *ignores other people's needs*.

The school's expectations for pupil behaviour

Children who are not prepared (or are unable) to conform have to accept the consequences, such as sanctions or punishments for unacceptable behaviour. Learning about behaviour (as with all learning) always takes place within a social context. Certain types of behaviour may be acceptable in one context but not in another (e.g. families may make allowances for their child's behaviour); however, different rules apply in school because adults must consider the needs of *all* pupils. What is acceptable in one situation may not be acceptable in another, even within the same school – for example, loud, boisterous behaviour *is* acceptable in the playground but *not* in the classroom. Conforming brings limitations to pupils' behaviour – for example, following school rules and participating in all curriculum areas, even those they do not like.

Other influences on pupil behaviour

The media (television, magazines and comics) and computer games can have positive or negative influences on pupil behaviour, depending on what the children see and how they are affected by it. Children exposed to violent images may see aggressive behaviour as an acceptable way to deal with others. Children who observe more assertive behaviour (with its emphasis on negotiation and compromise) are likely to demonstrate similar positive behaviour. Television programmes, characters and personalities provide powerful role models for children's behaviour. Just consider the effectiveness of advertising!

Peer pressure may have a negative influence on pupil behaviour as children may: persuade them to participate in dangerous activities including 'dares'; pressure them into socially unacceptable behaviour, e.g. lying, stealing or bullying; exclude or threaten them if they do not conform; encourage them to act in ways they never would as an individual, e.g. 'mob rule'. However, you can sometimes use peer pressure to encourage positive behaviour by highlighting the positive benefits of certain behaviour for the group, class or school.

Providing positive role models

Children model their attitudes and actions on the behaviour of others. They imitate the actions and speech of those they are closest to, e.g. acting at being 'mum', 'dad', 'nursery nurse', 'playworker' or 'teacher'; copying the actions and mannerisms of adults around the home, childcare setting or school. All adults working with children need to be aware of the significant impact they make to children's social (and emotional) development by providing positive **role models**. When working with pupils you should strike a balance between allowing for the children's increasing need for independence and providing adequate supervision with appropriate guidelines for socially acceptable behaviour. Observing the behaviour of parents and other significant adults (such as childcarers, teachers and teaching assistants) affects children's own behaviour, how children deal with their own feelings and how children relate to others. This is why it is so important for adults to provide positive role models for children's behaviour.

The benefits of positive behaviour

Promoting positive behaviour can bring many benefits to pupils, staff and schools. These benefits include: creating a positive framework with realistic expectations for pupils' behaviour; providing consistent care/education for pupils with clear rules and boundaries; the security and stability of a welcoming and structured environment; positive motivation through praise, encouragement and rewards; positive social interaction between pupils and staff; encouraging pupils' self-reliance, self-confidence and positive self-esteem; encouraging staff confidence in supporting pupils' learning; a positive atmosphere which makes educating pupils more interesting and enjoyable; opportunities for more effective thinking and learning leading to improved educational achievement and test/examination results.

There are also potential benefits for society such as: more positive social interactions including friendships, clubs, etc; re-development of community spirit and belief in citizenship; positive attitudes towards others, e.g. equal opportunities, racial harmony, etc. Research shows that pupils who have positive early years experiences are more likely to maintain an interest in education leading to further training/qualifications and are less likely to go on to experience 'juvenile delinquency' and adult unemployment (Ball, 1994).

EXAMPLES OF POSITIVE PUPIL BEHAVIOUR	EXAMPLES OF NEGATIVE PUPIL BEHAVIOUR
Sharing resources and adult's attention; taking turns	Not sharing; attention-seeking; jealousy
Working co-operatively	Disrupting activities, e.g. taking things without asking, fighting or arguing
Being friendly; helping/comforting others	Being aggressive/abusive, e.g. upsetting or hurting others, bullying
Concentrating on activities, e.g. remaining on task	Not concentrating on activities, e.g. being easily frustrated or distracted
Complying with adult requests	Being defiant and refusing reasonable adult requests
Contributing creative ideas	Overriding or ridiculing other people's ideas
Expressing self effectively	Expressing self inappropriately, e.g. emotional outbursts, whining or nagging
Being aware of danger	Having no sense of danger; being too compulsive
Being polite	Being rude, cheeky or interrupting others
Being responsible for own actions	Blaming others or lying about own actions
Being independent	Being easily led or too dependent on others
Being flexible	Resisting change or overly upset by change

Examples of positive and negative pupil behaviour

What is considered to be positive or acceptable children's behaviour depends on each adult's tolerance levels. Adult tolerance for different kinds of children's behaviour may depend on: their expectations for children's behaviour in relation to age/level of development; the social context in which the behaviour is demonstrated; and how the adult feels at that particular time.

EXERCISE: Copy the table below and list positive and negative behaviours that you consider to be appropriate to the age/level of development of the pupils you work with in school.

POSITIVE BEHAVIOUR	NEGATIVE BEHAVIOUR	CONTEXT/ ACTIVITY

Seven ways to encourage children's positive behaviour

You can help to encourage children's positive behaviour by:

1. **Keeping rules to a minimum**. Pupils will often keep to a few rules if they have some freedom. Explain why certain rules are necessary, e.g. for safety. All pupils should learn to understand the need for rules, but they also need to develop their own self-control and to make their own decisions regarding behaviour.

Pupils working co-operatively

2. **Being proactive**. This means preparing things in advance including having the correct materials and equipment ready for learning activities. You should also be clear about the behaviour guidelines for the pupils you work with and what your responsibilities are for dealing with any problems that might occur.

3. **Being positive**. Once ground rules have been set, encourage pupils to keep them through rewards. Reward positive behaviour using verbal praise and other positive incentives. Keep smiling! A sense of humour goes a long way.

4. **Ignoring certain behaviour**. It may be appropriate to ignore some unwanted behaviour, especially attention-seeking or behaviour that is not dangerous or life-threatening. Sometimes it is not possible or appropriate to ignore unwanted behaviour, e.g. if a pupil is in danger. With younger

▶

pupils it may be more effective to distract the child (e.g. by playing a game) or to divert their attention to another activity.

5. **Being consistent**. Once rules, goals and boundaries have been negotiated and set, stick to them. Pupils need to know where they stand; they feel very insecure if rules and boundaries keep changing for no apparent reason. The pupils need to understand that 'no' always means 'no', especially where safety is concerned.

6. **Knowing the pupils you work with**. An awareness of a pupil's home background, previous behaviour in another setting, including any special needs, influences the way you respond to potentially disruptive pupils. Use a variety of techniques; different pupils respond differently to different methods, e.g. a reminder of a ground rule may be sufficient or give a specific warning.

7. **Keeping calm!** Be calm, quiet, firm and in control; shouting only makes matters worse. If you feel you are losing control, count to five and then proceed calmly. You may need to use strategies like time out to give the pupil a chance to calm down, but keep it short, e.g. only a few seconds until the pupil is a little calmer.

 KEY TASK

List examples of methods you have used to encourage children's positive behaviour.

 NVQ LINKS:

Level 2 and Level 3: STL3.4

Implementing the school behaviour management policy

Section 61 of the *School Standards and Framework Act 1998* requires a governing body to ensure that its school pursues policies designed to promote positive behaviour. This includes making and reviewing a written statement of principles to guide the headteacher in determining measures for promoting positive behaviour in the school.

The school behaviour management policy

The school's behaviour policy should cover how the school promotes high standards of behaviour as well as promoting excellent attendance and tackling poor attendance. School policies for behaviour include: behaviour policy; attendance policy; anti-bullying policy. These policies can be combined into one document to form an overall school behaviour management policy.

The behaviour management policy should include:

✯ The school's aims and underlying principles for behaviour
✯ The roles and responsibilities of staff members

- ☆ A code of conduct for pupils
- ☆ How positive behaviour will be promoted
- ☆ How regular attendance will be encouraged
- ☆ Strategies to combat bullying
- ☆ How the policy will be implemented
- ☆ The use of rewards and sanctions
- ☆ The arrangements for supporting pupils and staff
- ☆ Monitoring and reviewing procedures for the policy.

The policy should ensure consistency by providing clear guidelines for all staff on its implementation as well as practical advice to parents and carers on how they can help. This information could be included in documents such as the staff handbook and the home-school agreement.

The behaviour management policy should be an integral part of the school curriculum. The policy must be based on clear values (e.g. respect, fairness and inclusion) that are also reflected in the school's aims, equal opportunities policy and special educational needs policy. To promote positive behaviour, the expectations in the behaviour management policy need to be taught explicitly as part of the curriculum. For example, pupils' moral, social, emotional and behavioural development could be encouraged through the religious education programme and designated PSHE lessons. Pupils should have regular explicit opportunities for learning about how to behave in accordance with the school's values and beliefs. In promoting positive behaviour schools should implement practical strategies for intervention, including using support available from the LEA, Education Welfare Service, police, Connexions service, multi-agency teams, complementary schools etc. (DfES, 2003b).

Staff responsibilities for managing pupil behaviour

Staff members are responsible for the behaviour of **all** pupils and not only those that they have been assigned to. Adults should always act as good role models for positive behaviour. Parents and pupils need to be informed of school expectations for behaviour. School and classroom rules need to be displayed and referred to. Pupils need to be encouraged to become self-disciplined, to be responsible for their own actions, in order to develop their confidence and independence. Pupils need to know the consequences of negative behaviour. Pupils need to understand that they can improve their behaviour and make a new start. Work within classrooms must take account of individual ability. Poor behaviour needs to be monitored with notes and dates put in social records. The class teacher should inform the parent(s) at an early stage if any problems occur with their child.

The teaching assistant's role in managing pupil behaviour

When managing pupil behaviour, you need to recognise and respond promptly and appropriately to anti-social behaviour; remember to follow school policies. For example, you may need to remind pupils about the school/class rules or protect other pupils and yourself from harm when challenging behaviour is demonstrated by a pupil. You will need to report any problems in dealing with unacceptable or challenging behaviour to the class or subject teacher. You should also be able to identify and report any pupil's uncharacteristic behaviour patterns to the appropriate person, e.g. class or form teacher (see below). As part of your role in supporting the management of pupil behaviour, you will need to provide constructive feedback on the effectiveness of the behaviour strategies including the improvements or setbacks of pupils with Behaviour Support Plans. You may also be asked to contribute to ideas for improvements for behaviour management strategies.

EXERCISE:
1. What are staff members' general responsibilities for managing pupil behaviour?
2. Summarise the role and responsibilities of the teaching assistant for managing pupil behaviour.

Factors affecting pupil behaviour

It is important to be aware of the factors that may cause a pupil's negative or inappropriate behaviour. No single factor causes a pupil's unwanted behaviour; there is usually a combination of factors. By identifying the contributing factors that make such behaviour more likely, adults working in schools can often avoid the additional factors that can result in unwanted behaviour.

Contributing factors include environmental, social or emotional factors such as: family bereavement or prolonged illness; divorce or separation; one-parent families or step-families; family violence; emotional damage through physical, verbal or sexual abuse; insecure early relationships; depression; changes, e.g. moving house, school; sibling jealousy or rivalry; inappropriate role models outside the setting; lack of parental care and control; financial problems, poverty or homelessness; negative early years experiences in previous settings.

Schools may have little or no control over these contributing factors but they do have control over **additional factors** such as: response to pupils' negative behaviour; inadequate preparation for and introduction to the setting/transition to other settings (see section on preparing pupils for transitions in Chapter 7); the demands of the school, e.g. unfamiliar routines, overly strict regimes; insensitivity or inflexibility towards individual needs; stressful, boring or frustrating learning activities; inappropriate learning activities; unrealistic adult expectations or limitations; inappropriate role models *within* the setting; poor staff-to-pupil ratio; very large group size; over-emphasis on competition and not enough on co-operation; unwarranted disapproval from staff or pupils; pupils being bullied (see section below on dealing with bullying).

There are also some **rare factors** that cause negative or inappropriate behaviour:

✶ **Psychosis:** a serious psychological disorder characterised by mental confusion, hallucination and delusions; in children symptoms include regression, speech loss and extreme hyperactivity.

- ☆ **Autistic spectrum disorders:** a rare and complex condition usually present from birth (although identification may not be made until 3 years+); autistic tendencies include speech loss or unusual speech patterns, isolation and withdrawal, intense dislike of environmental changes.
- ☆ **Attention deficit disorder:** a biological condition affecting children's behaviour and concentration.

Recognising behaviour patterns

You should be able to identify the sorts of behaviour patterns that might indicate problems such as child abuse, substance abuse or bullying. You should also know who to report these to – for example, the class teacher, or whoever is responsible for child protection in the school.

Behaviour patterns that might indicate problems in **younger pupils** include:

- ☆ Unusually aggressive behaviour towards people and/or property.
- ☆ Regression to earlier level of development, e.g. emotional outbursts, wetting or soiling.
- ☆ Defiance, e.g. refusing to comply with adult requests.
- ☆ Lack of co-operation during learning activities.
- ☆ Attention-seeking behaviour, e.g. excessive swearing.
- ☆ Being very passive or withdrawn.
- ☆ Wandering around the classroom aimlessly or staring into space.
- ☆ Repetitive or self-damaging behaviour, e.g. rocking, thumb-sucking, frequent masturbation, picking own skin, pulling out own hair, head-banging.
- ☆ Appearing very nervous and anxious.
- ☆ Inability to concentrate at usual level.
- ☆ Deterioration of school work.
- ☆ Refusing to eat and/or drink while at school.

Behaviour patterns that might indicate problems in **older pupils** include:

- ☆ Deterioration in the pupil's academic work.
- ☆ Gradual changes in their appearance or behaviour over a period of time.
- ☆ Rapid or acute increase in behavioural or emotional changes.
- ☆ Emotional instability and mood swings; irritability.
- ☆ Loss of confidence and heightened levels of anxiety.
- ☆ Unexplained, persistent lateness and absenteeism.
- ☆ Tiredness due to disturbed sleep.
- ☆ Signs of substance abuse, e.g. slurred speech, memory impairment, lack of co-ordination, poor concentration, irritability.
- ☆ Withdrawal from social contact.
- ☆ Inappropriate responses to normal situations.
- ☆ Noticeable changes in eating habits.

Concerns about a pupil's behaviour patterns should be discussed with colleagues but remember confidentiality. Adults in schools have a legal duty to report serious concerns about a pupil's welfare, e.g. possible signs and symptoms of abuse – each school has guidelines about this (see section on responding to concerns about possible abuse in Chapter 2).

Reporting concerns about pupil behaviour

You will need to recognise and respond promptly and appropriately to anti-social behaviour, remembering to always follow the school's agreed policies for managing pupil behaviour. You will need to report any problems in dealing with unacceptable or challenging behaviour to the class teacher.

Concerns about behaviour or discipline problems should be discussed with colleagues and sometimes with other professionals, but remember confidentiality. You may need specialist advice, guidance or support to provide the best possible approaches to responding to some pupils' behavioural and/or emotional difficulties. Every school has clear structures for reporting concerns about pupil behaviour to colleagues/other professionals and appropriate ways to deal with these concerns. Be aware of your own role and responsibilities within these structures.

Colleagues may include: the pupil's class, form or subject teacher; Key Stage/year group co-ordinator; special educational needs co-ordinator (SENCO); deputy headteacher; headteacher. Other professionals may include: health visitor; paediatrician; clinical psychologist; educational psychologist; social worker; education welfare officer; play therapist; or music therapist.

 KEY TASK

1. What sorts of behaviour patterns might indicate problems such as child abuse, substance abuse or bullying?

2. When and to whom should you report concerns relating to a pupil's welfare?

 **NVQ LINKS:**

Level 2 and Level 3: STL3.3

Supporting behaviour management strategies

Many pupils find it difficult to settle in school and to concentrate on their work because of behaviour problems. These pupils often challenge the authority of the teacher and the teaching assistant as well as their parents. Teachers and teaching assistants need to help these pupils learn how to behave in class because difficult behaviour makes it hard for teaching and learning to take place. In addition, disruptive behaviour demonstrated by one or two pupils can affect the learning opportunities for other pupils. Improving the behaviour of individual pupils helps schools to raise the educational standards for all pupils.

Most behaviour problems in class are of a low-level type that can be easily managed when teachers and teaching assistants use the correct strategies (see below). However, if this low level of behaviour is incorrectly managed then challenging confrontations can result. Learning to behave appropriately in school is essential because unless pupils can settle to learn they will not reach their full academic potential.

When supporting the management of pupil behaviour, you should consistently and effectively implement agreed behaviour management strategies. You will also need to provide constructive feedback on the effectiveness of the behaviour management strategies including the improvements or setbacks of pupils with Behaviour Support Plans.

School code of conduct for pupils

A school's behaviour management policy must set explicit standards of behaviour and attendance including a code of conduct for pupils. The purpose of the code should be to promote positive behaviour, so rules should be expressed in positive terms. The code should outline the school's expectations for pupil behaviour in the classroom and around the school. A system of rewards and sanctions should be used to support the code of conduct. Positive behaviour and regular attendance should not be taken for granted – they should be actively encouraged and reinforced (DfES, 2003b).

Example of school code of conduct for pupils

1. Treat everyone and everything with respect.

2. Try to understand other people's points of view.

3. Make it as easy as possible for everyone to learn and for the teacher to teach by: arriving on time with everything you need for the day; listening carefully, following instructions, not interrupting when your teacher is talking; helping each other when you can; working quietly and sensibly without distracting or annoying your classmates.

4. Move sensibly and quietly around the school. This means: never running, barging or shouting; opening doors or standing back to let people pass; helping to carry things.

5. Always speak politely to everyone, children and adults alike. Never shout.

6. Be silent whenever you are required to be. If the class is asked a question, put up your hand and answer. Do not call out.

7. Take pride in your personal appearance, attending school clean and dressed appropriately.

---

8. Keep the school clean and tidy so that it is a welcoming place we can all be proud of by: putting all litter in bins; keeping walls and furniture clean and unmarked; taking great care of displays, particularly of other people's work.

9. Leave toys, jewellery etc. at home as these can get lost or damaged or can cause arguments.

10. Always remember when out of school, walking locally or with a school group that the school's reputation depends on the way you behave.

EXERCISE: Find out about the code of conduct for the pupils in your school.

Setting goals and boundaries

As well as helping pupils to follow the school code of conduct, you will help them work towards specific goals and within certain boundaries as set by the teacher including individual, group or class targets for behaviour. **Goals** are the *expectations* for behaviour, usually starting with 'Do...'. **Boundaries** are the *limitations* to behaviour, often starting with '**Don't...**'.

Working with the teacher you should set goals and boundaries for the pupils that take into account: their ages and levels of development; their individual needs and abilities in different areas of the curriculum; the social context, e.g. the learning activity, group size.

Pupils are more likely to keep to goals and boundaries if they have some say about them. Pupils need to be active participants, not only in following rules but in establishing them. Having a feeling of ownership makes rules more real and gives pupils a sense of control. Tutorials or 'circle time' with pupils can provide opportunities for you to support the teacher in establishing and maintaining class rules as well as encouraging pupils to work co-operatively with each other.

When supporting the teacher in setting goals and boundaries consider the following:

1. **What is the goal or boundary?** Focus on the behaviour staff would like to change. Encourage pupils to talk about, draw a picture or write down what *they* would like to change. Remember to be positive.

2. **Why is the goal necessary?** To improve behaviour, to provide a happier atmosphere, to encourage co-operation or for safety reasons.

3. **Who does the goal or boundary apply to?** Does it apply to everyone in the school, just the group/class, or one particular individual?

4. **Where does the goal or boundary apply?** Does it apply everywhere in school, in a particular room/class, indoors or outdoors?

5. **When will the pupils start working towards the goal?** *When* will the boundary apply? Will it apply at all times in the classroom or school, or only at certain times?

6. **How will the goal or boundary be implemented?** *How* will the pupils be encouraged to keep to the goal or boundary? Include positive incentives such as smiley faces, stickers or merit/house points.

7. **What happens when the goal is achieved?** Ask the pupils what *they* would like. Rewards might include a badge, certificate, assembly praise or a special treat.

8. **Set new goal.** Start with the next goal or boundary which needs changing.

Setting goals and boundaries

KEY TASK

1. Think about the goals and boundaries that might be appropriate to the pupil or pupils you work with in your school.

2. If possible, encourage the pupil or pupils to draw up their own list of rules that promote positive behaviour.

NVQ LINKS:

Level 2:
STL3.4   STL4.1   STL4.3

Level 3:
STL3.4   STL19.2   STL20.1
STL20.2   STL20.3   STL37.1

Rewards and sanctions

The school behaviour policy should state how the school establishes a climate where praise and encouragement have precedence over the use of sanctions. A wide range of rewards should be available, especially the frequent use of praise during lessons and around the school to show instant recognition for positive behaviour, punctuality and regular attendance. You must know which rewards and sanctions you are free to use and those which you would have to negotiate with, or leave to, the teacher to apply.

Formal reward systems including credits, merits and prizes can also be used to recognise and congratulate pupils who are good role models for behaviour. Rewards should not be given just to the same 'good' pupils but also to pupils who demonstrate improvement in their own behaviour or attendance (DfES, 2003b).

Rewards

Rewards can provide positive incentives for positive behaviour. Pupils can be motivated by rewards such as: choice of favourite activity; special responsibility; smiley faces, stars or stamps; stickers or badges; merit points and certificates; mention in praise assembly; mention in headteacher's praise book; letter from headteacher to pupil's parents.

Rewards are most effective when they are:

✸ immediate and clearly linked to the pupil's behaviour, effort or achievement so that the pupil connects the reward with the behaviour

✸ meaningful and appropriate to the pupil's age/level of development, e.g. smiley faces and stickers are more real to younger pupils than merit or house points

✸ related to an individual's behaviour, effort or achievement rather than a group; every pupil needs the chance to obtain rewards for some positive aspect of their own behaviour

✸ recognised and consistently applied by all the staff in the school, e.g. some adults hand out rewards like confetti (making them meaningless), while others strictly ration them (making rewards virtually unobtainable) – either way pupils will not be motivated.

The difficulty with some school reward systems is that pupils who find it easier to behave appropriately may do very well, but those with emotional or behavioural difficulties may not. Reward systems that display stars or points for the whole group can be particularly damaging to pupils' self-esteem and often they do not indicate what the reward was for. An individual chart or book for each pupil can be better as they are then clearly competing against their own past efforts or improving their own behaviour.

For example, each pupil could have a small exercise book with a page a week for stickers, smiley faces or merit points which are clearly linked to the pupil's behaviour and/or learning. The teacher can negotiate with each pupil the targets they are expected to achieve that particular week. If the pupil achieves this target they receive an appropriate reward such as a certificate or choose a

Example cover

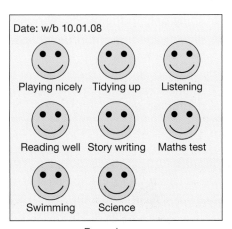

Example page

Example of individual pupil record of rewards

favourite activity. This makes it easier for pupils to see their individual efforts and achievements and can also help to set future goals for behaviour and learning.

Sanctions

While the emphasis should be on promoting positive behaviour through encouragement, praise and rewards, there may be times when these do not work. Sometimes it is necessary to impose sanctions for pupils whose behaviour goes beyond acceptable boundaries or who break the school/class/playground rules.

Schools should have a scale of sanctions for inappropriate behaviour. The school behaviour management policy should explain why these sanctions are necessary. Effective sanctions should be designed to discourage inappropriate behaviour rather than to punish pupils who break the rules. Consistency in the application of sanctions is essential and staff should use reprimands sparingly and fairly. Sanctions are more likely to discourage inappropriate behaviour if pupils see them as fair.

The school behaviour management policy should be supported with a range of sanctions for pupils who break the rules, ranging from letters to parents/carers, loss of privileges and detention right up to exclusion for the most serious or persistent inappropriate behaviour (DfES, 2003b).

Sanctions for inappropriate behaviour may include: staff registering disapproval and explaining why to the pupil(s); staff warnings to pupils that their behaviour is unacceptable; 'time out' involving isolation of the pupil for a short period; extra or alternative tasks for the pupil; pupil losing a privilege, e.g. loss of playtime; pupil writing a letter of apology or writing about what happened during an incident; parents being told at the end of the day or a letter being sent home outlining a serious incident; parents being invited into school to discuss a serious incident or when a pupil appears to be developing a pattern of poor behaviour; pupil being referred to their Key Stage co-ordinator, the SENCO, the deputy or headteacher.

Sanctions are most effective when they:

- ☆ balance against appropriate rewards
- ☆ are reasonable and appropriate to the pupil's action so that major sanctions do not apply to minor lapses in acceptable behaviour
- ☆ apply only to the pupils responsible and not the whole group/class
- ☆ discourage unwanted/unacceptable behaviour without damaging pupils' self-esteem
- ☆ are used as a last resort; every effort should be made to be positive and to encourage acceptable behaviour through positive rather than negative reinforcement.

EXERCISE:
1. What is the school's policy for rewards and sanctions relating to pupil behaviour? What rewards and sanctions have you seen in action? Which were the most effective and why?
2. Get a copy of the school policy for rewards and sanctions relating to behaviour. Highlight which rewards and sanctions can be applied by the teaching assistant.

The UN Convention on the Rights of the Child states that '*children have the right to be protected from all forms of physical and mental violence and deliberate humiliation*' (Article 19). Where parental expectations concerning punishment conflict with those of the school, staff should point out to parents the school's legal requirements under the Children Act 1989, which is no physical punishment. Physical or corporal punishment is not allowed in maintained schools, day nurseries and play settings:

'*Corporal punishment (smacking, slapping or shaking) is illegal in maintained schools and should not be used by any other parties within the scope of this guidance. It is permissible to take necessary physical action to prevent personal injury either to the child, other children or an adult or serious damage to property.*' (DH, 1991, The Children Act 1989; Volume 2, Section 6.22)

However, teachers (and others) are permitted '*... to use reasonable force to control or restrain pupils under certain circumstances. Other people may also do so, in the same way as teachers, provided they have been authorised by the headteacher to have control or charge of pupils*' (DH, 1999; p.16).

In addition, using physical punishment is never acceptable because it teaches children and young people that violence is an acceptable means for getting your own way. Shouting and verbal abuse are also totally unacceptable. Smacking and shouting do not work; adults end up having to smack harder and shout louder to get the desired behaviour. Children and young people do not learn how to behave better by being smacked or shouted at; they are just hurt and humiliated, which can have lasting damage on their self-esteem.

KEY TASK

1. Working with the teacher, set goals and boundaries for a pupil or group of pupils as part of a framework for positive behaviour.

2. Outline how you would implement this framework. Remember to emphasise the positive aspects of behaviour.

3. Devise a system of rewards for encouraging the pupils to demonstrate the targeted positive behaviour. If appropriate, include possible sanctions for unwanted/unacceptable behaviour.

NVQ LINKS:

Level 2:
STL3.4   STL4.1   STL4.3

Level 3:
STL3.4   STL19.1   STL19.2
STL20.1   STL20.2   STL20.3
STL37.1   STL37.3

Managing pupils' challenging behaviour

As part of your role as a teaching assistant you will be promoting the school's policies regarding pupil behaviour by consistently and effectively implementing agreed behaviour strategies as directed by the class teacher, SENCO or other professional. Teaching assistants need to be familiar with the ways teachers deal with pupils who demonstrate difficult behaviour to avoid giving conflicting messages to pupils.

Approaches to responding to persistent challenging or unwanted behaviour

1. **Think approaches not solutions**. There are no easy answers or quick solutions to dealing with challenging or unwanted behaviour. You may need to use a variety of approaches.

2. **Consider past experiences**. Children learn about behaviour through their early relationships and experiences; the effects these have depends on individual personality (see Chapter 3). No one's behaviour is static; they can acquire new behaviour patterns and discard behaviour which is ineffective or inappropriate.

3. **Remember adult influences on children's behaviour**. Adults working in schools have major influences on pupils' behaviour. Adult responses to pupil behaviour can make things better or worse. You may need to modify your own behaviour and responses.

4. **Be patient**. Changing pupil behaviour takes time, so do not expect too much all at once – take things one step at a time. Remember that behaviour may get worse before it gets better because some pupils will resist attempts to change their behaviour (particularly if they have behaved this way for some time) and will demonstrate even more challenging behaviour, especially if minor irritations are being ignored.

5. **Establish clear rules, boundaries and routines**. Pupils need to understand rules and the consequences if they do not follow the rules. Pupils need clear boundaries as to what is or is not acceptable behaviour, including frequent reminders about what these are.

6. **Be consistent**. Staff need to be consistent when responding to pupils with persistent unwanted behaviour or the pupils become confused. Adults need to discuss and agree on responses to the pupil's behaviour. Adults in schools need to work with the child's parents so the child sees that both are working together to provide a consistent framework for behaviour.

7. **Use diversionary tactics.** You can sometimes divert the pupil from an emotional or aggressive outburst or self-damaging behaviour. This does not always work, but often does. Be aware of possible triggers to unwanted behaviour and intervene or divert the pupil's attention *before* difficulties begin. Pupils can also be diverted by being offered alternative choices or being involved in decision-making.

8. **Encourage positive social interaction**. Help pupils to develop their social skills so they can join in activities with other pupils. Start off with one-to-one, then small groups and then larger groups. Play tutoring can help, e.g. using adult involvement to develop and extend social play. With older pupils encourage them to join school clubs.

9. **Help pupils find alternative ways to gain attention**. Most children want adult attention; it is the *way* they behave to gain attention that may need changing. Instead of being disruptive, pupils need to be encouraged to use more acceptable ways to get adult attention by asking or showing the adult that they have something to share.

10. **Help pupils to express their feelings.** Encourage pupils to express strong feelings such as anger, frustration or fear in positive ways – through play and communication. Older pupils need opportunities to express their grievances.

11. **Look at the environment**. Identify and, where possible, change aspects of the environment and routines within the classroom/school which may be contributing towards the pupil's unwanted behaviour.

12. **Label the behaviour not the pupil.** Make sure any response to unwanted behaviour allows the pupil to still feel valued without any loss of self-esteem, e.g. 'I like you, Tom, but I don't like it when you …'

13. **Be positive**. Emphasise the positive and encourage pupils to be positive too. Phrase rules in positive ways, e.g. 'do' rather than 'don't'. Think about which unwanted behaviour must be stopped and which can simply be ignored so that pupils are not being told 'No' or 'Don't do …' all the time. Encourage pupils to focus on positive aspects of school, e.g. friends, favourite subjects, school clubs.

14. **Remember punishments rarely work**. Punishments may satisfy the people giving them, but they are often of little value in changing pupil behaviour. Pupils may become devious or blame others in order to avoid being punished. Quiet reprimands are more effective than a public 'telling off', which only causes humiliation in front of other pupils and increases the pupil's resentment towards the adult. Rewarding positive behaviour is more effective than punishing unacceptable behaviour.

15. **Use praise, encouragement and rewards.** Set realistic and achievable goals and use pupils' interests to motivate them. Use regular positive feedback to encourage pupils to behave in acceptable ways and raise their self-esteem. Praise pupils' *efforts* as well as achievements. Find out which kinds of rewards matter to the pupils and use them.

16. **Avoid confrontation if at all possible**. Use eye contact and the pupil's name to gain/hold their attention. Keep calm, sound confident and in control. If the pupil is too wound up to listen, give them a chance to calm down, e.g. 'time out'.

17. **Give individual attention and support.** This encourages pupils to share their worries or concerns with a trusted adult. Time in involves giving pupils special individual attention to reinforce positive behaviour and decreases the need for them to gain adult attention through unwanted behaviour. It involves pupils talking one-to-one (or in a small group) with an adult about their day including reviewing positive aspects of the day.

18. **Use behaviour modification.** This involves using positive reinforcement to encourage acceptable behaviour; ignoring all but harmful unwanted behaviour. Work on one aspect of behaviour at a time and reward the pupil for any progress, no matter how small.

● KEY TASK

1. Observe a pupil who regularly demonstrates challenging or unwanted behaviour during group activities.

2. In your assessment include information on:
   - the pupil's behaviour during the activity
   - the pupil's communication skills
   - how the adult responds
   - how the other pupils respond to the pupil's behaviour.

3. Suggest ways to monitor the pupil's future behaviour.

4. Suggest ways to encourage the child's positive behaviour.

 NVQ LINKS:

Level 3:

STL18.1	STL19.1	STL19.2
STL20.1	STL20.2	STL29.1
STL29.2	STL37.1	STL37.2
STL37.3	STL41.1	STL41.2

Behaviour modification

Ivan Petrovich **Pavlov** was a Russian biologist who studied animal behaviour. His experiments involved teaching dogs to salivate in response to the sound of a bell. Before giving the dogs their food, Pavlov rang a bell. Eventually the dogs began to salivate when the bell rang even when there was no food. The dogs had learned to respond to the bell sound with their salivating reflex. This type of learned response or behaviour is called a *conditioned reflex.* Pavlov extended his ideas concerning conditioning to human psychology; he believed that human behaviour consists of many conditioned reflexes that are triggered by external influences.

B.F. **Skinner** was an American psychologist who discovered that the behaviour of rats could be controlled by food rewards. This idea of *operant conditioning* can be applied to any situation where the required behaviour is reinforced with a reward. Skinner believed that positive reinforcement (rewards) and negative reinforcement (sanctions) both contribute towards an individual's motivation for learning and behaviour.

The basic principles of behaviour modification are as follows:

- ☆ **P**raise and reward acceptable behaviour
- ☆ **R**educe the opportunities for unwanted behaviour
- ☆ **A**void confrontations
- ☆ **I**gnore minor unwanted behaviour
- ☆ **S**tructure appropriate sanctions
- ☆ **E**stablish clear rules, boundaries and routines.

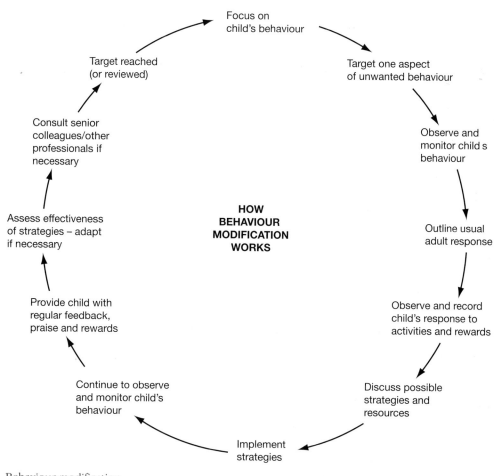

Behaviour modification

KEY TASK

1. Think about the basic principles of behaviour modification.
2. Look back at your behaviour observation on page 104 and focus on one aspect of that pupil's behaviour.
3. Outline a step-by-step approach to encourage the pupil to behave in more acceptable ways. Remember to include appropriate rewards (and sanctions).

NVQ LINKS:

Level 3:
STL18.1   STL19.1   STL19.2
STL20.1   STL20.2   STL29.2
STL37.1   STL37.2   STL37.3
STL41.1

Behaviour Support Plans

Persistent behavioural difficulties are recognised as special educational needs (SEN) and pupils with behavioural difficulties will require additional support in school. Teaching assistants are often used to provide this additional support. Providing support for pupils with behavioural difficulties is one of the most challenging roles that teaching assistants undertake. When supporting these pupils you may sometimes feel hopeless, annoyed or helpless. However, working with pupils with behavioural problems can also be very rewarding, as by providing support, you are helping them to develop the life skills and coping strategies they need.

You should always remember that a teaching assistant is not a teacher and that the teaching assistant's responsibilities are set within clear boundaries. The teacher who manages your work has the responsibility to ensure that appropriate behaviour and learning programmes are planned, followed and monitored. The teacher also has the responsibility to ensure that you are well supported in your role of supporting pupils who have behavioural difficulties.

Pupils with persistent behavioural difficulties usually have an Individual Education Plan (IEP) and/or an individual Behaviour Support Plan (BSP). A pupil's BSP should include the following information:

☆ The short-term targets for the pupil
☆ The strategies to be used
☆ The support to be put in place
☆ When the plan is to be reviewed
☆ The outcome of any action taken.

These plans will give you information about the support being provided to help the pupil and will often include details of your role in giving behaviour support. You may sometimes be involved in drawing up these plans, along with the teacher, the pupil and the parents or carers. You need to be clear about your exact role in implementing Behaviour Support Plans. For example:

- ✫ Helping the pupil to follow specific routines in particular lessons.
- ✫ Being vigilant at lesson changes, break times and lunchtimes that can provide stress points for pupils with difficult behaviour, as there is not as much structure as in lesson times.
- ✫ Fostering the participation of pupils in social and academic processes of a school.
- ✫ Helping the pupils to take a real part in school life both through positive friendships and achievement in learning.
- ✫ Providing support to enable the pupil to remain as a part of the full class/group for as much time as possible.

Support systems for pupils and staff

The school should have a range of strategies for responding to pupils who demonstrate challenging behaviour including:

- ✫ Regular pastoral reviews to identify pupils most at risk.
- ✫ Contact with parents in the early stages of any problem.
- ✫ Advice or support from senior colleagues and training in behaviour management.
- ✫ Referrals for specialist advice from agencies linked to the school (e.g. LEA Behaviour Support Team or Educational Psychology Service).
- ✫ Referrals to a learning support unit for a short period of additional support outside the classroom environment.
- ✫ Parent/carer consultations and family sessions.
- ✫ One-to-one counselling with a trained specialist.
- ✫ Support from learning mentors or trained teaching assistants.
- ✫ Strategies for responding to pupils with persistent unwanted behaviour.

(DfES, 2003b)

> EXERCISE:
> 1. What strategies may the school use when responding to pupils who demonstrate challenging behaviour?
> 2. Describe how *you* have responded to a pupil who demonstrates challenging behaviour.
> 3. What specialist advice on behaviour management is available within the school?

Dealing with bullying

Research suggests that 85% of children aged 5 to 11 years old have experienced bullying in some form, e.g. name-calling, being hit or kicked. In 2000 a survey of 11 to 16 year olds found that '*36% of children said they had been bullied in the last 12 months; 26% had been threatened with violence and 13% had been physically attacked*' (ATL, 2000). Bullying is such a serious problem that schools must have an anti-bullying policy that clearly sets out the ways in which they try to prevent bullying and deal with bullying behaviour when it happens.

Defining bullying behaviour

Bullying can be defined as behaviour that is deliberately hurtful or aggressive, repeated over a period of time and difficult for victims to defend themselves against. There are three main types of bullying: **physical** – hitting, kicking, taking belongings; **verbal** – name-calling, insulting, making offensive remarks; **indirect** – spreading nasty stories about someone, exclusion from social groups, being made the subject of malicious rumours, sending malicious emails or text messages on mobile phones.

Name-calling is the most common type of bullying. Pupils may be called nasty names because of their individual characteristics, ethnic origin, nationality, skin colour, sexual orientation or disability. Verbal bullying is common amongst both boys and girls. Boys experience more physical violence and threats when being bullied than girls. However, physical attacks on girls by other girls are becoming more common. Girls tend to use more indirect types of bullying which can be more difficult to detect and deal with (DfES, 2000a).

Any pupil can experience bullying but certain factors may make bullying more likely. While there is *never* an acceptable excuse for bullying behaviour, pupils are more likely to experience bullying if they: are shy or have an over-protective family environment; are from a different racial or ethnic group to the majority of pupils; appear different in some obvious respect, e.g. stammering; have special needs, e.g. a disability or learning difficulties; behave inappropriately, e.g. are a 'nuisance' or intrude on others' activities; possess expensive accessories, e.g. mobile phones or computer games.

Recognising when a pupil is being bullied

Pupils who are experiencing bullying may be reluctant to attend school and are often absent. They may be more anxious and insecure than others, have fewer friends and often feel unhappy and lonely. They can suffer from low self-esteem and negative self-image; they may see themselves as failures, e.g. stupid, ashamed and unattractive.

Possible signs that a pupil is being bullied include:

- ✯ Suddenly not wanting to go to school when usually enjoys it
- ✯ Unexplained cuts and bruises
- ✯ Possessions have unexplained damage or are persistently 'lost'
- ✯ Becoming withdrawn or depressed but will not say what is the matter.

While the above signs may indicate that a pupil is being bullied, they may also be symptomatic of other problems such as abuse (see responding to concerns about possible abuse in Chapter 2).

Helping pupils who are being bullied

The behaviour of some pupils can lead to them experiencing bullying, though this does not justify the behaviour of the bullies. For example, some pupils may: find it difficult to play with other pupils; be hyperactive; behave in ways that irritate others; bully weaker pupils; be easily roused to anger; fight back when attacked or even slightly provoked; be actively disliked by the majority of pupils in the school. School staff and the pupil's parents should work together to identify any such behaviour. The pupil needs help to improve personal and social skills including assertiveness techniques and conflict resolution.

You may be able to provide support for a pupil who is being bullied by:

* Encouraging the pupil to talk
* Listening to the pupil's problems
* Believing the pupil if they say they are being bullied
* Providing reassurance that it is not their fault; no one deserves to be bullied
* Discussing the matter with the pupil's class teacher or form tutor
* Taking appropriate action, following the school's policy on anti-bullying.

Dealing with persistent and violent bullying

Where a pupil does not respond to the strategies to combat bullying, the school should take tough action to deal with persistent and violent bullying. The school should have a range of sanctions to deal with this type of bullying. Everyone within the school should know what sanctions will be taken. These sanctions should be fair and applied consistently. You can help deal with bullying behaviour by:

* knowing the school's policy and strategies for dealing with bullying behaviour
* using appropriate sanctions for such behaviour, e.g. exclusion from certain activities
* providing help for the bully so they can recognise that this behaviour is unacceptable, e.g. discussion, mediation, peer counselling
* working with teachers and parents to establish community awareness of bullying
* making sure all pupils know that bullying will *not* be tolerated
* understanding that the school can permanently **exclude** pupils who demonstrate persistent bullying behaviour, especially physical violence.

KEY TASK

1. Outline your school's anti-bullying policy and main strategies for dealing with bullying behaviour.

2. Give a reflective account of how you have handled concerns about bullying. Remember confidentiality.

3. Devise an activity to encourage pupils to speak up about bullying, e.g. story, discussion, role-play, drama or poster-making.

 NVQ LINKS:

Level 2:		
STL3.4	STL4.1	STL4.3
Level 3:		
STL3.4	STL19.1	STL19.2
STL20.1	STL20.2	STL20.3
STL37.1	STL37.3	

STOP the bullies now!
LOOK out for your friends.
LISTEN to your friends who are sad or upset.
TALK to your teachers or parents.

Example of pupil's anti-bullying poster

Further reading

Blandford, S. (1998) *Managing discipline in schools.* Routledge Falmer.

Chaplain, R. (2003) *Teaching without disruption in secondary schools: a model for managing behaviour.* Routledge Falmer.

DfES (2003) *Advice on whole school behaviour and attendance policy.* DfES. (Available free from: www.standards.dfes.gov.uk.)

Docking, J. W. and MacGrath, M. (2002) *Managing behaviour in the primary school.* David Fulton Publishers.

Elliott, M. and Kilpatrick, J. (2002) *How to stop bullying: a Kidscape training guide.* Kidscape.

Glenn, A. *et al.* (2003) *Behaviour in the early years.* David Fulton Publishers.

Kay, J. (2006) *Managing behaviour in the early years.* Continuum International Publishing Group.

Mortimer, H. (2002) *Behavioural and emotional difficulties.* Scholastic.

Petrie, P. (1997) *Communicating with children and adults: interpersonal skills for early years and playwork.* Hodder Arnold.

Rogers, B. (2000) *Behaviour management: a whole school approach.* Paul Chapman Publishing.

Train, A. (2004) *ADHD: how to deal with very difficult children.* Souvenir Press Ltd.

5 Promoting positive working relationships

Key points:

- ✳ Developing positive working relationships with pupils
- ✳ Understanding children's needs and rights
- ✳ Promoting equality and inclusion
- ✳ Supporting pupils with special educational needs
- ✳ Communicating with children
- ✳ Supporting children in developing relationships
- ✳ Encouraging pupils to recognise and deal with feelings
- ✳ Developing positive working relationships with adults
- ✳ Communicating with adults
- ✳ Confidentiality matters
- ✳ Handling disagreements with other adults.

Developing positive working relationships with pupils

Being a teaching assistant involves working closely with individuals and groups of children. Your relationships with pupils must be professional without being too distant. When working with groups of children you should give individual attention to each child and ensure that *all* the children feel welcome and valued within the school. This includes encouraging pupils to answer questions, ask questions, make suggestions and contribute ideas as appropriate to their ages, needs and abilities.

You can help to develop and promote positive working relationships with **pupils** by:

- ✩ remembering that the social, intellectual, physical welfare and emotional well-being of all pupils is the prime purpose and first concern of the school
- ✩ acting with compassion and impartiality
- ✩ expressing any criticism of pupils in a sensitive manner and avoiding hurtful comments of a personal nature
- ✩ never abusing, exploiting or undermining the staff/pupil relationship

* respecting the confidentiality of information relating to pupils unless the disclosure of such information is either required by law or is in the best interests of that particular child (see section below on confidentiality matters)

* ensuring that any necessary records on the pupils are based on factual, objective and up-to-date information (see section on maintaining pupil records in Chapter 12).

Positive interactions with pupils

As a teaching assistant you should know and understand what is meant by the terms 'appropriate' and 'inappropriate' behaviour when interacting with pupils, including the relevant legal requirements (see section on rewards and sanctions in Chapter 4). To work well as a teaching assistant you need to genuinely care about children. In addition to meeting children's physical and intellectual needs you need to provide emotional security by showing a genuine interest in everything the children say and do as well as providing comfort when children are upset or unwell. Children can sense when they are with someone who really cares about them. Personal friendships with children or their parents are best avoided as they can complicate your professional relationships within the school. However, if you are working in your local community this may not always be possible. If you *are* friends with children and/or their families outside the school try to keep your personal and professional lives separate. For example, do not give the child preferential treatment within the school or gossip with parents about what occurs in the school (see section below on confidentiality matters).

Ten ways to develop positive relationships with pupils

You can develop positive relationships with pupils by:

1. Remembering children's names and pronouncing them correctly

2. Being approachable and willing to listen to pupils

3. Listening and responding to pupils in ways which let children feel they are understood

4. Giving time to pupils as individuals within the school

5. Avoiding stereotype judgements about individual pupils concerning race, gender, ability, religion

6. Getting a pupil's own explanation concerning behaviour before criticising them; do not jump to conclusions

7. Communicating with pupils in a sensitive way, e.g. do not interrupt them rudely or talk over them (see section below on effective communication with pupils)

8. Showing pupils that they are valued and important people

9. Being alert to children's feelings

10. Looking at the world from a child's point of view!

KEY TASK

Outline how you contribute to developing and promoting positive relationships with pupils in your school.

 NVQ LINKS:

Level 2: STL4.1

Level 3: STL20.1

Understanding children's needs and rights

In the past decade there has been a major shift in attitude towards children's **rights**. Previously children's rights were mainly concerned with children's basic welfare needs. Now as well as their basic rights to life, health and education, children are viewed as having a much wider range of rights including the right to engage in play activities, to express their views and to participate in making decisions that affect them directly.

Children's rights, as stated in the UN Convention on the Rights of the Child, are clear and universal: they apply to all children. Also, while children's individual **needs** may differ, they all have the same rights. Children's rights are based on their needs, but emphasising rights rather than needs demonstrates a commitment to viewing and respecting children as valued citizens (The Children's Rights Alliance for England: www.crae.org.uk).

All children are special and unique; *all* children have individual needs because they perceive the world differently and interact with others in different ways. All children (including identical twins) have different life experiences which affect their view of the world. Children experience different social and environmental factors which, along with their genetic differences, shape their personalities, knowledge and skills. Children may be individuals but they exist as part of various social groups, e.g. family, local community, school and wider society. Adults working with children must appreciate the uniqueness of every child while ensuring that the needs of both the individual and the group are met (Brennan, 1987).

For example, how children react to learning in the school environment depends on their individual needs and life experiences. Some children may find the school environment challenging or even exciting and are well motivated to learn. Others may find the school environment daunting and may experience learning difficulties. Still others may find this type of learning environment uninviting or boring and may demonstrate signs of difficult behaviour.

All children have these essential needs:

- ☆ **Physical care:** regular, nutritious meals; warmth; rest and sleep
- ☆ **Routines:** a regular pattern to their day, with any changes explained
- ☆ **Independence:** encouragement to do things for themselves and make choices
- ☆ **Communication:** encouragement to talk and interact with others
- ☆ **Encouragement and praise:** for trying as well as achieving
- ☆ **Love:** from parents/carers which is unconditional, e.g. expecting nothing back
- ☆ **Education:** appropriate to their age and level of development
- ☆ **Sincerity and respect:** honest and courteous treatment
- ☆ **Stimulation:** opportunities to explore their environment and tackle new challenges.

All children have individual *learning* needs which require: opportunities to explore their environment; adult assistance to aid their knowledge and understanding; activities which are appropriate to their abilities and development. *All* children also have *social and emotional* needs which should be met by the setting: assistance in adjusting to new play and learning environments; help in relating comfortably with other children and adults; opportunities to interact/play with other children; opportunities to find out about people and the world they live in. Some children have *special or additional needs* which mean that they may require: special equipment or resources; modified surroundings, e.g. wheelchair access, ramps; extra learning support to access the National Curriculum; a special or modified curriculum. These children have **special educational needs** arising from: a physical disability; a learning difficulty; an emotional or behavioural problem (see section below on children with special educational needs).

Example of child's poster about children's rights

The United Nations Convention on the Rights of the Child

As a teaching assistant you should know and understand the basic requirements of the *United Nations Convention on the Rights of the Child*. These rights are for children and young people (up to the age of 18 years). The United Nations (UN) approved the Convention on the Rights of the Child on 20 November 1989, the UK government ratified (agreed to uphold) it on 16 December 1991. Countries that have ratified the Convention are legally bound to do what it states and to make all laws, policy and practice compatible with the Convention. The only two countries in the world that have not signed the Convention are the USA and Somalia. There are 54 articles in the UN Convention on the Rights of the Child. The articles cover four different groupings of rights: survival, protection, development and participation. Each article outlines a different right. (For more information see the *Children's Rights and Responsibilities Leaflet* – available free from **www.unicef.org.uk/tz/resources/assets/pdf/rights_leaflet.pdf**.)

> **EXERCISE:**
> 1. Find out more about the UN Convention on the Rights of the Child.
> 2. Check whether copies of the Convention and related materials are available in your school and/or the college library.
> 3. Design a poster and/or leaflet outlining the Articles most relevant to education settings, e.g. Articles: 1–4, 12–15, 19, 23, 28–31 and 39. You could encourage the pupils in your school to design their own posters/leaflets about these rights.

National legislation relating to children's rights

As a teaching assistant you should know and understand the basic requirements of national legislation relating to children's rights. **The Children Act 1989** came into force on 14 October 1991 and is concerned with families and the care of children, local authority support for children and their families, fostering, childminding and day care provision. *The Children Act 1989* is particularly important because it emphasises the importance of putting the child first. In summary, the Act states that:

- ✰ what is best for the child must always be the first consideration
- ✰ whenever possible children should be brought up in their own family
- ✰ unless the child is at risk of harm, a child should not be taken away from their family without the family's agreement
- ✰ local authorities must help families with children in need
- ✰ local authorities must work with parents and children
- ✰ courts must put children first when making decisions
- ✰ children being looked after by local authorities have rights, as do their parents.

The Children Act 1989 provides the legislative framework for the child protection system in England and Wales. *The Children (Northern Ireland) Order 1995* and *The Children (Scotland) Act 1995* share the same principles as *The Children Act*

1989 but contain their own guidance. ***The Children Act 2004*** introduced changes to the structure and organisation of the child protection system in England and Wales. For information about the 2004 Act see www.everychildmatters.gov.uk/strategy/guidance/.

The national framework for children's services

The *Children Act 2004*, together with *Every Child Matters: Change for Children* published in December 2004 by the Department for Education and Skills (DfES), sets out the Government's direction for 150 local programmes of change to be led by local authorities and their key partners. Many local areas have already started their local change programmes, which bring together local authority, health, criminal justice services, voluntary and community organisations and other local partners to deliver improved services for children.

Every Child Matters: Change for Children sets out the national framework of outcomes for all children, to protect them, to promote their well-being and to support the development of their full potential. The document sets out the action needed locally and the ways in which the Government will work with and support local authorities and their partners (DfES, 2004).

What the outcomes mean

1. **Be healthy:** physically healthy; mentally and emotionally healthy; sexually healthy; healthy lifestyles; choose not to take illegal drugs.

2. **Stay safe:** safe from maltreatment, neglect, violence and sexual exploitation; safe from accidental injury and death; safe from bullying and discrimination; safe from crime and anti-social behaviour in and out of school; have security, stability and are cared for.

3. **Enjoy and achieve:** ready for school; attend and enjoy school; achieve stretching national educational standards at primary school; achieve personal and social development and enjoy recreation; achieve stretching national educational standards at secondary school.

4. **Make a positive contribution:** engage in decision-making and support the community and environment; engage in law-abiding and positive behaviour in and out of school; develop positive relationships and choose not to bully or discriminate; develop self-confidence and successfully deal with significant life changes and challenges; develop enterprising behaviour.

5. **Achieve economic well-being:** engage in further education, employment or training on leaving school; ready for employment; live in decent homes and sustainable communities; access to transport and material goods; live in households free from low incomes.

(DfES, 2004)

This national framework will enable organisations providing services to children (including hospitals, schools, the police and voluntary groups) to access the same information and work together to protect children from harm and help them achieve what they want and need. Children will have a greater say about the issues that affect them both as individuals and collectively.

Promoting equality and inclusion

All schools have an equal opportunities policy with procedures to ensure that it is implemented. You must follow your school's policy and procedures together with any relevant legal requirements when dealing with these issues. As a teaching assistant you should:

☆ challenge discrimination or prejudice when necessary (for example, if a colleague makes a derisory comment about a person's race, culture or disability, you should tell them why it is unacceptable to express their views in this way)

☆ state that you will not condone views that discriminate against another person

☆ provide support for children and adults who experience discrimination or prejudice by encouraging them to respond with positive action.

EXERCISE: How have you challenged (or would you challenge) discrimination or prejudice in school?

Legislation relating to equality and inclusion

You must know and understand the basic requirements of legislation relating to equality and inclusion, e.g. equal opportunities, disability discrimination and special educational needs (see below). The *Sex Discrimination Act 1975* and the *Race Relations Act 1976* made it unlawful to discriminate on the grounds of sex, race, colour, ethnic or national origin. These Acts, with subsequent amendments, established statutory requirements to: prevent discrimination; promote equality of opportunity; provide redress against discrimination.

Amendments to these Acts and the *Disability Discrimination Act 1995* have developed and extended anti-discrimination legislation. The Disability Discrimination Act (DDA) protects people with disabilities in education, employment, access to goods, facilities and services, e.g. service providers have to make reasonable adjustments for disabled people, such as providing extra help and adjusting the physical features of their premises to overcome physical barriers to access (www.drc-gb.org).

Part IV of the DDA was amended by the *Special Educational Needs and Disability Act 2001* (see below) and includes new duties for education providers to ensure that they do not discriminate against people with disabilities which came into effect in September 2002. The *Disability Discrimination Act 2005* amends the DDA 1995 and places a duty on public bodies to promote equality of opportunity for people with disabilities. The Disability Equality Duty came into force in December 2006. The *Race Relations (Amendment) Act 2000* introduced new statutory duties for the public sector including actively promoting race equality. Under a new European Union directive the grounds for discrimination go beyond the three main areas of race, gender and disability (which are discussed in this chapter) to include age, religious belief and sexual orientation. Individual rights are also protected by the *Data Protection Act 1998, Human Rights Act 1998* and *Freedom of Information Act 2000*. Useful websites with summaries of equal opportunities and disability discrimination legislation include:

- ✯ Commission for Racial Equality: www.cre.gov.uk
- ✯ Disability Rights Commission: www.drc-gb.org
- ✯ Equal Opportunities Commission: www.eoc.org.uk

EXERCISE: Find out about the legislation covering equality and inclusion and how it relates to your school, e.g. the school's equal opportunities policy, inclusion policy and/or special educational needs policy.

Anti-discriminatory and inclusive practice

Anti-discriminatory practice in the school can be defined as words and actions which prevent discrimination and prejudice towards any individual or group of people and actively promote equal opportunities. This means ensuring that all pupils, parents, colleagues and other professionals are treated in an unbiased, fair and non-prejudiced way. This includes ensuring that all the school's policies, procedures and strategies demonstrate a positive and inclusive attitude towards all individuals regardless of age, gender, race, culture or disability.

Inclusive practice in the school can be defined as words and actions which encourage the participation of *all* pupils (including those with disabilities or from other minority groups) within a mainstream setting. This means ensuring that all pupils are valued as individuals and are given appropriate support to enable them to participate fully in the play and learning activities provided by the school.

As a teaching assistant you should know how to judge whether the school is inclusive and supportive of diversity. You should be able to demonstrate that you support inclusion and diversity through your words, actions and behaviours in the school. Inclusion is about the child's right to: attend the local mainstream setting; be valued as an individual; be provided with all the support needed to thrive in a mainstream setting. Inclusive provision should be seen as an extension of the school's equal opportunities policy and practice. It requires a commitment from the whole staff, parents and pupils to include the full diversity of children in the local community. This may require planned restructuring of the whole school environment to ensure equality of access.

1. Find out about your school's policies and practices for inclusion including equal opportunities and special educational needs.
2. Briefly outline the school's procedures for inclusion and anti-discriminatory practice including your role in implementing these procedures.

NVQ LINKS:

Level 2:
STL4.1   STL11.2   STL12.1
STL12.2   STL12.3

Level 3:
STL20.1   STL34.2   STL35.2
STL36.2   STL36.3   STL38.1
STL38.2   STL39.1   STL40.1
STL41.1   STL42.1   STL44.1
STL47.1

Positive attitudes towards cultural diversity, gender and disability

Children are influenced by images, ideas and attitudes that create prejudice and lead to discrimination or disadvantage. Children are not born with these attitudes; they *learn* them. You have an important role to play in promoting children's positive attitudes towards themselves and other people. In addition, you must not have stereotyped views about children's potential or have low expectations of children based on culture, gender or disability. As a teaching assistant you should:

- ☆ recognise and eliminate racial discrimination
- ☆ have high but realistic expectations for *all* children
- ☆ maximise each child's motivation and potential
- ☆ encourage each child to feel a positive sense of identity
- ☆ ensure the learning environment reflects positive images
- ☆ challenge stereotypes in the media, literature and everyday life
- ☆ give all children the opportunities to play with a wide variety of toys, games and play equipment
- ☆ ensure that children do not think they are superior to others
- ☆ expect the same standards of behaviour from all children regardless of culture, gender or disability
- ☆ recognise children with disabilities as individuals, not by their condition or impairment (e.g. child *with* autistic tendencies, not autistic child)
- ☆ encourage the 'able' world to adapt to those with disabilities, not the other way round.

Twelve ways to promote positive images of children and the wider society

You can help the teacher to provide an environment, activities and experiences that promote positive images of children and reflect the wider society in the following ways:

1. Share books and stories about real-life situations with people the children can identify with.

2. Use posters, pictures, photographs, displays, jigsaws, puzzles, toys and other play materials which reflect positive images of race, culture, gender and disability.

3. Provide activities that encourage children to look at their physical appearance in a positive light, e.g. games looking in mirrors; self-portraits (ensuring paints provided for all skin tones); drawing round each other to create life-size portraits.

4. Provide activities that encourage children to focus on their abilities in positive ways, e.g. 'I can …' tree with positive statements about what each child can do.

5. Provide activities which encourage children to express their likes and dislikes, plus confidence in their own name and who they are, e.g. circle games such as The name game where each child takes it in turn to say 'My name is …and I like to … because …' or Circle jump where each child takes a turn at jumping into the circle, making an action that they feel expresses them and saying 'Hello, I'm …'; then the rest of the children copy the action and reply 'Hello … [repeating the child's name]'.

6. Provide opportunities for sharing experiences about themselves and their families through topics like All about me and by inviting family members such as parents/grandparents to come into the setting to talk about themselves and their backgrounds.

7. Provide opportunities for imaginative/role play which encourages children to explore different roles in positive ways, e.g. dressing-up clothes, cooking utensils, dolls and puppets that reflect different cultures.

8. Visiting local shops, businesses and community groups that reflect the cultural diversity of the setting and the local community.

9. Inviting visitors into the setting to talk positively about their roles and lives, e.g. (female) police officer or fire fighter, (male) nurse, people with disabilities or from different ethnic groups. (Note: Avoid tokenism; include these visitors as part of on-going topics.)

10. Celebrate cultural diversity through the festivals of the faiths in the local community, e.g. Diwali (Hindu), Channuka (Jewish), Christmas (Christian), Eid (Muslim).

11. Value language diversity by displaying welcome signs and other information in community languages.

12. Provide positive examples of:

    ● Black and Asian people and women from all ethnic groups in prominent roles in society, e.g. politicians, doctors, lawyers, teachers, entrepreneurs

- Black and Asian people's past contributions to politics, medicine, science, education, etc. Look at important historical figures like Martin Luther King, Mahatma Gandhi, and Mary Seacole

- People with disabilities participating fully in modern society such as Stephen Hawking, Marlee Matlin and the late Christopher Reeve as well as famous people from the past like Louis Braille, Helen Keller and Franklin D. Roosevelt.

 KEY TASK

1. Compile a resource pack that promotes positive images. You might include the following information and resources: posters, wall charts, photographs and pictures; booklets and leaflets; suggested activities to promote positive images; book list of relevant children's books and stories; list of useful organisations and addresses.

 **NVQ LINKS:**

Level 3:
STL20.1   STL35.1   STL36.2
STL38.1   STL38.2   STL47.1

2. Plan, implement and evaluate at least one activity suggested in your resource pack.

National legislation relating to children with special educational needs

The Education Act 1993 defines children with special educational needs as:

(a) Having a significantly greater difficulty in learning than the majority of children of the same age
(b) Having a disability which either prevents or hinders the child from making use of educational facilities of a kind provided for children of the same age in schools within the area of the local education authority
(c) An under five who falls within the definition at (a) or (b) above or would do if special educational provision was not made for the child.

The Special Educational Needs and Disability Act 2001 amends Part 4 of the *Education Act 1996* to make further provision against discrimination, on the grounds of disability, in schools and other educational establishments. This Act strengthens the right of children with special educational needs (SEN) to be educated in mainstream schools where parents want this and the interests of other children can be protected. The Act also requires local education authorities (LEAs) to make arrangements for services to provide parents of children with SEN with advice and information. It also requires schools to inform parents where they are making special educational provision for their child and allows schools to request a statutory assessment of a pupil's SEN (www.drc-gb.org).

The Special Educational Needs Code of Practice 2001 replaces *The 1994 Code of Practice on the Identification and Assessment of Special Educational Needs* and gives practical advice to Local Education Authorities, maintained schools and others concerning their statutory duties to identify, assess and provide for children's special educational needs. The new code came into effect on 1 January 2002. This code keeps a great deal of the guidance from the first Code of Practice but includes developments in education since 1994 and also utilises the experiences of schools and LEAs. The central aim of the government's special needs policy is to enable *all* children to have the opportunities available through inclusive education. The new code re-enforces the right for children with SEN to receive education within a mainstream setting and advocates that schools and LEAs implement a graduated method for the organisation of SEN. The code provides a school-based model of intervention for children with special educational needs. The five stages of the 1994 code have been replaced with: Early Years Action or School Action (old Stages 1 and 2); Early Years Action Plus or School Action Plus (old Stage 3); and Statutory Assessment (old Stages 4 and 5).

The code also includes new chapters on: Parent Partnership and Disagreement Resolution; pupil participation including the *UN Convention on the Rights of the Child*; early years with extra information; the Connexions Service for young people aged 13 to 19 years. Accompanying the new code is the *Special Educational Needs Toolkit* which expands on the guidance contained in the code. This 'toolkit' is not law but does provide examples of good practice that LEAs and schools can follow.

Supporting pupils with special educational needs

As a teaching assistant you should be actively involved in contributing to the inclusion of children with special needs, including those with hearing or visual impairment, communication difficulties, learning difficulties, emotional difficulties or behavioural difficulties. (For detailed information on supporting pupils with special needs see Chapter 11.)

Ten ways to support pupils with special educational needs

You can help pupils with special educational needs to participate in all activities by:

1. Providing a stimulating language-rich childcare environment which is visually attractive, tactile and interactive

2. Maximising the use of space in the setting to allow freedom of movement for all children (including those who are physically disabled or visually impaired)

3. Ensuring accessibility of resources including any specialist equipment

4. Providing opportunities for all children to explore different materials and activities

5. Encouraging children to use the abilities they do have to their fullest extent

6. Providing sufficient time for children to explore their environment and materials; some children may need extra time to complete tasks

7. Encouraging independence, e.g. use computers, word processing, tape recorders

---

8. Praising all children's efforts as well as achievements

9. Supporting families to respond to their children's special needs

10. Accessing specialist advice and support for children with special needs.

EXERCISE: Devise a leaflet for a new teaching assistant on how to organise the classroom to ensure an effective and inclusive learning environment. Include at least ten key points.

Communicating with children

It is important to communicate with children in a manner that is clear and concise and appropriate to their ages, needs and abilities. This involves: using words and phrases that children will understand; actively listening to children; responding positively to children's views and feelings; clarifying and confirming points to reinforce children's knowledge and understanding. When communicating with children: ask and answer questions to prompt appropriate responses from them and to check their understanding; encourage them to ask questions and contribute their own ideas; adapt communication methods to suit their individual language needs if they have special needs such as a hearing impairment or they are bilingual. (For more information on supporting pupils with special language needs see Chapters 10 and 11.)

Effective communication with children

The first step towards effective communication with children (and adults, too, of course) is being able to listen attentively to what they have to say. Nearly all breakdowns in communication are due to people not listening to each other. Effective communication requires good inter-personal skills such as:

- ☆ **Availability** – make time to listen to pupils
- ☆ **Attentive listening** – concentrate on what pupils are saying
- ☆ **Appropriate use of non-verbal skills** – facing the pupil, leaning slightly towards them, smiling, nodding, open-handed gestures not clenched fists
- ☆ **Follow the rules of turn-taking** in language exchanges; every person needs to have their say while others listen
- ☆ **Politeness and courtesy** – no shouting, no talking over other people, avoiding sarcasm (especially with younger pupils, who do not understand it and can be frightened by your strange tone of voice)
- ☆ **Being relaxed, confident and articulate**
- ☆ **Using appropriate vocabulary** for your listener(s)
- ☆ **Encouraging others to talk** by asking 'open' questions
- ☆ **Responding positively** to what is said
- ☆ **Being receptive** to new ideas

- ☆ **Being sympathetic** to other viewpoints (even if you totally disagree with them!)
- ☆ **Providing opportunities** for meaningful communication to take place.

Effective communication also involves pupils being able to understand and use **the language of learning**. That is, the language needed to: understand concepts; participate in problem-solving; develop ideas and opinions. You need to be able to utilise language effectively yourself in order to encourage and extend pupils' learning. A sound knowledge of child development (see Chapter 3) plus the realistic organisation of the school, classroom, activities and time are essential components for effective communication with pupils.

Active listening

Communication is a two-way process that depends on the sender (talker) and on the receiver (listener). Research has shown that adults tend to be poor listeners. Adults working in schools do too much talking and not enough listening to pupils' talk. While most primary schools appreciate the benefit of 'listening time', many secondary schools do not (Hutchcroft, 1981). Active listening depends on: listening carefully to pupils' talk; considering the mood of the participants; minimising distractions in the immediate surroundings.

Asking and answering questions

You need to develop your skills at being able to initiate and sustain pupils' talk by providing questions, prompts and cues, which encourage and support the pupils' language and learning without doing the thinking for them. Some questions require only limited responses or answers from pupils. These 'closed' questions usually receive one-word answers such as 'yes' or 'no' or the name of a person/object. These types of questions do not help pupils to develop their own language and communication skills. 'Open' questions, on the other hand, are a positive way to encourage a variety of responses allowing more detailed answers, descriptions and accounts of pupils' personal experiences, feelings and ideas. For example: the question 'Did you ride your bike?' can be answered only by 'yes' or 'no'. Instead you could ask 'Where did you go on your bike?' and then use questions like 'What happened next?' to prompt further responses.

As well as asking questions, you need to be able to *answer* pupils' questions. Encouraging pupils to ask questions helps them to explore their environment more fully, to look for reasons/possible answers and to reach their own conclusions as to why and how things happen. Always treat their questions seriously. Try to answer them truthfully and accurately. If you honestly do not know the answer, then say so and suggest an alternative way for the pupil to obtain an answer. For example, 'I don't know where that animal comes from, let's look in the encyclopaedia or on the Internet to find out.' Or 'I'm not sure what that word means exactly; go and look in your dictionary to see if it's in there.' You should encourage pupils to find their own answers as appropriate to their age and level of development. Give them information in an appropriate form, which will increase their vocabulary and add to their knowledge/understanding of their world. Your answers should use words that are appropriate to the pupil. For example, if a younger pupil asks 'Why does it rain?' you need to give a simple reply such as 'Clouds are full of water which falls back to the ground as drops of rain', while an older pupil can be given a more technical description of cloud formation and rainfall.

KEY TASK

1. Listen to adults talking with children in a variety of situations, both within and outside your school (e.g. on buses, in shops, in the street, in the playground). Pay particular attention to the questions asked by the adults *and* the children, and *how* they are answered.

2. Consider these points:
   - Which inter-personal skills were used?
   - How effective was the communication?
   - Did the adult use active listening skills?
   - What did the children learn about language, the activity and/or the environment?

NVQ LINKS:

Level 2:
STL2.3   STL4.1   STL4.3

Level 3:
STL20.2   STL25.3

The importance of praise and encouragement

Praise and encouragement are essential components when communicating with children. All children (especially young children) need immediate and positive affirmations or rewards to show that their learning and development are progressing in accordance with the adult's (and child's) expectations. Adults should emphasise the positive aspects of children's learning and development. You can support children in managing failure and disappointment by emphasising the importance of taking part, trying their personal best and praising and/or rewarding children for their *efforts* not just their achievements. Children gain confidence and increased positive self-esteem when they receive praise/rewards for their efforts and achievements including encouragement to try new activities and experiences.

There are four main methods used to praise and encourage pupils:

1. **Verbal**, e.g. 'praise' assemblies; positive comments about the child's behaviour or activities such as 'Well done, Tom! This is a lovely story! Tell me what happened next.'

2. **Non-verbal**, e.g. body language: leaning forward or turning towards a child to show interest in what the child is communicating; facial expressions: smiling; sign language: 'good boy/girl!'

3. **Symbolic**, e.g. 'smiley faces' for a carefully done work or positive behaviour; stickers for being a good listener or for reading well; stars or merit points for attempting and/or completing tasks.

4. **Written**, e.g. merit certificates; written comments in headteacher's book; newsletter recording achievements; comments written (or stamped) on child's work such as 'Well done!' or 'Good work!'.

Supporting children in developing relationships

As a teaching assistant you will support children in developing positive relationships with other children and adults. Observing the behaviour of parents and other significant adults (teachers, teaching assistants, playworkers and so on) affects children's behaviour, how children deal with their own and other people's feelings and how children relate to others.

This is why it is so important for adults to provide positive role models for children's behaviour. Positive interactions with adults (and other children) in various settings encourage children to demonstrate positive ways of relating to others and using appropriate social skills. To develop positive relationships every child needs: Security; Praise; Encouragement; Communication; Interaction; Acceptance; Love (**SPECIAL**).

You should set limits and firm boundaries as agreed with children, families, colleagues and other professionals. To do this you will need to effectively communicate and exchange information with children according to their ages, needs and abilities. This includes understanding the possible effects of communication difficulties and attention deficit disorders. You will also need to be able to implement agreed behaviour procedures and strategies when dealing with children who continue to demonstrate challenging behaviour.

Supporting children in developing agreements about behaviour

Adults should not use aggressive or bullying tactics when trying to encourage appropriate behaviour in children. Firm discipline includes warmth and affection to show children they are cared for and accepted for who they are regardless of any inappropriate behaviour they may demonstrate. The school should provide an appropriate framework for socially acceptable behaviour with rules that have to be followed by all. Language plays an important part in encouraging children to behave in acceptable ways as it enables them to: understand verbal explanations of what is and is not acceptable behaviour; understand verbal explanations of why certain behaviour is not acceptable; express their own needs and feelings more clearly; avoid conflicts when handled by sensitive adults; reach compromises more easily; have a positive outlet for feelings through discussion and imaginative play.

As part of your role as a teaching assistant you will be helping to promote the school's policy, procedures and strategies regarding children's behaviour by consistently and effectively implementing agreements about ways to behave, e.g. ground rules and/or a children's code of conduct (see section on supporting behaviour management strategies in Chapter 4). You will support children in developing agreements about ways of behaving as appropriate to the requirements of the school *and* the children's ages and levels of development.

Agreements about ways of behaving should be introduced following consultation with colleagues, children and parents. A copy of the **home-school agreement** should be sent home and parents (and if appropriate, children) asked to sign as an indication of agreement and support. The agreement should be displayed throughout the school as appropriate. The agreement should be brief and easy to learn, and it should include rules that the school will enforce. The reason for each rule should be obvious, but staff should also explain these as appropriate to the age and level of development of the children they work with. The agreement may be applied to a variety of situations and should be designed to encourage children to develop responsibility for their own behaviour. Developing agreements about ways of behaving should include negotiating appropriate goals and boundaries for behaviour (see section on setting goals and boundaries in Chapter 4).

Encouraging pupils to recognise and deal with feelings

An essential aspect of supporting children in developing relationships is helping children to recognise and deal with their own feelings and those of other people. **Feelings** can be defined as: an *awareness* of pleasure or pain; physical and/or psychological *impressions; experience of personal emotions* such as anger, joy, fear or sorrow; and *interpersonal emotions* such as affection, kindness, malice or jealousy.

In British society we are often encouraged to keep our feelings to ourselves. Males may be discouraged from showing the more sensitive emotions; females may be discouraged from demonstrating the more aggressive emotions. Babies and very young children naturally demonstrate clearly how they feel by crying, shouting and rejecting objects. They will openly show affection and other emotions such as jealousy or anger. Young children do not understand that others can be physically or *emotionally* hurt by what they say or do. Gradually, children become conditioned to accept that the feelings and needs of others *do* matter.

We need to ensure that children do not forget their own feelings and emotional needs by becoming too concerned with the feelings of others or trying to please others. Children need to know that it is natural to feel a wide range of emotions and that it is acceptable to express strong feelings such as love and anger openly as long as they do so in positive and appropriate ways.

As a teaching assistant you can help pupils to recognise and express their feelings through the following:

* *Books, stories and poems* about feelings and common events experienced by other children/young people to help them recognise and deal with these in their own lives.
* *Creative activities* to provide positive outlets for feelings, e.g. pummelling clay to express anger; painting/drawing pictures or writing stories and poems which reflect their feelings about particular events and experiences.
* *Physical play or sports* involving vigorous physical activity that allow a positive outlet for anger or frustration.
* *Drama or role-play* activities to act out feelings, e.g. jealousy concerning siblings; worries over past experiences; fears about future events such as a visit to dentist.

Babies and very young children are naturally *egocentric*; their belief that the world revolves around them and their wishes often makes them appear selfish and possessive. As children develop they begin to think and care about others as well as themselves. We have all experienced jealousy in our relationships with others, e.g. with siblings, friends, neighbours, colleagues, employers. Unchecked jealousy can be a very destructive and hurtful emotion that prevents children (and adults) from developing respect and care for others.

You can help pupils to cope with any feelings of jealousy they may have towards others by:

* ✶ *avoiding comparisons between pupils (especially siblings).* For example, do not make comments like 'You're not as quiet as your brother' or 'Why can't you behave more like that group of children?'
* ✶ *encouraging pupils to focus on their own abilities.* Emphasise co-operation and sharing rather than competition. Comparisons should be related to improving their own individual skills
* ✶ *understanding the reasons for a pupil's jealousy.* Children feel better when adults acknowledge their feelings. Do not make children feel guilty about being jealous
* ✶ *treating all pupils with respect and fairness.* Take into account each pupil's individual needs. Pupils may require different amounts of adult attention at different times. Equality of opportunity does not mean treating everyone exactly the same, as this would mean ignoring individual needs; it means treating individuals fairly and providing the same *chances*
* ✶ *reassuring pupils that they are accepted for* who *they are regardless of what they* do. Try to spend a few minutes with each pupil in your group. Give regular individual attention to help reduce jealousy and increase emotional security.

> EXERCISE: Describe an activity which supports pupils in understanding other people's feelings, e.g. sharing a story or poem about feelings and common events experienced by other children. Give an example from your own experiences of working with pupils.

Dealing with pupils' emotional outbursts

You should work with the teacher to provide a calm and accepting environment which allows pupils to experience and express their feelings safely (see above section on encouraging pupils to recognise and deal with feelings). Sometimes pupils (especially young children) are overwhelmed by their emotions and will act inappropriately or regress to previous patterns of behaviour. When children are unable to use language to express their feelings (e.g. because they lack the appropriate words, are too worked up, have behavioural/emotional difficulties or other special needs) they are more prone to demonstrate their emotional responses in physical ways, e.g. biting, scratching, kicking, shouting, screaming, throwing things, throwing themselves on the floor, etc. An emotional outburst or 'temper tantrum' can be very frightening to the child and others in the group or class. Adults too can find children's emotional outbursts difficult to deal with.

When dealing with a pupil's emotional outbursts it is essential that you:

★ remain calm yourself; speak quietly but confidently, shouting only makes things worse
★ ignore the emotional outburst as much as possible while maintaining pupil safety
★ avoid direct confrontations
★ give the pupil time and space to calm down
★ reassure the pupil afterwards but do not reward them
★ when the pupil has calmed down talk about what upset them in a quiet manner
★ suggest to the pupil what they could do instead if they feel this way again.

The best way to deal with emotional outbursts is to minimise the likelihood of them happening in the first place: avoid setting up situations where emotional outbursts are likely to happen, e.g. making unrealistic demands or doing complex activities when a pupil is tired; give advance warning, e.g. prepare the pupil for new experiences; give a five-minute warning that an activity is coming to an end and that you want them to do something else; provide reasonable choices and alternatives to give the pupil a sense of responsibility and control, e.g. choice of activity to do next; choice of materials; encourage the pupil to express their feelings in more positive ways (see section above on encouraging pupils to recognise and deal with feelings).

KEY TASK

1. Outline your school's policy for dealing with a pupil's emotional outburst.
2. Describe how *you* have dealt with a pupil's emotional outburst.
3. Give examples of opportunities in your school which allow pupils to experience and express their feelings safely.

 NVQ LINKS:

Level 2:
STL2.2   STL3.4   STL4.1
STL4.3

Level 3:
STL20.1   STL20.2   STL20.3
STL3.4   STL19.1   STL19.2
STL41.1   STL41.2   STL45.1

Helping pupils to deal with conflict situations

All pupils will experience situations where they feel that life is not fair. They will have disagreements and disputes with other pupils. Initially children rely on adults to help resolve these disputes, but gradually they learn how to deal with these for themselves. Pupils need to learn how to use language to reach agreements so that as far as possible their needs and other people's can be met fairly. Pupils need to learn that resolving conflicts does not mean getting your own way all the time (being aggressive) or allowing others to get their own way all the time (being submissive/passive). There is a better way that allows everyone to reach a satisfactory compromise – being **assertive**.

Ways to resolve conflicts:

- Fight/Bully = Aggressive → 'I win so you lose'
- Submit/Retreat = Submissive/Passive → 'I lose because you win'
- Discuss/Negotiate = Assertive → 'I win and you win'

Point out to pupils that shouting or physical violence never resolves conflicts, they usually make matters worse and only demonstrate who is the loudest or strongest or has more power. Conflicts need to be discussed in a calm manner so that a mutually agreed compromise can be reached.

You can use books, stories and videos that depict a potential conflict situation such as:

- ☆ sharing or borrowing toys
- ☆ deciding on rules for a game or choosing a game
- ☆ choosing partners or teams fairly
- ☆ knocking over models or spoiling work *accidentally*
- ☆ disrupting other children's activities *deliberately*.

Discuss with the pupils afterwards:

- ☆ what caused the conflict or disagreement
- ☆ how they were resolved
- ☆ what the best solutions were
- ☆ how they would have resolved it.

Younger pupils can do this with appropriate situations and guidance from sensitive adults. Using puppets and play people can also help. Where pupils are used to doing role play or drama, adults can get them to act out how to resolve conflicts in peaceful ways.

EXERCISE:
1. Describe how you have dealt with a conflict situation.
2. Look at the conflict situations listed above. Suggest how these could be resolved to achieve a 'win/win' result.

Developing positive working relationships with adults

Developing and promoting positive working relationships with adults is important because this helps to maintain a positive learning environment that benefits pupils, parents and staff. Positive working relationships will also reflect the school's aims such as: providing a caring environment that fosters co-operation and respect; encouraging children's all-round development; delivering play and learning opportunities in stimulating and appropriate ways; working in partnership with parents and the local community.

As a teaching assistant, you should have a strong commitment to pupils, colleagues, parents and the local community. You and your colleagues should behave at all times in a manner that demonstrates personal courtesy and integrity. You should actively seek to develop your personal skills and professional expertise.

You can help to develop and promote positive working relationships with **colleagues** by:

- ✯ having a duty of care towards your colleagues
- ✯ demonstrating an awareness of the work-related needs of others
- ✯ remembering confidentiality in discussions with colleagues concerning problems associated with their work
- ✯ respecting the status of colleagues, particularly when making any assessment or observations on their work
- ✯ never denigrating a colleague in the presence of others
- ✯ if relevant to your role, using maximum frankness and good faith in all matters relating to appointments to posts and providing references that are fair and truthful.

You can help to develop and promote positive working relationships with each parent and carer by:

- ✯ helping parents and carers to feel welcome and valued in the setting
- ✯ seeking to establish a friendly and co-operative relationship with parents and carers
- ✯ never distorting or misrepresenting the facts concerning any aspect of their children's care, learning and development
- ✯ respecting the joint responsibility that exists between the setting and parents/carers for the development and well-being of their children
- ✯ respecting parental rights to enquiry, consultation and information with regard to the development of their children.

Communicating with adults

You should use language that other adults (including parents/carers, colleagues, parent helpers, volunteers and students) are likely to understand. Try to avoid 'jargon' or technical language unless you are sure that they too understand its meaning. Any requests for information from colleagues or parents that are beyond your knowledge and expertise or any difficulties in communicating with colleagues or parents should be referred to the appropriate person, e.g. the class/subject teacher, SENCO or headteacher. You may need guidance on how to handle sensitive situations regarding your interactions with some colleagues or parents especially when a derogatory remark is made about another colleague/parent or when the school policies are disregarded (see section below on handling disagreements).

Sharing information with parents and carers

Parents usually know more about their children and their children's needs so it is important to listen to what parents have to say. You should therefore actively encourage positive working relationships between parents (or designated carers) and the school. As a teaching assistant, you could provide a useful liaison between parents and their children's teacher because some parents may find you easier to talk to than the teacher. Some parents may find you more approachable especially if you live in the local community and your children go/went to the same school.

Sharing information with parents

When communicating with parents use their preferred names and modes of address, e.g. the correct surname, especially when a woman has changed her name following divorce or remarriage. Only give information to a parent that is consistent with your role and responsibilities within the school – do not give recommendations concerning the pupil's future learning needs directly to the parents if this is the responsibility of the teacher, senior colleague or other professional. Any information shared with parents must be agreed with the teacher and must comply with the confidentiality requirements of the school. When sharing information about a pupil with their parents ensure that it is relevant, accurate and up-to-date.

Some adults may find it difficult to communicate effectively with others, e.g. those with hearing impairment or physical disabilities affecting their ability to articulate sounds. Some parents may speak little or no English. Teaching assistants who have additional communication skills may be very useful in the school, e.g. being able to use sign language to communicate with an adult who has a hearing impairment or bilingual teaching assistants who can liaise with parents whose community language is not English. Teaching assistants who share local community languages may help parents and carers to feel more welcome in the school and help to avoid possible misinterpretations concerning cultural differences.

Sharing information is an essential part of working with pupils and their parents or carers. Adults working with pupils need essential information *from* parents, including:

☆ **Routine information,** e.g. medical history/conditions such as allergies; cultural or religious practices which may have implications for the care and education of the pupil such as special diets, exclusion from R.E. and assemblies; who collects the pupil (if applicable) including the transport arrangements (such as taxi or minibus) for a pupil with special needs.

- ✱ **Emergency information,** e.g. contact telephone numbers for parents/carers, GP.
- ✱ **Other information,** e.g. factors which may adversely affect the pupil's behaviour in the school including family difficulties and crises such as divorce, serious illness or bereavement.

Remember to pass on information from parents to the relevant member of staff. Always remember **confidentiality** with regard to information provided by parents or carers (see below).

Adults working with pupils will also need to *give* parents information on:

- ✱ the main aims and objectives of the school
- ✱ age range of pupils
- ✱ class sizes and staff to pupil ratios
- ✱ staff names, roles and qualifications
- ✱ school hours and term dates/school holidays
- ✱ admission and settling in procedures
- ✱ record keeping and assessment
- ✱ test/examination targets and results
- ✱ an outline of approaches to learning (e.g. the National Curriculum)
- ✱ the facilities for indoor and outdoor play including arrangements for swimming
- ✱ arrangements for pupils with special needs including the administration of medicines
- ✱ school discipline and behaviour management including rewards and sanctions used
- ✱ school procedures regarding food, drink, meal/snack times
- ✱ rules regarding school uniform, dress code and jewellery.

This information is usually given to parents and carers in the play setting's brochure, prospectus or information pack. Information can also be given to parents and carers via letters, notice boards, newsletters and open days.

KEY TASK

1. Give examples of how your school shares information with parents.
2. Get a copy of the school's brochure, prospectus or information pack.
3. What are your school's policy and procedures for parents wishing to discuss their child's progress with a teacher?

 NVQ LINKS:

Level 2:
STL4.4   STL12.3

Level 3:
STL20.4   STL38.3   STL60.1
STL60.2

Sharing information with colleagues

You will be working as part of a team with other professionals, including other teaching assistants, teachers and SENCOs. Your colleagues will need regular information about your work, e.g. feedback about play and learning activities as well as updates about pupil participation and/or developmental progress. Some of this information may be given orally – for example, outlining a pupil's participation and developmental progress during a particular learning activity or commenting on a child's behaviour. Even spoken information needs to be given in a professional manner, e.g. to the appropriate person (the teacher), in the right place (not in a corridor where confidential information could be overheard) and at the right time (urgent matters need to be discussed with the teacher immediately while others may wait until a team meeting). Some information will be in written form, e.g. activity plans, notice boards, newsletters, staff bulletins and records. (See also section on effective communication with colleagues in Chapter 6.)

Confidentiality matters

Confidentiality is important with regard to sharing information. Only the appropriate people should have access to confidential records. Except where a pupil is potentially at risk, information should not be given to other adults or agencies unless previously agreed. Where the passing of confidential information is acceptable then it should be given in the agreed format. You must always follow the school's policy and procedures regarding confidentiality and the sharing of information. Check with the class teacher or headteacher if you have any concerns about these matters. You should also be aware of any legal requirements with regard to record-keeping and accessing information in your school, e.g. Data Protection Act.

The basic provisions of the Data Protection Act

Under the *Data Protection Act 1998* all settings processing personal information must comply with the eight enforceable principles of good practice. Personal data must be:

* fairly and lawfully processed
* processed for limited purposes
* adequate, relevant and not excessive
* accurate
* not kept longer than necessary
* processed in accordance with the data subject's rights
* secure
* not transferred to countries without adequate protection.

The Data Protection Act also safeguards the storage of data kept on computers including hard drives and floppy disks. All records relating to personal information must be kept securely within the setting and the person to whom the records refer should have access to them. However, under the Data Protection Act 1998 certain information is exempt from disclosure and should not be shared with other service providers. This includes: material whose disclosure would be likely to cause serious harm to the physical or mental health or emotional condition of the child or someone else; information about whether the child is or has been subjected to or may be at risk of suspected child abuse; information that may form part of a court report; references about pupils supplied to another school, any other place of education or training, any national body concerned with student admissions.

The school's requirements regarding confidentiality

You may find that the parents or carers of the pupils you work with will talk to you about their problems or give you details about their family. Senior staff at your school may also tell you confidential information to help you understand the needs of particular pupils and so enable you to provide more effective support. If a parent or colleague gives you confidential information you must not gossip about it.

However, you may decide to pass on information to colleagues on a *'need to know'* basis; for example, to enable other members of staff to support the pupil's care, learning and development more effectively or where the pupil might be in danger. If you think that a pupil is at risk then you **must** pass on confidential information to an appropriate person, e.g. the class teacher or the member of staff responsible for child protection issues in your school. If you decide to pass on confidential information then you should tell the person who gave you the information that you are going to do this and explain that you have to put the needs of the child first. Remember that every family has a right to privacy and you should only pass on information in the genuine interests of the child or to safeguard their welfare. (See section on the confidentiality of information relating to abuse in Chapter 2.)

KEY TASK

1. What are the policy and procedures regarding confidentiality in your school?
2. Make a list of the key points.

NVQ LINKS:

Level 2:

| STL1.3 | STL3.2 | STL3.4 |
| STL4.4 | STL5.1 | STL9.2 |

Level 3:

STL3.2	STL3.4	STL20.4
STL21.1	STL23.3	STL24.2
STL27.3	STL29.1	STL55.1
STL55.2		

Handling disagreements with other adults

As a teaching assistant you need to be able to recognise and respond to any problems that affect your ability to work effectively. This includes dealing appropriately with disagreements and conflict situations that affect your working relationships with other adults. Conflicts and disagreements are a part of everyone's working lives. If communication and working relationships break down, then conflict situations may arise which seriously damage the atmosphere in the school. Conflicts and disagreements can occur between: you and pupils; you and parents or carers; you and colleagues; you and other professionals. Most conflicts in the workplace arise due to: concerns about duties and responsibilities; disagreements about pupil behaviour; disagreements about management issues; clashes concerning different lifestyle choices; clashes between personalities.

Conflicts can also arise due to prejudice or discrimination. Incidents of such attitudes or behaviour must be challenged, as they are not only undesirable but also unlawful. However, it is essential to follow the school's policy and procedures together with any relevant legal requirements when dealing with these issues.

Many disagreements and conflicts can be resolved through open and honest discussion. This will involve arranging a mutually convenient time to talk to the other adult about the problem and may include the class teacher or headteacher. Sometimes another person can act as a **mediator** to help those involved to reach a satisfactory agreement or compromise. Where serious difficulties or conflict situations cannot be resolved, then the school will have a grievance procedure to deal with it. This usually involves talking to your line manager (e.g. class teacher) about the problem in the first instance; they will then refer the matter to the senior management team/headteacher. If the problem concerns your line manager, then you may need to talk to the headteacher directly. You may also need to put your concerns in writing. If the matter cannot be resolved at this stage then, depending on the nature of the conflict, the school governors, the local education authority and relevant trade unions may be involved. Check with your line manager and/or the staff handbook for the exact procedures in your school.

KEY TASK

1. Describe how you have responded (or would respond) to a disagreement or conflict situation with another adult in your school (be tactful and remember confidentiality).

2. Outline the grievance procedures for staff in your school.

NVQ LINKS:

Level 2: STL4.4   STL5.1
Level 3: STL20.4   STL21.1

Further reading

Alderson, P. (2000) *Young children's rights: exploring beliefs, principles and practice.* Jessica Kingsley Publishers.

DfES (2004) *Every child matters: change for children.* DfES [Available free online at www.everychildmatters.co.uk.]

Hobart, C. and Frankel, J. (2003) *A practical guide to working with parents.* Nelson Thornes.

Johnstone, D. (2001) *An introduction to disability studies.* David Fulton Publishers.

Lindon, J. (2006) *Equality in early childhood: linking theory and practice.* Hodder Arnold.

O'Hagan, M. and Smith, M. (1999) *Early years child care and education: key issues.* Bailliere Tindall.

Petrie, P. (1997) *Communicating with children and adults: interpersonal skills for early years and playwork.* Hodder Arnold.

Ramsey, R. D. (2002) *How to say the right thing every time: communicating well with students, staff, parents and the public.* Corwin Press.

Tassoni, P. (2003) *Supporting special needs: understanding inclusion in the early years.* Heinemann.

6 Developing professional practice

Key points:

* ❋ Providing effective support for your colleagues
* ❋ Effective teamwork
* ❋ Providing leadership for your team
* ❋ Allocating and checking work in your team
* ❋ Leading and motivating volunteers
* ❋ Reflecting on and developing practice
* ❋ Professional development and training opportunities
* ❋ Providing information to improve policies, practices and provision
* ❋ Mentoring in the workplace
* ❋ Supporting competence achieved in the workplace.

Providing effective support for your colleagues

To provide effective support for colleagues you need to know: the school's principles and values (see page vii); the school's expectations for children's development and learning (see Chapter 3); the aims and objectives for children's learning (see Chapter 9); the school's expectations for pupil behaviour (see Chapter 4); the inclusion policy for pupils with special needs (see Chapter 11); your role and responsibilities as a teaching assistant (see Chapter 1).

Effective teamwork

Much of adult life involves working with other people, usually in a group or team. Individuals within a team affect each other in various ways. Within the team there will be complex interactions involving different personalities, roles and expectations as well as hidden agendas that may influence the behaviour of individual members of the team. Teamwork is essential when working closely and regularly with other people over a period of time.

Effective teamwork is important because it helps all members of the team to do the following:

- ☆ **T**ake effective action when planning and/or assigning agreed work tasks
- ☆ **E**fficiently implement the agreed work tasks
- ☆ **A**gree aims and values which set standards of good practice
- ☆ **M**otivate and support each other
- ☆ **W**elcome feedback about their work
- ☆ **O**ffer additional support in times of stress
- ☆ **R**eflect on and evaluate their own working practices
- ☆ **K**now and use each person's strengths and skills.

(See also section on group dynamics in Chapter 7.)

Working as part of a team

As a teaching assistant, you need to know and understand the different roles of the team members in your school and the process of decision-making within the team. A teaching assistant in a primary, secondary or special school is part of a team which will include some or all of the following: other teaching assistants; class or subject teachers; deputy headteacher; headteacher; special educational needs co-ordinator (SENCO); specialist teachers, e.g. to support pupils with sensory or physical impairment; parent helpers and/or other volunteers; students on placement from college; pupils on work experience from secondary school.

You need to be very clear about the organisational structure of the school as information from different people can be confusing or even contradictory. In particular, you need to know who is your line manager; that is, the person who manages your work in school. Your line manager may not necessarily be the class teacher; depending on the size of the school and the responsibilities of senior staff, your line manager could be the headteacher, deputy head, head of department or Key Stage co-ordinator. If your work mostly involves supporting pupils with special educational needs then the SENCO may well be your line manager. Whoever your line manager is, you must always follow the directions of the teacher in whose class you are working with pupils. When the class teacher and your line manager are not the same person, their roles and responsibilities need to be understood both by them and by you (for more detailed information on the teaching assistant's role and responsibilities see Chapter 1).

Working in partnership with the teacher

Advanced planning (with clear objectives) and the detailed preparation of work are central to the effective delivery of the curriculum and to providing appropriate support for pupils' learning. Teachers need to involve teaching assistants in the planning and preparation of their work by having regular planning meetings about once a term or every half-term. In addition, each day the teacher and the teaching assistant should discuss:

- ☆ the teacher's lesson plans
- ☆ the learning objectives for the pupils
- ☆ the teaching assistant's contribution to the lesson
- ☆ the type and level of support for the pupils.

These regular planning meetings and discussions will help to avoid confusion as both the teacher and the teaching assistant will then be clear about the exact tasks to be performed and the level of support to be provided. Short discussions after lessons are also helpful as teaching assistants can provide feedback to the teacher about the progress of pupils during group or individual activities. This feedback can make a valuable contribution to the teacher's assessment of pupils and help with the future planning of learning activities (see Chapter 9).

Teaching assistants also need to be familiar with the ways individual teachers deal with pupils who demonstrate difficult behaviour to avoid giving conflicting messages to pupils. While all staff in a school should work within the framework of the school's behaviour management policy, individual teachers may have different approaches to responding to difficult behaviour based on their own teaching style and the individual needs of their pupils (see Chapter 4).

Working with the special educational needs co-ordinator

Many teaching assistants are responsible for supporting pupils with special educational needs. As part of this responsibility the teaching assistant should be aware of:

* ☆ each pupil's special educational needs
* ☆ how these needs affect the pupil
* ☆ the special provision and learning support required
* ☆ their role in helping the pupil to access the curriculum.

This role will involve working with the teacher responsible for pupils with special educational needs – the special educational needs co-ordinator. Regular meetings, usually once a week, help the teaching assistant and the SENCO to provide effective support for the learning and participation of pupils with special educational needs. Teaching assistants may also be involved in contributing to and reviewing Individual Educational Plans or Behaviour Support Plans because they spend more time working with individual pupils with special educational needs than the class teacher (see Chapter 11).

> EXERCISE:
> 1. Draw a diagram to show the organisational structure of your school including where you (as a teaching assistant) and your line manager fit into this structure.
> 2. Outline the role and main responsibility of each member of your particular team.

Effective communication with colleagues

You should know how to communicate effectively with members of your team. Effective communication is essential for developing effective team practice. Look back at the list of inter-personal skills needed for effective communication with children (and adults) in Chapter 5. Effective lines of communication are also important to ensure that all members of the team receive the necessary up-to-date information to enable them to make a full contribution to the life of the school. As a teaching assistant you may feel particularly isolated if you work only part-time, work in only one class or support an individual pupil with special educational needs. Make sure you check school notice boards, newsletters and/or staff bulletins for important information. You can also use informal opportunities such as break or lunch times to share information, experiences and ideas with the SENCO, teachers or other teaching assistants. Regular lines of communication are particularly important if more than one teaching assistant works with the same pupil or pupils. You might find a communications book or file may be useful as well as regular meetings with other teaching assistants. If you are a new (or student) teaching assistant you may benefit from the knowledge and understanding of existing teaching assistants; if you are an experienced teaching assistant you can make a valuable contribution to the induction or on-going training of new teaching assistants possibly acting as a mentor.

How to participate in team meetings

As a teaching assistant you will also be involved in regular team meetings with the teacher (or teachers) in whose class you work and/or the SENCO. These meetings will enable you to make relevant contributions to provide more effective support for both the teacher and pupils. You may discuss specific plans the teacher has made relating to the pupils' learning, the progress made by pupils including their achievements and any difficulties plus the appropriate resources and support approaches.

You may also be invited to more general staff meetings. Where there are logistical problems in all teaching assistants being able to attend all staff meetings, you may be welcome to attend any meeting but be specifically invited to attend meetings where issues are to be discussed that are directly relevant to *your* work in schools.

You need to prepare for meetings carefully, especially if you have been asked to provide information, for example, on the progress of a pupil with whom you work. Even if you are not required to make a specific contribution you still need to look at the meeting agenda and any relevant reports in advance so that you can participate in discussions during the meeting. At team meetings, participate in ways which are consistent with your role as a teaching assistant. Ensure your contributions are relevant and helpful to the work of the team. Express your opinions in a clear, concise manner and demonstrate respect for the contributions made by other team members. Make notes during the meeting to remind yourself of any action *you* need to take as a result of the issues discussed and decisions made by the team.

Team meeting

KEY TASK

1. Participate in a team meeting relevant to your role in school; for example, a planning meeting to discuss a week's or half term's learning activities for the pupils. (When doing this task, for reasons of confidentiality, avoid meetings where problems concerning specific pupils are referred to in detail.)

2. Make notes on the key points discussed at the meeting. With the team leader's permission include a copy of the agenda.

Then consider the following points:

- What preparation did you need to make before the meeting?
- What was your contribution to the meeting?
- What action did you need to take as a result of the meeting (e.g. were you set specific tasks and if so, what were they)?

NVQ LINKS:

Level 2:
STL1.1   STL2.4   STL4.2
STL4.4   STL5.1

Level 3:
STL18.1   STL20.4   STL21.1
STL23.1   STL24.1   STL27.1
STL52.3   STL61.1   STL62.1
STL62.2

Making an effective contribution to your team

In order to make a more effective contribution to your team you need to: develop and maintain confidence in your own abilities; maintain or improve your self-esteem; practice assertiveness techniques; take care of your emotional well-being.

Self-esteem is developed from childhood; some children and adults have feelings of low self-esteem which have negative effects on their confidence in their own abilities. You may need to develop your own feelings of self-worth to improve your self-esteem (see Chapter 7 and the suggestions for further reading at the end of this chapter).

Assertive people gain control over their lives by expressing personal feelings and exerting their rights in such a way that other people listen. Assertive individuals also show respect for other people's feelings. Practising assertiveness techniques involves the following:

1. Being aware of your own feelings.
2. Putting your feelings into words.
3. Connecting how you feel with the actions of others.
4. Being aware of the other person's feelings.
5. Arranging a specific time and place for a discussion.
6. Making a statement showing you are aware of their feelings.
7. Listening actively to their feedback.

(Houghton and McColgan, 1995)

Working with children or young people is a rewarding but often challenging or even stressful occupation. You need to take responsibility for your own emotional well-being and take the necessary action to tackle or reduce stress in your life. For example: develop assertiveness techniques; take regular exercise including relaxation; have a healthy diet; manage time effectively.

Time management

Effective time management involves being clear about what you need to do and that you are able to do it. Unrealistic work goals lead to work tasks piling up, unnecessary stress, feeling overwhelmed, and time being wasted in unnecessary disagreements due to tempers flaring.

Ten essential steps to effective time management

1. Decide to use time more effectively.

2. Check what you need to do, then prioritise: urgent/essential down to unimportant.

3. Make 'to do' lists in order of priority.

4. Estimate the time needed for tasks realistically.

5. Say 'No' or delegate if you cannot do a task in the time specified.

6. Forward plan using a good diary.

7. Organise how you intend to do each task.

8. Do it!

9. Monitor or revise plans if necessary.

10. Value other people's time by being punctual for meetings and appointments.

Efficient organisation of the learning environment can also contribute to more effective time management. For example:

- ✫ A chalk or white board may be used to indicate where people are.
- ✫ Check that cupboards, desk drawers, filing cabinets, etc. are clearly labelled.
- ✫ Remember 'A place for everything and everything in its place'!
- ✫ Keep everything you need for specific tasks in one place.
- ✫ Store items you use regularly in accessible places.
- ✫ Throw away rubbish!
- ✫ Find out if there is a quiet room/area for undisturbed work or discussions.

Ten ways to provide effective support for colleagues

You can provide effective support for your colleagues by:

1. Working with other members of staff as part of a team.

2. Working in partnership with them to prepare and maintain the learning environment.

3. Working in partnership with parents and carers.

4. Knowing and following relevant school policies and procedures.

5. Attending staff or team meetings.

6. Helping to monitor and evaluate children's participation and developmental progress.

7. Providing feedback about children's play, learning and behaviour.

8. Helping with resources and school administration.

9. Recognising and using personal strengths and abilities.

10. Developing skills through work-based training and other courses.

KEY TASK

1. Describe how you have asked for help, information or support from your colleagues.

2. Give examples of how you have offered support to colleagues including:

    - teaching assistants working at the same level as you

    - your line manager (e.g. the class teacher or SENCO)

    - staff for whom you are responsible (e.g. new teaching assistants, students, parent helpers, volunteers).

 NVQ LINKS:

Level 2:
STL4.2   STL4.4   STL5.1
STL5.2

Level 3:
STL20.4   STL21.1   STL21.2
STL62.1   STL62.2   STL63
STL64   STL66

[single element units]

Providing leadership for your team

Your team should have a clear structure with duties carried out by different members of the team. Team members should know what their key responsibilities are within the team (see Chapter 1). They should also know and understand the legal, regulatory and ethical requirements of the education sector (see Chapters 2 and 5).

Leadership styles and leadership skills

To provide effective leadership for your team you need to know and understand leadership styles and leadership skills. **Leadership styles** affect the behaviours, beliefs and attitudes of the people working together as a team. Leadership style is also important in creating a positive atmosphere in the workplace by reducing work stress and promoting job satisfaction. There are three different leadership styles: autocratic, laissez-faire and democratic.

1. *Autocratic leadership:* This style of leadership involves demonstrating a lack of confidence and trust in colleagues. The team leader imposes decisions without consulting or involving other team members. There is little effective communication and few opportunities to be involved in the decision-making process within the setting. Team members feel that they are expected to follow instructions on their working practices without being critical or reflective.

2. *Laissez-faire leadership:* This style of leadership involves allowing colleagues to make their own decisions but providing some support as required. The whole team is responsible for day-to-day management including budgeting and evaluating the effectiveness of the work in the setting. Team members may feel stressed and under pressure especially if there is a lack of guidance and support.

3. *Democratic leadership:* This style of leadership involves encouraging team members to contribute to the development of the setting's policies, procedures and practices including the recruitment of staff. The team leader acknowledges and values the individual skills and contributions of each team member. Colleagues feel motivated and actively share their knowledge and experience for the mutual benefit and support of team members.

(Houghton and McColgan, 1995)

An effective team leader needs a range of **leadership skills** including the ability to:

- ✰ respond to the individual needs of team members
- ✰ promote team spirit and co-operation between colleagues
- ✰ motivate the team members to carry out agreed tasks
- ✰ allow team members to express their ideas and opinions
- ✰ enable the team to devise action plans and effective strategies
- ✰ direct the team towards making decisions

* use the skills and experience of all team members effectively
* be supportive to fellow team members
* give positive feedback to team members.

(O'Hagan and Smith, 1994)

EXERCISE:
1. What would you say is your leadership style?
2. List your own leadership skills.

Basic management skills

To manage your team effectively you also need to know and understand basic management skills. Basic management skills can be divided into four main categories:

1. ***Managing people:*** Helping to recruit and/or retain colleagues; motivating staff; providing training opportunities; managing difficult team members and dealing with personality clashes; dealing with grievance and disciplinary issues; working with parents and carers; supporting children with challenging behaviour.
2. ***Managing activities:*** Effective planning and organisation, e.g. activity plans, work rota, monitoring children's care, learning and development.
3. ***Managing resources:*** Obtaining and organising appropriate resources.
4. ***Managing information:*** Record-keeping; day-to-day administration, e.g. daily attendance registers.

EXERCISE:
1. Make a list of your management skills.
2. Are there any particular skills that you need to work on and improve?

Team objectives

You also need to know and understand the purpose, objectives and plans of your team including: how to set and achieve team objectives which are SMART (Specific, Measurable, Achievable, Realistic and Time-bound) in consultation with team members; and how to demonstrate to team members how their personal work objectives contribute to team objectives (see section on providing learning opportunities for colleagues in this chapter). You should also be aware of the types of support and advice that team members may require (see section above on providing effective support for colleagues).

KEY TASK

Describe how you set and achieve team objectives in consultation with your team members.

NVQ LINKS:

Level 3:
STL62.1   STL62.2   STL63
STL64 [single element units]

Allocating and checking work in your team

When managing routines and activities within your responsibility, you must have a clear knowledge and understanding of the following: effective planning and organisation within the school; allocating work in your team including job rotation and effective delegation; monitoring work in your team; monitoring children's care, learning and development; making the best use of the available resources.

Effective planning and organisation within the school

Staff meetings are essential for effective planning and organisation within the school. Such meetings also provide regular opportunities to share day-to-day information and to solve any problems. Staff meetings should be held regularly – about once every 4–6 weeks. Ensure that there is an agenda for the meeting and that the minutes of the meeting are recorded and can be easily accessed by staff. Encourage colleagues to share best practice, knowledge and ideas on developing appropriate learning activities in the school. As well as general staff meetings you should also have regular team meetings for the more detailed planning of activities as well as the allocation of work within your area of responsibility (for more detailed information on planning activities see Chapters 1, 3, 8 and 9).

You can allocate work and responsibilities in a variety of ways. For example:

- ☆ **Responsibility for supporting pupils in a particular age range:** Each teaching assistant (or group of teaching assistants) is responsible for supporting pupils in a particular age range within the school and promoting children's care, learning and development within a particular Key Stage or year group. The teaching assistant(s) will provide support for the individual needs of the pupils in that Key Stage or year group including appropriate adult supervision or intervention as and when necessary.

- ☆ **Responsibility for supporting pupils in a particular curriculum area:** The teaching assistant may be responsible for a particular curriculum area or activity, e.g. literacy, numeracy or ICT activities. The teaching assistant stays with the same activity throughout the day/week and is responsible for: selecting and setting out materials or helping pupils to access these for themselves; encouraging pupil interest and participation in the activity; providing appropriate adult supervision or intervention as required; and helping pupils to clear away afterwards.

☆ **Responsibility for supporting a small group of pupils:** Each teaching assistant is responsible for a small group of pupils as their key person or key worker. The teaching assistant helps them to settle into the school. The teaching assistant is responsible for: greeting their group of pupils on arrival; encouraging the children's care, learning and development in the school; establishing and maintaining a special relationship with each child and their family.

☆ **Responsibility for supporting an individual pupil:** A teaching assistant may have special responsibility for a pupil with a disability. The teaching assistant will be responsible for: ensuring that pupil's particular needs are met in an inclusive way within the school; ensuring the pupil has the necessary materials to participate in routines and activities including any specialist equipment; establishing and maintaining a special relationship with the pupil and their family.

Effective delegation

Effective delegation is another important factor in allocating the work of your team. Delegation involves motivating your colleagues to carry out specific tasks to enable you to focus on the jobs that you need to do. Delegation also enables you to make use of the particular strengths and skills of your colleagues. Remember developing effective delegation takes time and practice.

Eight steps to effective delegation

You can demonstrate effective delegation by doing the following:

1. *Finding the right person:* consider existing and potential abilities, attitude, personality.

2. *Consulting first:* allow your colleagues to be involved in deciding what is to be delegated.

3. *Thinking ahead:* do not wait for a crisis to occur and then delegate; try to delegate in advance.

4. *Delegating whole tasks:* where possible, delegate a complete task to a colleague, rather than just a small section of a task.

5. *Specifying expected outcomes:* make it clear what outcomes are expected from your colleagues.

6. *Taking your time:* especially if you have been under-delegating or are dealing with less experienced staff. A gradual transfer of responsibility will allow both you and your colleagues to learn what is involved.

7. *Delegating the good and the bad:* if you delegate the tasks that are pleasant to do and also those that are not so pleasant, your colleagues will have the opportunity to gain valuable, realistic experience of many types of jobs.

> 8. *Delegating, then trusting:* when you delegate a task to a colleague, together with the responsibility for getting it done, you then need to trust that person to complete the job to your specified and mutually agreed requirements.
>
> (Wandsworth EYDCP, 2001)

KEY TASK

1. Give examples of effective planning and fair allocation of work within your area of responsibility. You could include copies of planning sheets, minutes from a staff or team meeting and a work rota.
2. Describe how you use effective delegation to motivate your colleagues to carry out specific tasks.

 NVQ LINKS:

Level 3:
STL62.1 STL62.2 STL63
STL64 STL65 STL66

Monitoring the work of your team

When monitoring the progress and quality of work of individuals within your team or area of responsibility, you should encourage your colleagues to take responsibility for their own work tasks and to use existing feedback systems to keep you informed of work progress. When establishing procedures for monitoring work include the following: formal procedures (e.g. reports, formal meetings, mentoring, staff appraisals, supervision); informal procedures (e.g. observations, informal meetings, conversations); the type of information required (e.g. checklists, evaluation sheets, progress reports); when the information will be delivered to you or others in the team (e.g. daily, weekly, monthly, half-termly, termly, annually); the form of the information (e.g. verbal, written, email, audio-visual); where and how the information will be delivered (e.g. meeting, face-to-face, presentation, electronic); the amount of detail required (Wandsworth EYDCP, 2001).

Staff appraisals

Staff appraisals or reviews are a formal way to keep up-to-date with the work performance of colleagues and to identify their ongoing training needs. Staff appraisals usually take place once a year. Staff appraisals should have an agreed format, e.g. a form to be completed by the teaching assistant prior to the appraisal meeting that will form the basis of discussion at the actual appraisal meeting.

Outline the methods you use to monitor the work of colleagues and provide feedback on their performance. For example: staff and/or team meetings; staff appraisals.

 **NVQ LINKS:**

Level 3:
STL62.1   STL62.2   STL63
STL64   STL65   STL66

Leading and motivating volunteers

You may be involved in supporting the work of volunteers in the school such as parent helpers and work experience students. This involves briefing volunteers on their responsibilities, helping them to resolve any problems and giving them feedback on their work. The formal aspects of planning, organising and monitoring volunteer work in school is usually carried out by the teachers with whom they work.

Leading volunteers

Briefing volunteers should include an induction process to provide new volunteers with the opportunity to learn about the school and what is expected of them. It can be helpful to compile an induction pack including the following:

- ☆ A welcome letter
- ☆ Principles and values
- ☆ Copies of essential policies and procedures, for example: equal opportunities, health and safety, child protection, fire and emergency procedures
- ☆ Information about the school's administration, e.g. registration and consent forms, monitoring forms, risk assessment, time sheets
- ☆ Names of staff and their main roles and responsibilities
- ☆ The management structure of the school
- ☆ Details of who to contact if they have any problems
- ☆ General information and publicity about the school
- ☆ Floor plan of the building.

You should provide opportunities for volunteers to reflect on their work performance and to review any difficulties they may have as well as to discuss issues that may not be appropriate to raise at a team meeting. Plan regular 'keep in touch' sessions with each volunteer, with agreed and clear ground rules including the confidentiality of these sessions. Keep written records of the sessions and ensure that they are kept in a locked file. A suggested format for a 'keep in touch' session is as follows: discuss current feelings about the volunteer work; review of work since last session, including any goals set; discuss current work including successes and difficulties; provide support or access to training as required (Wandsworth EYDCP, 2001).

Motivating volunteers

Motivating volunteers is an essential part of supporting the work of volunteers in the school. Motivation is a key factor in creating a positive learning environment and maintaining positive working relationships within the school. Remember that everyone is an individual and each volunteer will respond to different motivating factors. Find and use the motivating factors for the volunteers you work with.

Seven ways to motivate volunteers

You can help to motivate volunteers more effectively by:

1. Identifying and trying to understand the individual needs and personal goals of volunteers.

2. Remembering that volunteers work in the school on an unpaid basis so rewards other than higher pay are more appropriate for getting volunteers to work more effectively, e.g. providing opportunities for relevant training.

3. Setting work targets that are realistic and achievable but also providing volunteers with some challenges to prevent boredom and increase job satisfaction. Involve colleagues in setting their own targets, e.g. using SMART objectives (see page 154).

4. Always consulting volunteers before changing agreed targets.

5. Always using praise or other rewards to acknowledge volunteers' achievements.

6. Using group pressure to influence motivation in positive ways, e.g. involving volunteers in group decision-making to strengthen their commitment.

7. Keeping volunteers regularly informed about what is happening in the school.

 KEY TASK

Outline the methods you use to lead and motivate the work of volunteers including the following:

- Briefing volunteers on work requirements and responsibilities
- Helping volunteers to solve problems during volunteering activities
- Giving feedback to volunteers on their work.

 NVQ LINKS:

Level 3:
STL66.1   STL66.2   STL66.3

Reflecting on and developing practice

In order to reflect on and develop practice you need to know and understand the following: effective practice; being an effective, reflective practitioner; using best practice benchmarks such as the Key Elements of Effective Practice (KEEP); evaluating your personal effectiveness; developing your personal development objectives; professional development and training opportunities.

Identifying effective practice

Effective practice requires committed, enthusiastic and reflective practitioners with a breadth and depth of knowledge, skills and understanding. To be an effective, reflective practitioner, you should use your own learning to improve your work with pupils and their families in ways which are sensitive, positive and non-judgemental. Through initial and on-going training and development, you can develop, demonstrate and continuously improve your: relationships with both children and adults; understanding of the individual and diverse ways that children develop and learn; knowledge and understanding in order to actively support and extend children's learning in and across all areas and aspects of learning; practice in meeting all children's needs, learning styles and interests; work with parents, carers and the wider community; work with other professionals (DfES, 2005).

The Key Elements of Effective Practice (KEEP) provides a framework for early years practitioners to: reflect on their work; understand what effective practice looks like; record their qualifications; formulate their self-development plan; allow managers to understand staff experience/qualifications and training needs to support the development of the setting. KEEP supports self-appraisal, appraisal, quality assurance, self-evaluation and performance management as it links the needs of children, parents, the setting *and* practitioners (DfES, 2005). See: www.standards.dfes.gov.uk/primary/publications/foundation_stage/keep/.

KEEP has been developed alongside and is consistent with *The Common Core of Skills and Knowledge for the Children's Workforce* which sets out the six areas of expertise that everyone working with children, young people and families should be able to demonstrate. For details see www.everychildmatters.gov.uk/deliveringservices/commoncore/.

 KEY TASK

Outline the standards of professional practice expected from you and your colleagues. (This information may be included in a code of practice for staff which may be in the staff handbook and/or set out in best practice benchmarks such as KEEP.)

 NVQ LINKS:

Level 2: STL5.2
Level 3: STL22.1

Evaluating your personal effectiveness

You need to know and understand clearly the exact role and responsibilities of your work as a teaching assistant (see Chapter 1). Review your professional practice by making regular and realistic assessments of how well your working practices match your role and responsibilities. Share your self-assessments with those responsible for managing and reviewing your work performance, e.g. during your regular discussions/meetings with your colleagues or with your line manager. You should also ask other people for feedback about how well you fulfil the requirements and expectations of your role. You can also reflect on your own professional practice by making comparisons with appropriate models of good practice, e.g. the work of more experienced teaching assistants within the school.

Self-evaluation

Self-evaluation is needed to improve your own professional practice and to develop your ability to reflect upon activities and modify plans to meet the individual needs of the pupils you work with. When evaluating your own practice you should consider the following questions:

- ✯ Was your own particular contribution appropriate?
- ✯ Did you choose the right time, place and resources?
- ✯ Did you intervene enough or too much?
- ✯ Did you achieve your goals (e.g. objectives/outcomes for the pupil or pupils and yourself)? If not, why not? Were the goals too ambitious or unrealistic?
- ✯ What other strategies/methods could have been used? Suggest possible modifications.
- ✯ Who should you ask for further advice (e.g. class teacher, SENCO, headteacher, other professional)?

KEY TASK

1. How do you monitor the processes, practices and outcomes from your work?

2. Give examples of how you evaluate your own practice including: self-evaluation; reflections on your interactions with others; sharing your reflections with others; using feedback from others to improve your own evaluation.

3. Describe how you have used reflection to solve problems and improve practice.

NVQ LINKS:

Level 3:

STL18.1	STL20.4	STL21.1
STL21.2	STL22.1	STL23.3
STL24.2	STL27.3	STL29.1
STL61.1	STL61.2	STL62.2

Developing personal development objectives

You should take part in continuing professional development by identifying areas in your knowledge, understanding and skills where you could develop further. This involves being able to identify your own SMART personal development objectives:

* **S**pecific: identify exactly what you want to develop such as the particular skills you need to update or new skills you need to acquire, e.g. first-aid or ICT skills.
* **M**easurable: define criteria that can be used to measure whether or not your objectives have been achieved, e.g. best practice benchmarks, course certificate of attendance or qualification.
* **A**chievable: avoid being too ambitious; set objectives which you know are attainable.
* **R**ealistic: be realistic about what you want to develop.
* **T**ime-bound: plan a realistic time frame within which to achieve your objectives.

EXERCISE: Identify your own SMART personal development objectives.

You should discuss and agree these objectives with those responsible for supporting your professional development, e.g. your line manager. This includes developing and negotiating a plan to develop your knowledge, skills and understanding further, e.g. a personal development plan. For example, you may consider that some of your work tasks require modification or improvement and discuss possible changes with your line manager. Or you may feel that you lack sufficient knowledge and skills to implement particular activities and need to discuss opportunities for you to undertake the relevant training. To achieve your personal development objectives you should make effective use of the people, resources (e.g. the Internet, libraries, journals) and other professional development or training opportunities available to you (see below).

When assessing your personal development and training needs you need to consider:

* your existing experience and skills
* the needs of the pupils you work with
* any problems with how you currently work
* any new or changing expectations for your role
* information and/or learning needed to meet best practice, quality schemes or regulatory requirements.

A professional portfolio highlighting your existing experience and qualifications can form the basis for assessing your training needs. This portfolio will also be a tangible record of your professional development and will help to boost your self-esteem.

Staff appraisals can also help you to identify your training needs. Once your training needs have been identified, you need to agree with your line manager on an appropriate training course or qualification that will help to meet these training needs.

KEY TASK

Describe how you assess your personal development and training needs. Include information on: your existing strengths and skills; skills and knowledge you need to improve; plans for improving your work; preparing for future responsibilities.

NVQ LINKS:

Level 2: STL5.2

Level 3:
STL21.1   STL21.2   STL22.1
STL28.1   STL28.2

Professional development and training opportunities

Good quality and appropriate professional development and training opportunities can have a huge, positive impact on workplace performance which in turn can greatly enhance the learning experiences of the pupils within the school. To be effective, staff development should take into account the needs of individual staff members and the needs of the school as a whole. You should have a Personal Development Plan or Continuing Professional Development Plan that includes training and personal development goals and how these relate to the aims of the school.

When considering professional development you may have a choice of training options including: attending training courses at the local educational development centre or local college, e.g. literacy and numeracy seminars or ICT courses; attending sessions run by outside providers, e.g. first-aid training; and attending in-house training, e.g. INSET days.

Another aspect of professional development involves sharing knowledge, skills and experience with others, e.g. acting as a mentor (see above) or training as an NVQ assessor. Training opportunities should be also be offered to parents and carers as well as staff members including meetings with speakers, discussion groups and reading materials, e.g. books, factsheets and information packs.

The areas of training and development identified by teaching assistants include: knowledge of curriculum subject content; supporting literacy activities; supporting numeracy activities; behaviour management; supporting specific special needs; working with parents; developing ICT skills. Teaching assistants indicate that they prefer practical training opportunities and many of the courses available are skills or competency-based. Research shows that some of the most effective training for teaching assistants takes place in schools as part of their INSET provision. However, it is not always possible to teach the necessary skills in schools, especially those relating to specific special needs. Many LEAs provide training courses for teaching assistants employed directly by them or those recruited by individual schools.

Specific training and recognised qualifications for teaching assistants are also available:

- ✮ NVQ/SVQ Levels 2 and 3 Supporting Teaching and Learning in Schools
- ✮ CACHE Levels 2 and 3 Certificates for Teaching Assistants (CTA2 and CTA3)
- ✮ OCR Level 2 Certificate in Supporting Teaching and Learning
- ✮ CACHE Specialist Teacher Assistant award (STA)
- ✮ Higher Level Teaching Assistant (HLTA)
- ✮ OCR Certificate for Literacy and Numeracy Support Assistants
- ✮ City & Guilds Learner Support 7321 course.

Training courses and qualifications can have a positive influence on improving the status of teaching assistants as well as enabling them to share examples of good practice with others who support teaching and learning. Schools also benefit from having teaching assistants who are able to improve their expertise and increase their job satisfaction.

 KEY TASK

1. Find out about the professional development and training opportunities for teaching assistants in your local area.
2. Give examples of how you have accessed professional development and training opportunities.

 NVQ LINKS:

Level 2: STL5.2

Level 3:
STL21.2   STL22.2   STL28.1
STL28.2

Supporting the professional practice of colleagues

Part of your role may involve supporting the professional practice of colleagues. This could include: providing information to improve policies, practices and provision; providing learning opportunities for colleagues; mentoring in the workplace; and supporting competence achieved in the workplace.

Providing information to improve policies, practices and provision

As part of your role you may be involved in contributing to policy review and the improvement of practices and procedures as a member of the school team. Monitoring and evaluation helps those working in the school to understand how the policies and procedures are working in practice, to check the quality of work and provision of routines, play opportunities and learning activities, as well as to plan for the future. Monitoring and evaluation can also help to make day-to-day working within the school more effective.

Monitoring and evaluation help to ensure that the school's policies and procedures are working in practice and that the routines, play opportunities and learning activities provided have the desired effect. Evaluation is also a way to let any providers of grants or funds know about the work of the school. Evaluation is about looking at the work of the school, how the work was done and what the results were. Evaluation provides the opportunity to review the work of the school, to make any necessary adjustments or improvements and to celebrate success. As a teaching assistant, you may be involved in providing information and advice to aid the development of strategies, policies, practice and provision.

When evaluating school provision, you will need to collect, record and analyse information using the agreed evaluation methods and criteria. After you have analysed the information you have gathered, you will need to report the evaluation results to the relevant colleague including any recommendations for changes or improvements to practices and procedures. You should remember to follow the school's policies and procedures for collecting, recording, reporting and storing information (see Chapter 12).

KEY TASK

1. Describe how you provide information and advice to aid the development of strategies, policies, practice and provision.

2. Give examples of how you collect and present information to aid monitoring, review and improvement of performance.

NVQ LINKS:

Level 3: STL61.1   STL61.2

Providing learning opportunities for colleagues

Good quality and appropriate staff development and training can have a huge, positive impact on workplace performance which, in turn, can greatly enhance the learning experiences of the pupils. To be effective, staff development should take into account the needs of individual staff members and the needs of the school as a whole. When providing learning opportunities for your colleagues, you should start by identifying their learning needs, e.g. what additional knowledge and skills do they need to work more effectively? Staff appraisals can help you to identify these learning needs. Once their learning needs have been identified, you need to agree with your colleague(s) on an appropriate training course or qualification that will help to meet their learning needs.

When considering staff development you will have a choice of training options including: sending staff on existing training courses (as a group or individually); inviting trainers in to the setting to run sessions for you; running in-house training. Another aspect of staff development is to look at ways that your colleagues can pass on their knowledge, skills and experience to other teaching assistants, e.g. training as NVQ assessors. Training opportunities may also include meetings with speakers, discussion groups and reading materials, e.g. books, factsheets and information packs.

Each member of staff should have a Personal Development Plan or Continuing Professional Development Plan that includes training and personal development goals and how these relate to the aims of the childcare setting. (For more information see the section above on professional development and training opportunities.)

 KEY TASK

Describe how you identify the learning needs of your colleagues and provide training opportunities to meet these needs.

 NVQ LINKS:

Level 3:

STL21.1	STL21.2	STL63
STL64	STL67	STL68.1
STL68.2	STL68.3	STL69.1
STL69.2		

Mentoring in the workplace

Mentoring is a structured approach to supporting a colleague by pairing an experienced member of the team with a less experienced member of the team. Mentoring is a very effective way for colleagues to share knowledge, skills and experience. Mentoring involves: 'shadowing' (e.g. watching the work of a more experienced colleague); learning 'on the job' (e.g. developing new skills; asking and answering every day questions); introducing other people in the school; providing guidance and constructive criticism; agreeing and setting daily objectives; reviewing progress; providing feedback to senior staff on progress; identifying further training needs; and providing friendly and reassuring support.

The aims of the mentoring process may include: to provide help and advice on all aspects of the practitioner's role; to support the transfer of skills, e.g. putting theory into practice by applying knowledge and learning to practical tasks in the workplace; to provide constructive feedback on routines and activities; to help in identifying and planning personal development; to provide a friendly support outside the management framework.

The stages involved in planning the mentoring process are as follows:

1. Identify the development needs and expectations of trainees.
2. Recruit mentors and provide them with training and guidance on mentoring activities.
3. Match mentors with trainees to form mentoring pairs.
4. Mentoring pair negotiates a mentoring agreement based on development needs.
5. Devise an Individual Development Plan based on development objectives.
6. Implement individual development plans.
7. Mentoring agreement concluded.
8. Evaluate the individual development plan and the mentoring process.

The mentoring relationship

The roles and responsibilities of the mentor and trainee should be agreed including agreements about the timing and location of discussions and meetings as well as regular reviews of the trainee's progress and development. You could use a learning log or diary to monitor the mentoring relationship on a regular basis.

The role and responsibilities of the mentor include: setting up a mutually agreed mentoring contract; planning a series of one-to-one meetings with the trainee; keeping a brief record of mentoring meetings and discussions; using email as well as other communications to keep in touch with the trainee; sharing knowledge and skills with the trainee; demonstrating practical skills; providing opportunities for the trainee to practice new skills while ensuring the safety of the trainee, the children and other adults at all times; reviewing the trainee's progress and revising development objectives as appropriate.

The role and responsibilities of the trainee include: being an active participant in the mentoring process; identifying their development needs; initiating discussions and meetings with the mentor; taking responsibility for their own development; being open to constructive criticism; using email as well as other communications to keep in touch with the mentor; observing the practice of experienced practitioners including the mentor; practising new skills while ensuring the safety of the children and other adults at all times; reviewing their progress with the mentor and revising their development objectives as appropriate; keeping their line manager informed.

You could use a 'mentoring contract' as a useful starting point for the mentoring relationship. (For an example see **www.hebs.scot.nhs.uk/learningcentre/trainers/mentoringworkshop.cfm**.)

To be an effective mentor you need the following important skills and personal qualities: good interpersonal skills including being a good listener (see page 123); good coaching/counselling skills; appropriate workplace experience; honesty and integrity; being well informed about the work of the setting and other relevant agencies; enthusiasm; patience; reliability; being a reflective practitioner; commitment to supporting trainees.

KEY TASK

1. Which training programmes are available in your setting, e.g. NVQs, modern apprenticeships, etc?
2. What resources, facilities, information and support are available to help trainees?
3. What is the code of practice for mentoring in your setting?
4. Which documents and activities are available to help trainees in the early stages of mentoring?
5. Describe how you could provide mentoring support for a less experienced member of staff.

 NVQ LINKS:

Level 3:
STL67 [single element unit]
STL68.1   STL68.2   STL68.3
STL69.1   STL69.2

Supporting competence achieved in the workplace

You may be involved in supporting individuals to develop and demonstrate competence in the workplace. This involves agreeing work patterns which give trainees opportunities to develop and show their competence, agreeing which aspects of competence can be assessed in the workplace, identifying opportunities for assessing competence in the workplace, watching them perform tasks in the workplace and giving guidance and feedback on their performance.

 KEY TASK

Outline the methods you use to support competence achieved in the workplace. Include information on how you:

- assess performance in the workplace against agreed standards (e.g. National Occupational Standards)
- give staff members support in the workplace and feedback on their performance.

 NVQ LINKS:

Level 3:
STL67 [single element unit]
STL68.1   STL68.2   STL68.3
STL69.1   STL69.2

Further reading

Clegg, B. and Birch, P. (2002) *Crash course in managing people.* Kogan Page.

Hartley, M. (2005) *The assertiveness handbook.* Sheldon Press.

Kerry, T. (2001) *Working with support staff: their roles and effective management in schools.* Pearson Education.

Lindenfield, G. (2000) *Self-esteem: simple steps to developing self-reliance and perseverance.* Harper Collins.

Lyus, V. (1998) *Management in the early years.* Hodder Arnold.

Miller, L. *et al.* (2005) *Developing early years practice.* David Fulton Publishers.

O'Hagan, M. and Smith, M. (1999) *Early years child care and education: key issues.* Bailliere Tindall.

Petrie, P. (1997) *Communicating with children and adults: interpersonal skills for early years and playwork.* Hodder Arnold.

Ramsey, R. D. (2002) *How to say the right thing every time: communicating well with students, staff, parents and the public.* Corwin Press.

Roet, B. (1998) *The confidence to be yourself.* Piatkus.

7 Promoting children's well-being and resilience

Key points:

❊ Enabling pupils to relate to others
❊ Encouraging positive social interactions
❊ Encouraging children's self-reliance
❊ Encouraging children's self-esteem
❊ Encouraging children's resilience
❊ Supporting children and young people during transitions.

Enabling pupils to relate to others

Promoting children's well-being and resilience involves helping children to: develop and sustain healthy lifestyles; keep safe and maintain the safety of others; develop and maintain positive self-esteem; take responsibility for their own actions; have confidence in themselves and their own abilities; make and keep meaningful and rewarding relationships; be aware of their own feelings and those of others; consider and respect the differences of other people; be active participants as citizens of a democratic society. Promoting children's health and well-being can be particularly helpful for children who are experiencing negative social or environmental factors. For example, actively promoting children's well-being may help to reduce the numbers of young people involved in teenage pregnancies, alcohol/drug misuse, truancy and crime (Goleman, 1996).

Encouraging positive social interactions

Having at least one secure and personal relationship with a parent or carer enables children to form other relationships. Consistent, loving care from a parent/carer who is sensitive to the child's particular needs enables children to feel secure and to develop self-worth. Observing the behaviour of parents and other significant adults (e.g. childcarers, playworkers, teachers and teaching assistants) affects children's own behaviour including how they relate to others. A child's ability to relate to others may also be affected by: special needs, e.g. communication and/or social interaction difficulties; family circumstances such as separation or divorce; death, abandonment or other permanent separation from parent or main carer. All children need affection, security, acceptance, encouragement, patience and a stimulating environment. Children deprived of these in the first five to six years of life may find it difficult to relate to other people throughout childhood (and even adulthood). However, children are amazingly resilient and subsequent sustained relationships with caring adults in a supportive environment can help children overcome early parental separation, rejection or neglect.

Adults who provide inconsistent or inappropriate care may unwittingly encourage difficult behaviour in children which can lead to adults spending less time interacting with the child resulting in the child having poor communication skills as well as difficulties in establishing and maintaining positive relationships with other people. While positive social interactions with adults (and other children) in various settings will lead to children being able to demonstrate positive ways of relating to others and using appropriate social skills.

Group dynamics

As a teaching assistant, you should understand how *group dynamics* affect the various stages of group development; that is, pupil interaction and their behaviour within social groups. As well as coping within the demands of the curriculum, pupils are dealing with their peers and the social world of other pupils. Friendship and membership of a peer group seem especially important. Each individual has different personal characteristics that affect their ability to communicate effectively and work comfortably alongside others. From your experiences of working with pupils you may have identified their differing characteristics that influence their willingness or reluctance to interact within a group.

EXERCISE:
1. Think about the personal characteristics of the pupil or pupils you work with.
2. How do they interact in group situations?
    *   Do they take turns at speaking and listening?
    *   Do they work co-operatively?
    *   Do they try to impose their own ideas on the group?

Where the group size is appropriate to the task and the group dynamics are right, the contribution levels from pupils will be fairly even. Pupils usually know when it is their turn to speak and are aware if anyone has not had an opportunity to contribute and will try to involve that member of the group. Most pupils understand that to effectively work together it is important to utilise the offerings of all members of the group – even when this means considering different viewpoints and conflicting ideas. To achieve this level of positive social interaction and effective learning experience, the composition of any group is very important. Pupils may not work well with certain others; they may ask to work with pupils they know well in order to make better progress.

Opportunities for learning should be flexible and available in a variety of groupings: one-to-one; pairs/small groups; large groups; whole class. This allows for individual differences within the class and gives every pupil opportunities to develop many different learning skills in a variety of meaningful ways. Group work allows pupils to: identify and solve problems; select relevant information; collaborate socially to increase own knowledge; structure effective discussions; evaluate conflicting ideas; develop communication skills (Prisk in Pollard, 1987: p. 97).

Stages in group development

You also need to be aware of the stages in the development of groups and how these affect group dynamics. Research suggests that groups and teams grow and develop through a four-stage cycle:

1. **The forming stage:** A group starts by learning about others in the group. First impressions are important and adults should assist pupils in this early stage by providing appropriate introductions, 'ice breaking' activities and an induction programme. The adult acts as the leader of the group to ensure participation by all pupils.

2. **The storming stage:** Group members establish their positions within the group and decide on group functions. There may be arguments and personality clashes between certain members of the group. The adult can assist by providing opportunities for group discussion which tackle these matters in an open and positive manner, helping pupils to sort minor disagreements between themselves (as appropriate to their age/level of development) and acting as an impartial referee if necessary. This can be a difficult stage but it is essential to the healthy development of the group as more serious conflicts may emerge later on if the group does not work through this stage.

3. **The norming stage:** Group members reach agreement on how to work together including establishing group rules and individual responsibilities. Teaching assistants may help with the formation of group rules in line with the school/class rules as directed by the teacher. Adults also plan and organise the group's working practices including the timetable, provision of learning activities and the rota for routine classroom tasks such as tidying up, collecting the register, etc.

4. **The performing stage:** Group trust is established and the group works well together. At this stage the group is usually positive, enthusiastic, co-operative and energetic with group members supporting each other. Adults can assist by providing opportunities for the group to work together in ways which foster a spirit of co-operation rather than competition (see below). Adults need to use praise and encouragement to help maintain positive group interactions.

(Houghton and McColgan, 1995)

Remember that pupils will need to work through these stages again when changes arise, e.g. a pupil leaves or joins the group. You also need to be aware of the possible problems that can arise within a group and how to identify any signs of tension. These include: frequent arguments about differing views and ideas; uncertainty concerning group purpose or activity; confusion over roles and responsibilities within the group; lack of participation by some group members; poor concentration among group members.

Encouraging pupils to share and co-operate

Encouraging children to take turns is also an essential element of helping them to interact positively with other children. From about the age of three, young children begin to co-operate with other children in play activities. By about five years they should be quite adept at playing co-operatively with other children. Gradually children should be able to participate in more complex co-operative play including games with rules as their understanding of abstract ideas increases.

We live in a highly competitive society; we all want to be the best, fastest, strongest or cleverest. The media (television, magazines and newspapers) focuses our attention on being the best. Most sports and games have only one *winner*, which means all the other participants are *losers*. To win is the aim of all contestants. *Winning* makes the individual feel good, confident and successful; *losing* makes the individual feel bad, inadequate and unsuccessful. Competitive games can prepare children for the competitiveness of real life. However, competition can also contribute to children's: negative self-image and low self-esteem; aggressive behaviour; lack of compassion for others; and an overwhelming desire to win at *any* cost.

Competitive sports and games can be beneficial to children's social development as long as they emphasise: co-operation and working as a team; mutual respect; agreeing on rules and following them; that participation and the pleasure of taking part are more important than winning; doing their *personal* best.

As well as being competitive people can also be sociable and co-operative; we like to be part of a group or groups. Co-operative activities encourage children to: be self-confident; have high self-esteem; relate positively to others; work together and help others; make joint decisions; participate fully (no one is left out or eliminated); have a sense of belonging.

Ten ways to enable pupils to relate positively to others

You can enable pupils to relate positively to others by encouraging them to do the following:

1. Celebrate our individual differences. We are all important, valued and unique individuals.

2. Listen and be attentive to what others have to communicate.

3. Regard and value the needs and rights of others.

4. Recognise and respect the culture and beliefs of others.

5. Be considerate and courteous towards others.

6. Help and care for each other as much as we are able.

7. Co-operate and work together to reach the best solutions.

8. Share and take turns; remember compromise equals wise.

9. Praise and encourage others to raise their self-esteem.

10. Inspire respect in others through our own kindness, fairness and honesty.

KEY TASK

Plan and implement an activity that encourages pupils to relate to others, e.g. work co-operatively during group activities.

 NVQ LINKS:

Level 2:
STL2.2 STL3.4

Level 3:
STL3.4 STL4.1 STL4.3
STL20.1 STL20.2 STL20.3
STL41.2 STL45.1

Encouraging children's self-reliance, self-esteem and resilience

As a teaching assistant, you should encourage children's self-reliance, self-esteem and resilience by: engaging with and providing focused attention to individual pupils; treating pupils with respect and consideration as individual people in their own right; showing empathy to pupils by demonstrating understanding of their feelings and points of view. You should encourage pupils to take decisions and make choices (see section below on involving pupils' decision-making). You should communicate with pupils openly and honestly in ways that are not judgemental. You should help pupils to choose realistic goals that are challenging but achievable (see section on setting goals and boundaries in Chapter 4). You should praise specific behaviour that you wish to encourage as well as directing any comments, whether positive or negative, towards the demonstrated behaviour not the pupil (see sections on rewards and sanctions in Chapter 4).

You should work with colleagues and other professionals, as required, to encourage children's self-esteem and resilience, e.g. providing opportunities to encourage children's self-reliance, positive self-esteem and self-image (see below). You may need to work with other professionals (e.g. counsellors, psychologists or social workers) to promote the well-being and resilience of pupils with additional needs (see Chapter 11).

Encouraging children's self-reliance

Encouraging children's self-reliance is an important part of helping them to develop their independence and resilience which will enable children to face life's demands and challenges in preparation for their adult lives. Encouraging self-reliance involves helping children to develop: *independence* (or autonomy), e.g. the ability to think and act for oneself; *dependence* on own capabilities and personal resources; *competence* in looking after self; *trust* in own judgement and actions; *confidence* in own abilities and actions.

Eight ways to encourage children's self-reliance

You can encourage children's self-reliance in the following ways:

1. Provide *freedom* for pupils to become more independent.

2. Be *patient* and provide *time* for pupils to do things for themselves, e.g. let younger pupils dress themselves (i.e. for P.E.): although it takes longer, it is an essential self-help skill. Pupils with physical disabilities may need sensitive support in this area.

3. *Praise* and *encourage* their efforts at becoming more independent.

4. Be aware of *individual needs* for independence; every pupil is different and will require encouragement relevant to their particular level of development. Do not insist pupils be more independent in a particular area until they are ready.

5. Be sensitive to *changing needs* for independence. Remember a pupil who is tired, distressed or unwell may require more adult assistance than usual.

6. Offer *choices* to help pupils feel more in control. As they develop and mature, increase the scope of choices. Involve the pupils in *decision-making* within the school (see below).

7. Provide *play opportunities* that encourage independence, e.g. dressing-up is a fun way to help younger pupils learn to dress independently.

8. Use *technology* to encourage independence, e.g. specialist play equipment; voice-activated word processing; motorised wheelchairs.

Pupil demonstrating self-help skills

KEY TASK

1. Observe a pupil demonstrating self-help skills such as: washing hands; getting dressed/undressed (e.g. for PE); tidying up.

2. Assess the pupil's ability to perform the skill independently. Outline the adult's role in developing the pupil's self-reliance in this area.

 NVQ LINKS:

Level 2:
STL2.1   STL2.2

Level 3:
STL45.2   STL45.4

Involving children and young people in decision-making

As a teaching assistant, you should know and understand the importance of encouraging pupils to make choices and involving pupils in decision-making. This includes encouraging pupils to take responsibility for everyday tasks within the school. Younger pupils are quite capable of making their own decisions and this helps to develop their independence and extends their own communication skills even further. For example, pupils as young as four years old can: be responsible for tidying up their own activities, getting equipment out (under adult supervision for safety reasons, of course); choose their own activities; select and follow written and/or pictorial instructions for tasks/activities to be done that session.

Children have the right to be consulted and involved in decision-making about matters that affect them (UN Convention on the Rights of the Child, Article 12 – see page 115). Children should have opportunities to be involved in the planning, implementation and evaluation of policies that affect them or the services they use (CYPU, 2001). Involving pupils in decision-making within your school will help you to support the teachers in providing better educational provision based on the children's real needs rather than adult assumptions about children's needs. It will also help the school to promote social inclusion by encouraging the pupils to participate as active citizens in their local community.

You could involve pupils in decision-making in the following ways:

1. *Suggestion box* for their comments and complaints about the provision including play opportunities.
2. *Questionnaires and surveys* to find out their opinions about the setting's policies and procedures including any gaps in the provision.
3. *Consultation exercises*, e.g. discussion groups; drama and role-play activities, music and games to provide opportunities for children to express ideas.
4. *Direct involvement*, e.g. taking part in staff development and recruitment activities, assessing new initiatives, mentoring other children, providing information via leaflets, posters and IT for other children.

(CYPU, 2001)

KEY TASK

1. How does your school involve children and young people in decision-making?
2. What opportunities are provided to enable young people to be active citizens?

NVQ LINKS:

Level 2:
STL4.1   STL4.3   STL15.3

Level 3:
STL20.1   STL20.2   STL45.2
STL45.4   STL47.1   STL47.2

Encouraging children's positive self-esteem

A person's self-esteem is changeable; sometimes we feel more positive about ourselves than at other times. Even if we have had past experiences that resulted in negative or poor self-esteem, we can overcome this and learn to feel more positive about ourselves. Self-esteem involves: feelings and thoughts about oneself (positive or negative); respect or regard for self (or lack of it); consideration of self; self-worth (i.e. value of self); self-image (i.e. perception of self). How we feel about ourselves depends on a number of factors: *who* we are with at the time; the social context, e.g. *where* we are; current and past *relationships*; past *experiences* (especially in early childhood).

We cannot *see* self-esteem, but we can assess children's (and adults') levels of self-esteem by their emotional responses, attitudes and actions. People with positive or high self-esteem are usually: calm and relaxed; energetic, enthusiastic and well-motivated; open and expressive; positive and optimistic; self-reliant and self-confident; assertive; reflective (e.g. aware of own strengths and weaknesses); sociable, co-operative, friendly and trusting. People with negative or low self-esteem tend to be: anxious and tense; lacking in enthusiasm, poorly motivated and easily frustrated; secretive and/or pretentious; negative and pessimistic; over-dependent, lacking in confidence and constantly seeking the approval of others *or* over-confident, arrogant and attention-seeking; aggressive *or* passive; self-destructive *or* abusive towards others; resentful and distrustful of others.

Possible reasons for low self-esteem

All children begin with the *potential* for *high* self-esteem, but their interactions with others contribute to whether positive self-esteem is encouraged or diminished. Experiences in early childhood have the most significant affect on children's self-esteem; sometimes these effects may not become apparent until adolescence or adulthood when serious psychological and social problems may result due to very low self-esteem. Children (and adults) are very resilient and can learn to have greater self-esteem even if their earlier experiences were detrimental to their esteem. Factors which lead to low self-esteem include: being deprived of basic needs or having these needs inadequately met; having feelings denied or ignored; being put down, ridiculed or humiliated; participating in inappropriate activities; feeling that their ideas and opinions are unimportant; being over-protected, under-disciplined or excessively disciplined; being physically or sexually abused (Lindenfield, 1995).

EXERCISE:
1. Think of as many *positive* words to describe yourself using the same initial as your first name, e.g. *caring, creative,* Carlton; *magnificent, marvellous,* Miriam; *sensitive, sharing,* Shazia; *terrific, tremendous* Tom.
2. You could also try this with friends, colleagues or a group of pupils.

Factors affecting self-image and identity

The development of self-image is strongly linked to self-esteem. Self-image can be defined as the individual's view of their own personality and abilities including the individual's *perception* of how other people view them and their abilities. This involves recognising ourselves as *separate* and *unique* individuals with characteristics which make us different from others. Self-image also involves a number of factors which influence how we *identify with* other people. For example: gender, culture, race, nationality, religion, language, social status/occupation, disability/special needs, early childhood experiences and relationships.

Children develop their self-image through interactions with others starting with family members and gradually including childcarers, teachers, teaching assistants, friends, classmates. Through positive interactions, children learn to value themselves and their abilities *if* they receive approval, respect and empathy. Early childhood experiences and relationships may have positive or negative influences on children's self-image.

Research shows that intelligence or physical attractiveness are *not* factors in children's self-image or self-esteem; very intelligent or attractive children may still have poor self-esteem and self-image. The main reason for poor self-image and low self-esteem is the treatment that children receive from their parents (Fontana, 1984). Children with positive self-image: tend to come from homes where they are regarded as significant and interesting people; have their views invited and listened to; have parents with high, but reasonable and consistent expectations; receive firm discipline based on rewards and sanctions *not* physical punishment. Children with negative self-image: tend to come from homes where no one takes any real interest in them; have parents with limited, negative or unreasonable expectations; are given little consistent guidance and/or care; receive too little discipline or overly strict discipline or a confusing mixture of the two.

However, it is not just parents who influence children's self-image and self-esteem. Adults working with children (such as childcarers, playworkers, teachers and teaching assistants) also influence children's self-image and self-esteem through their attitudes, words and actions. In schools pupils soon become aware that certain levels of performance are expected by adults and begin to compare their own achievements with those of other pupils. If pupils regularly feel that their achievements do not compare favourably with those of other pupils, then they begin to experience a sense of failure and inferiority. Pupils may react to this feeling by either passively accepting that they are a failure and being reluctant to attempt new learning activities *or* rebelling against and rejecting all learning activities that remind them of failure.

Adults have important roles to play in children's development of self-image and identity. Children are able to see and feel not only the way adults interact with them personally, but also the way adults interact with other children and adults at home, in the childcare setting or at school. Young children are very capable and accurate at assessing what adult expectations of them are and of behaving accordingly! The constraints of class size, time and resources mean that many classrooms *do* group pupils according to ability. Nursery and primary education are now more curriculum and assessment orientated, e.g. early learning goals, Foundation Stage profile, the National Curriculum including the literacy and numeracy hours, and Standard Assessment Tasks (SATs).

Some children may experience particular difficulties in developing a positive self-image. For example: children with special needs; children from ethnic minorities; children who are/have been abused. These children may be experiencing prejudice and/or discrimination on a regular basis which affects their ability to maintain a positive self-image.

As a teaching assistant you need to be aware of your own self-image and the importance of having positive self-esteem. This may mean that you need to deal with issues regarding your own self-image and to raise your own self-esteem before you can encourage children's positive self-image.

EXERCISE:
1. Think about the factors which influence your own self-image (e.g. male or female; full or part-time student; employment status; nationality and race; any special needs; early experiences and relationships).
2. How do you think these factors influence your self-image and the ways you *think* other people see you? (For example, some people may consider studying for a teaching assistant qualification appropriate for a woman, but a male studying the same course may be regarded differently.)

Encouraging children's positive self-esteem and self-image

By praising *all* children and encouraging them to feel good about themselves and their achievements, adults can help *all* children to establish and maintain a positive self-image. Developing and implementing inclusive policies, procedures and strategies will also help (see section on promoting equality and inclusion in Chapter 5).

Ten ways to encourage positive self-esteem and self-image

1. Treat every pupil as an individual; every pupil has unique abilities and needs.

2. Be positive by using praise and encouragement to help pupils to focus on what they are good at.

3. Help pupils to maximise their individual potential.

4. Encourage pupils to measure their achievements by comparing them to their *own* efforts.

5. Have high but realistic expectations of *all* pupils.

6. Take an interest in each pupil's efforts as well as achievements.

7. Encourage positive participation during learning activities, e.g. sharing resources, helping others and contributing ideas.

8. Give pupils opportunities to make decisions and choices.

9. Promote equality of opportunity by providing positive images of children, young people and adults through books, stories and songs.

10. Remember to label the behaviour not the pupil as this is less damaging to their self-esteem, e.g. 'That was an unkind thing to say' rather than 'You are unkind'.

EXERCISE:
1. Design your own 'personal flag'. Use words and pictures to describe the following: my happiest memory; my best qualities; my significant achievements; my current goal.
2. If possible, try this activity with a pupil or small group of pupils.

Example of child's personal flag

Encouraging children's resilience

The pressures of modern living in the 21st century affect the emotional well-being and resilience of both children and adults. For example:

1. Parents in the UK work longer hours than in any other country in Europe; consequently working parents have less time to spend with their children.
2. National Curriculum demands have led to a return to more formal methods of teaching, with increased emphasis on academic achievement for all children, e.g. literacy and numeracy hours, end of Key Stage tests.
3. Technological advances and concerns about personal safety mean many children and young people spend more time in front of televisions, computers and games consoles than playing out with friends.

Academic intelligence or achievement has very little to do with emotional well-being. According to research intelligence quotient (IQ) contributes 20% to the factors that lead to success in life while other factors contribute to the other 80%. These other factors include: environmental and social factors (see section below on factors that affect resilience); luck, e.g. being in the right place at the right time or wrong place at the wrong time; emotional intelligence or competence (Goleman, 1996).

In Britain we tend to place great importance on people's qualifications and job status. We need to put more emphasis on people's emotional intelligence or well-being as this would lead to people having better life skills, e.g. making better use of leisure time, maintaining positive relationships, being able to pass exams, getting satisfying and challenging jobs, and being better parents.

Emotional intelligence or emotional well-being involves developing: positive self-esteem and self-image; emotional strength to deal with life's highs and lows;

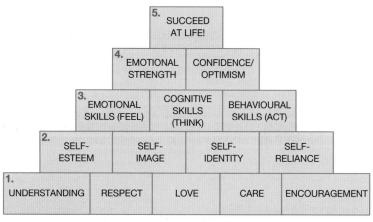

Key:
1. These **foundation stones** are established by parents, grandparents and carers in childhood; as adults we can regain them through partners/spouses, close friends, etc.
2. These **self-building blocks** are influenced by others including family, carers, teachers, teaching assistants, playworkers, friends, peers, colleagues, etc. throughout life.
3. These **skills** can be developed as a child and/or as an adult.
4. These **qualities** can be demonstrated as a child and/or as an adult.
5. **Individual achievements** in different areas of life as a child and as an adult.

Emotional building blocks

confidence to face the world with optimism; awareness of own feelings and those of other people.

We all need to feel valued – that who we are and where we come from are respected; that our ideas and abilities are important. On this solid emotional platform the building blocks for a stimulating and fulfilling life can be successfully constructed. Even if these building blocks are damaged by life experiences, personal difficulties, tragedy or trauma they can be rebuilt in childhood, adolescence and even adulthood.

Factors that affect resilience

Children vary in their responses to a set of circumstances. Some children may do well even in extremely adverse circumstances while others may not be able to cope with small amounts of stress. Rutter describes resilience as *'the phenomenon of overcoming stress or adversity'* (DH, 2000). Resilience (or protective) factors cushion children from the worst effects of adversity and may help a *'child or young person to cope, survive and even thrive in the face of great hurt and disadvantage'* (Bostock, 2004).

Resilience factors are things which help children and young people withstand adversity and to cope in unfavourable circumstances or times of difficulty. Resilience factors include the following:

- ✦ Positive attachment experiences, e.g. caring relationship with parents and/or carers.
- ✦ Positive relationships with caring, concerned and sincere adults (such as childcarers, teachers, teaching assistants) can also increase self-esteem.
- ✦ Positive early years/school experiences including participation in activities they enjoy to build positive self-esteem.
- ✦ Recognition, respect and rewards for special skills and talents that everyone has as unique individuals, e.g. nurturing academic, artistic, musical, sporting and vocational abilities through activities both in the setting and in spare time.
- ✦ Opportunities to take responsibility or contribute to decisions which affect one's life, e.g. involvement in discussions/reviews to develop services for children/young people.
- ✦ A sense of direction that provides stability and control by building up a picture of what the future might hold, e.g. helping to develop goals and how to reach these goals.

(Bostock, 2004)

Promoting children's emotional well-being and resilience

As a teaching assistant you can promote children's emotional well-being and resilience by working with the teacher to provide opportunities for pupils to: learn about their feelings; understand the feelings of others; develop their creative abilities, e.g. art and craft, drama, musical activities; participate in physical activities, games and sport; interact with other pupils and make friends, e.g. play together; and develop emotional intelligence.

Five ways to promote children's emotional well-being and resilience

You can help pupils to develop emotional well-being and resilience by doing the following:

1. **Developing their self-awareness**, including helping pupils to establish a positive self-image and to recognise their own feelings.

2. **Helping them to handle and express feelings** in appropriate ways, e.g. through creative, imaginative and physical play.

3. **Encouraging their self-motivation** by helping pupils to establish personal goals, e.g. developing self-control and self-reliance.

4. **Developing their empathy for other people** by encouraging pupils to recognise the feelings, needs and rights of others.

5. **Encouraging positive social interaction** by helping pupils to develop effective interpersonal skills through play and other co-operative group activities in the school and in the local community.

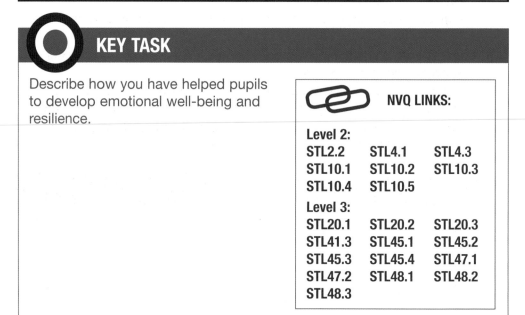

⬤ KEY TASK

Describe how you have helped pupils to develop emotional well-being and resilience.

🔗 **NVQ LINKS:**

Level 2:
STL2.2	STL4.1	STL4.3
STL10.1	STL10.2	STL10.3
STL10.4	STL10.5	

Level 3:
STL20.1	STL20.2	STL20.3
STL41.3	STL45.1	STL45.2
STL45.3	STL45.4	STL47.1
STL47.2	STL48.1	STL48.2
STL48.3		

Supporting children and young people during transitions

The process of adjusting to a new situation is known as a **transition**. Transitions involve the experiences of change, separation and loss. A transition may involve the *transfer* from one setting to another or changes within the same setting. For example: home to childminder's home, nursery, playgroup or school; one year group or Key Stage to another, e.g. Reception to Year 1, Key Stage 1 to 2;

mainstream to or from special school; secondary school to college or work; staff changes due to illness, maternity leave, promotion, retirement, etc. A transition may also involve other significant transfers or *changes* in the child's life such as: death or serious illness of a family member or close friend; parental separation or divorce; moving house; puberty; going into hospital; death of a favourite pet; arrival of a new baby or step-brothers and sisters; going on holiday (especially visiting another country).

Planning for transitions

The school should have policies and procedures for helping pupils adjust to a new setting including the following:

- ☆ Identification of the changes in expectations and activities required of the pupil(s).
- ☆ Review of relevant information with an individual pupil.
- ☆ Work with parents and carers to ensure a full understanding of the process.
- ☆ Identification of the support the pupil will need to make a successful adjustment including any special requirements.
- ☆ Preparation of a transition plan that assists others to develop a full understanding of the experiences and achievements of the pupil.
- ☆ An effective induction programme that helps pupils to understand the new expectations and activities.
- ☆ Assessment of the pupil's current levels of achievement and learning experience to provide a programme that will provide continuity in learning.
- ☆ Prompt transfer of information to aid effective planning, following agreed confidentiality protocols and legislative requirements.

 KEY TASK

How does your setting support children and young people during transitions?

For example: transferring to/from a new setting or to a different group within the same setting (e.g. moving to a new year group or Key Stage in a school); meeting a new teacher or teaching assistant; starting college or work; going into hospital for a planned operation or treatment; supporting unexpected or unplanned transitions such as bereavement or divorce.

 **NVQ LINKS:**

Level 3:
STL45.1   STL45.2   STL45.4
STL49.1   STL49.2

Preparing pupils for transitions

To cope with, prepare for and accept transfers and transitions, children need: reassurance from adults to maintain their feelings of stability, security and trust; adult assistance to adjust to different social rules and social expectations; help in adapting to different group situations. To alleviate some of the anxiety and stress experienced by children during transitions, appropriate preparation is now seen as an essential part of successful transitions in most settings including nurseries and schools. Most settings have established procedures for preparing children for transitions.

Preparing **pupils aged 3–11 years** for transitions:

* Talk to the pupils and explain what is going to happen.
* Listen to the pupils and reassure them that it will be fine.
* Read relevant books, stories and poems about transitions, e.g. starting primary school or moving to secondary school.
* Watch appropriate videos/television programmes that demonstrate the positive features of the new school.
* Provide opportunities for imaginative play to let pupils express their feelings and fears about the transition.
* Organise introductory visits for the pupils and their parents/carers so that the children can become familiar with the school and the adults who will care for and support them.
* Provide information appropriate to both pupils and parents, e.g. information pack/brochure plus activity pack for the pupil.
* Obtain relevant information about each pupil, e.g. correct name and address, contact details, medical information, any special dietary requirements.
* Plan activities for an induction programme (the pupil's first day/week in the new school).

Preparing **pupils aged 11–16 years** for transitions:

* Encourage pupils and parents to attend open days and evenings for school/college.
* Year 6 could be taught by different primary teachers to prepare them for the difference in teaching and learning style, e.g. from topic-based to subject-based.
* Start a project towards the end of the summer term to be completed in the first few weeks of secondary to give a sense of continuity.
* Year 7 teachers could visit and teach Year 6 pupils in primary schools during the summer term.
* Teaching assistants could visit new school/year group and work alongside teachers particularly if going to have responsibility for pupil or pupils with special needs.
* Taster days for pupils to experience the layout and routine of the new school/college, e.g. moving to different classrooms for lessons with different subject teachers through fun activities in science, IT and sport.
* Discussions between different Key Stage staff about individual pupils' performance.
* Exchange of relevant documentation, e.g. SATs test results, teacher assessments, any special educational needs information including Individual Education Plans, Behaviour Support Plans, Statements, etc.

- ☆ Pupil's record of achievement including their school work, interests and hobbies.
- ☆ Encourage pupils with behaviour problems to look at this as a new start.
- ☆ School brochure including information on homework and bullying as these are often key areas of concern.
- ☆ Obtain relevant information from parents.
- ☆ Provide opportunities for work experience to help pupils with transition from learning environment to world of work.
- ☆ Provide opportunities for careers advice and information on further education/training.

KEY TASK

Describe the procedures in your school for preparing pupils for transitions. Include possible strategies for supporting the preparation of pupils for transfer or transition. Consider these points:

- The pupil's level of social interaction (e.g. age and ability to communicate).
- The pupil's potential behaviour based on your existing knowledge of the pupil (e.g. are they likely to be co-operative or disruptive?).
- The pupil's possible emotional responses and how to deal with them.

 NVQ LINKS:

Level 3:
STL45.1   STL45.2   STL45.4
STL49.1   STL49.2

Strategies for helping pupils settle into a new setting

The first days (or even weeks) that pupils spend in a new school require a sensitive approach from adults to enable the pupils to cope with separation from their parents and/or their adjustment to new routines and school staff.

Ten ways to help pupils settle in a new setting

1. Follow a clear, structured daily routine to provide stability and security for the pupils.

2. Provide opportunities for pupils to express their feelings and concerns over separating from parents or starting in new school/year group/Key Stage.

3. Work with the teacher to identify pupils' individual needs during the transition period.

4. Provide activities and experiences appropriate to these needs.

5. Show an active interest in the pupils' activities.

6. Give particular praise and encouragement for effort not just achievement.

7. Work with the teacher and pupils to establish clear boundaries and rules.

8. Reassure younger pupils about their parents' eventual return.

9. Prepare parents for possible temporary effects of the transition, e.g. children may demonstrate their feelings of anxiety by being clingy, hostile and aggressive or by regressing to previous developmental level.

10. Settling in can often be more stressful for parents than their children; encouraging parents to be calm and confident will help their children who can sense their anxiety.

Factors affecting adjustment to new settings

Children's responses to transitions often depend on the way they are prepared for new settings. The need for preparation was not recognised in the past; children started school and were left to cope with the situation with little or no preparation and parental involvement was positively discouraged.

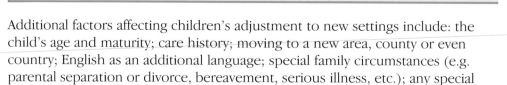

EXERCISE: Can you remember your first day at primary or secondary school? How were you helped to adjust to this new setting?

Additional factors affecting children's adjustment to new settings include: the child's age and maturity; care history; moving to a new area, county or even country; English as an additional language; special family circumstances (e.g. parental separation or divorce, bereavement, serious illness, etc.); any special educational needs; returning to the setting after a prolonged illness or accident.

Possible problems in adjusting to new settings

Many children experience anxiety and stress when they first attend a new setting due to:

* separating from their parent or carer
* encountering an unfamiliar group of children who may have established friendships
* adapting to length of time in the setting, e.g. half-day in nursery to full-day in school
* experiencing a culture and/or language different from home or previous setting
* coping with unfamiliar routines and rules
* worrying about doing the wrong thing
* participating in unfamiliar activities/routines such as PE, playtime and lunchtime
* being overwhelmed or scared by an unfamiliar physical environment

* experiencing difficulties in following more structured activities and adult directions
* concentrating on activities for longer than previously used to.

The transition from primary to secondary school may cause additional concerns due to:

* lack of sufficient information about individual pupils on transfer
* discontinuity of Year 6 and 7 curriculum in spite of the National Curriculum
* having several subject teachers instead of one class teacher
* decrease in pupil performance after transfer.

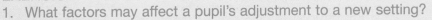

EXERCISE:
1. What factors may affect a pupil's adjustment to a new setting?
2. What possible problems might a pupil experience when adjusting to a new setting?

Five ways to respond to problems with adjusting to a new setting

You should recognise possible problems that pupils may experience when adjusting to a new setting and respond to these appropriately by doing the following:

1. Offering reassurance and information as required by individual pupils to help them learn about the setting.

2. Using strategies designed to help pupils join in activities and adjust to the setting, e.g. ice-breakers, co-operative games, etc.

3. Encouraging other pupils to interact with and welcome new arrivals, e.g. 'buddy' system, showing new pupils where resources are, asking them to join in with their games at playtime, etc.

4. Recognising the signs of distress (e.g. tearfulness, withdrawal or reluctance to participate in activities, complaining of 'tummy ache', toileting 'accidents') and responding appropriately as agreed with the teacher.

5. Reporting to the teacher promptly any problems in helping pupils adjust to the setting.

EXERCISE: Describe how a teaching assistant could respond to a pupil with problems in adjusting to a new setting. If possible, give examples from your own experiences of supporting pupils in adjusting to a new setting.

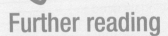

Further reading

Bayley, R. *et al.* (2003) *Smooth transitions: building on the foundation stage.* Featherstone Education Ltd.

Broadhead, P. (2003) *Early years play and learning: developing social skills and co-operation.* Routledge Falmer.

Children and Young People's Unit (2001) *Learning to listen: core principles for the involvement of children and young people.* DfES. [Available online at www.dfee.gov.uk/cypu.]

DfES (2005) *Social and emotional aspects of learning.* DfES. [Available online at www.standards.dfes.gov.uk.]

Dowling, M. (2000) *Young children's personal, social and emotional development.* Paul Chapman Publications.

Fabian, H. (2002) *Children starting school: a guide to successful transitions and transfers for teachers and assistants.* David Fulton Publishers Ltd.

Kamen, T. (2000) *Psychology for childhood studies.* Hodder Arnold.

Lindenfield, G. (2000) *Confident children: help children to feel good about themselves.* HarperCollins.

Lindenfield, G. (2000) *Self-esteem: simple steps to developing self-reliance and perseverance.* HarperCollins.

Lindon, J. (2007) *Understanding children and young people: development from 5–18 years.* Hodder Arnold.

Newman, T. and Blackburn, S. (2002) *Transitions in the lives of children and young people: resilience factors.* Scottish Executive.

8 Supporting children's play

Key points:

✳ The importance of play

✳ The role of play in children's learning and development

✳ Identifying children's play needs and preferences

✳ Planning and preparing play spaces

✳ Providing for a range of play types – physical, exploratory and imaginative play

✳ Obtaining resources for play spaces

✳ Supporting self-directed play

✳ Helping children and young people to manage risk during play.

The importance of play

Play is an essential part of children's development and learning. It is the central way in which children explore and develop an understanding of their environment. Children learn through play. The term 'play' is often used to refer to children's activities that are considered unimportant and frivolous by many people, especially parents. It is up to adults working with children to stress the importance of play to those who are sceptical about its benefits. Play can help children's development and learning by providing opportunities for: self-chosen and well-motivated learning; challenging and interesting experiences; taking responsibility for their own learning; gaining confidence and independence; co-operative work between children; developing a wide range of physical skills; developing problem-solving skills; encouraging imagination and creativity.

The role of play in children's learning and development

Early learning involves learning through stimulating play activities with appropriate adult support to provide young children with the essential foundations for later learning. Young children who are pushed too hard by being forced to do formal learning activities before they are ready may actually be harmed in terms of their development and they may also be put off literacy, numeracy and other related activities. Young children need a combination of real and imaginary experiences to encourage early learning. This is why play is an important aspect of young children's development and learning. Young children need to handle objects and materials to understand basic concepts, for example in mathematics, using objects for counting and addition such as buttons, cones and plastic cubes. Once children have plenty of practical experiences they can cope more easily with abstract concepts such as written sums or mental arithmetic. Children use play opportunities to encourage and extend the problem-solving abilities that are essential to developing their intellectual processes.

Play activities provide informal opportunities for children to develop ideas and to understand concepts through active learning and communication. Language is a key component in children's thinking and learning. Play is an invaluable way to provide opportunities for language and to make learning more meaningful, especially for young children. Play enables children to learn about concepts in a safe and non-threatening environment. Play activities help to promote all aspects of children's development.

Children's social play

Children go through a recognised sequence of social play. Younger children tend to engage in more solitary or parallel play activities because they are more egocentric, while older children are capable of more co-operative play activities as they can take turns, share play equipment and follow rules more easily. There will be times when quite young children can be engaged happily in play activities with some interaction with other children (associative play) such as dressing-up, home corner, doing jigsaws, simple construction or painting. There will be occasions when older children become engrossed in solitary or parallel play activities with no interaction with other children, e.g. doing detailed drawings and paintings, building intricate constructions that require complete concentration to the exclusion of everyone else.

> **The sequence of social play**
> - *Solitary play:* playing alone
> - *Parallel play:* playing alongside other children without interaction
> - *Associative play:* playing alongside other children with limited interaction
> - *Co-operative play:* playing together
> - *Complex co-operative play:* playing together including following agreed rules.

A child's level of social interaction during play activities depends on: the individual child; the child's previous experiences of play; the play activity itself; the social context, e.g. the setting and other people present. Play also helps develop children's social and emotional skills by providing opportunities for: learning and developing new social skills; practising and improving existing social skills; experimenting with new situations, e.g. anticipating what they *might* do in new situations; preparing for new experiences; acting out past experiences; expressing emotions in positive ways.

Seven ways to promote children's learning and development through play

You can help to promote children's learning and development through play by working with the teacher to do the following:

1 Plan play carefully and think about what the pupils will learn from the activities.

2 Provide challenging and interesting play opportunities appropriate to the ages, needs, interests and abilities of the pupils.

3 Provide varied play resources and encourage the pupils to use them.

4 Participate in the pupils' play activities to stimulate language and extend learning.

5 Encourage the pupils' imagination and creative ideas.

6 Encourage social interaction during play, e.g. the pupils may need coaxing to join or guidance on taking turns and sharing.

7 Link play activities to real-life situations, e.g. link shop play with real shopping trips.

KEY TASK

1. Give an example of a play opportunity you have used (or could use) to promote children's learning and development.

2. Suggest other play opportunities which might encourage the children's learning and development.

 NVQ LINKS:

Level 2:

STL1.1	STL1.2	STL1.3
STL10.1	STL10.2	STL10.3
STL10.4	STL10.5	STL15.2

Level 3:

STL18.1	STL18.2	STL53.1
STL53.2	STL53.3	STL53.4
STL54.2	STL54.3	

Identifying children's play needs and preferences

Play is not an extra – something to be done to keep children quiet or occupied while adults are busy or as a reward for children when other tasks have been done. Play is an essential part of children's (and young people's) development and learning. Children's play needs to include opportunities to do the following:

☆ Access safe play spaces

☆ Engage in a wide range of play activities and use a variety of play resources

* Learn about and understand the physical world
* Develop individual skills and personal resources
* Communicate and co-operate with others
* Develop empathy for others
* Make sense of the world in relation to themselves
* Do their own learning, in their own time and in their own way.

You should be able to identify children's play needs and preferences. Play needs are the individual needs of children for play. Preferences are children's choices with regard to play. You can help to identify children's play needs and preferences by: researching playwork theory and practice to find out about children's play and development; observing children playing; interacting with children. You should also consult children about their play needs and preferences by talking with them and asking for their suggestions about play spaces and resources.

Play objectives

When supporting children's play, it is helpful to know and understand the indicators and objectives that can be used to evaluate play provision. Knowledge and understanding of the **play objectives** in *Best play: what play provision should do for children* (see Further reading at the end of this chapter) will help you to research and identify a range of play spaces and resources that will meet children's play needs and preferences.

The play objectives:

1. The play provision extends the choice and control that children have over their play, the freedom they enjoy and the satisfaction they gain from it.

2. The play provision recognises children's need to test boundaries and responds positively to that need.

3. The play provision balances the need to offer risk and the need to keep children safe from harm.

4. The play provision maximises the range of play opportunities.

5. The play provision fosters children's independence and self-esteem.

6. The play provision fosters children's respect for others and offers opportunities for social interaction.

7. The play provision fosters the child's well-being, healthy growth and development, knowledge and understanding, creativity and capacity to learn.

(NPFA *et al.*, 2000: p.18)

You can use these play objectives to evaluate play needs and preferences in the following ways: observing and recording the play types demonstrated by the children and the relationships within the setting; listening to the children about their views on play spaces and the resources available in the setting; monitoring the policies and procedures and how these work in practice in the setting; evaluating and reviewing activity plans, play opportunities and resources as well as the policies and procedures in the setting (NPFA *et al.*, 2000).

In addition to the play objectives in *Best Play* you can evaluate play provision by using the **characteristics of VITAL play opportunities** from *Getting serious about play: a review of children's play*. For example, you should consider these 'VITAL' key elements of successful play opportunities:

* Value-based * In the right place * Top quality * Appropriate * Long-term

Characteristics of VITAL play opportunities:

1. **Value-based:** Children and young people's interests and rights are respected; all children and young people are welcomed, whatever their ability or background, especially those from disadvantaged groups; children and young people's skills and abilities are respected.

2. **In the right place:** Close to children and young people's homes and schools or on well-used travel routes; in safe locations; located in places that children, young people and the wider community are happy with.

3. **Top quality:** Safe, welcoming and providing choice and variety; well-designed in relation to surrounding area and local community; has balanced approach to managing risk; well managed and maintained.

4. **Appropriate:** Shaped by local needs and circumstances; complementing other local opportunities; taking account of all sectors of the local community; well planned.

5. **Long-term:** Sustainable beyond the lifetime of immediate funding; set up to be valued and respected parts of the social fabric of the neighbourhood.

(DCMS, 2004: p.19 – reproduced under the terms of the Click-Use Licence)

 KEY TASK

1. Collect information on the play needs and preferences of the children and/or young people in your setting using these methods: research playwork theory and practice; observe the children and/or young people playing; consult the children and/or young people about their play needs and preferences.

 **NVQ LINKS:**

Level 3: STL54.1

2. Use this information to identify their play needs and preferences, e.g. make suggestions for possible play opportunities and resources.

3. You could present this information in a booklet or information pack on children's play for parent helpers, volunteers and students.

Planning and preparing play spaces

In order to plan and prepare play spaces it is essential for you to know about the range of different types of play spaces that support and enrich the potential for children's play. **Play spaces** are areas that support and enrich the potential for children to play (SkillsActive, 2004).

Plan and create play spaces: for physical play; for affective play; that are transient or permanent.

Types of play spaces include the following:

1. **Care and education settings** run by professional staff such as childcarers, playworkers and teaching assistants providing play opportunities, e.g. private and local authority day nurseries, out-of-school clubs providing extra-curricular activities, extended schools.
2. **'Formal' play provision** run by professional play staff and parent helpers/volunteers, e.g. playgroups, holiday playschemes.
3. **'Open access' play facilities** operated by professional playworkers but where children and young people come and go as they please, e.g. adventure playgrounds, some holiday playschemes, and playbuses.
4. **'Informal' play facilities** that are not staffed, e.g. public parks, play areas and playgrounds, skate parks, basketball courts, football pitches and playing fields.
5. **Non-designated play spaces** used by children and young people especially when there are no other play spaces available, e.g. local streets, outside shops, abandoned buildings, open spaces.

(DCMS, 2004)

EXERCISE:
1. Find out about the existing play spaces available in your local area.
2. What additional play spaces and resources do you think should be made available to meet the play needs and preferences of the children in your local area?

An inclusive play environment

Planning play spaces that meet children's play needs

You need to be able to plan play spaces that meet children's play needs. When planning play spaces you should remember that: the play environment should be welcoming and provide maximum opportunities for children to make choices; play resources should be varied with sufficient quantities so that children do not have to wait too long to play with materials or equipment; children should have lots of opportunities for social interaction with other children and adults (Lindon, 2002).

You will need to plan how the setting will be organised, both indoors and outdoors, and what play opportunities and resources will be available. However, your planning must take account of children's play needs and be flexible enough to allow them to enjoy play in their own way, and to make their own choices and decisions about play. This includes being able to adapt play opportunities according to the ages, abilities and needs of the children and/or young people in your setting.

EXERCISE: Think about the planning and creation of play spaces in your setting.

When planning and creating play spaces you should remember these important points:

1. Plan play spaces based on children's play needs and preferences, e.g. find out about children's play and development, observe children's play activities.
2. Involve children in the creation of play spaces, e.g. consult them about the play opportunities and play resources they would like in the setting.
3. Create play spaces that children can adapt to their own needs, e.g. flexible play areas to allow children to spread out during their play.
4. Allow children to choose and explore play spaces for themselves, e.g. selecting their own play activities and play resources.
5. Allow children to develop through play in their own ways, e.g. freedom to explore and enjoy their chosen play activities in their own way and in their own time.
6. Allow children's play to continue uninterrupted, e.g. participate in their play as and when invited to do so; intervene in children's play only in order to maintain their physical safety or emotional security.
7. Address the possible barriers to accessing play spaces that some children may experience, e.g. ensure the play setting is inclusive and encourages participation by all the children including those from ethnic minority backgrounds and those with disabilities.

Providing for a range of play types

You should know and understand how to provide opportunities for a wide range of play types. Play types can be grouped into three main areas of play:

1. **Physical play**: play activities that provide opportunities for children to develop their physical skills. For example: locomotor play, mastery play, rough and tumble play.
2. **Exploratory play**: play activities that provide opportunities for children to understand the world around them by exploring their environment and experimenting with materials. For example: exploratory play, creative play, object play.

3. **Imaginative play:** play activities that provide opportunities for children to express feelings and to develop social skills. For example: communication play, deep play, dramatic play, fantasy play, imaginative play, role play, social play (see section on the sequence of children's social play), symbolic play.

Physical play

Children should have plenty of opportunities for physical play such as play apparatus, outdoor play, ball games, and swimming. By using their whole bodies children learn to control and manage them. The more practice children get to develop gross motor skills, the more agile, co-ordinated and safe they will be, as they get older. Using lots of energy in physical play is also fun and relaxing. Children also need opportunities to develop their fine motor skills and hand-eye co-ordination, e.g. playing with stacking toys and jigsaws. Physical play enables children to: develop body awareness and awareness of spatial relationships; understand positional relationships, e.g. in and out, over and under; develop gross motor skills; develop fine motor skills.

EXERCISE: Give examples of physical play opportunities from your own experiences of working with children.

Examples of play opportunities to meet children's physical play needs

1. **Outdoor play opportunities** should be provided for children everyday, e.g. playing in the outdoor play area, going for walks, going to the park or visiting an adventure playground. As well as the benefits of fresh air, outdoor play offers children more space to develop gross motor skills such as running, hopping, jumping, skipping, throwing and catching a ball, playing football, doing somersaults and cartwheels.

2. **Play apparatus** can be used indoors or outdoors depending on the size of the equipment and the space available. Larger play equipment that cannot be easily (or safely) accommodated inside the setting can be used in outdoor play, e.g. climbing apparatus. When using play equipment whether in the play setting or at a playground you must ensure that it is safe for use as well as appropriate for the children's ages and sizes. Always check play apparatus *before* use (see Chapter 2).

3. **Jigsaw puzzles** help children with shape recognition as well as developing fine motor skills and hand-eye co-ordination. Children can tackle standard jigsaws with a few large pieces, increasing the number of pieces as the children grow and improve their physical skills.

4. **Ball games** provide children with opportunities to develop ball skills such as throwing a ball, kicking a ball, catching a ball. Younger children need large, lightweight balls to practise their throwing and catching skills. As they get older, smaller balls, beanbags and quoits can be used to develop their skills of throwing with more accuracy. Older children can be encouraged to participate in team sports such as five-a-side football or basketball.

5. **Swimming** is an excellent all-round physical activity. Children are usually ready to learn to swim by the age of four or five years old. If the setting does not have its own swimming pool, it may be possible to arrange regular outings to a local swimming pool. If not, try to encourage the children in your setting to use their local pool with their families or friends depending on their ages/swimming abilities.

Exploratory play

Exploratory play encourages and extends children's discovery skills. Play is an important way to motivate children and to assist thinking and learning in a wide variety of settings. Children learn from play situations that give them 'hands-on' experience. Exploratory play encourages children to use their senses to discover the properties of different materials in pleasurable and meaningful ways. For example, playing with sand encourages children to consider textures and the functions of sand – getting the right consistency of sand to build sand castles, too wet or too dry and the sand will not stick together. Exploratory play enables children to: understand concepts such as shape and colour; explore the properties of materials, e.g. textures; understand volume/capacity and physical forces through sand and water play; develop problem-solving skills; devise and use own creative ideas.

EXERCISE: Give examples of exploratory play opportunities from your own experiences of working with children.

Examples of play opportunities to meet children's exploratory play needs

1. **Painting** with brushes, sponges, string; finger painting, bubble painting, 'butterfly' or 'blob' painting, marble painting, wax resist painting; printing (e.g. with leaves, potatoes, cotton reels) and pattern-making (e.g. with rollers, stamps).
2. **Drawing** using pencils, crayons, felt tips or chalks on a variety of materials including different kinds of paper, card, fabric and wood. Include colouring activities linked to the children's interests by drawing your own colouring sheets, buying ready made colouring books or using free printable colouring pages from the Internet.
3. **Model making** using commercial construction kits (e.g. *Lego Explore, Mega Bloks, Stickle Bricks*), wooden blocks or clean and safe 'junk' materials to enable children to create their own designs.
4. **Collage** using glue and interesting materials to create pictures involving different textures, colours and shapes, and provide an enjoyable sensory experience too.
5. **Clay, playdough and plasticine** can be used creatively; they are tactile too.
6. **Cooking** provides a similar experience to working with playdough or clay except that the end product is (usually) edible. Remember to include 'no cook' activities such as icing biscuits, making sandwiches or peppermint creams.

7. **Making music** can provide opportunities for children to explore different sounds and to experiment freely with the musical instruments. Provide a portable box/trolley with a range of percussion instruments including: drum, tambourine, castanets, wood blocks, shakers, bell stick, Indian bells, triangle, xylophone and chime bars.

8. **Water play** with plain, bubbly, coloured, warm or cold water helps children learn about the properties of water, e.g. it pours, splashes, runs, soaks. Provide small containers to fill and empty, as well as a sieve and funnel.

9. **Sand play** provides opportunities for exploring the properties of sand, e.g. wet sand sticks together and can be moulded, while dry sand does not stick and can be poured. Use 'washed' or 'silver' sand (not builder's sand which might contain cement). Provide small containers, buckets, sieves and funnels.

Imaginative play

Imaginative play provides opportunities for children to release emotional tension and frustration or express feelings such as anger or jealousy in positive ways. Imaginative play also encourages children to look and feel things from another person's viewpoint as well as developing communication skills to interact more effectively with others. Imaginative play activities such as role play and dressing-up enable children to overcome fears and worries about new experiences or people, to feel more important and powerful, and to feel more secure by being able to temporarily regress to earlier levels of development. Imaginative play enables children to: develop language and communication skills; practise and rehearse real-life situations; improve self-help skills such as getting dressed; express feelings in positive ways; share ideas and co-operate with other children.

EXERCISE: Give examples of imaginative play opportunities from your own experiences of working with children.

Examples of play opportunities to meet children's imaginative play needs

1. **Role play** includes *domestic play*, e.g. playing/imitating 'mum' or 'dad'; pretending to be a baby while other children act as parents; later imitates other role models such as carers, playworkers, teachers, characters from television, books; *shop play*, e.g. post office, hairdressers, café where can explore other roles. Pretending to visit the dentist, clinic, optician or hospital, setting up a home corner, a health centre or hospital can also provide for this type of play. Also include *drama* activities.

2. **Dressing-up activities** include pretending to be parents, carers, playworkers, teachers, film/television super-heroes, characters from games consoles, kings and queens, allows children to experiment with being powerful and in control. Pretending to be someone else can also help children to understand what it is like to be that person and encourages empathy and consideration for others.

3. **Dolls and puppets** can help children to deal with their feelings, e.g. jealousy over a new baby can be expressed by shouting at a teddy or doll. Puppets are also a useful way of providing children with a 'voice' and may encourage shy or withdrawn children to express themselves more easily.

4. **Miniature worlds** include play with small-scale toys such as dolls' houses, toy farms and toy zoos as well as vehicle play where children can act out previous experiences or situations while sharing ideas and equipment with other children; this can also help them establish friendships.

KEY TASK

1. Give examples of your involvement in planning and creating the following: play spaces for physical play; play spaces for affective play; transient play spaces; permanent play spaces.

NVQ LINKS:

Level 3:
**STL54.1   STL54.2   STL54.3
STL54.4**

2. Include information on how the play spaces: meet children's play needs and preferences; can be adapted by children to meet new needs; provide for a range of play types; are accessible to all children including those with disabilities; meet health and safety requirements.

3. Your examples might include: child observations; work plans/activity plans; summaries of discussions with children; relevant policies and procedures, e.g. equal opportunities, health and safety, etc.

Obtaining resources for play spaces

Every setting should be equipped with play resources appropriate to the age range of the children. You should know how to obtain and/or create the resources needed for a range of play spaces. You may need to work within the budget available for resources and if necessary find alternative ways to obtain or create resources. Children benefit from a wide range of play resources, not just those that are commercially produced. Depending on the setting, you should be able to provide a wide selection of play resources. For example:

* ☆ *Recycled materials* to provide opportunities for children to construct models, etc.
* ☆ *The outdoor environment* to provide opportunities for exploring the natural world, e.g. gardening, visiting local parks and playgrounds.
* ☆ *Natural materials* to provide opportunities for exploring different materials and their properties, e.g. sand, water, cooking ingredients.
* ☆ *Homemade materials* for creative activities, e.g. homemade playdough (encouraging children to make the playdough themselves enriches their play and learning experience).

- ✭ *Clean unwanted clothing* for dressing-up activities (recycling again!), not just commercially produced outfits.
- ✭ *Space* for children's imaginary games that require little or no props.
- ✭ *Commercially produced resources* which are well made, durable and safe for children's use as well as being good value for money, e.g. construction kits and tools, climbing equipment, child-size domestic play equipment. Remember quality not quantity is more important.

Remember to make use of any community resource facilities such as book loans from local libraries (usually free to non-profit organisations) and borrowing play equipment from toy libraries. Contact the local authority or disability charities for information on schemes they may operate for hiring or purchasing specialist play equipment for children with disabilities.

A designated member of staff should have specific responsibility for replenishing supplies of consumables (e.g. pencils, paper and card, paint, cooking ingredients) as necessary. Stock levels should be monitored on a regular basis. Staff and children should know how to use all play resources correctly and safely, with care and respect; and with regard for Health and Safety and waste. Care should be taken to ensure that play resources reflect the cultural and linguistic diversity of the local community, and that all children have equality of access. Visual aids should also be available. For example: videos; maps; posters; pictures; interesting objects or artefacts related to topics or themes; computer software. Display materials for use in play areas and around the setting should also be available (see section on organising classroom resources in Chapter 12).

KEY TASK

1. List the main play resources available in your setting under these headings: consumables; equipment; finance; adult resources.

NVQ LINKS:

Level 3: STL54.2

2. What are your responsibilities for obtaining and/or creating the necessary resources for your setting?

Supporting self-directed play

You should aim to provide minimum intervention in play activities while keeping children safe from harm. You should help to create a play environment that will stimulate self-directed play and provide maximum opportunities for children and/or young people to experience a wide variety of play types. You can enrich their play experiences in the following ways: planning and creating play spaces that meet their play needs and preferences; obtaining and/or creating resources for a range of play spaces; fostering positive attitudes; providing new materials and tools to stimulate their exploration and learning; participating in their play if and when invited.

You should use information on play needs and preferences to plan appropriate play opportunities. You can write down your plans for play opportunities on a planning sheet or in an activity file. Your plans may be brief or detailed depending on the requirements of your setting. Some activities may require more detailed preparation and organisation than others, e.g. arts and crafts, cooking, outings, etc.

A plan for a play activity could include the following:

Title: A brief description of the activity.

1. **When?** Date and time of the activity.

2. **Where?** Where the activity will take place, e.g. indoor play area, outdoor play area, local park or playground.

3. **Why?** Outline why you have selected this particular activity, e.g. identified children's play needs and preferences through research, observation or consultation.

4. **What?** What you need to prepare in advance, e.g. selecting or making appropriate resources; buying ingredients, materials or equipment.

5. **How?** How you will organise the activity. Consider any safety requirements. Think about tidying up after the activity, e.g. encouraging the children to help tidy up.

Evaluate the activity afterwards, e.g. the children's response to the activity, the skills and/or learning demonstrated by the children, the effectiveness of your preparation, organisation and implementation. Make a note of your evaluation on the planning sheet or in the activity file. These notes will prove helpful when planning future play opportunities and for providing information to colleagues at regular meetings.

While careful planning of appropriate play opportunities is important, your planning should be flexible enough to allow for each child's individual interests and for unplanned, spontaneous opportunities for play. For example, an unexpected snowfall can provide a wonderful opportunity to explore and talk about snow as well as enabling the children to express delight and fascination for this type of weather. (There is more about planning activities in Chapter 3.)

EXERCISE: How do you plan for self-directed play in your setting?

Providing appropriate support for self-directed play

You should know how to provide appropriate support for self-directed play. You can provide appropriate types of support for self-directed play in the following ways:

- ✫ Provide flexible planning and minimal adult supervision.
- ✫ Enable children to choose from a broad range of play opportunities and resources.
- ✫ Enable them to choose whether or not they wish to be involved in play activities.
- ✫ Give them freedom to choose how they use the available materials.
- ✫ Provide them with access to a wide range of materials and allow them to determine their own play in their own way.
- ✫ Provide plenty of space for their play activities, especially for physical games and imaginative play.
- ✫ Encourage them to sort out fair ways to take turns on play equipment.
- ✫ Keep the numbers of children in group activities to a reasonable size to enable everyone to enjoy play.
- ✫ Create a stimulating and enjoyable play environment that also maintains their physical safety and emotional well-being.
- ✫ Provide challenging play opportunities to avoid boredom; risk-taking is part of the enjoyment of play.

(Lindon, 2002)

Identifying and responding to play cues

You should know and understand the main stages of the play cycle. The play cycle is the course of play from start to finish, e.g. from the first play cue to completion of play. You should be able to identify when and how to respond to play cues as part of the play cycle.

Play cues are *'facial expressions, language or body language that communicate the child or young person's wish to play or invite others to play'* (SkillsActive, 2004). You should observe children's play and respond appropriately to their play cues.

Child s Play Cue	Playworker's Response
First play cue: child smiles and uses eye contact (facial expression) to indicate wish to play.	Asks the child which particular play activity they want to do. Child chooses an activity and selects own resources.
Second play cue: child makes specific verbal request (language) for adult to join in with the play activity.	Joins in as per the child s request, e.g. having a 'cup of tea' in the playhouse.
Final play cue: child points (body language) to another play activity indicating wish to play something else.	Checks there is space for the child to do the desired play activity. Child selects resources for this activity and new play cycle begins.

Child's Play Cue/Adult's Response

Defining a play frame

A play frame is *'a material or non-material boundary that keeps the play intact'* (SkillsActive, 2004). For example, a material boundary could be an actual physical boundary such as a specific play area, e.g. a play shop; a non-material boundary may be something imaginary such as a 'magic circle'. In a play setting, you must be able to hold children's play frames as necessary, e.g. maintaining a play frame by adopting an appropriate role during children's play such as a customer during shop play.

KEY TASK

1. Describe how you have supported self-directed play using the following types of play spaces: play spaces for physical play; play spaces for affective play; transient play spaces; permanent play spaces.

 **NVQ LINKS:**

Level 3:
STL54.1   STL54.2   STL54.3

2. How have you observed and responded to a child's play cues?
3. Give two examples of how you have held children's play frames.

Helping children and young people to manage risk during play

When working with children and/or young people, you should help them to manage risk during play as appropriate to their ages and levels of development. Children need opportunities to explore and experiment through play and to try out new, exciting play activities. Many play activities have risks especially physical activities such as climbing, exploring and swimming. *'Risky activity, and risk-taking itself, is recognised as an essential part of growing up'* (CAPT, 2002). Always follow the relevant setting policies and procedures, e.g. health and safety policy; risk assessment and risk management procedures.

As children play, they will make mistakes and accidents will happen. By exploring their environment and experimenting with their physical skills and intellectual abilities, children develop confidence and competence in their own abilities. Play spaces and play opportunities should be sufficiently challenging and have different levels of difficulty to enable children to fully explore these challenges. Without these challenges and opportunities to assess risks, children will not develop the survival skills they need later in life (ILAM, 1999).

Seven ways to help children to manage risk during play

You can help children to manage risk during play by doing the following:

1. Assessing and managing the levels of risk in play areas either through supervision or design.
2. Helping individual children to make a realistic assessment of their abilities to avoid them being under- or over-confident.

3. Taking precautions to reduce the severity of injuries if children make inaccurate judgements, e.g. provide appropriate safety surfaces in outdoor play areas to reduce impact of falls.

4. Informing children of the potential dangers of play activities so that they can make their own decisions.

5. Providing opportunities for children to take calculated risks, e.g. challenging climbing frames, adventure playgrounds.

6. Providing appropriate safety information.

7. Consulting and involving the children in developing play activities that are challenging and interesting to them.

 KEY TASK

1. Outline your setting's policies and procedures that are relevant to managing risk during play activities, e.g. health and safety policy; risk assessment and risk management procedures.

 NVQ LINKS:

Level 3: STL54.4

2. List examples of how you help children to manage risk during play according to these policies and procedures *and* the ages/levels of development of the children you work with.

Further reading

Brown, F. (ed.) (2002) *Playwork: theory and practice.* Open University Press.

Bruce, T. (2001) *Helping young children learn through play.* Hodder Arnold.

Dunn, K. *et al.* (2003) *Developing accessible play space: a good practice guide.* ODPM. [Available free online at www.communities.gov.uk.]

Kamen, T. (2005) *The playworker's handbook.* Hodder Arnold.

Kidsactive (2000) *Side by side: guidelines for inclusive play.* Kidsactive.

Lindon, J. (2001) *Understanding children's play.* Nelson Thornes.

National Playing Fields Association, Children's Play Council and Playlink (2000) *Best play: what play provision should do for children.* NPFA. [Available free online at www.ncb.org.uk.]

9 Supporting curriculum delivery

Key points:

* ❋ Understanding pupil development and learning
* ❋ How children think and learn
* ❋ Learning styles
* ❋ Factors affecting learning
* ❋ Curriculum frameworks
* ❋ Curriculum plans
* ❋ Making assessments
* ❋ Using ICT to support teaching and learning.

Understanding pupil development and learning

An understanding of intellectual development is essential for teaching assistants because it helps them to assist the teacher in supporting learning activities through: a well-organised and structured learning environment; careful planning and preparation of learning activities; the provision of appropriate learning resources; effective communication with pupils during learning activities; high adult expectations for learner development; accurate evaluation of learning activities and assessment of pupil abilities.

How children think and learn

Research into how children think and learn has made adults more aware of the need to: observe and assess children's development very carefully; listen to children and the way they express ideas; take account of children's interests and experiences when planning learning opportunities.

General principles of Jean Piaget's cognitive theories

1. Children are *actively* involved in structuring their own cognitive development through exploration of their environment. Children need real objects and 'concrete experiences' to discover things for themselves.

2. The adult's role is to provide children with appropriate experiences in a suitable environment to facilitate the children's instinctive ability to think and learn.

3. Cognitive development occurs in four set stages, which are universal – they apply to all forms of learning and across all cultures. These four stages are: **sensori-motor**; **pre-operations**; **concrete operations**; and **formal operations** (see diagram below).

4. Children will learn only when they are 'ready' for different experiences as determined by their current stage of cognitive development.

5. Children's use of language demonstrates their cognitive achievements, but does not control them. Piaget did not see language and communication as central to children's cognitive development because this development begins at birth before children can comprehend or use words. He *does* see the importance of language at later stages.

6. Children are **egocentric**. They are unable to see or understand another person's viewpoint. This also means they are unable to convey information accurately or effectively to others.

7. Piaget believed that children interact with their environment to actively construct their knowledge and understanding of the world. They do this by relating new information to existing information. Piaget called this interaction **assimilation** – the need for further information; **accommodation** – the need for organised information; **adaptation** – the need for revised/updated information (see second diagram below). All new information has to be built on existing information; there needs to be some connection between them. *Similar* information can be stored as it relates to existing information.

8. Piaget described internal mental processes as schemas and the ways in which they are used when thinking as operations. Mental processes or schemas do not remain static; they continually develop as we acquire new information and extend our understanding of the world.

---

1. Sensori-motor (0–2 years)
- babies and very young children learn through their senses, physical activity and interaction with their immediate environment
- they understand their world in terms of actions.

---

2. Pre-operations (2–7 years)
- young children learn through their experiences with real objects in their immediate environment
- they use symbols (e.g. words and images) to make sense of their world.

---

3. Concrete operations (7–11 years)
- children continue to learn through their experiences with real objects
- they access information (using language) to make sense of their immediate and wider environment.

---

4. Formal operations (11–adult)
- children and adults learn to make use of abstract thinking (e.g. algebra and physics).

Piaget's stages of cognitive development

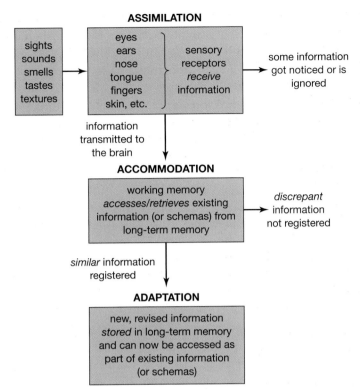

ASSIMILATION

| sights sounds smells tastes textures | → | eyes ears nose tongue fingers skin, etc. | } | sensory receptors *receive* information | → | some information got noticed or is ignored |

information transmitted to the brain ↓

ACCOMMODATION

working memory *accesses/retrieves* existing information (or schemas) from long-term memory

→ *discrepant* information not registered

similar information registered ↓

ADAPTATION

new, revised information *stored* in long-term memory and can now be accessed as part of existing information (or schemas)

Understanding Piaget's ideas of assimilation, accommodation and adaptation

EXERCISE:
1. Make a list of the main points of Piaget's theories of cognitive development.
2. Which points do you think accurately describe children's thinking and learning?
3. Give examples from your experiences of working with pupils.

The learning process: a social constructivist view

The social constructivist view of the learning process takes into account more recent research concerning how children think and learn within the context of home, school and the wider environment. Social constructivism integrates children's cognitive and social development within a useful framework. It moves away from the idea that the development of children's cognitive abilities occurs in stages at particular ages and that adults simply provide the means for this natural process. Rather adults assist children's cognitive development as part of the **social process** of childhood. Age is not the critical factor in cognitive development; assisted learning can and does occur at *any* age. The **key factor** is the learner's *existing* knowledge and/or experience in connection with the *current* problem or learning situation.

Like Piaget, L.S. Vygotsky was concerned with the active process of intellectual development. Vygotsky argued that cognitive development was a matter not just of the maturation of intellectual processes, but of 'active adaptation' to the environment. The interaction *between* the child and *other* people forms the basis of the developing intellectual processes *within* the child. This social interaction enables children to develop the intellectual skills necessary for thought and logical reasoning. Language is the key to this interaction. Through language and communication children learn to think about their world and to modify their actions accordingly.

Vygotsky (and later Bruner) viewed the adult as supporting children's cognitive development within an appropriate framework (see scaffolding below). Adults support children's learning by assisting the children's own efforts and thus enabling children to acquire the necessary skills, knowledge and understanding. As children develop competent skills through this **assisted learning**, the adults gradually decrease their support until the children are able to work independently. With adult assistance young children are able to complete tasks and to solve problems which they would not be able to do on their own. It is important that adults recognise when to provide support towards each child's next step of development and when this support is no longer required. Vygotsky used the idea of the zone of proximal development or area of next development to describe this framework of support for learning. The zone of proximal development can be represented in four stages (Tharp and Gallimore, 1991).

For example, a pupil learning to read may progress in this way:

- ✰ **Stage 1: Assistance from others:** Learns phonic, decoding and comprehension skills with assistance of parents, teachers, nursery nurses and/or teaching assistants.
- ✰ **Stage 2: Self-help:** Sounds out difficult/unfamiliar words, reads aloud to self, lips move during silent reading, etc.
- ✰ **Stage 3: Auto-pilot:** Reads competently using internal prompts.
- ✰ **Stage 4: Relapses to previous stages:** When learning new words, reading complicated texts or learning to read in a different language may require further assistance.

Jerome Bruner (like Vygotsky) emphasises the importance of the adult in supporting children's thinking and learning. Bruner uses the term scaffolding to describe this adult support. Picture a builder using scaffolding to support a house while it is being built. Without the scaffold the house could not be built; but once the house is finished, the scaffolding can be removed. The adult supports the child's learning until they are ready to stand alone. Bruner also emphasises the adult's *skills* of recognising where and when this support is needed and when it should be removed. The structuring of children's learning should be flexible; the adult support or scaffold should not be rigid; it needs to change as the needs of the child change, that is as the child gains knowledge and understanding and/or acquires skills. Bruner believed that any subject can be taught to any child at any age as long as it is presented in an appropriate way. Learning does not occur in pre-determined stages, but is dependent on linking knowledge to children's existing knowledge in a holistic way.

Bruner's *sequence* of cognitive development is divided into three areas:

* ★ **Enactive:** understanding the world through action (relates to Piaget's sensori-motor stage).
* ★ **Iconic:** manipulation of images or 'icons' in child's thinking about the world (corresponds to Piaget's pre-operational stage).
* ★ **Symbolic:** use of language and symbols to make sense of the world (similar to Piaget's operational stage).

Bruner also views language as central to cognitive development and stresses how language is used to represent experiences and how past experience/knowledge is organised through language in ways which make information more accessible.

EXERCISE:
1. Summarise the main points of Vygotsky's and Bruner's theories concerning children's thinking and learning.
2. Think about how these ideas are related to your experiences of working with pupils.

Learning experiences

Every learning experience can be viewed as a journey, travelling along different pathways to reach our destination or learning goal (Drummond, 1994). At different points of a learning experience the learning may be:

* ★ very easy – speeding along a clear motorway
* ★ interesting, but uncertain in parts – taking the scenic route
* ★ very difficult and complicated – stuck in a traffic jam on 'spaghetti junction'
* ★ totally confusing – trying to find the correct exit from a big road traffic island
* ★ completely beyond us – entering a no-through road or going the wrong way down a one-way street.

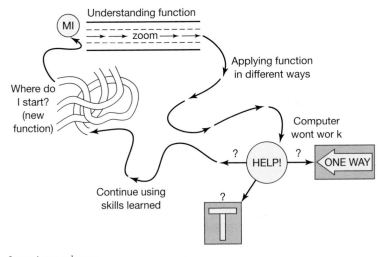

Learning pathways

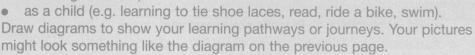

EXERCISE: Think about your own experiences of learning:
- as an adult (e.g. learning to drive, cook, study; becoming a teaching assistant)
- as a child (e.g. learning to tie shoe laces, read, ride a bike, swim).

Draw diagrams to show your learning pathways or journeys. Your pictures might look something like the diagram on the previous page.

Patterns of learning

The experience of learning is a never-ending cycle; learning new skills continues indefinitely. Once one skill is gained in a particular area, further skills can be learned. For example, once pupils have learned basic reading skills, they continue to develop their literacy skills even as adults by: increasing their vocabulary; improving spelling; decoding unfamiliar words; reading and understanding more complex texts.

EXERCISE: Think about the learning experiences of the pupils in your school. Select two pupils and draw diagrams of their learning experiences. Compare them with your own experiences of learning. Are there any similarities or differences?

As well as the circular nature of learning experiences, you may also have noticed the importance of *active participation* in all learning experiences.

Active learning

Active participation is essential in all effective learning experiences. For example, watching someone else use a computer or read a book can only help so much; to develop the relevant skills, pupils need hands-on experience of using computers or handling books. Active learning is an important part of all learning experiences – not just for children but for adults as well. For example, at college or school you may find that learning situations take the form of workshops, group activities and discussions rather than formal lectures. It is essential that pupils become actively involved in the learning process. Learning needs to be practical not theoretical. Pupils need concrete learning experiences, that is, using real objects in a meaningful context. Children (and adults) learn by doing. In all learning situations it is important to provide information in small portions with plenty of discussion and activity breaks to maintain interest and concentration. This is because the average attention span of a child is about 5 to 10 minutes and can be as little as 2 to 3 minutes. Play is an essential part of the active learning process. Through active learning, pupils use play opportunities to encourage and extend the problem-solving abilities that are essential to developing their intellectual processes. Play activities provide informal opportunities for pupils to develop ideas and to understand concepts through active learning and communication (see section on the importance of play in Chapter 8).

Learning styles

Pupils have different ways of processing information. Pupils use the skills of looking, listening or touching in varying amounts depending on their individual learning style. For example, some pupils require visual stimulation; some respond well to verbal instructions while others need more 'hands on' experiences. In addition, different times of the day affect individual levels of concentration; some pupils work better in the morning, others in the afternoon. You need to be aware of the individual learning styles of the pupils you work with in order to plan and provide appropriate learning activities. Recognising learning styles will help you to understand the ways pupils learn and to assist them in achieving educational success.

Visual learners gather information through observation and reading. Pupils with this learning style may find it difficult to concentrate on spoken instructions, but respond well to visual aids such as pictures, diagrams and charts. They tend to visualise ideas and remember the visual details of places and objects they have seen. According to research, about 65% of people have this learning style.

Auditory learners process information by listening carefully and then repeating instructions either out loud or mentally in order to remember what they have learned. Research suggests that about 30% of people use this style of learning. Pupils with this learning style tend to be the talkers as well as the listeners in group and/or class situations and benefit from being able to discuss ideas. Auditory learners can be easily distracted by noise and may concentrate better with background music to disguise potentially disruptive noises.

Kinesthetic learners process information through touch and movement. All young children rely on this learning style to a large extent hence the importance of active learning (see below) especially in the early years. About 5% of people continue to use this style even as adults. Pupils with this learning style will benefit from physical interaction with their environment with plenty of emphasis on learning by doing.

Pupils are not restricted to learning in only one way as they can learn to use different learning styles for different activities within the curriculum. However, research shows that working outside their preferred learning style for extensive periods can be stressful. Providing opportunities for pupils to use their preferred learning style wherever practical increases their chances of educational success (Tobias, 1996).

As well as relying on one particular style of learning, people also tend to use one of two styles of processing information: either analytic or global. **Analytic learners** process information by dividing it into pieces and organising it in a logical manner, e.g. making lists, putting things in order, following clear instructions or rules, completing/handing in work on time. Analytic learners prefer order and a planned, predictable sequence of events or ideas. **Global learners** process information by grouping large pieces of information together and focusing on the main ideas rather than details, e.g. drawing spidergrams, using pictures or key words, ignoring or bending rules including missing deadlines. Global learners prefer spontaneity and activities which allow them creative freedom.

Factors affecting learning

Intellectual development is affected by other factors besides the pupil's chronological age. Factors affecting learning can include: lack of play opportunities; unrewarding learning activities; lack of opportunities to use language and communication skills; inappropriate learning activities; introduction to formal learning situations at too early an age; English as an additional language. Some pupils may not develop their intellectual processes in line with the expected pattern of development for their age due to special needs such as: communication and/or interaction difficulties; learning difficulties; behavioural, social or emotional difficulties (see Chapter 11).

The inability to concentrate, to work independently or to use investigative skills may make it very difficult for some pupils to participate fully in learning activities. This may lead to subsequent learning difficulties in curriculum areas such as English, mathematics, science, technology, and so on. Some pupils may be inaccurately thought to have learning difficulties, when they are really experiencing a lack of appropriate intellectual stimulation. Children with little or no intellectual stimulation cannot develop their own thinking skills or formulate new ideas. It is vital that all pupils have access to a stimulating learning environment that enables them to learn in exciting and challenging ways. Intellectual stimulation through appropriate learning activities allows pupils to develop their intellectual abilities and to fulfil their potential as individuals.

Curriculum frameworks

As appropriate to your particular role, you will need to prepare curriculum plans according to the curriculum frameworks for education for your home country: England, Northern Ireland, Scotland or Wales. For example, in England the curriculum frameworks for education are the Early Years Foundation Stage (0 to 5 years) and the National Curriculum Key Stages 1 to 4 (5 to 16 years).

The Early Years Foundation Stage

Orders and regulations under section 39 of the Childcare Act 2006 will bring the **Early Years Foundation Stage** (EYFS) into force in September 2008. EYFS brings together *Curriculum Guidance for the Foundation Stage* (2000), the *Birth to Three Matters* (2002) framework and the *National Standards for Under 8s Daycare and Childminding* (2003). All early years providers are required to use the EYFS to ensure a coherent and flexible approach to children's care, learning and development that will enable young children to achieve the five *Every Child Matters* outcomes: staying safe; being healthy; enjoying and achieving; making a positive contribution; and achieving economic well-being (see page 116).

The EYFS is based around four themes and each **theme** is linked to an important principle:

- ✰ **A Unique Child:** Every child is a competent learner from birth who can be resilient, capable, confident and self-assured.
- ✰ **Positive Relationships:** Children learn to be strong and independent from a base of loving and secure relationships with parents and/or a key person.
- ✰ **Enabling Environments:** The environment plays a key role in supporting and extending children's development and learning.
- ✰ **Learning and Development:** Children develop and learn in different ways and at different rates and all areas of learning and development are equally important and inter-connected.

(www.standards.dfes.gov.uk/eyfs)

The Childcare Act 2006 provides for the EYFS learning and development requirements to comprise three elements:

- ✰ **The early learning goals:** the knowledge, skills and understanding which young children should have acquired by the end of the academic year in which they reach five years old.
- ✰ **The educational programmes:** the matters, skills and processes which are required to be taught to young children.
- ✰ **The assessment arrangements:** the arrangements for assessing young children to ascertain their achievements (see section below on making assessments).

There are six areas covered by the early learning goals and educational programmes. None of these areas can be delivered in isolation from the others. They are equally important and depend on each other to support a rounded approach to child development. All the areas must be delivered through planned, purposeful play, with a balance of adult-led and child-initiated activities. The six areas of learning and development are:

1. Personal, Social and Emotional Development
2. Communication, Language and Literacy
3. Problem Solving, Reasoning and Numeracy
4. Knowledge and Understanding of the World
5. Physical Development
6. Creative Development.

For more information about the EYFS in England see www.standards.dfes.gov.uk/eyfs. In Wales the framework for early years can be found in *Desirable Outcomes for Children's Learning before Compulsory School Age*. (http://accac.org.uk/uploads/documents/110.pdf). There is currently no framework for babies and children under three in Wales. In Scotland the framework for under-threes, is *Birth to three: supporting our youngest children* (**www.ltscotland.org.uk/earlyyears/ images/birth2three_tcm4-161671.pdf**). There is no legally established early years curriculum in Scotland but the Scottish Executive Education Department (SEED) provides guidelines for schools, e.g. *A Curriculum Framework for Children 3 to 5* (**www.ltscotland.org.uk/earlyyears/images/CF3to5_tcm4-115469.pdf**). The Scottish curriculum is currently going through the national review, *A Curriculum for Excellence*, with the aim of developing a streamlined curriculum for 3 to 18 year olds. In Northern Ireland the relevant curriculum framework is *Curricular Guidance for Pre-School Education* (**www.deni.gov.uk/pre_school_guidance_pdf**). There is currently no framework for babies and children under three in Northern Ireland.

The National Curriculum

The National Curriculum sets out the statutory requirements for the knowledge and skills that every child is expected to learn in schools. The National Curriculum framework enables teachers to provide all school-aged children with challenging learning experiences, taught in ways that are both balanced and manageable. The National Curriculum sets out the standards to be used to measure the progress and performance of pupils in each subject to help teachers plan and implement learning activities that meet the individual learning needs of pupils.

The National Curriculum applies to children of compulsory school age in schools in England and Wales. The National Curriculum sets out what pupils should study, what they should be taught and the standards that they should achieve. It is divided into Key Stages:

- ✵ **Key Stage 1:** 5 to 7 year olds (Year groups: 1 and 2)
- ✵ **Key Stage 2:** 7 to 11 year olds (Year groups: 3, 4, 5 and 6)
- ✵ **Key Stage 3:** 11 to 14 year olds (Year groups: 7, 8 and 9)
- ✵ **Key Stage 4:** 14 to 16 year olds (Year groups: 10 and 11)

The National Curriculum's subjects: The National Curriculum consists of three **core subjects**: English; mathematics; science. Plus six **foundation subjects**: information and communication technology (ICT); design and technology; history; geography; art and design; music; physical education (PE).

In addition to these subjects the National Curriculum in secondary schools includes citizenship and modern foreign languages. The Key Stage 4 curriculum has changed following consultation on the White Paper, *14–19: Opportunity and excellence*. The main changes include: a new science programme; design and technology and a modern foreign language are no longer compulsory at Key Stage 4; schools must make entitlement curriculum areas (e.g. the arts, design and technology, the humanities and modern foreign languages) available to all students who wish to study them; a new statutory requirement for work-related learning and a non-statutory framework setting out the minimum experience that schools should provide for work-related learning. See: *Changes to the Key Stage 4 curriculum: guidance for implementation from September 2004* (**www.nc.uk.net/nc_resources/html/ks4_changes.pdf**).

There is also a non-statutory framework for personal, social and health education (PSHE). religious education (RE) is outside the National Curriculum framework but all schools must make provision for RE using an accredited scheme of work. Each Key Stage and subject area of the National Curriculum has: programmes of study; attainment targets and level descriptions.

Programmes of study: Programmes of study give detailed information about what pupils should be taught in each subject at every Key Stage. The programmes of study provide the framework for planning schemes of work in schools. The National Literacy and Numeracy Strategies, as well as examples of schemes of work, demonstrate how the programmes of study and attainment targets can become practical plans for effective teaching and learning.

Attainment targets and level descriptions: Each attainment target defines the 'knowledge, skills and understanding which pupils of different abilities and maturities are expected to have by the end of each Key Stage' (Education Act 1996, section 353a). Except for citizenship, attainment targets contain nine level descriptions of increasing difficulty including a description for exceptional pupil performance. Each description explains the types and range of pupil performance at that particular level. These descriptions form the criteria for assessments of pupils' performance at the end of each Key Stage except Key Stage 4.

You should know the relevant National Curriculum guidelines for teaching and learning relevant to the pupils you work with. In England the relevant framework is: *National Curriculum in England* – see the National Curriculum online website at **www.nc.uk.net** and the National Curriculum documents available in schools. In Wales the relevant framework is the *National Curriculum in Wales* – see the Department of Education, Lifelong Learning and Skills website at **http://old.accac.org.uk/index_eng.php**. In Scotland there is no legally established National Curriculum but the Scottish Executive Education Department provides guidelines for schools, e.g. the *5–14 National Guidelines* – see Learning and Teaching Scotland Online Service at **www.ltscotland.org.uk**. The Scottish curriculum is currently going through a national review called A *Curriculum for Excellence* with the aim of developing a streamlined curriculum for 3 to18 year olds and implementing new approaches to assessment. The *Northern Ireland Curriculum* (for pupils aged 4 to 16) is the relevant curriculum for those working in schools in Northern Ireland – see Department of Education, Northern Ireland website at **www.deni.gov.uk**.

EXERCISE: What is the curriculum framework for the pupils you work with?

Curriculum plans

Schools should be able to explain their approach to the curriculum and to show how they meet the statutory requirements for all learners, including any variations to meet the needs of individual pupils. Detailed information about a school's curriculum plans can be found in: policy statements for the whole curriculum and for each subject of the curriculum; schemes of work and teaching plans for pupils in each Key Stage; class or group timetables; Individual Education Plans.

Developing curriculum plans involves planning learning activities that will provide all pupils with appropriate opportunities to learn, which reflect the range of needs, interests and the past achievements of pupils in each year group at each Key Stage.

Curriculum plans include:

- ✮ **Policy statements** showing the balance between different parts of the curriculum at each Key Stage.
- ✮ **Practical guidelines** for staff assisting the delivery of each curriculum subject, e.g. general information about resources and important teaching points.
- ✮ **Long-term plans** showing the content and skills in the programmes of study for every subject at each Key Stage and how these are covered, including links between subjects as well as progression, consolidation and diversification for pupils across units (e.g. between units in the DfES/QCA schemes of work).
- ✮ **Medium-term plans** defining the intended learning outcomes for units of work including information on learning activities, recording and assessment methods.
- ✮ **Short-term plans** setting out detailed information on learning activities for pupils in each class on a weekly and daily basis, including lesson plans and/or activity plans with details of specific targets, organisation, resources and strategies to support learning.

(QCA, 2001a)

Depending on your role in the school, you will be involved in the planning and preparation of schemes of work and teaching plans by having regular planning meetings with colleagues, e.g. weekly, monthly, once a term or half-term. You will need to prepare plans which take into account the pattern of pupil attendance (e.g. part-time or full-time) and their need for a balanced programme of activities.

Long-term plans

Long-term plans are usually drawn up in preparation for the year ahead. A long-term plan should provide an overview of the range of learning opportunities for pupils and should include the content and skills in each curriculum area or subject. For example: the aspects of learning within the six areas of learning in The Foundation Stage or the Programmes of study for every subject at each Key Stage of the National Curriculum.

Long-term plans may include an **overall curriculum plan** (usually linked to a topic or theme) demonstrating how the school intends to encourage and extend the learning of pupils within a curriculum framework, e.g. the National Curriculum. Long-term plans should include links between subjects/areas of learning as well as progression, consolidation and diversification for pupils (e.g. between units in the DfES/QCA schemes of work). Long-term plans should show progression for learning and development, e.g. from year group to year group within each Key Stage.

Many schools (especially in the early years) use a central topic or theme to link teaching and learning across the curriculum. A **topic web** can be a useful starting point for schemes of work and activity/lesson plans. Using a topic web

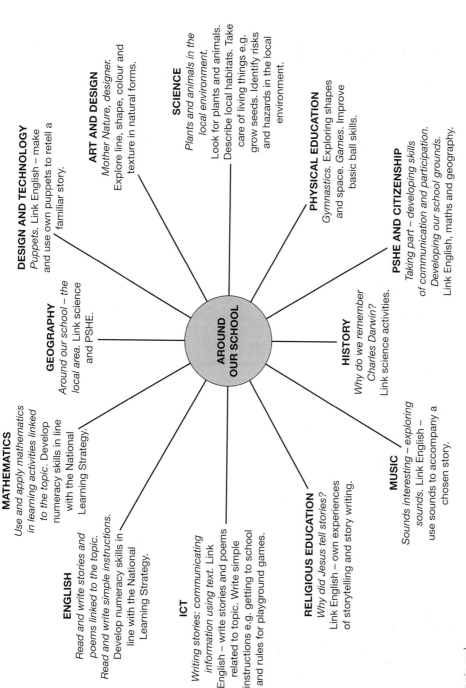

Topic web

can help ensure that each area of the curriculum is covered and emphasises an integrated approach to curriculum planning with play at the heart of learning and development.

Medium-term plans

Medium-term plans are used to bridge the gap between the outline of the long-term plan and detailed short-term plans. Medium-term plans define the intended learning outcomes for areas of learning or units of work including information on learning activities, recording and assessment methods. For example, the intentions for learning for each school term for each year group in a Key Stage. Medium-term plans involve the detailed planning and preparation of **schemes of work** that are central to the effective delivery of the curriculum and to the provision of appropriate support for learning. These plans enable staff to devise and implement learning activities in their short-term planning that promote progress and achievement for all pupils. Staff may need to adjust the balance in the curriculum to focus on particular areas of learning so that their planning takes account of group or Individual Education Plans.

Short-term plans

Short-term plans should be based on the long-term plan and medium-term plans as well as ongoing observations and assessments of pupils including discussions with colleagues and parents. Staff should use this information to plan appropriate activities and experiences for pupils.

Short-term plans provide details of learning activities on a weekly, daily and lesson-by-lesson basis. Planning appropriate learning activities involves: identifying the intended learning outcomes that promote inclusion, participation and achievement for all pupils; using information about pupil interests, skills and prior achievements to structure the content and progress of activities/lessons; taking into account individual learning and development needs including different learning styles (see page 203); including targets from Individual Education Plans for pupils with special educational needs; defining the roles and responsibilities of the staff involved; insuring that adequate and appropriate resources are available; using ICT to support children's learning and development.

KEY TASK

Provide examples of the planning you and the teacher(s) use within the curriculum framework applicable to the pupils in your school. Include information on:

 NVQ LINKS:

Level 2:
STL1.1   STL2.4

Level 3:
STL18.1   STL23.1   STL24.1
STL27.1   STL34.1   STL50.2

- long-term plans, e.g. overall curriculum plan, topic web
- medium-term plans, e.g. schemes of work, timetables
- short-term plans, e.g. activity plans, lesson plans.

Making assessments

As well as being able to observe children's development you also need to help the teacher assess children's development based on observational findings and other reliable information from pupils, parents, carers, colleagues and other appropriate adults. You must be able to make formative and summative assessments (see below) and record your assessments as appropriate to the policies and procedures of your school. You should share your findings with pupils and their parents as appropriate to your role. You should also refer any concerns about pupils to the teacher, senior colleagues and/or relevant external agencies when required. Always remember to follow the school's confidentiality and record-keeping requirements.

Formative assessments are initial and on-going assessments. Formative assessments identify future targets for the individual and groups as appropriate to the ages, developmental needs and abilities of pupils and the requirements of the school. Formative assessments are continuous and inform planning provision to promote children's development and learning. Examples of formative assessments include: pupil observations; tick charts/lists; reading records; maths records; daily target records for pupils with Individual Education Plans.

Summative assessments are assessments that summarise findings. Summative assessments involve more formal monitoring of pupil progress. Summative assessments should be used appropriately and allow judgements to be made about each pupil's achievement. Summative assessments are usually in the form of criterion-based tests or tasks. Examples of summative assessments include: Foundation Stage Profile; Standard Assessment Tasks (SATs); teacher assessments; annual school reports; reviews of pupils with special educational needs. (See also the section on providing information on pupil progress and responses in Chapter 1.)

The Early Years Foundation Stage Profile

The Practice Guidance for the Early Years Foundation Stage provides detailed formative assessment suggestions in the 'Look, listen and note' sections of the areas of learning and development. Early years practitioners should: make systematic observations and assessments of each child's achievements, interests and learning styles; use these observations and assessments to identify learning priorities and plan relevant and motivating learning experiences for each child; match their observations to the expectations of the early learning goals.

The EYFS Profile is a way of summing up each child's development and learning achievements at the end of the EYFS. It is based on practitioners' ongoing observation and assessments in all six areas of learning and development. Each child's level of development must be recorded against the 13 assessment scales derived from the early learning goals. Judgements against these scales, which are set out in Appendix 1 of the *Statutory Framework for the Early Years Foundation Stage*, should be made from observation of consistent and independent behaviour, predominantly children's self-initiated activities (**www.standards.dfes.gov.uk/eyfs**).

National Curriculum assessment

Pupils are assessed by National Curriculum tests, commonly known as standard assessment tasks or SATs, at the end of each Key Stage:

- ✵ Key Stage 1 tests in English and mathematics are taken at age 7 (Year 2)
- ✵ Key Stage 2 tests in English, mathematics and science are taken at age 11 (Year 6)
- ✵ Key Stage 3 tests in English, mathematics and science are taken at age 14 (Year 9)
- ✵ Key Stage 4 is assessed by GCSE levels of achievement at age 16 (Year 11).

In addition to the National Curriculum tests, formal teacher assessments are used to measure each pupil's progress. Teacher assessments judge children's performance over a longer period. Teacher assessment is an essential element of the National Curriculum assessment process. The standard assessment tasks give a 'snapshot' of each pupil's level of attainment at the end of the Key Stage. Teacher assessment covers the full scope of the Programmes of study as demonstrated by each pupil's performance in a wide range of learning activities in the classroom. Teacher assessment also includes information about pupil performance and attainment gained through discussion and observation. The results from teacher assessment are reported along with the results for the standard assessment tasks. Both national and teacher assessment have equal standing and provide a balanced view of each pupil's attainment (QCA/DfES, 2002).

In Northern Ireland, Statutory Assessment arrangements (under the 1989 Education Reform Order) support the Northern Ireland Curriculum and include a 'snapshot' of each pupil's performance at three fixed points: age 8 (Year 4 to the end of Key Stage 1); age 11 (Year 7 to the end of Key Stage 2) and age 14 (Year 10 to the end of Key Stage 3) (see www.deni.gov.uk).

For curriculum assessment guidelines in Scotland see *Promoting Learning: Assessing Children's Progress 3 to 5 and Curriculum and Assessment in Scotland, National Guidelines: Assessment 5–14* (see www.ltscotland.org.uk).

Examples of statutory assessment:

- ✵ **Early Years Foundation Stage Profile:** EYFS Profiles should be completed in accordance with advice and support from the local education authority.
- ✵ **Standard assessment tasks** (SATs) in English and mathematics at Key Stage 1 and English, mathematics and science at Key Stages 2 and 3; these must be administered in accordance with the instructions from QCA.
- ✵ **For each pupil in the final year of each Key Stage, a teacher assessment** must be made of the level achieved in each of the attainment targets in English, mathematics and science.
- ✵ **Teacher assessments in all applicable attainment targets** must be made continuously throughout all Key Stages.
- ✵ **Differentiation:** Assessment activities should be differentiated to ensure all pupils have access to the task. Pupils may be assessed orally if they are unable to produce a piece of written work.
- ✵ **Annual school reports** (see below).

Examples of internal assessment:

- ☆ **Teacher assessments:** Teacher assessments should be made systematically and continuously throughout each Key Stage. A variety of assessment techniques should be used to give all pupils the opportunity to demonstrate what they know, understand or can do. Teacher assessments should be carried out as part of normal classroom activities, using both formal and informal assessment opportunities. Results of assessments in core subjects will be recorded on individual record sheets.

- ☆ **Record folders:** For example, literacy sheets including reading records; numeracy sheets; any on-going records; handwritten notes, e.g. pupils causing concern or needing extra challenges when measured against learning objectives.

- ☆ **Records of achievements:** For example, commendations; certificates; samples of work including a piece of writing reflecting progress over half a term related to the National Literacy Strategy objectives (six pieces per year).

KEY TASK

1. What are the assessment requirements of the curriculum framework applicable to the pupils you work with in school?

2. What are your role and responsibilities in the assessment process?

NVQ LINKS:

Level 2:

STL1.3	STL4.4	STL9.1
STL9.2	STL14.3	

Level 3:

STL18.1	STL20.4	STL23.3
STL24.2	STL27.3	STL29.1
STL30.1	STL30.2	STL36.1
STL55.1	STL55.2	STL60.2

School reports

In education settings it is a legal requirement that parents receive a written report at least once a year detailing the progress of their children in the National Curriculum subjects plus RE. General comments should also be made concerning the child's general progress and behaviour along with other achievements in the school including extra-curricular activities. All relevant personnel should be encouraged to contribute to these reports. School reports also contain teacher assessment and test level or examination results at the end of each Key Stage according to current statutory requirements. Each report must also detail the number of authorised and unauthorised absences since the last report.

A pupil's annual report should:

- ☆ be written clearly and concisely with out too much jargon
- ☆ summarise the pupil's performance since the last report

- ☆ outline the pupil's level of attainment in the National Curriculum subjects. National Curriculum levels of attainment are required only in the core subjects in Years 2, 6 and 9. However, parents are informed if their child is working below, at or above National Curriculum levels in the remaining year groups. For pupils in Key Stage 4, the school report will outline the pupil's expected GCSE results (Year 10) and actual GCSE results (Year 11)
- ☆ set out what the pupil has actually learned not just what they have been taught during the school year
- ☆ highlight positive achievements and progress made by the pupil
- ☆ identify the pupil's weaknesses and suggests positive future action
- ☆ set realistic targets to motivate the pupil for the coming school year.

Reports are usually given to parents in July and staff should be available to discuss pupil reports by appointment at a special parents' evening arranged for this purpose. Parents should be invited to write comments about their children's reports on a separate slip that is returned to and kept by the school along with a copy of each report.

EXERCISE:
1. Outline your school's policy and procedures for reporting pupil progress to their parents.
2. What are your responsibilities for reporting pupil progress to their parents?

Using ICT to support teaching and learning

In today's technological society, information and communication technology (ICT) is an increasingly important part of the school curriculum. As a teaching assistant, you may use ICT to support teaching and learning in the classroom. When supporting classroom use of ICT equipment, you should ensure the safe and correct use of ICT equipment by yourself and others. Supporting the use of ICT equipment involves: following the correct operating procedures and routines; following the school's policy for using ICT in the school; helping pupils to develop a range of ICT skills including competence and independence when using ICT equipment; checking that equipment is being used correctly and is in safe working order; reporting any faults to the appropriate person; ensuring that equipment is left safe and secure after use.

The provision of ICT equipment in school

There should be a wide range of ICT equipment available within the school. Computer hardware includes laptops, notebooks, PDAs, personal computers, monitors and keyboards. Computer accessories or peripherals include modems links, printers, scanners, adapted keyboards, computer-activated toys, concept keyboards, touch screens, digital camera and digital projector. Computer software packages include CD-ROMs, 'paint' programs, presentation programs, data-handling programs and word-processing programs. ICT equipment also includes electronic communication systems, interactive whiteboards, overhead projector (OHP), television and radio, recording and playback equipment, e.g. audio cassette/CD and video/DVD players and recorders.

The location of ICT equipment

Each classroom may have a small number of computers with appropriate peripherals and the school should provide pupils with access to up-to-date computer systems that are connected to the Internet (used under strict supervision – see below). In addition to using the computers in their own classrooms, pupils may have regular timetabled access to an ICT suite. Pupils may also have access to computers in the library or learning support base to help them complete coursework, projects and homework; these facilities may be available before/after school and/or during lunchtimes. This can be very useful for pupils who have no access to computers at home or pupils who need additional support to develop their ICT skills.

The school may have a designated television room or each Key Stage may have a portable television and video/DVD unit. Staff usually book the use of the television unit or room in advance, using a special timetable located in the relevant Key Stage staffroom. Every classroom will usually have its own cassette/CD player. A list of the television and radio programmes currently recorded by the school should be available from the ICT co-ordinator. Requests for other programmes to be recorded should be submitted in writing to the ICT co-ordinator.

EXERCISE:
1. Find out what ICT equipment is available for use in your school.
2. Where is ICT equipment kept in your school?

Following operating procedures and safety requirements

You should know the operating procedures and safety requirements of the school before using any equipment. Ensure you have copies of the school's policies and procedures for dealing with ICT equipment. You may already be familiar with some ICT equipment which you have at home except perhaps for the OHP. You should still check that the school equipment is similar, e.g. switches may be in different places or the sequence of operation may be different. You must always use the appropriate consumables as cheap tape or paper for some machines can be damaging. You must follow the setting up and operating instructions as indicated for the machine you are using as some actions can damage equipment. For example, an OHP should not be moved until the bulb cools down as this will shorten the life of the bulb or cause it to explode (Watkinson, 2003: p.125). (See section on safety checks in the learning environment in Chapter 2.)

The school policy for use of ICT in school

The school should have a policy for use of ICT in school including virus controls (to protect computer systems and files from viruses that can corrupt or destroy important information) and access to the Internet (e.g. software filters to restrict access to inappropriate websites). This should include guidelines on preventing access to unsuitable material via the Internet and maintaining the safety of pupils who access the Internet.

As schools develop intranets and provide access to them for staff and pupils both in school and at home, there is a need to ensure that the school's system is safe and that visitors can only access information appropriate for their use. It is essential that schools have a firewall and/or password-protected system to prevent pupils and others from accessing personal or financial information. The school should have an Acceptable Use Policy that is regularly updated to take account of emerging technologies. The school should send information to parents regarding ICT use in the school. Pupils and parents (where appropriate) should give their consent for pupils to use the Internet in school. The school should take reasonable measures to monitor the use of emails by pupils and staff (Becta, 2004: p.7).

Supporting the development of ICT skills in pupils

Pupils need to be able to use ICT to support their learning across all areas of the National Curriculum. Developing ICT skills helps prepare pupils for the world, which is rapidly being transformed by technology. They need to learn the ICT skills necessary for work and everyday life, e.g. using the Internet and email or computer programs for business or home.

Pupils use ICT in school to: access information; develop their ideas; communicate with others; work together to solve problems. At primary school pupils will learn how to control a computer including using a computer for word-processing, developing pictures using 'paint' software, making tables or graphs, and accessing information via the Internet. Once pupils leave secondary school they will have used computers throughout their school career in various ways including using the Internet and email, digital cameras and scanners, recording equipment as well as computer software. The majority of pupils will have reached a standard equivalent to GCSE and many will have taken and passed a GCSE in ICT.

ICT not only includes computers but also extends to the whole range of audio-visual aids, including audiotape, video film/DVDs and educational broadcasts. ICT is, of course, more than a teaching tool. For many pupils with special educational needs it is an essential communication aid, e.g. Dictaphone, specially adapted computers.

ICT skills in primary schools

In **Key Stage 1** pupils learn how to use ICT to find out information, then to share and exchange information. Pupils become familiar with some computer hardware and software, e.g. learning how to use a word-processor and 'paint' software. They store information on computers, present it in different ways, and talk about how ICT can be used both in and out of school. By about age 7 years, most pupils can be expected to: use ICT to handle information in different ways, including gathering it, organising it, storing it and presenting it to others; start to feel comfortable using computer software in their everyday work, e.g. writing and modifying their class work using a word-processor or other computer packages and make use of graphics and sound; use programmable toys, putting together computerised instructions in the right order; explore what happens using ICT (DfEE, 2000a).

In **Key Stage 2** pupils use a range of ICT tools and information sources, such as computer software and the Internet, to support their work in other subjects. Pupils develop research and communication skills. They learn that information needs to be accurate and relevant and that information on the Internet may sometimes be neither. They are taught how to check the quality of information, learning how to filter good information from bad and how to present information in a way that suits the needs of their audience. Pupils also explore and compare the different ways ICT is used in and out of school. By about age 11 years, most pupils can be expected to: use ICT to present information and share ideas in different ways, including using email; check the reliability of information; think carefully about their audience when presenting and communicating information; write and test simple computer programs to control and monitor events (for example, children might create programs that monitor temperature change, or switch on a light bulb when light levels drop below a certain point); use simulation software and spreadsheets to test theories and explore patterns in data (DfEE, 2000a).

ICT skills in secondary schools

In **Key Stage 3** pupils develop skills and confidence to help them use new technology and information sources independently. Pupils learn how to search for information more thoroughly, accessing the right kind of information for their work and checking its accuracy. Pupils use new technology to record and test data in different ways and to present information in a way that meets the needs of their audience, e.g. on the web or through video conferencing. They think critically about their use of ICT, judging when it has only a limited use. By about age 14 years, most pupils can be expected to: use information from a range of sources to improve their work; improve and develop their work and ideas; use ICT to present ideas in different ways to suit different audiences; make up sequences of computerised instructions to carry out different tasks, e.g. to control the movement of automatic doors or the temperature in greenhouses; use models to make predictions, and test these predictions to check their accuracy, for example, pupils might use spreadsheets to model the running of a school tuck shop at a charity event, or use simulation software to model more complicated activities, such as scientific experiments; and discuss the impact of ICT on themselves and society (DfEE, 2000b).

During **Key Stage 4** – pupils become more responsible for choosing and using ICT tools and information sources. They use a wide range of ICT applications confidently and effectively, and are able to work independently much of the time. They choose and design ICT systems to suit particular needs and may design and implement systems for other people to use. They work with others to carry out and evaluate their work (www.nc.uk.net).

You can find out more about the ICT requirements in the Programmes of study for the Key Stage(s) for the pupils you work with – see the National Curriculum documents available in the school or the National Curriculum online website at www.nc.uk.net.

KEY TASK

1. Observe a pupil during an activity involving the use of ICT skills.

2. In your assessment include information on the following:
   - Did the pupil achieve the learning objectives set? If not, why not?
   - Were the learning objectives too easy or too hard for the pupil?
   - Which ICT skills were demonstrated by the pupil?
   - How did any staff involvement affect the pupil's achievement?

3. Include a copy of any observation and assessment sheets used, the teacher's activity plan with learning objectives for the pupil(s) and an example of the work completed by the pupil demonstrating their ICT skills, e.g. print out of work or CD with saved work.

NVQ LINKS:

Level 2:

STL1.3	STL7.2	STL8.2
STL9.1	STL9.2	

Level 3:

STL18.1	STL18.2	STL8.2
STL23.3	STL24.2	STL27.3
STL28.3	STL29.1	

Pupil demonstrating ICT skills

Promoting independence in the use of ICT

The organisation of ICT equipment is an important consideration. For example, to encourage independent learning, classroom resources should be organised in ways that allow pupils to locate the learning materials they need and to put them away afterwards. Learning materials should be clearly labelled and stored where they are accessible to the pupils. You need to arrange with the teacher the strategies and resources to be used to promote independent learning.

Once pupils have been supported in developing their research skills and are familiar with the ways in which information can be retrieved from the Internet or a CD-ROM, many will be able to work in quite an independent way to access and retrieve the information they are seeking. Your role may change so that you question the pupils, offer them opinions on their work and give them new challenges (Becta, 2006).

Ten ways to promote independence in the use of ICT equipment by pupils

1. Encourage pupils to find out about different ICT equipment and their uses, e.g. photocopier, digital camera, answer machine, scanner, walkie-talkies.

2. Use ICT equipment to stimulate interest and prompt discussion, e.g. display photographs taken with a digital camera; make a slide show of photographs.

3. Encourage pupils to use the ICT equipment available as independently as possible, e.g. using a digital camera to take photographs, opening image on computer and printing out.

4. Demonstrate how to use a paint program and encourage pupils to create their own pictures using it.

5. Encourage pupils to investigate moving a programmable toy including using the language of direction – forwards, backwards and turn.

6. Provide opportunities for pupils to explore the functions of an electronic musical keyboard.

7. Demonstrate how to use a cassette player or CD player so that pupils can listen to music or talking books by themselves.

8. Demonstrate how to use interactive books on the computer and provide opportunities for pupils to explore these independently.

9. Provide opportunities for pupils to use computer software in their everyday work, e.g. use a word-processing or presentational program to present their work.

10. Use ICT as communication aids for pupils, e.g. computers and adapted keyboards or concept keyboards for pupils with special needs.

⬤ KEY TASK

1. Plan an activity to encourage a pupil to work more independently using ICT skills. Include the following: a description of the activity; the learning objectives; the organisation and resources required; your role in supporting the pupil. You could use your observation on page 218 as the starting point for the activity.

2. If possible, ask the class teacher for permission to implement the activity. Evaluate the activity afterwards.

 NVQ LINKS:

Level 2:

STL1.1	STL1.2	STL1.3	STL2.4
STL4.1	STL4.3	STL6.1 (literacy)	
STL6.2 (numeracy)	STL7.1	STL7.2
STL8.1	STL8.2	STL9.1	STL9.2

Level 3:

STL18.1	STL18.2	STL20.1	STL20.2
STL8.1	STL8.2	STL23.1	STL23.2
STL23.3	STL24.1	STL24.2	STL25.1
STL25.2	STL25.3 (literacy)	STL26.1
STL26.2 (numeracy)	STL27.1	STL27.2
STL27.3 (early years)		

Further reading

Dean, J. (2005) *The teaching assistant's guide to primary education.* Routledge Falmer.

DfES (2005) *Working together: teaching assistants and assessment for learning.* DfES.

DfES (2007) *Primary and secondary national strategies: pedagogy and personalisation.* DfES.

[Note: the DfES publications are available free online at www.standards.dfes.gov.uk.]

Dupree, J. (2005) *Help students improve their study skills: a handbook for teaching assistants in secondary schools.* David Fulton Publishers Ltd.

Galloway, J. (2004) *ICT for teaching assistants.* David Fulton Publishers Ltd.

Hutchin, V. (2007) *Supporting every child's learning across the early years foundation stage.* Hodder Murray.

Kamen, T. (2000) *Psychology for childhood studies.* Hodder Arnold.

Lindon, J. (2005) *Understanding child development: linking theory and practice.* Hodder Arnold.

10 Supporting literacy and numeracy activities

Key points:

* National frameworks and curriculum guidelines for English
* Developing literacy skills
* Resources to support literacy development
* The teaching assistant's role in supporting literacy skills
* Supporting pupils with special literacy and/or language needs
* National frameworks and curriculum guidelines for mathematics
* Developing numeracy skills
* Resources to support numeracy development
* The teaching assistant's role in supporting numeracy skills
* Supporting pupils with special numeracy needs
* Enabling pupils to access the wider curriculum.

National frameworks and curriculum guidelines for English

You should know the relevant national regulatory frameworks and curriculum guidelines for teaching English (or Welsh) and mathematics relevant to the pupils you work with (information about curriculum frameworks is in Chapter 9).

The Primary Framework for literacy and mathematics

In October 2006 the *Primary Framework for literacy and mathematics* replaced *The National Literacy Strategy Framework for Teaching YR to Y6 (1998)* and *The National Numeracy Strategy for Teaching Reception to Y6 (1999)*, which both apply to pupils aged 3 to 11 years. The renewed Framework builds on the learning that has taken place since the original Frameworks for teaching literacy and mathematics were introduced in 1998 and 1999.

The renewed literacy and mathematics Frameworks are different from the 1998/1999 Frameworks in the following ways: electronic versions; and simplified learning objectives. The online version of the *Primary Framework for literacy and mathematics* can be accessed at **www.standards.dfes.gov.uk/ primaryframeworks**. The **electronic Framework** provides a resource that will be added to and expanded with additional support and material as the Framework project develops. This will include any necessary revisions to the Early Years elements following the EYFS consultation (DfES, 2006b). Simplified **learning objectives** give a broad overview of the literacy and mathematics curriculum in the primary phase. The learning objectives are aligned to 12 strands (literacy) and 7 strands (mathematics) to demonstrate progression in each strand. These strands link directly to the Early Learning Goals and aspects of English in the National Curriculum. Covering the learning objectives will allow children to reach the Early Learning Goals for Communication, Language and Literacy, and Mathematics, and the appropriate National Curriculum levels for Key Stages 1 and 2. The learning objectives will be taught through the full range of texts described in the National Curriculum for English and mathematics. The **strands** are as follows:

ENGLISH (12 STRANDS)	MATHEMATICS (7 STRANDS)
Speak and listen for a wide range of purposes in different contexts	1. Using and applying mathematics
	2. Counting and understanding number
1. Speaking	3. Knowing and using number facts
2. Listening and responding	4. Calculating
3. Group discussion and interaction	5. Understanding shape
4. Drama	6. Measuring
Read and write for a range of purposes on paper and on screen	7. Handling data
5. Word recognition: decoding (reading) and encoding (spelling)	
6. Word structure and spelling	
7. Understanding and interpreting texts	
8. Engaging and responding to texts	
9. Creating and shaping texts	
10. Text structure and organisation	
11. Sentence structure and punctuation	
12. Presentation	

(DfES, 2006b)

The literacy hour

Pupils have daily lessons for literacy where they are taught the knowledge, skills and understanding set out in the National Curriculum for English. The guidance in the renewed Framework still places emphasis on carefully planned, purposeful, well-directed teaching and learning. When the literacy framework was first published the context demanded that attention was given to the structure and organisation of the lesson. Now the challenge is about improving and refining what is in place. The literacy hour has been successful in structuring the pace of learning and planning for progression through Key Stages 1 and 2. The literacy hour provides a structure for teaching in Key Stages 1 and 2 which can be adapted and revised to be sufficiently flexible to meet the learning needs of all pupils. The daily literacy hour may sometimes be planned as individual lessons. The renewed Framework promotes planning across a sequence of lessons that offers pupils continuity with a blend of approaches that sustain the challenge and maintain an interest in learning (DfES, 2006b).

The Secondary National Strategy Key Stage 3 and Key Stage 4

Key Stage 3 is a crucial point in a pupil's education as evidence indicates that if pupils perform well in the National Curriculum tests at age 14, they will achieve success in their GCSEs. Equipping pupils with effective literacy skills is also the key to raising standards across all curriculum subject areas and to preparing pupils for adult life. *The Framework for teaching English: Years 7, 8 and 9* aims to improve the achievements of 11 to 14 year old pupils. The objectives for Years 7, 8 and 9 provide a framework for progression and cover all aspects of the National Curriculum for English (see: **www.standards.dfes.gov.uk/keystage3**). The Secondary National Strategy Key Stage 4 provides detailed information on raising standards in GCSE including guidelines on improving the planning and teaching of English at Key Stage 4 (see **www.standards.dfes.gov.uk/keystage4**). The Key Stage 3 Framework and the Key Stage 4 guidelines are based on the Programmes of study for English in the revised National Curriculum 2000.

> EXERCISE: What are the national frameworks and curriculum guidelines for teaching English (and Welsh where applicable) relevant to your school?

National Curriculum targets for English

During **Key Stage 1** pupils learn how to express their ideas and experiences clearly and creatively using spoken and written forms of language. Pupils listen to and read stories, poems and rhymes from all over the world as well as using books to discover new information.

During **Key Stage 2** pupils learn to listen to and discuss the ideas of others in addition to presenting their own ideas. Pupils read for pleasure and to discover new information as well as being able to discuss their opinions about what they have read. Pupils should now be able to put their thoughts into writing more easily due to increased understanding of language structure, spelling and punctuation.

During **Key Stage 3** pupils should continue to extend the effective use of the four key English skills by speaking clearly, listening closely, reading carefully and writing fluently. These skills will help pupils to express themselves creatively and increase their confidence about speaking in public and writing for others. Pupils should read classic and contemporary prose and poetry from around the world, examining how writers use language and considering the social/moral issues raised.

During **Key Stage 4** pupils learn to use language confidently, both in their academic studies and for the world beyond school. Pupils use and analyse complex features of language; they are keen readers who can read many kinds of text and make articulate and perceptive comments about them. (For detailed information on the targets for English in all Key Stages see the National Curriculum online: **www.nc.uk.net**.)

KEY TASK

Observe a pupil during a literacy activity in Key Stage 1, 2, 3 or 4. Then answer these questions:

- Did the pupil achieve the learning objectives set? If not, why not?
- If the pupil has achieved the learning objectives, what effect has it had (e.g. on the pupil's behaviour, learning, any special need)?
- Were the learning objectives too easy or too hard for the pupil?
- How did any staff involvement affect the pupil's achievement?
- Was the lesson or activity plan successful? If not, why not?

NVQ LINKS:

Level 2:
STL6.1   STL9.1   STL9.2

Level 3:
STL25.1   STL25.2   STL25.3
STL29.1

Developing literacy skills

As a teaching assistant you may be involved in helping pupils to develop their literacy skills. Working under the direction of the teacher you should provide support for pupils' literacy development during whole class, group and individual learning activities including: discussing with the teacher how the learning activities will be organised and what your particular role will be; providing the agreed support as appropriate to the different learning needs of pupils; giving feedback to the teacher about the progress of pupils in developing literacy and language skills.

What is literacy?

Literacy means the ability to read and write. The word 'literacy' has only recently been applied as the definitive term for reading and writing especially since the introduction of the National Literacy Strategy in schools. It makes sense to use the term 'literacy' as the skills of reading and writing do complement one another and are developed together. Reading and writing are forms of communication based on spoken language. Pupils need effective speaking and listening skills in order to develop literacy skills. Literacy unites the important skills of reading, writing, speaking and listening.

Why is literacy important?

Developing literacy skills is an essential aspect of development and learning. Without literacy skills individuals are very restricted in their ability to: function effectively in school, college or at work; access information and new ideas; communicate their own ideas to others; participate fully and safely in society. Education depends on individuals being able to read and write. Nearly all jobs and careers require at least basic literacy (and numeracy) skills. Our society also requires people to use literacy skills in everyday life: reading signs, e.g. street names, shop names, traffic signs and warning signs; reading newspapers, magazines, instructions, recipes, food labels; dealing with correspondence, e.g. reading and replying to letters, household bills, bank statements, wage slips and benefits; using computers, the Internet and email; writing shopping lists, memos and notes.

At the centre of all learning are two key skills: literacy and numeracy. Literacy is probably the more important of the two as pupils need literacy to access other areas of the curriculum. For example, to tackle a mathematics problem they might need to read the question accurately before applying the appropriate numeracy skills or they may need to record the results of a science experiment in a written form.

Developing speaking and listening skills

Speaking and listening are part of the National Curriculum Programmes of study for English: 'Speaking and listening', 'Reading' and 'Writing'. These three areas all focus on language and how it is used in the different modes (see section on promoting children's communication skills and language development in Chapter 3). Each mode has its own distinct features but speaking and listening, reading and writing are interdependent. Speaking and listening skills involve:

- ✫ *Speaking:* being able to speak clearly and to develop and sustain ideas in talk.
- ✫ *Listening:* developing active listening strategies and critical skills of analysis.
- ✫ *Group discussion and interaction:* taking different roles in groups, making a range of contributions and working collaboratively.
- ✫ *Drama:* improvising and working in role, scripting and performing, and responding to performances.

(DfES, 2003c)

All areas of the school curriculum provide opportunities for the development of children's speaking and listening skills. The skills used will vary according to the curriculum area. For example, pupils may be involved in learning activities that encourage them to: describe, interpret, predict and hypothesis in mathematics and science; express opinions and discuss design ideas in art, design and technology; discuss cause and effect in history and geography; discuss social or moral issues in PSHE and RE.

Describe how you have helped pupils to develop their speaking and listening skills in at least one of the following: discussion during news, circle time or tutorials; playing a game with a child or small group of children; sharing a story, poem or rhyme.

NVQ LINKS:

Level 2:

STL1.2	STL2.3	STL4.3
STL6.1	STL7.2 (ICT)	STL8.2 (ICT)
STL10.1		

Level 3:

STL18.1	STL20.2	STL8.2 (ICT)
STL23.2	STL25.3	STL27.2 (early years)

Developing reading skills

Reading is the process of turning groups of written symbols into speech sounds. In English this means being able to read from left to right, from the top of the page to the bottom and being able to recognise letter symbols plus their combinations as words. Reading is not just one skill; it involves a variety of different abilities: visual and auditory discrimination; language and communication skills; word identification skills; conceptual understanding; comprehension skills; memory and concentration.

Being able to read does not happen suddenly. Reading is a complex process involving different skills, some of which (e.g. visual discrimination and communication skills) the individual has been developing since birth. Being able to use and understand spoken language forms the basis for developing reading skills. A child who has a wide variety of early language experiences will have developed many of the skills needed for learning to read (see section on promoting children's communication skills and language development in Chapter 3).

Children who are pushed too hard by being forced to read and write before they are ready may actually be harmed in terms of their literacy development as they can be put off reading, writing and other related activities. The area of learning **communication, language and literacy** included in the early learning goals for the EYFS provides guidelines to help early years staff (and parents) understand the importance of informal approaches to language and literacy.

There is no set age at which children are magically ready to read although most children learn to read between the ages of 4 and 6 years old. The age at which a child learns to read depends on a number of factors: physical maturity and co-ordination skills; social and emotional development; language experiences especially access to books; interest in stories and rhymes; concentration and memory skills; opportunities for play.

Reading skills checklist:

1. Can the child see and hear properly?

2. Are the child's co-ordination skills developing within the expected norm?

3. Can the child understand and follow simple verbal instructions?

4. Can the child co-operate with an adult and concentrate on an activity for short periods?

5. Does the child show interest in the details of pictures?

6. Does the child enjoy looking at books plus joining in with rhymes and stories?

7. Can the child retell parts of a story in the right order?

8. Can the child tell a story using pictures?

9. Can the child remember letter sounds and recognise them at the beginning of words?

10. Does the child show pleasure or excitement when able to read words in school?

If the answer is 'yes' to most of these questions, the child is probably ready to read; if the answer is 'no' to any of the questions, the child may need additional support or experiences in those areas before they are ready to read.

Reading approaches

The *whole word or 'look and say' approach* involves teaching pupils to recognise a small set of key words (usually related to a reading scheme) by means of individual words printed on flashcards. Pupils recognise the different words by shape and other visual differences. Once pupils have developed a satisfactory sight vocabulary, they go onto the actual reading scheme. The whole word approach is useful for learning difficult words which do not follow the usual rules of English language. The drawback is that this approach does not help pupils to work out new words for themselves.

With the *phonics approach* pupils learn the sounds that letters usually make. This approach helps pupils establish a much larger reading vocabulary fairly quickly as they can 'sound out' new words for themselves. The disadvantage is that there are many irregular words in the English language; one letter may make many different sounds, e.g. b*ough*, r*ough*, thr*ough*. However, pupils do better with the phonics approach than any other approach.

The *apprenticeship approach*, also known as the 'story' or 'real books' approach, does not formally teach pupils to read. Instead the pupil sits with an adult and listens to the adult read; the pupil starts reading along with the adult until the pupil can read some or the entire book alone. This approach does not help pupils with the process of decoding symbols. There has been much criticism of this approach, but it has proved effective in this country and New Zealand as part of the 'Reading Recovery' programme for older, less able readers.

Most adults helping pupils to develop reading skills use a combination of the 'look and say' approach to introduce early sight vocabulary and then move onto the more intensive phonics approach to establish the pupils' reading vocabulary. It is important for you to be flexible to meet the individual literacy needs of pupils. You should also work with parents to develop their children's reading skills.

EXERCISE:
1. How did you learn to read? How did your own children (if any) learn to read?
2. What are the approaches to teaching reading in your school?
3. Consider the similarities and differences between these approaches.

Developing writing skills

Writing is the system we use to present *'speech in a more permanent form'* (Moyle, 1976). There are two elements to writing: the **mechanical skill of letter formation**, that is writing legibly using recognised word and sentence structures including appropriate spaces between words and punctuation marks; and the **creative skill of 'original composition'**, that is, deciding what to write and working out how to write it using appropriate vocabulary to express thoughts and ideas which may be fact or fiction (Taylor, 1973).

Children will experience written language through books and stories and learn that writing is made up of symbols or patterns organised on paper in a particular way. In English this means 26 letters in the alphabet written from left to right horizontally. Children also learn, by watching adults and other children at home, in the childcare setting and/or in school, that writing can be used for:

* recording past events and experiences, e.g. news, outings, visitors, special events
* exchanging information, e.g. notes, memos, letters, postcards
* functional writing, e.g. shopping lists, recipes, menus, recording experiments or data
* sharing stories and ideas, e.g. story writing, poetry.

Children do not learn to write just through exposure to a writing environment. Writing is a skill that has to be taught. Learning to write involves learning specific conventions with regard to letter shapes, the sequence of letters in words, word order in sentences, the direction of writing, etc. It is usual to teach writing skills alongside reading. This helps children to make the connection between written letters and the sounds they make when read. Most of the activities used to develop children's reading skills will also help their writing skills. In addition, children need plenty of opportunities to develop the *co-ordination* skills necessary for writing: hand-eye co-ordination; fine manipulative skills for pencil control; being able to sit still with the correct posture for writing.

Developing writing skills is much more difficult than reading because of the considerable physical and cognitive demands of writing, for example, co-ordinating movements to write; writing legibly, e.g. letters of consistent size and shape; putting gaps between words; using the correct punctuation and sentence structure; following the correct spelling requirements; writing material of the required length which also makes sense. Remember that some pupils may have special needs which require writing using alternative means or specialist equipment, e.g. Braille, voice-activated computer or word processor (see section below on supporting pupils with special literacy needs).

EXERCISE:
1. How did you learn to write?
2. Which activities for developing pupils' writing skills are used in your school?

Ten ways to help pupils to develop their literacy skills

You can help pupils to develop their literacy skills by doing the following:

1. **Providing plenty of opportunities for pupils to talk** – children who are effective communicators often transfer these skills to reading and writing. Provide plenty of opportunities for discussion such as: circle time; story time; problem-solving during activities; follow-up to activities, e.g. after television programmes or stories; co-operative group work; games and puzzles; talking about key features when on outings.

2. **Sharing books, stories, poems and rhymes to introduce pupils to different literary styles or genres** including picture books, storybooks, 'big' books, novels, poetry books, information books, dictionaries, encyclopaedias and atlases. This also includes looking at other types of printed materials, e.g. newspapers, magazines, comics, signs. These will encourage pupils' listening skills and auditory discrimination and provide stimulus for discussion and literacy activities as well introducing or extending their vocabulary.

3. **Encouraging pupils to participate in appropriate opportunities for play** especially activities that encourage language and communication, e.g. role/pretend play such as dressing-up, home corner, shop play, creative activities (see Chapter 8).

4. **Using displays as a stimulus for discussions and to consolidate learning**, e.g. wall and interactive tabletop displays with interesting objects to talk about, look at and/or play with as well as recorded sounds to listen to including voices, music, songs, rhymes and musical instruments.

5. **Providing opportunities for pupils to follow and give instructions** such as: introducing or extending knowledge on a specific skill; specifying

tasks (verbal and/or written on a board); listening to step-by-step instructions; explaining worksheets, work cards or textbooks; verbal instructions during an activity to keep pupils on task or providing extra support for individual pupils; delivering verbal/written messages, errands.

6. **Encouraging pupils to participate in games to develop auditory and visual discrimination** like sound lotto and 'guess the sound' using sounds of everyday objects or musical instruments. Encourage pupils to participate in matching games and memory games to develop visual discrimination and memory skills, e.g. snap, matching pairs, jigsaws and games like 'I went shopping…'. Provide fun activities to develop letter recognition such as: 'I spy…' using letter sounds; going on a 'letter hunt' (looking around the classroom for things beginning with a particular letter); hang up an 'alphabet washing line'; singing alphabet songs and rhymes.

7. **Providing opportunities for the pupils to write for different purposes and for different audiences** such as: writing about their own experiences as appropriate to their age and level of development, e.g. news and recording events; creating their own stories and poems as a means of expressing their feelings and ideas; using class or group topics as well as the pupils' own interests to stimulate their ideas for stories and poems; using storybooks as a starting point for the pupils' own creative writing. Provide pupils with opportunities to write in different styles such as: writing letters; writing reports; writing step-by-step instructions; designing posters, signs and notices. Encourage pupils to use independent spelling techniques, e.g. word banks, personal word books and dictionaries.

8. **Using alternative writing methods** to release younger pupils or those with co-ordination difficulties (such as dyspraxia) from their physical limitations of writing, e.g. allowing them to dictate their ideas while an adult acts as scribe or use a tape recorder or word-processor.

9. **Considering the individual interests and abilities of pupils** including valuing children's home experiences/cultural backgrounds and being aware of possible developmental or psychological difficulties that may affect their speaking and listening skills by carefully observing children's development and learning (see section below on supporting children with special language needs).

10. **Using information and communication technology** (ICT) including television, CD-ROMs and the Internet as additional stimuli for discussions and ideas. ICT can also be used to introduce or reinforce information on topics and themes within the setting. Remember that ICT is not a substitute for other forms of communication such as conversation and children's play (see Chapter 9).

KEY TASK

Give examples of activities you have used to help pupils develop their literacy skills.

 NVQ LINKS:

Level 2:

STL1.2	STL2.3	STL4.3	STL6.1
STL7.2 (ICT)	STL8.2 (ICT)	STL10.1	

Level 3:

STL18.1	STL20.2	STL8.2 (ICT)	STL23.2
STL25.1	STL27.2 (early years)		

Resources to support literacy development

The classroom needs to provide the space and opportunities for effective communication to take place and to enable pupils to use the different modes of language (see page 75) while participating in all aspects of the school curriculum. Classroom organisation and groupings will encourage and support active participation by: grouping and regrouping pupils for different activities in order to develop their literacy skills; supporting pupils in each group, e.g. competent readers and writers; using a range of grouping strategies, e.g. mixed/like ability, language, interest, random, gender, age. The classroom organisation should encourage the practice and development of all four language skills (speaking and listening, reading and writing) through: collaborative activities that involve talk; opportunities for feedback to others; activities matched to pupils' needs and abilities; activities that have a clear sense of progression. Suitable areas and resources should be provided to facilitate the development of pupils' literacy skills.

Areas for the **primary classroom** include:

* **Writing tables:** enabling pupils to use a variety of writing tools (crayons, pencils, pens, pastels, chalks) on different shapes, sizes and types of paper (e.g. plain, coloured, graph paper).
* **Displays:** interest tables; displays of pupils' work and construction models; wall displays and posters to provide a stimulus for language and learning.
* **Sand and/or water trays plus other science and mathematics equipment:** to encourage exploration and conversation.
* **Pretend play areas:** home corner, shop, café, post office or space station to encourage language and communication skills through imaginative play.
* **Book displays and story corner:** to promote pupils' interest in books and to develop their literacy skills.
* **Computers:** to extend the pupils' range of literacy skills, e.g. word-processing, referencing skills.

Areas for the **secondary classroom** include:

- ✴ **Suitable writing tables and writing materials for the curriculum area:** pens for writing activities; pens, pencils and plain or graph paper for recording results in mathematics, science and geography.
- ✴ **Displays:** interest tables; wall displays including pupils' own work; posters to stimulate discussion and further learning.
- ✴ **Varied and interesting science or mathematics equipment/ materials:** to stimulate exploration and discussion during experiments.
- ✴ **Books relevant to the curriculum area:** to promote interest in books, to develop literacy skills across the curriculum and to extend knowledge of the curriculum area.
- ✴ **Computers:** to extend literacy skills, e.g. word-processing, researching and referencing; to extend knowledge in other areas such as graphs, statistics, etc.

Visual aids should play an essential part in the presentation and introduction of lessons or topics, for example: DVDs; maps; posters; pictures; interesting objects related to the topic or theme; computer graphics. Displays in the classroom and around the school should reflect linguistic and cultural diversity. Dual language textbooks should be available and in use where appropriate.

EXERCISE: List the resources available in your school to support literacy development.

The teaching assistant's role in supporting literacy skills

The teaching assistant plays a key role in supporting the teacher and pupils during literacy activities. You need to find out from the teacher how the literacy activities are to be organised and your specific role in supporting various learning activities including class discussions, group activities and tasks for individuals. You must be able to: understand the intended learning outcomes for the pupils; agree the support strategies to be used for each pupil; obtain the resources required; implement the agreed strategies; provide feedback and encouragement during the activity; monitor the progress of the pupils; report any problems to the teacher.

Pupil sharing books with a teaching assistant

Strategies to help pupils develop literacy skills

Support strategies to help pupils to develop their literacy skills include:

- ✫ using targeted prompts and feedback to encourage independent reading and writing
- ✫ encouraging pupils to participate in shared reading and writing activities
- ✫ developing phonic knowledge and skills to help pupils read and spell accurately
- ✫ using specific reading or writing support strategies, e.g. paired reading, writing frames
- ✫ using specific reading or writing support programmes, e.g. graded reading books, Additional Literacy Support (see below)
- ✫ repeating instructions given by the teacher
- ✫ taking notes for a pupil while the teacher is talking
- ✫ explaining difficult words and phrases to a pupil
- ✫ promoting the use of dictionaries
- ✫ reading and clarifying textbook/worksheet activity for a pupil
- ✫ reading a story to an individual pupil or small group
- ✫ playing a word game with an individual pupil or small group
- ✫ directing computer-assisted learning programmes
- ✫ assisting pupils with special equipment, e.g. hearing aid or a Dictaphone
- ✫ encouraging shy or reticent pupils to participate in conversations and discussions
- ✫ providing any other appropriate assistance during an activity
- ✫ monitoring pupil progress during an activity
- ✫ reporting problems and successes to the teacher.

Factors affecting support for literacy activities

Despite careful planning and organisation, you may have problems in providing support for pupils during literacy activities. You should know and understand the sorts of problems that might occur. For example: difficulties with the quantity, quality, suitability or availability of learning resources; issues relating to space, comfort, noise levels or disruptions within the learning environment; factors that may affect a pupil's ability to learn during literacy activities, e.g. social and cultural background, special educational needs such as learning difficulties or behaviour problems (see sections below on supporting pupils with special literacy and

Pupils engaged in a literacy activity

language needs). You will need to be able to deal with any problems you may have in providing support for pupils as planned. For example: modifying or adapting an activity; providing additional activities to extend their learning; providing an alternative version of the activity; presenting the materials in different ways; offering a greater or lesser level of assistance; coping with insufficient materials or equipment breakdown; dealing with unco-operative or disruptive pupils.

KEY TASK

Give a detailed account of an activity you have used to help pupils to develop their literacy skills. Include information on:

- the organisation of the activity including the resources used
- how you implemented the agreed strategies for each pupil
- how you provided feedback and encouragement during the activity
- how you monitored the progress of the pupils
- the learning outcomes achieved by the pupils
- how you reported any problems in providing support to the teacher.

NVQ LINKS:

Level 2:
STL1.2   STL1.3   STL2.3
STL4.3   STL6.1   STL7.2 (ICT)
STL8.2 (ICT)   STL10.1

Level 3:
STL18.1   STL20.2   STL8.2 (ICT)
STL23.2   STL23.3   STL24.2
STL25.1   STL25.2   STL25.3
STL27.2 (early years) STL27.3 (early years)

Supporting pupils with special literacy needs

Some pupils may have special literacy needs due to cognitive and learning difficulties or sensory impairment or physical disabilities (see Chapter 11). Some pupils may have special literacy needs due to behavioural difficulties (see Chapters 4 and 11) or special language needs, e.g. English as an additional language (see below). The range of pupils with special educational needs (SEN) varies from school to school. Many pupils with SEN may not have special literacy needs and will not require extra or different literacy support. However, many classes will have one or more pupil with identified SEN who requires a modified approach to the National Literacy Strategy.

There are two broad groups of pupils with special literacy needs:

1. A larger group of pupils who experience minor difficulties in learning, which is reflected in their attainment of levels of literacy which are below those expected for pupils of their age. The structure provided by the National Literacy Strategy can benefit these pupils. The pupils can usually overcome these difficulties through normal teaching strategies and will

soon develop the essential literacy skills that will enable them catch up and work at a comparable level to the rest of their year group.

2. The second smaller group includes pupils with severe and complex learning difficulties that require the use of different teaching strategies. These pupils may require different levels of work from the rest of their year group. They may need to be taught at a different pace for all or most of their school years. Some pupils with SEN will always need access to systems such as symbols, signing, Braille or electronic communicators.

(DfES, 1998)

Some pupils with identified SEN may work at earlier levels than those specified in the National Literacy Strategy Framework for their year group. Some pupils with SEN will need to work on one term's work for several terms. With structured, intensive teaching, some of these pupils will gradually progress through the levels in the Framework and will eventually be able to work at the levels appropriate to their age. Some pupils will require work on the development of particular literacy skills, or to work on some skills for longer than others, for example, pupils with speech and language difficulties may need to work on programmes devised by a speech therapist or specialist language teacher.

EXERCISE:
1. Describe how you could provide support for a pupil with special literacy needs.
2. Use examples from your own experience if applicable.

Supporting pupils with special language needs

All pupils have *individual* language needs, but some pupils may have *additional* or *special language needs* that affect their ability to communicate effectively with others. Being able to structure and use language is an enormous task for everyone; it takes the first seven to eight years of life to learn how to form all the different sounds correctly. Some sounds are more difficult to pronounce than others, for example: s, sh, scr, br, cr, gr and th. Most children have problems with these sounds at first, but eventually are able to pronounce them properly.

Some pupils may have difficulties with structuring language, e.g. problems with:

✴ **phonology:** the articulation of sounds, syllables and words (as mentioned above)

✴ **grammar** or **syntax:** words, phrases or sentence structure

✴ **semantics:** *understanding* language (**receptive** difficulties): and/or *using* language (**expressive** difficulties).

Many of the activities already suggested in this chapter will be suitable for *all* pupils including those with special language needs. Some pupils, especially those with severely delayed or disordered language development, may need specialist help from a speech and language therapist. (For more detailed information see the section on supporting pupils with communication and interaction needs in Chapter 11.)

KEY TASK

Describe how you have (or could have) provided support for pupils with special language needs in your school. Include examples for pupils with additional communication and/or interaction needs.

NVQ LINKS:

Level 2:
STL2.3	STL4.3	STL6.1
STL10.1	STL12.1	STL12.2
STL12.3		

Level 3:
STL18.1	STL20.2	STL25.1
STL25.2	STL25.3	STL27.2 (early years)
STL33.1	STL38.1	STL38.2
STL39.1	STL39.2	STL40.1
STL42.1	STL42.2	

Supporting bilingual pupils

Bilingual means 'speaking two languages' which applies to some pupils (and staff) in schools in the United Kingdom. 'Multilingual' is used to describe someone who uses more than two languages. The term 'bilingual' is widely used for all pupils who speak two or more languages.

Promoting language diversity

We live in a multicultural society where a huge variety of languages are used to communicate. We are surrounded by different accents, dialects and other ways of communicating such as sign language. All pupils should have an awareness and understanding of other people's languages, while still feeling proud of their own *community language* and being able to share this with others. Pupils in schools where only English (or Welsh) is spoken still need an awareness of other languages to appreciate fully the multicultural society they live in.

You must respect the languages of *all* the pupils in your school by working with the teacher to provide an environment which promotes language diversity through: welcoming signs in community languages; learning essential greetings in these languages; displaying

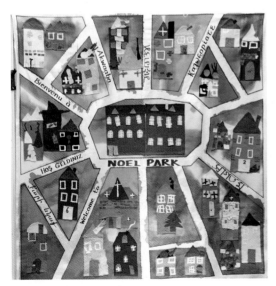

Promoting language diversity

photographs and pictures reflecting multicultural images; using labels with different languages/writing styles; sharing books, stories and songs in other languages; providing multicultural equipment, e.g. ethnic dolls, dressing-up clothes, cooking utensils; celebrating festivals; preparing and sharing food from different cultures.

While promoting language diversity we need to remember that we live in a society where English is the dominant language; developing language and literacy skills in English is essential to all pupils if they are to become effective communicators both in and outside the school. Most children starting nursery or school will speak English even if they have a different cultural background. However, there are some children who do start nursery or school with little or no English because they are new to this country or English is not used much at home.

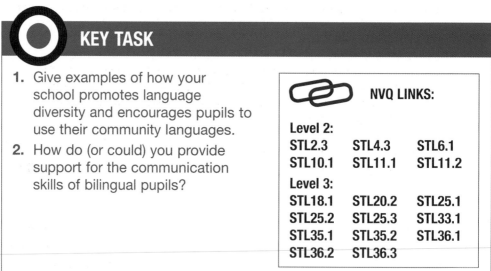

KEY TASK

1. Give examples of how your school promotes language diversity and encourages pupils to use their community languages.

2. How do (or could) you provide support for the communication skills of bilingual pupils?

NVQ LINKS:

Level 2:
STL2.3   STL4.3   STL6.1
STL10.1   STL11.1   STL11.2

Level 3:
STL18.1   STL20.2   STL25.1
STL25.2   STL25.3   STL33.1
STL35.1   STL35.2   STL36.1
STL36.2   STL36.3

Pupils with English as an additional language

Since the introduction of The National Literacy Strategy, the preferred term for bilingual pupils is *pupils with English as an additional language* (EAL). There is a broad range of pupils with EAL including pupils who are: literate in English and do not require extra provision; able to converse in English but need help to use language in their school work; literate in languages other than English but need a little extra support with literacy; learning to speak English as well as learning to read and write it; below the levels of language or literacy expected for their age and require adapted materials to meet their language and/or literacy needs.

There are four important factors to consider when providing support for pupils with EAL:

1. **There are different and changing levels of competence involved in speaking two or more languages.** For example, some pupils are still learning their first language while adding words to their second language. Very young children often do 'language mixing' which involves combining words from two or more languages when involved in conversations or discussions.

2. **Different situations prompt the use of one language over another.**
Pupils who are more fluent in English often use whichever language is appropriate to a particular situation. For example: they might speak to one grandparent using Standard English; speak to another grandparent using Mirpuri and Punjabi; conversations with parents and siblings might involve a mixture of Punjabi and English; and language at the setting might involve the use of a local dialect such as that used in the 'Black Country' in the West Midlands.

3. **The range of communication and literacy skills may be different in each language.** Pupils may be aware of different writing systems being used by their families and in the local community. They may be able to speak a particular language and not be able to write in that language. Pupils may have seen writing which went from right to left as in the Arabic or Hebrew scripts not just from left to right as with English; or they may be used to vertical rather than horizontal writing systems such as Mandarin Chinese or Japanese. Developing literacy skills can be a confusing experience for some pupils with EAL who could be learning to read and write in English in school while learning the same skills in Punjabi at home or in a community school *and* also learning Arabic when studying the Koran at Saturday school.

4. **Changing circumstances can affect a pupil's use of their community language.** For example, moving to a different area where cultural attitudes may be different so that more or less of the pupil's community language is used.

(Whitehead, 1996)

Pupils with English as an additional language do not see their use of different languages as a difficulty. Adults working in schools need to maintain this attitude and to encourage bilingual pupils to see their linguistic abilities as the *asset* it really is in our multicultural society.

You can support pupils with English as an additional language by:

☆ encouraging the pupils to use their community languages some of the time; this promotes security and social acceptance which will make learning English easier

☆ asking the teacher to invite parents/grandparents to read or tell stories in community languages or to be involved with small groups for cooking, sewing or craft activities

☆ using songs and rhymes to help introduce new vocabulary

☆ using other areas of the curriculum to develop language skills in a meaningful context, e.g. focus on words used when working on the computer or during science experiments

☆ using play activities and/or games to encourage and extend language.

As well as communication, language and literacy activities you can use other areas of the curriculum to develop language skills in a meaningful context, e.g. use play activities and/or games to encourage and extend language or focus on words used when working on the computer or during science experiments.

Specialist language support staff can help to ensure that EAL learners are encouraged to apply what they have learnt in the literacy hour across the curriculum. Language support teachers should work with teachers and other staff (e.g. nursery nurses, teaching assistants) to select resources and texts that meet the needs of EAL learners.

It is important to distinguish between pupils who have additional language learning needs and those who also have special educational needs (SEN). Some pupils with EAL may also be assessed as having special educational needs. (See section on identification, assessment and provision for pupils with SEN in Chapter 11.)

KEY TASK

Design and make a booklet about supporting the learning and development of pupils in bilingual or multilingual settings. Include information on the following: the community languages used by the pupils in your school; the school's activities and resources available to support pupils with EAL, e.g. dual language books; bilingual story sessions; language support staff; multilingual resources from the community centre or local education development centre, etc.

NVQ LINKS:

Level 2:
| STL2.3 | STL4.3 | STL6.1 |
| STL10.1 | STL11.1 | STL11.2 |

Level 3:
STL18.1	STL20.2	STL25.1
STL25.2	STL25.3	STL33.1
STL35.1	STL35.2	STL36.1
STL36.2	STL36.3	

National frameworks and curriculum guidelines for mathematics

You should know the relevant national regulatory frameworks and curriculum guidelines for teaching mathematics relevant to the pupils you work with. (Information on curriculum frameworks is in Chapter 9.) See the beginning of this chapter for details of the *Primary Framework for literacy and mathematics*.

The daily mathematics lesson

Pupils have daily lessons for mathematics where they are taught the knowledge, skills and understanding set out in the National Curriculum for mathematics. The guidance in the renewed Framework still places emphasis on carefully planned, purposeful, well-directed teaching and learning. When the numeracy framework was first published the context demanded that attention was given to the structure and organisation of the lesson. Now the challenge is about improving and refining what is in place. The daily mathematics lesson has been successful in structuring the pace of learning and planning for progression through Key Stages 1 and 2. The daily mathematics lesson provides a structure for teaching in Key Stages 1 and 2 which can be adapted and revised to be sufficiently flexible to meet the learning needs of all pupils. The daily mathematics lesson may sometimes be planned as individual lessons. The renewed Framework promotes planning across a sequence of lessons that offers pupils continuity with a blend of approaches that sustain the challenge and maintain an interest in learning (DfES, 2006b).

The Secondary National Strategy Key Stage 3 and Key Stage 4

The Framework for teaching mathematics: Years 7, 8 and 9 aims to improve the achievements of 11 to 14 year old pupils (see: **www.standards.dfes.gov.uk/ keystage3**). The objectives for Years 7, 8 and 9 provide a framework for progression and cover all aspects of the National Curriculum for mathematics. The Framework sets out yearly teaching programmes illustrating how objectives for teaching mathematics can be planned from Year 7 to Year 9. The framework provides advice on teaching strategies, inclusion and differentiation, and the assessment of pupil progress. The Secondary National Strategy Key Stage 4 includes guidelines on improving the planning and teaching of mathematics at Key Stage 4 (see: **www.standards.dfes.gov.uk/keystage4**). The Key Stage 3 Framework and the Key Stage 4 guidelines are based on the Programmes of study for mathematics in the revised National Curriculum 2000.

EXERCISE: What are the national frameworks and curriculum guidelines for teaching mathematics relevant to your school?

National Curriculum targets for mathematics

During **Key Stage 1** pupils learn to count and do basic number calculations such as addition and subtraction. Pupils learn how to talk about mathematical problems and work out how to solve them through practical activities. Pupils demonstrate their thinking and problem-solving skills by using objects, pictures, diagrams, simple lists, tables, charts, words, numbers and symbols. They do mental calculations (e.g. work out sums in their heads) without relying on calculators. They handle and describe the various features of basic shapes. They learn to estimate and measure a range of everyday objects.

During **Key Stage 2** pupils learn more about numbers and the number system including doing more difficult number calculations such as multiplication and division. Pupils talk about mathematical problems and decide on strategies to tackle them. Pupils demonstrate their thinking and problem-solving skills by using mathematical language, diagrams, words, numbers and symbols. Pupils learn how to use calculators to solve certain mathematical problems but they are expected to solve most problems using mental calculations (e.g. working out sums in their heads) or writing them down on paper. They handle and describe the various features of more complex shapes. They learn to answer questions by selecting, organising and presenting appropriate data using tables, charts, and graphs.

During **Key Stage 3** pupils learn more about numbers and the number system, more complex calculations, different ways of solving mathematical problems, and algebra. Pupils talk about mathematical problems and decide on strategies to tackle them. Pupils demonstrate their thinking and problem-solving skills by using more complex mathematical language, diagrams, words, numbers and symbols. Pupils learn to use scientific calculators to solve complex mathematical problems but they are still expected to solve most problems using mental calculations (e.g. working out sums in their heads) or writing them down on paper. They learn more about shapes and co-ordinates, constructing shapes (geometry) and measurement. They continue to answer questions by selecting, organising and presenting appropriate data using tables, charts and graphs. Pupils learn to solve increasingly demanding mathematical problems, including problems that require a step-by-step approach to reach a solution.

In **Key Stage 4** there are two Programmes of study for mathematics: **foundation** and **higher**. Pupils may be taught either the foundation or higher programme of study. The foundation programme of study is intended for those pupils who have not attained a secure Level 5 at the end of Key Stage 3. Pupils studying at the **foundation** level should: consolidate their understanding of basic mathematics, which will help them to tackle unfamiliar problems in the workplace and everyday life and develop the knowledge and skills they need in the future; become increasingly proficient in mathematical calculations; collect data, learn statistical techniques to analyse data and use ICT to present and interpret the results. The higher programme of study is intended for students who have attained a secure Level 5 at the end of Key Stage 3. Pupils studying at the **higher** level should: use short chains of deductive reasoning, develop their own proofs, and begin to understand the importance of proof in mathematics; see the importance of mathematics as an analytical tool for solving problems; refine their calculating skills to include powers, roots and numbers expressed in standard form; learn to handle data through practical activities, using a broader range of skills and techniques, including sampling; develop the confidence and flexibility to solve unfamiliar problems and to use ICT appropriately. (For detailed information on the targets for all Key Stages see the National Curriculum online at **www.nc.uk.net**.)

KEY TASK

Observe a pupil during a mathematics activity in Key Stage 1, 2, 3 or 4. Then answer these questions:

- Did the pupil achieve the learning objectives set? If not, why not?
- If the pupil has achieved the learning objectives, what effect has it had (e.g. on the pupil's behaviour, learning, any special need)?
- Were the learning objectives too easy or too hard for the pupil?
- How did any staff involvement affect the pupil's achievement?
- Was the lesson or activity plan successful? If not, why not?

NVQ LINKS:

Level 2:
STL6.2   STL9.1   STL9.2

Level 3:
STL26.1   STL26.2   STL29.1

Developing numeracy skills

As a teaching assistant you may be involved in helping pupils to develop their numeracy skills. Working under the direction of the teacher you should provide support for pupils' numeracy development during whole class, group and individual learning activities including: discussing with the teacher how the learning activities will be organised and what your particular role will be; providing the agreed support as appropriate to the different learning needs of pupils; giving feedback to the teacher about the progress of pupils in developing mathematical knowledge and skills.

What is numeracy?

The term 'numeracy' was introduced in about 1982 to describe what was previously called arithmetic. Individuals who are competent at arithmetic have always been described as 'numerate'; now this competency is called 'numeracy'. Numeracy is more than an ability to do basic arithmetic. Numeracy is a proficiency that involves confidence and competence with numbers and measures. It requires an understanding of the number system, a repertoire of computational skills and an inclination and ability to solve number problems in various contexts. Numeracy also demands practical understanding of the ways in which data is gathered, by counting and measuring, and is presented in graphs, diagrams and tables.

Why is numeracy important?

Being able to do number calculations confidently is an essential life skill; it helps people function effectively in everyday life. It is also very important as a first step in learning mathematics. We use numeracy in everyday life including: shopping – checking change, buying the right quantities, getting value for money; cooking – weighing ingredients; decorating – calculating the amount of wallpaper, paint, carpet or other materials needed for the required areas; sewing – measuring materials; using graph paper to plot designs; journeys and holidays – understanding transport timetables, planning the best route, calculating mileage or the time a journey will take, working out how much petrol is needed for a car journey, etc.

Learning numeracy skills is the central part of mathematics, but children are also taught about geometry (e.g. space and shapes) and the beginnings of algebra (e.g. number patterns). Children need to develop numeracy skills that involve confidence and competence with numbers and measures including: knowledge and understanding of the number system; knowing by heart various number facts, e.g. multiplication tables; using a range of mathematical skills; making mental calculations; being able to solve number problems in a variety of contexts; presenting information about counting and measuring using graphs, diagrams, charts and tables.

Developing mathematical skills

Pupils need to develop the following mathematical skills: using and applying mathematics; counting and understanding number; knowing and using number facts; calculating; understanding shape; measuring; handling data.

Using and applying mathematics

Pupils learn to select an appropriate mathematical skill to tackle or solve a problem. They learn to use words, symbols and basic diagrams to record and give details about how they solved a problem. Pupils develop problem-solving skills in order to work out the best approach to finding a mathematical solution. They learn which *questions* to ask as well as developing the appropriate skills to answer mathematical problems such as: What is the problem? Which mathematical skill needs to be used? Will a graph, chart or diagram help find the solution?

Counting and understanding number

Many children learn number names and how to count before they begin school. At home and/or in early years settings (e.g. day nursery or playgroup) they do counting activities and sing number songs and rhymes. During the primary school years pupils develop and extend their counting skills. Younger pupils begin with numbers 0 to 20 which are the most difficult to learn as each number name is different; numbers from 20 onwards have recognisable patterns which makes learning numbers up to 100 or more much easier. Pupils begin by counting forwards and then backwards from 20; once they are confident with this they learn to count forwards and backwards in sets of 2, 5 and 10 which helps with doing sums and the early stages of learning multiplication.

Knowing and using number facts

Primary pupils should learn to recognise and use: number symbols and words for whole numbers 1 (one) to 20 (twenty) by 4 to 5 years; all the whole numbers to 100 (one hundred) plus halves and quarters by 6 to 7 years; numbers to 10,000 including more fractions and decimal places by 8 to 9 years; all whole numbers, fractions, decimals plus percentages by 10 to 11 years. During the primary school years, pupils also develop knowledge and understanding of the mathematical language relevant to numbers: smaller, bigger; more/less than; even and odd numbers; factors and prime numbers, etc.

From about 4/5 years old pupils begin to learn how to make mathematical calculations using real objects to add and subtract small whole numbers. Gradually they recognise number patterns which make doing calculations easier, e.g. being able to add 4 + 8 means they can also add 400 + 800. Memorising number facts also helps with calculations, e.g. learning multiplication tables by heart.

Calculating

By age 10/11 years pupils should have learned addition, subtraction, multiplication and division using whole numbers, fractions, decimals and negative numbers. As well as learning mental calculations pupils also learn the standard written methods for calculation operations.

Remember the aim for older children is to calculate mentally and to become less reliant on fingers and apparatus. Older children should be encouraged to consider mental methods first through strategies such as: 'Think first, and try to work it out in your head. Now check on your number line' (DfES, 1999). Children with special needs may need particular equipment, books and materials for mathematics activities (see section below on supporting pupils with special numeracy needs).

Understanding shape

In addition to developing competency with numbers, pupils learn to recognise and name geometrical shapes; they also learn about the properties of shapes, e.g. a triangle has three sides; a square has four right angles. Pupils learn about directions, angles and plotting points on a graph.

Measuring

Pupils learn to measure mass, distance, area and volume using appropriate units, e.g. kilograms, metres, centimetres or litres. Measuring also includes learning to tell the time in hours and minutes.

Handling data

Handling data is an essential skill in this technological age and using computers is an important aspect of mathematics today. Pupils learn to gather, arrange and convert data into useful information, e.g. working out the likelihood of rain so we know when to wear a raincoat or take an umbrella.

EXERCISE:
1. How did you develop your mathematical skills? How did your own children (if any) develop their mathematical skills (for example: singing number songs and rhymes; practical maths activities such as sorting shapes, measuring or shopping; playing number games; learning by rote such as reciting times tables; learning formal number operations such as addition, subtraction, multiplication and division)?
2. What are the methods used to teach mathematics in your school?
3. Consider the similarities and differences between these methods.

Ten ways to help pupils to develop their mathematical skills

You can help pupils to develop their mathematical skills by doing the following:

1. **Encouraging pupils to use and apply mathematics to tackle and solve everyday practical mathematical problems**, e.g. giving change in shop play and real shopping trips (addition and subtraction); exploring volume and capacity during sand and water play filling various containers to encourage understanding of full, empty, half-full, half-empty, nearly full, nearly empty, more/less than, the same amount, then introduce idea of standard measures, e.g. litre of juice, pint of milk. Using weighing and measuring activities such as: shop play (using balance scales to compare toys and other items); real shopping (helping to weigh fruit and

vegetables); sand play (heavy and light); cooking activities (weighing ingredients to show importance of standard measures).

2. **Providing opportunities for pupils to use and apply mathematics in the school and wider environment** such as orientation exercises, nature walks, geography and environmental studies can develop numeracy skills; educational visits can also contribute to mathematics across the curriculum, e.g. visits to science museums.

3. **Encouraging younger pupils to explore numbers** through playing games like dominoes, 'snakes and ladders' and other simple board games; looking for shapes/sizes and making comparisons, price tags and quantities in shop play and real shopping trips; number songs and rhymes like '*One, two, three, for five, Once I caught a fish alive...*'.

4. **Supporting pupils engaged in counting, calculating and solving mathematical problems**, e.g. addition and subtraction then multiplication and division. Supporting older pupils in employing standard methods to perform mental and written calculations including addition, subtraction, multiplication and division using whole numbers, fractions, decimals and percentages.

5. **Prompting pupils to communicate their reasoning about problems and explaining their solutions** using objects, pictures, diagrams, numbers, symbols and relevant mathematical language, e.g. using letter symbols in algebra, setting up and using simple equations to solve problems.

6. **Supporting pupils' use of calculator functions to complete complex calculations** and understand the answers calculators give in relation to the initial mathematical problem.

7. **Encouraging pupils to compare, estimate and measure a range of everyday objects**, e.g. developing an understanding of length by comparing everyday objects/toys and using mathematical language such as tall/taller/tallest, short/shorter/shortest, long/ longer/longest, same height, same length; measuring objects using appropriate units such as centimetres, metres, kilograms or litres.

8. **Helping pupils to tell the time:** o'clock, half-past and quarter-past the hour; with older pupils telling the time in hours and minutes and solving problems relating to time using a 12-hour or 24-hour clock.

9. **Encouraging pupils to explore shape and space** through activities such as: games involving shape recognition; handling and describing the various features of basic shapes (e.g. use correct names for basic 2-D and 3-D shapes; know how many sides, corners or right angles a shape has); physical activities involving whole-turns, half-turns and quarter-turns or right angles as well as spatial awareness, e.g. PE, movement, dance.

Helping older pupils to learn more about shapes and co-ordinates, constructing shapes (geometry), and measurement including using a ruler, protractor and compasses to create lines, angles and 2-D or 3-D shapes.

10. **Using ICT to encourage or extend pupils' knowledge, understanding and skills in mathematics**, e.g. playing shape recognition games; writing instructions to create and change shapes on a computer; providing opportunities for pupils to select, collect, organise and present appropriate data using lists, charts, graphs, diagrams, tables, surveys, questionnaires and CD-ROMs.

 KEY TASK

Give examples of activities you have used to help pupils to develop their mathematical skills.

 NVQ LINKS:

Level 2:
STL1.2   STL2.3   STL4.3
STL6.1   STL7.2 (ICT)
STL8.2 (ICT)   STL10.1

Level 3:
STL18.1   STL20.2   STL8.2 (ICT)
STL23.2   STL25.3   STL27.2 (early years)

Resources to support numeracy development

A wide range of equipment and materials provide essential resources for supporting the development of pupils' mathematical skills both in and outside the classroom:

1. **Boards and charts:** Large white board for whole class/group teaching and individual white boards for pupils with appropriate marker pens; flip chart and marker pens or chalkboard and chalk; over-head projector, transparencies and appropriate pens.

2. **Number lines:** Large number line for teaching purposes at a suitable level for the pupils; a 'washing line' of numbers hung across the room that can be added to/altered; table top number lines, marked and unmarked, for individual use; for younger pupils, number tracks with the spaces numbered to 20, rather than number lines with the points numbered; by end of Key Stage 1 number lines should be to 100; for older pupils, number lines should include negative numbers; by the end of Key Stage 2 need marked and unmarked number lines on which decimals and fractions can be placed.

3. **Number cards:** Pack of **digit cards** 0 to 9 for each pupil to hold up when answering questions in a whole-class setting, two-digit numbers can be formed from cards held side-by-side; **place value cards** with nine cards printed with multiples of 100 from 100 to 900, nine with multiples of 10 from 10 to 90, and ten with the numbers 0 to 9, two- or three-digit numbers can be built up by overlapping cards of different widths; **addition and subtraction cards** for number bonds, first bonds to 5, then to 10, extending to 20; **symbol cards** for '+' and '–' that can also be held up in response to questions about the operation needed to solve a problem; large **100 square**, displayed where pupils can clearly see and touch it.

4. **Mathematics equipment and materials: Small apparatus** such as counters, interlocking cubes, wooden cubes, pegs and pegboards, straws, rulers, coins, dominoes, dice; variety of **squared paper**; selection of **number games**: range of **measuring equipment**; sets of **shapes**; various **construction kits**; **pencils and pens** for recording; **calculators** when required.

5. **Books: Interest books on mathematics** and **mathematical dictionaries** suitable for the age of the pupils; **mathematics schemes** such as Cambridge Maths, Nuffield Maths and Letts Maths; **other useful books** for activities and practice exercises for class work and homework.

EXERCISE: List the resources available in your school to support numeracy development.

The teaching assistant's role in supporting numeracy skills

Pupils in a mathematics lesson

The teaching assistant has a key role in providing support for the teacher and pupils during numeracy activities. You need to find out from the teacher how the numeracy activities are to be organised and your specific role in supporting various learning activities including whole-class oral/mental maths activities, group work and tasks for individuals. You must be able to: understand the intended learning outcomes for the pupils; agree the support strategies to be used for each pupil; obtain the resources required; implement the agreed strategies; provide praise and encouragement during the activity (see page 125); monitor the progress of the pupils; report any problems in providing support to the teacher.

Strategies to help pupils develop numeracy skills

Support strategies to help pupils to develop their mathematical knowledge and skills include the following:

- ✫ Using questions and prompts to encourage mathematical skills
- ✫ Repeating instructions given by the teacher
- ✫ Taking notes for a pupil while the teacher is talking
- ✫ Explaining and reinforcing correct mathematical vocabulary
- ✫ Reading and clarifying textbook/worksheet activity for a pupil
- ✫ Introducing follow-on tasks to reinforce and extend learning, e.g. problem-solving tasks, puzzles
- ✫ Playing a mathematical game with an individual pupil or small group
- ✫ Helping pupils to use computer software and learning programmes
- ✫ Helping pupils to select and use appropriate mathematical resources, e.g. number lines, measuring instruments
- ✫ Assisting pupils with special equipment, e.g. hearing aid or a Dictaphone
- ✫ Encouraging shy or reticent pupils to participate in conversations and discussions
- ✫ Providing any other appropriate assistance during an activity
- ✫ Monitoring pupil progress during an activity
- ✫ Reporting problems and successes to the teacher.

You must know and understand the sorts of problems that might occur when supporting pupils during learning activities and how to deal with these problems (see page 13). If a pupil is experiencing difficulties during a mathematics activity you should consider the following:

1. Does the pupil understand the task?
2. Has the pupil learned how to do the relevant technique (e.g. counting, adding, learning times tables by repeating them)?
3. Does the pupil know which technique to use to solve the mathematical problem?

The pupil needs to understand the mathematical problem and decide which techniques are required to solve it. You can help the pupil develop problem-solving skills by encouraging them to: understand the problem, e.g. explain the task using visual aids or equipment; plan to solve the problem, e.g. suggest possible ways or draw

Pupils engaged in a numeracy activity

diagrams; attempt the solution, e.g. try a technique; review the problem and solution, e.g. reconsider the problem, check the answer makes sense.

KEY TASK

Give a detailed account of an activity you have used to help pupils to develop their mathematical knowledge and skills. Include information on the following:

- The organisation of the activity including the resources used.
- How you implemented the agreed strategies for each pupil.
- How you provided feedback and encouragement during the activity.
- How you monitored the progress of the pupils.
- The learning outcomes achieved by the pupils.
- How you reported any problems in providing support to the teacher.

NVQ LINKS:

Level 2:

STL1.2	STL1.3	STL2.3
STL4.3	STL6.2	STL7.2 (ICT)
STL8.2 (ICT)	STL10.1	STL10.5

Level 3:

STL18.1	STL20.2	STL8.2 (ICT)
STL23.2	STL23.3	STL24.2
STL26.1	STL26.2	STL27.2 (early years)
STL27.3 (early years)		

Factors affecting support for numeracy activities

Some pupils have difficulties with numeracy because the language used in mathematics may be too complex for them to understand the task. Poor memory skills can prevent some pupils from learning procedural techniques, e.g. times tables. Frequent experiences of failure during numeracy activities can make some pupils anxious, discouraged and lacking in confidence so that they fall behind in their numeracy development.

Mathematical skills involve a wide range of specific capabilities, any of which can prove difficult for particular pupils and affect their mathematical development. It is important to find out what the pupil knows and where the problem lies. It is important to make sure that the pupil's problem with numeracy is not in fact a problem with literacy. For example, some pupils may: not be able to understand the written question; have handwriting or directional problems resulting in inaccurate recording and errors; have poor motor skills causing miscalculations when using a calculator.

It is also important not to under-estimate what pupils can do mathematically simply because they are learning English as an additional language (see below). They should be expected to make progress in their mathematical learning at the same rate as other pupils of the same age.

Supporting pupils with special numeracy needs

Some pupils may have special numeracy needs due to special educational needs (SEN) such as cognitive and learning difficulties, behavioural difficulties, sensory impairment or physical disabilities (see Chapter 11). The range of pupils with SEN varies from school to school. Many pupils with SEN may not have special numeracy needs and will not require extra or different numeracy support. However, many classes will have one or more pupil with identified SEN who requires a modified approach to the National Numeracy Strategy. There are two broad groups of pupils with special numeracy needs:

1. A larger group of pupils who experience minor difficulties in learning, which is reflected in their attainment of levels of numeracy which are below those expected for pupils of their age. The structure provided by the National Numeracy Strategy can benefit these pupils. The pupils can usually overcome these difficulties through normal teaching strategies and will soon develop the essential numeracy skills that will enable them to catch up and work at a comparable level to the rest of their year group.

2. The second smaller group includes pupils with severe and complex learning difficulties that require the use of different teaching strategies. These pupils may require different levels of work from the rest of their year group. They may need to be taught at a different pace for all or most of their school years. Some pupils with SEN will always need access to systems such as symbols, signing, Braille or electronic communicators.

(DfES, 1999)

Some pupils with identified special educational needs may work at earlier levels than those specified in the National Numeracy Strategy Framework for their year group. Some pupils with SEN will need to work on one term's work for several terms. With structured, intensive teaching, some of these pupils will gradually progress through the levels in the Framework and will eventually be able to work at the levels appropriate to their age.

Many pupils with special educational needs (e.g. pupils with physical disabilities or sensory impairment) will not require a separate learning programme for mathematics. For most of them access, materials, equipment and furniture may require adapting to meet their particular needs so that they can work alongside the rest of their class. They should work on the same objectives for their year group with emphasis on access and support. Adaptations that may be necessary include: sign language; Braille and symbols; tactile materials; technological aids; adapted measuring equipment.

Support staff (including specially trained teaching assistants) can provide assistance for pupils with special numeracy needs by: signing to support a pupil with hearing impairment during shared numeracy activities; supporting a pupil during group work to develop specific numeracy skills; asking questions aimed at the appropriate level; giving the pupil some extra help in a group; sitting next to the pupil to keep them on task.

Supporting pupils with learning difficulties

Pupils with learning difficulties will usually require constant repetition and revision of previous learning in mathematics. This is especially important in terms of language and mental operations. The understanding of language of mathematics and the ability to calculate mentally are essential to the development of numeracy skills. Pupils with learning difficulties may not have adequate language and mental strategies, which may have contributed to their problems with formal, standard methods of representing calculations. Some pupils with specific learning difficulties (e.g. dyscalculia) may not understand key concepts in numeracy (see section on supporting pupils with specific learning difficulties in Chapter 11).

Pupils with English as an additional language

Whole-class sessions can provide helpful adult models of spoken English and opportunities for careful listening, oral exchange and supportive, shared repetition. Group work provides opportunities for intensive, focused teaching input. You may need to repeat instructions for pupils with English as an additional language (EAL) and to speak more clearly, emphasising key words, particularly when you are describing tasks that they are to do independently. Encourage them to join in things that all pupils do in chorus: counting, reading aloud whole number sentences, chanting, finger games, songs about numbers, and so on. The structure of rhymes and the natural rhythm in songs or poems, play an important part in developing number sense in any culture. Use stories and rhymes from a range of cultural backgrounds.

KEY TASK

Describe how you have (or could have) provided support for pupils with special numeracy needs in your setting. Include examples for pupils with learning difficulties and pupils with English as an additional language.

NVQ LINKS:

Level 2:

STL1.2	STL1.3	STL2.3
STL4.3	STL6.2	STL10.1
STL10.5	STL11.1	STL11.2
STL12.2	STL12.3	

Level 3:

STL18.1	STL20.2	STL8.2 (ICT)
STL23.2	STL23.3	STL24.2
STL26.1	STL26.2	STL27.2 (early years)
STL27.3 (early years)	STL33.2	
STL35.1	STL35.2	STL36.1
STL36.2	STL36.3	STL38.1
STL38.2	STL39.1	STL40.1
STL40.2	STL42.1	

Enabling pupils to access the wider curriculum

In addition to helping pupils to develop their literacy and numeracy skills as part of the curriculum for English and mathematics, you may be involved in providing literacy and numeracy support to enable pupils to access the wider curriculum. To provide this type of support you will need to know and understand: the literacy and numeracy requirements for the learning activities; the level of support needed by pupils to meet these requirements; your specific role in providing literacy and numeracy support; how to recognise and respond to any difficulties experienced by pupils.

KEY TASK

Describe how you have (or could have) provided literacy and numeracy support to help pupils access different subjects within the curriculum.

  NVQ LINKS:

Level 3:
STL25.1   STL25.2   STL25.3
STL26.1   STL26.2   STL33.1
STL33.2   STL27.1   STL27.2
STL27.3 (early years)

Further reading

DfES (2000) *Working with teaching assistants: a good practice guide.* DfES.

DfES (2001) *Early literacy support programme: materials for teachers working in partnership with teaching assistants.* DfES.

Elkin, S. (2007) *Teaching assistant's guide to literacy.* Continuum International Publishing Group Ltd.

Fielder, S. (2007) *Teaching assistant's guide to numeracy.* Continuum International Publishing Group Ltd.

Fox, G. and Halliwell, M. (2000) *Supporting literacy and numeracy: a guide for learning support assistants.* David Fulton Publishers.

Palmer, S. and Bayley, R. (2004) *Foundations of literacy: a balanced approach to language, listening and literacy skills in the early years.* Network Educational Press Ltd.

Siraj-Blatchford, J. and Clarke, P. (2000) *Supporting identity, diversity and language in the early years.* Open University Press.

Williams, S. and Goodman, S. (2000) *Helping young children with maths.* Hodder Arnold.

Wright, R. J. *et al.* (2002) *Teaching number: advancing children's skills and strategies.* Paul Chapman Publishing.

11 Supporting pupils with additional needs

Key points:

* Identification, assessment and provision for pupils with special educational needs (SEN)
* Individual Education Plans
* The role of the special educational needs co-ordinator (SENCO)
* The role of the class teacher in supporting pupils with SEN
* The teaching assistant's role in supporting pupils with SEN
* Liaising with parents regarding their children with SEN
* Liaising with other professionals regarding pupils with SEN
* Supporting pupils with communication and interaction needs
* Supporting pupils with cognition and learning needs
* Supporting pupils with behavioural, social and emotional development needs
* Supporting pupils with sensory and/or physical needs.

Identification, assessment and provision for pupils with SEN

Supporting pupils with disabilities and/or special educational needs (SEN) involves establishing the strengths and needs of pupils in partnership with their families and in collaboration with other agencies. It also involves the identification and provision of appropriate resources to enable inclusion and participation.

You must know, understand and follow the relevant legislation regarding pupils with disabilities and SEN. This includes supporting the school in carrying out its duties towards pupils with SEN and that parents are notified of any decision that SEN provision is to be made for their child. (See section on national legislation relating to children with special educational needs in Chapter 5.)

Some children may have been identified as having special educational needs prior to starting school, e.g. children with physical disabilities, sensory impairment or autism. Some children may not be making sufficient progress within the early learning goals/National Curriculum targets or may have difficulties which require additional support within the school. Additional support for pupils with SEN in education settings may be provided through *Early Years or School Action, Early Years or School Action Plus* and *Statutory assessment.*

Early Years or School Action

Pupils identified as having special educational needs may require support in addition to the usual provision of the school. The special educational needs co-ordinator (SENCO), in consultation with colleagues and the pupil's parents will decide what additional support is needed to help the pupil to make progress. Additional support at *Early Years or School Action* may include: the provision of different learning materials or special equipment; some individual or group support provided by support staff (e.g. early years practitioners/nursery nurses or teaching assistants); devising and implementing an Individual Education Plan (see below).

Early Years or School Action Plus

Pupils with special educational needs may require additional support which involves external support services. The SENCO, in consultation with colleagues, the pupil's parents and other professionals will decide what additional support is needed to help the pupil to make progress. Additional support at *Early Years or School Action Plus* may include: the provision of specialist strategies or materials; some individual or group support provided by specialist support staff (e.g. early years practitioners/nursery nurses or teaching assistants with additional training in SEN); some individual support provided by other professionals, e.g. physiotherapist, speech and language therapist; access to LEA support services for regular advice on strategies or equipment, e.g. educational psychologist, autism outreach worker; devising and implementing an Individual Education Plan (see below).

Statutory Assessment

A few pupils with SEN in the school may still make insufficient progress through the additional support provided by *Early Years or School Action Plus.* When a pupil demonstrates significant cause for concern, the SENCO, in consultation with colleagues, the pupil's parents and other professionals already involved in the pupil's support, should consider whether to request a statutory assessment by the LEA. The LEA may decide that the nature of the provision necessary to meet the pupil's special educational needs requires the LEA to determine the pupil's special education provision through a **statement of special educational need**.

Individual Education Plans (IEP)

All education settings should differentiate their approaches to learning activities to meet the needs of individual pupils. The strategies used to enable individual pupils with SEN to make progress during learning activities should be set out in an IEP whether they receive additional support in the school as part of *Early Years Action, Early Years Action Plus* or *statement of special educational need.*

A pupil's IEP should identify three or four individual targets in specific key areas, for example, communication, literacy, numeracy or behaviour and social skills. When supporting the teacher in developing Individual Educational Plans, remember to have high expectations of pupils and a commitment to raising their achievement based on a realistic appraisal of children's abilities and what they can achieve. You may be involved in regularly reviews of Individual Educational Plans in consultation with the pupil's class teacher/form tutor, the SENCO, the pupil and their parents, e.g. at least three times a year. A pupil's IEP should include the following information:

* Pupil's strengths
* Priority concerns
* Any external agencies involved
* Background information including assessment details and/or medical needs
* Parental involvement/pupil participation
* The short-term targets for the pupil
* The provision to be put in place, e.g. resources, strategies, staff, allocated support time
* When the plan is to be reviewed
* The outcome of any action taken.

Documentation and information about the Special Educational Needs Code of Practice including *Early Years or School Action*, *Early Years or School Action Plus* and the statementing process should be available from the school office or the SENCO.

KEY TASK

Outline your school's procedures for ensuring that Individual Education Plans for pupils are in place and regularly reviewed. Provide examples of the relevant forms, e.g. an Individual Education Plan; review sheets for pupil comments, parent comments and staff comments; record of review. Remember confidentiality.

 NVQ LINKS:

Level 2:
STL12.1   **STL12.2**   **STL12.3**

Level 3:
STL38.1   **STL38.2**   **STL38.3**

Roles and responsibilities in supporting pupils with SEN

As a teaching assistant you should contribute to the inclusion of pupils with disabilities and special educational needs (SEN). (For detailed information on inclusion including a definition of special educational needs and the relevant legislation relating to children with disabilities and special educational needs, see Chapter 5.) You may be involved in supporting the teacher in developing individual plans to meet each pupil's needs and requesting additional resources or a statutory assessment where appropriate (see above section on identification, assessment and provision for pupils with SEN). You may also be involved in supporting pupils appropriately through transitions to ensure continuity of learning experiences (see Chapter 7).

The role of the special educational needs co-ordinator

All schools must have a special educational needs co-ordinator (SENCO) who is the Responsible Person as defined within the **Special Educational Needs Code of Practice**. Pupils with special educational needs require additional support in the school and usually have Individual Education Plans (IEPs). These plans will give information about the support being provided to help the pupil and will include details of the roles and responsibilities of staff members in providing appropriate learning and/or behaviour support. The SENCO is responsible for drawing up these plans, along with the teacher, support staff (e.g. teaching assistant), the pupil and their parents or carers.

The SENCO also has the following responsibilities for managing pupil behaviour and learning:

☆ To provide support and guidance to all staff to help them manage pupil behaviour and learning effectively.

☆ To ensure that adequate training is provided to all staff to improve behaviour management strategies and the implementation of learning activities.

☆ To ensure that (as far as is practical) all resources required are made available to facilitate appropriate learning experiences and effective behaviour management.

☆ To monitor the changing needs of pupils as they progress through the school.

☆ To liaise with external agencies.

☆ To ensure that there are programmes for identifying the needs of new pupils.

The role of the class teacher in supporting pupils with SEN

The class teacher should plan and organise an effective learning environment which: promotes equality and inclusion (see Chapter 5); promotes positive behaviour (see Chapter 4); supports *individual* pupil development and learning (see Chapters 3 and 9). The class teacher should carefully monitor pupils' behaviour and learning in order to provide appropriate learning activities. When a pupil experiences difficulties with participating in learning activities and/or behaving appropriately, the class teacher should follow the relevant school strategies.

The class teacher has the following responsibilities for managing pupil behaviour and learning:

☆ To identify each pupil's needs and skill levels.

☆ To make the SENCO aware of any concerns about a pupil's behaviour and/or learning.

- ☆ To advise the child's parents of any concerns about behaviour and/or learning.
- ☆ To provide reports for external agencies.
- ☆ To monitor and assess learning/behaviour and maintain appropriate records.
- ☆ To fill in and maintain the Special Educational Needs Register.
- ☆ To fulfil all other duties required of the class teacher by the Code of Practice.
- ☆ To ensure that the delivery of the curriculum enables *all* pupils, including those with special educational needs, to experience success.

The teaching assistant's role in supporting pupils with SEN

As a teaching assistant you should help pupils with special educational needs (SEN) to participate in the full range of activities and experiences (see section on promoting equality and inclusion in Chapter 5). You need to know and understand the details about particular disabilities or SEN as they affect the pupils in your school. Pupils with additional needs in your school may include pupils with: communication and interaction needs; cognition and learning needs; behavioural, emotional and social development needs; sensory impairment; physical disabilities (see relevant sections below).

Learning mentors

Learning mentors work with school pupils and college students to help them overcome barriers to learning and so have a better chance of achieving to their potential. Learning mentors play a key role in supporting children and young people with special needs, working closely with teachers and a range of support agencies. Learning mentors use regular one-to-one and group sessions with the pupils/students, to agree targets and strategies (e.g. to improve academic work, attendance, behaviour and relationships). They help pupils/students develop coping strategies, enhance their motivation, raise their aspirations and encourage them to re-engage in learning. Learning mentors should take into account the range of complex issues that are often behind problems with learning and achievement such as bereavement, lack of confidence/low self-esteem, low aspirations, mental health issues, relationship difficulties, bullying, peer pressure, family issues/concerns. (For more detailed information see section on learning mentors on the Standards website at **www.standards.dfes.gov.uk/learningmentors**.)

EXERCISE: Describe your role and responsibilities for supporting children and/or young people with special educational needs in school.

Liaising with parents regarding their children with SEN

When liaising with parents about the special educational needs of their children you should consider the family's home background and the expressed wishes of the parents. You must also follow the setting's policies and procedures with regard to special educational needs, e.g. inclusion strategies, policies, procedures and practice (see section on understanding children's needs and rights in Chapter 5). You may need to give parents positive reassurance about their children's care and education. Any concerns or worries expressed by a child's parents should be passed immediately to the appropriate person in the school, e.g. the class teacher and/or SENCO. If a parent makes a request to see a colleague or other professional, then you should follow the relevant school policy and procedures (see section on sharing information with parents and carers in Chapter 5).

EXERCISE: Give examples of how your school exchanges information with parents with regard to their children with special educational needs, e.g. information packs, regular reviews, Individual Education Plans, home-school diaries.

Liaising with other professionals regarding pupils with SEN

The teaching assistant can make a valuable contribution to the school by providing effective support for colleagues and by liaising with parents. In addition, teaching assistants are involved in the network of relationships between staff at the school and other professionals from external agencies such as:

- ✫ **Local education authority**, e.g. educational psychologist, special needs support teachers, special needs advisors, specialist teachers, education welfare officers
- ✫ **Health services**, e.g. paediatricians, health visitors, physiotherapists, occupational therapists, speech and language therapists, play therapists, school nurses, clinical psychologists
- ✫ **Social services department**, e.g. social workers; specialist social workers: sensory disabilities, physical disabilities, mental health or children and families
- ✫ **Charities and voluntary organisations**, e.g. AFASIC, British Dyslexia Association, Council for Disabled Children, National Autistic Society, RNIB, RNID, SCOPE.

EXERCISE: Find out which external agencies and other professionals are connected with the care and support of pupils with SEN at your school.

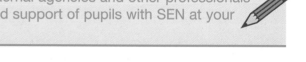

Pupils with special educational needs will often have support from external agencies. The teaching assistant is part of the educational support team, which also includes the teacher and the specialist. To provide the most effective care and support for the pupil, it is essential that the working relationships between the specialist, teacher and teaching assistant run smoothly and that there are no contradictions or missed opportunities due to lack of communication. With guidance from the teacher, teaching assistants can be involved with the work of the specialists in a number of ways: planning support for the pupil with the teacher; assisting pupils to perform tasks set by a specialist; reporting the pupil's progress on such tasks to the teacher.

Any interactions with other professionals should be conducted in such a way as to promote trust and confidence in your working relationships. Your contributions towards the planning and implementation of joint actions must be consistent with your role and responsibilities as a teaching assistant in your school. You should supply other professionals with the relevant information, advice and support as appropriate to your own role and expertise. If requested, you should be willing to share information, knowledge or skills with other professionals. You should use any opportunities to contact or observe the practice of professionals from external agencies to increase your knowledge and understanding of their skills/expertise in order to improve your own work in supporting pupil's learning and development.

KEY TASK

Compile an information booklet suitable for new teaching assistants which includes the following:

- The teaching assistant's role and responsibilities for supporting pupils with special educational needs in the school.
- Links with other professionals from external agencies established by your school.
- Liaising with parents and carers.
- Working with other professionals to support pupils.
- Sources of further information, e.g. special needs organisations, books, websites.

NVQ LINKS:

Level 2:

STL4.1	STL4.2	STL4.3
STL4.4	STL12.1	STL12.2
STL12.3	STL14.3	

Level 3:

STL19.2	STL20.1	STL20.2
STL20.3	STL20.4	STL34.1
STL37.1	STL37.2	STL37.3
STL38.1	STL38.2	STL38.3
STL39.1	STL39.2	STL40.2
STL41.2	STL41.3	STL50.1
STL50.2	STL50.3	STL50.4
STL51.1	STL51.2	STL60.1
STL60.2	STL62.1	STL62.2

Supporting pupils with communication and interaction needs

All pupils have *individual* language needs, but some may have *additional* or special needs that affect their ability to communicate and interact effectively with others. For example: autistic spectrum disorders; behavioural and/or emotional difficulties; cognition difficulties affecting the ability to process language; hearing impairment; physical disabilities affecting articulation of sounds. Depending on their individual language experiences, some pupils may not have reached the same level of language development as their peers or they may lack effective communication skills. Some pupils' language development may even be ahead of what is usually expected for their age. (See section on promoting children's communication skills and language development in Chapter 3.)

Identifying pupils with additional communication and/or interaction needs

Lisping is a common problem for many young children when they are learning to speak; it is caused by the child's inability to articulate a certain sound and so the child substitutes with another similar sound. Lisping usually stops without the need for adult intervention. Sometimes lisping may be a sign of a physical problem such as hearing loss, cleft palate or faulty tongue action in which case specialist advice is needed.

Some children may experience a period of **stammering**, usually around three years old. This is called *dysfluency* and is part of the normal pattern of language development. Dysfluency means that the young child cannot articulate thoughts into words quickly enough hence the stammer. About 5% of children stammer, but it can be difficult to identify them, because children who stammer are often reclusive and reluctant to talk. Most children eventually conquer this communication difficulty especially with the assistance of well-prepared and sympathetic staff as well as the help of speech and language therapists; only 1% of children will continue to stammer as adults.

Delayed language development may be due to environmental or social factors such as poverty, race and culture, parental background or limited early language experiences. These factors may restrict some children's opportunities to explore their environment and to develop language and communication skills through positive and stimulating interactions with others. Children with delayed language development go through the same stages of language development as other children, but at a slower rate. **Disordered language development** is more likely to be caused by: minimal brain damage affecting areas relating to language; physical disabilities affecting articulation of sounds; sensory impairment affecting hearing or visual abilities (see below); cognitive difficulties affecting the ability to process language (see below); autistic spectrum disorders (see below).

A child with a **cleft lip and/or palate** has structural damage to their top lip, palate or both, due to the failed development of these areas of the mouth during the early weeks in the womb. The condition is clearly diagnosed at birth. A series of operations is essential to correct this impairment; this may result in significant language delay as correct speech cannot be articulated until the gaps in the lips and/or palate have been successfully mended. Later speech and language therapy may be necessary.

Some pupils may choose not to speak. This is sometimes known as **selective mutism**. These pupils may be shy, withdrawn and uncommunicative for the following reasons: lack of confidence in group situations or lack of social skills; lack of experience in using English to communicate; emotional trauma; physical or sexual abuse. Check that there is no underlying cause for the pupil's reluctance or refusal to speak, e.g. hearing loss, or stressful event such as going into hospital or a death in the family. Most pupils who are uncommunicative lack confidence in themselves and their ability to relate to others, so it is important to develop their self-esteem (see Chapter 7) and to improve their social skills (see Chapter 3). Do not try to *make* a pupil speak when they are reluctant to do so as this may only cause further anxiety. Give the pupil *opportunities* to speak in a welcoming and non-threatening environment; sometimes they may contribute, sometimes they will not. Even if the pupil does not say anything, make sure they can still observe and listen to what is going on.

Here are some things to look out for when identifying a pupil's communication difficulties: difficulty understanding in one-to-one situations; difficulty understanding in group or class situations; difficulty following instructions; difficulty in pronouncing sounds (e.g. 'wabbit' instead of 'rabbit'); reluctance or refusal to speak; giving one-word answers; repeating sentences; difficulty learning by rote (e.g. rhymes, songs, alphabet, times tables); poor memory skills; inappropriate answers.

Autistic spectrum disorders

Autistic spectrum disorders (ASD) cover a wide range of communication and interaction difficulties from severe mental impairment to slight problems with social interaction. Recent research suggests that as many as 1 in 100 children may have ASD including those with high functioning autism and Asperger Syndrome. It is not known if the current apparent increase in the numbers of children with ASD is real or due to the increased awareness of ASD and the increase in professionals able to give a competent diagnosis. ASD affects four times as many boys as girls. The causes are not known, but autistic tendencies are usually present from birth, although they may not be formally identified until the child attends nursery or school. Children with Asperger Syndrome are at the more able end of the autistic spectrum; they are very intelligent, but they may have communication difficulties which may be disguised as emotional and behavioural problems.

Children with ASD have difficulty in relating to other people; they do not understand the thoughts, feelings and needs of others. In addition, they are usually unable to express their own thoughts, feelings and needs effectively to others. This presents difficulties in acquiring communication skills and being able to understand the social world. Children with severe ASD may not develop language at all. Children with ASD may appear indifferent to others or undemonstrative and often do not like physical contact. Children with ASD may have difficulties with: using verbal and/or non-verbal communication; being aware of other people, which affects their ability to communicate effectively; paying attention to other people (often more interested in objects) which affects their listening and comprehension skills; socialising with other children.

Strategies to support pupils with additional communication and/or interaction needs

Adults working in schools can do a great deal to help pupils with communication difficulties. Many of the language activities already suggested in this book (see sections on promoting children's communication skills and language development in Chapter 3 and developing speaking and listening skills in Chapter 10) are suitable for *all* pupils including those with communication difficulties. Some pupils, especially those with disordered language development, may need specialist help from a speech and language therapist. Here are some possible strategies you can use when supporting pupils with communication difficulties:

- ☆ Keep information short and to the point
- ☆ Avoid complex instructions
- ☆ Speak clearly and not too quickly
- ☆ Be a good speech role model
- ☆ Build up the child's confidence gradually (e.g. speaking one-to-one, then small group)
- ☆ Develop concentration skills, e.g. play memory games
- ☆ Encourage reluctant children to speak, but *do not insist* they talk
- ☆ Use stories and CDs to improve listening skills
- ☆ Use rhythm to sound out name/phrases, music and songs
- ☆ Using pictorial instructions and visual cues
- ☆ Teach social skills as well as communication skills
- ☆ Provide structured play opportunities and learning activities
- ☆ Keep to set routines
- ☆ Prepare for new situations carefully
- ☆ Use the child's favourite activities as rewards
- ☆ Get specialist advice and support, e.g. AFASIC, National Autism Society; health visitors; Portage worker; special needs advisor; specialist teacher; speech and language therapist.

Teaching assistant supporting pupil with additional communication needs

 KEY TASK

Provide examples of how you have encouraged (or could encourage) a pupil with additional communication and/or interaction needs to participate in the full range of activities and experiences in your school, e.g. adapting learning activities or using specialist resources to enable the pupil's full participation.

NVQ LINKS:

Level 2:
STL12.1   STL12.2   STL14.1
STL14.2   STL14.3

Level 3:
STL38.1   STL38.2   STL39.1
STL39.2

Supporting pupils with cognition and learning needs

All pupils have *individual* cognition and learning needs, but some may have *additional* or special needs that affect their ability to participate effectively in learning activities. For example, some pupils may not develop their intellectual processes in line with the expected pattern of development for their age for a variety of reasons: autistic spectrum disorders (see above); attention deficit disorders (see below); emotional difficulties (see below); cognitive and learning difficulties. Additional cognitive and learning needs can be divided into two main areas: general learning difficulties and specific learning difficulties (see below). (See also section on promoting children's intellectual development in Chapter 3.)

Supporting pupils with general learning difficulties

The term 'slow learners' is sometimes used to describe pupils with below average cognitive abilities across all areas of learning; the term **general learning difficulties** is preferable. The wide range of general learning difficulties is divided into three levels:

1. **Mild learning difficulties:** pupils whose learning needs can be met using resources within mainstream settings.
2. **Moderate learning difficulties:** pupils whose learning needs can be met using additional resources in designated classes/special units within mainstream settings or in special schools.
3. **Severe or profound learning difficulties:** pupils whose learning needs require the resources and staff usually available only in special schools.

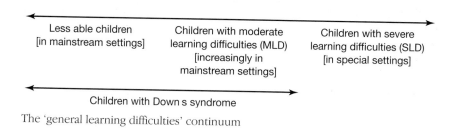

The 'general learning difficulties' continuum

Pupils with general learning difficulties often have delayed development in other areas; they may be socially and emotionally immature and/or have problems with gross/fine motor skills. Pupils with general learning difficulties need carefully structured learning opportunities where new skills are introduced step-by-step. Pupils with this type of cognitive difficulty may have problems processing information; they have difficulty linking their existing knowledge and past experiences to new learning situations which makes it difficult to reach solutions or to develop ideas.

Identifying pupils with general learning difficulties

Pupils with general learning difficulties are usually identified by the adults working with them at an early stage. Here are some common signs to look out for: delay in understanding new ideas/concepts; poor concentration/shorter than usual attention span; inability to remember new skills without constant repetition and reinforcement; poor listening skills; lack of imagination and creativity; difficulty following instructions in large group situations; difficulty comprehending abstract ideas; limited vocabulary; often give one-word answers; problems with memory skills; poor co-ordination affecting hand-eye co-ordination, pencil control; need lots of practical support and concrete materials; delayed reading skills, especially comprehension; delayed understanding of mathematics and science concepts.

Pupils with general learning difficulties (especially in mainstream settings) are often aware that their progress is behind that of their peers. This can be very damaging to their self-esteem. Some pupils may feel they are incapable of learning anything at all. Adults need to convince such pupils that they *can* and *will* learn as long as they keep trying and do not give up.

Praise and encouragement are essential to *all* children's learning. All pupils, regardless of ability, are motivated by achieving success. Make sure the learning activities provided are appropriate by using observations and assessments to plan activities (as appropriate to your setting) which are relevant to each pupil's abilities and interests. Praise and encouragement are especially important to raise the self-esteem of pupils who find learning difficult (see the importance of praise and encouragement in Chapter 5).

Strategies to support pupils with general learning difficulties

The following strategies may help to make learning activities more positive experiences for pupils with general learning difficulties:

- ✫ Build on what the pupils already know.
- ✫ Let the pupils work at their own pace.
- ✫ Provide activities that can be completed in the time available without the pupils feeling under pressure.
- ✫ Divide the learning into small steps in a logical sequence.
- ✫ Present the same concept or idea in various ways to reinforce learning and understanding.
- ✫ Use repetition frequently; short daily lessons are more memorable than one long weekly session.
- ✫ Demonstrate what to do as well as giving verbal instructions.
- ✫ Use real examples and practical experiences/equipment wherever possible.
- ✫ Keep activities short and gradually work towards increasing their concentration.
- ✫ Encourage active participation in discussion and group activities to extend language and communication skills.
- ✫ Provide more stimuli for learning activities rather than expecting the pupils to develop new ideas entirely by themselves.
- ✫ Help the pupils to develop skills in accessing information, e.g. use technology such as computers, Internet; and also libraries, reference books; museums.
- ✫ *Listen* to the pupils and take on board their points of view.
- ✫ Get specialist advice and support, e.g. MENCAP; educational psychologist; health visitor; Portage worker; special needs advisor; specialist teacher; occupational therapist.

Supporting pupils with specific learning difficulties

Pupils with specific learning difficulties show problems in learning in one particular area of development. For example: a pupil with **dyslexia** has difficulties in acquiring literacy skills; a pupil with **dyscalculia** has difficulties in acquiring numeracy skills; a pupil with **dyspraxia** has difficulties with the way the brain processes information which affects the co-ordination of movement.

Identifying pupils with dyslexia

Pupils with dyslexia have difficulties in acquiring literacy skills and consequently other aspects of learning may be affected. It is estimated that 4% of pupils are affected by dyslexia.

Look out for these signs of possible specific learning difficulties in the **under-fives**: delay or difficulty in speech development; persistent tendency to mix-up words and phrases; persistent difficulty with tasks such as dressing; unusual clumsiness and lack of co-ordination; poor concentration; family history of similar difficulties. However, many young children make similar mistakes; specific learning difficulties is only indicated where the difficulties are severe and persistent or grouped together (BDA, 1997).

Look out for these possible signs of specific learning difficulties in **5 to 9 year olds**: particular difficulties in learning to read, write and spell; persistent and continued reversing of letters and numerals (e.g. 'b' for 'd', 51 for 15); difficulty telling left from right; difficulty learning the alphabet and multiplication tables; difficulty remembering sequences, e.g. days of the week/months of the year; difficulty with tying shoelaces, ball-catching and other co-ordination skills; poor concentration; frustration, possibly leading to behavioural difficulties; difficulty following verbal and/or written instructions (BDA, 1997).

Look out for these possible signs of specific learning difficulties in **9 to 12 year olds**: difficulties with reading including poor comprehension skills; difficulties with writing and spelling including letters missing or in wrong order; problems with completing tasks in the required time; being disorganised at school (and at home); difficulties with copying from chalkboard, whiteboard or textbook; difficulties with following verbal and/or written instructions; lack of self-confidence and frustration (BDA, 1997).

Look out for these possible signs of specific learning difficulties in **12 to 16 year olds**: reads inaccurately and/or lacks comprehension skills; inconsistency with spelling; difficulties with taking notes, planning and writing essays; confuses telephone numbers and addresses; difficulties with following verbal instructions; severe problems when learning a foreign language; frustration and low self-esteem (BDA, 1997).

Strategies to support pupils with dyslexia

The following strategies may help when working with pupils with specific learning difficulties:

* Ensure the pupil is near you or at the front of the class/group.
* Check unobtrusively that copy-writing, note-taking, etc. is done efficiently.
* Use 'buddy' system, i.e. another pupil copies for this one.
* Give positive feedback and encouragement, without drawing undue attention to the pupil.

✯ Use computers to help the pupil (e.g. word-processing with spell-check facility).

✯ Help the pupil to develop effective strategies and study skills which may differ from those used by other pupils.

✯ Get specialist advice and support, e.g. British Dyslexia Association; educational psychologist; health visitors; special needs advisor; specialist teacher; occupational therapist.

(BDA, 1997)

Identifying pupils with dyscalculia

The term **dyscalculia**, meaning difficulty in performing mathematical calculations, is given to a specific disorder in the ability to do or learn mathematics. Pupils with dyscalculia will experience difficulty with understanding number concepts and the relationships of numbers as well as using application procedures. Pupils with dyscalculia may have difficulties with the following:

✯ Distinguishing between mathematics signs and symbols (e.g. 1, 2, £, etc.).

✯ Distinguishing between digits that are similar in shape (e.g. 6 and 9, 7 and 1, 2 and 5) when reading and writing numbers.

✯ Sequencing, e.g. saying times tables, predicting next number in a series, use of number line, following a sequence of instructions (e.g. when doing a two-stage calculation).

✯ Remembering the range of alternative words and phrases for number operations (e.g. *add, plus* and *sum* are all addition terms).

✯ The correct use of place value and the direction of number operations (e.g. subtraction starting with smallest place value, division starting with highest place value).

✯ Mathematics word problems including reading and language processing difficulties or losing track of number operation mid-process, especially if this is being done mentally.

✯ Organising and setting out calculations in writing.

✯ Memorising and recalling maths facts (e.g. recalling tables, mental arithmetic).

(DfES, 2003a)

Strategies to support pupils with dyscalculia

✯ Concrete materials (e.g. real objects) are important for all pupils but especially for pupils with learning difficulties. Pupils need real objects and experiences to help them develop an understanding of the abstract concepts used in mathematics.

✯ Use flash cards and illustrated wall displays to demonstrate the specific mathematical vocabulary for a particular task.

✯ Keep written instructions and explanations on worksheets to a minimum.

✯ Mathematics has a strong visual element so make frequent use of a number line, 100 square, number apparatus, pictures, diagrams, graphs and computer programmes.

✭ Use games and puzzles where pupils can quickly pick up the rules after watching a demonstration.

(DfES, 2003a)

Identifying pupils with dyspraxia

Pupils with dyspraxia have a difficulty in the way the brain processes information, which results in messages not being properly or fully transmitted so that the co-ordination of movement, perception and thought are affected. Dyspraxia is a difficulty in formulating the plan rather than a primary problem of motor execution.

Dyspraxia may be shown by marked delays in achieving motor milestones (e.g. crawling or walking), dropping things, difficulties with balance, 'clumsiness', or poor performance in sports or handwriting. Pupils with dyspraxia may have problems using knives and forks, tying shoelaces or holding a pencil. When hand-writing, they may also show difficulties with directionality and pressure on the page. Visual and perceptual difficulties (e.g. copying from the board or following sequential instructions) can also be symptoms of dyspraxia.

Strategies to support pupils with dyspraxia

✭ Give clear and unambiguous instructions.

✭ Break down activities into small steps.

✭ Arrange a 'buddy system'.

✭ Allow extra time for completing work.

✭ Teach the pupil strategies for remembering things.

✭ Use activities and strategies to encourage development and limit the impact of difficulties in school as suggested by the pupil's occupational therapist.

✭ Get specialist advice and support from The Dyspraxia Foundation.

KEY TASK

Provide examples of how you have encouraged (or could encourage) a pupil with general or specific learning difficulties to participate in the full range of activities and experiences in your school, e.g. encouraging the pupil to participate in learning activities or modifying learning activities to meet the pupil's individual learning needs.

NVQ LINKS:

Level 2:
STL12.1 STL12.2 STL14.1
STL14.2 STL14.3

Level 3:
STL38.1 STL38.2 STL40.1
STL40.2 STL62.2

Supporting gifted and talented pupils

Gifted and talented pupils are those who have one or more abilities developed to a level significantly ahead of their year group (or have the potential to develop these abilities). The term **gifted** refers to pupils who may excel in academic subjects such as English, mathematics, science or history. **Talented** refers to those pupils who may excel in areas requiring more practical abilities, such as art, drama, music or sport. Some gifted and talented pupils may be intellectually able but also appear on the Special Educational Needs (SEN) register for behavioural, literacy or physical difficulties.

Identifying gifted and talented pupils

Behaviours indicating higher ability, giftedness and talent may not be readily observable, for a number of reasons, for example: pupils may not have had sufficient opportunity to demonstrate their ability; pupils may hide their ability in order to 'fit in' with their peers; pupils may under-achieve for other reasons such as learning difficulties which mask their higher ability and talent. Certain characteristics may be demonstrated by gifted and talented pupils but these characteristics are indicative and not definitive; remember all children are unique individuals.

A gifted or talented pupil may:

* be a good reader
* be very articulate or verbally fluent for their age; give quick verbal responses
* have a wide general knowledge
* learn quickly
* be interested in topics which one might associate with an older child
* communicate well with adults – often better than with their peer group
* have a range of interests, some of which are almost obsessions
* show unusual and original responses to problem-solving activities
* prefer verbal to written activities
* be logical
* be self-taught in their own interest areas
* have an ability to work things out in their head very quickly
* have a good memory that they can access easily
* be artistic or musical or excel at sport
* have strong views and opinions
* have a lively and original imagination/sense of humour
* be very sensitive and aware
* focus on their own interests rather than on what is being taught
* be socially adept
* appear arrogant or socially inept
* be easily bored by what they perceive as routine tasks
* show a strong sense of leadership
* not necessarily be well behaved or well liked by others.

(DfES, 2004)

Strategies to support gifted and talented pupils

Gifted and talented pupils need additional challenges and innovative ideas to stretch their cognitive capabilities with access to advanced resources. They also require plenty of opportunities for independent, original and creative thought/action. Remember the pupils' social and emotional needs as well as their intellectual needs. Try to avoid making them feel different or extraordinary as this may make it difficult for them to mix with other pupils in the school.

Gifted and talented pupils can be more effectively supported by giving them the following:

- ✯ Space to make their own contributions in situations that are open ended.
- ✯ The opportunity to take risks with the possibility of failure in non-threatening and well-organised situations.
- ✯ Contact with other people like them.
- ✯ A share of the teacher's time that is fair, focused and appropriate to their needs.
- ✯ Activities that require them to spend a balance of time both working with urgency and reflecting quietly on their work; the opportunity and time to research for themselves.
- ✯ Questioning structured to employ their higher-order thinking skills with similar answers to their questions.
- ✯ Minimal instruction when possible, allowing them to use initiative and problem-solving skills, and opportunities to develop their work in directions they have chosen themselves.
- ✯ Encouragement to use a range of alternative methods and approaches and organisational and presentation techniques.
- ✯ Work set in ways that involve challenging creativity and imagination.
- ✯ Schemes of work that incorporate starting points for work sometimes with clear steps and sometimes open-ended.
- ✯ An appreciation that social and emotional maturity does not always equate with intellectual ability.
- ✯ A range of differentiation and enrichment activities and strategies.

(NAGC, 2007)

KEY TASK

Provide examples of how you have encouraged (or could encourage) gifted or talented pupils to extend their learning, e.g. providing additional challenges and/or access to advanced resources.

 NVQ LINKS:

Level 3:
STL34.1   STL34.2

Supporting pupils with behavioural, social and emotional development needs

All pupils have *individual* behavioural, social and emotional needs, but some may have *additional* or special needs that affect their ability to interact appropriately with others and/or participate effectively during routines and activities. For example, some pupils may have behavioural, social and/or emotional difficulties which hinder their ability to: follow specific routines or instructions for activities; interact positively with other pupils or adults; participate in play and learning opportunities; express their feelings appropriately.

Identifying pupils with behavioural, social and emotional difficulties

The adult's response to a pupil's behaviour is as important as the behaviour itself. Different people have different attitudes to what is or is not acceptable behaviour. The social context also affects adult attitudes towards children's behaviour (see Chapter 4). All adults should consider certain types of behaviour unacceptable. These include behaviour which causes: physical harm to others; self-harm; emotional/psychological harm to others; destruction to property.

Pupils whose unwanted behaviour is demonstrated through aggressive or disruptive behaviour are usually the ones to attract the most adult attention, as they are easily identified and hard to ignore. Pupils who demonstrate unwanted behaviour in a withdrawn manner may be overlooked especially by inexperienced adults or in very busy settings (see sections on recognising behaviour patterns and other influences on pupil behaviour in Chapter 4).

Most pupils with behavioural, social and emotional development needs respond favourably to a positive approach. However, some pupils may have been identified and assessed as having particular emotional and behavioural difficulties:

- ☆ **Pupils with emotional difficulties:** can be difficult to include; may have learning difficulties (see below).
- ☆ **Disruptive pupils:** disrupt the teaching and learning process; a nuisance; short concentration span; attention-seeking behaviour (see Chapter 4).
- ☆ **Disaffected pupils:** lacking in motivation; cannot see the point of learning; appears totally uninterested and doesn't want to be in school; difficult to re-engage; difficult to motivate; does not seem to appreciate any efforts the teacher might make (see below).
- ☆ **Pupils with Attention Deficit Disorders:** pupils with ADD have short concentration span; divergent mind; difficult to engage/motivate. Pupils with ADHD have similar difficulties to pupils with ADD, but are more complex and difficult to manage; ignore 'classroom rules' (see below).

Pupils with emotional difficulties

Pupils may experience emotional difficulties for a variety of reasons. Some emotional difficulties are part of the usual pattern of children's emotional development and are only temporary. For example: emotional outbursts (see Chapter 5); common childhood fears; reactions to family or friend's accident/illness, child's own accident/illness or pet illness/death; adjusting to transitions such as starting nursery/school or the arrival of new baby or step-sibling (see Chapter 7); pressures at home or school; concerns about tests or exams; worries about local, national or international crises witnessed in the media.

Some pupils may experience emotional difficulties of a more lasting nature. For example, emotional difficulties as a result of traumatic experiences such as: child abuse (see Chapter 2) or bullying (see Chapter 4); parental separation and divorce (especially when there are disputes about child support and/or residency); terminal illness or bereavement in a child's family; domestic violence; armed conflict; witnessing a violent or catastrophic event, e.g. shooting, stabbing, car crash or natural disaster.

Disaffected pupils

Indicators of disaffection in school range from disruptive behaviour to unauthorised absence and persistent truancy. Schools should regularly review the progress of pupils to identify any pupils at risk of failure at school, in partnership with the Education Welfare Service and other agencies. Where there are signs of disaffection, early intervention by the school may prevent problems from worsening. It is important that schools closely monitor attendance so that any patterns of non-attendance are identified and dealt with, e.g. tackling and preventing pupil absenteeism before it reaches the point where the pupil is referred to the Education Welfare Service. Pupils who do not respond to school actions to combat disaffection may be at serious risk of permanent exclusion or criminal activity.

A whole school approach to attendance and absence is essential to handling signs of disaffection and should include: a strong school attendance ethos; clear absence policies; effective systems to monitor attendance; promoting the importance and legal requirements of good attendance to pupils and their parents; early intervention when pupil absences give cause for concern; support systems for vulnerable pupils; rewards for good and improved attendance.

Pupils with Attention Deficit Disorders

Attention Deficit Disorder can occur with or without hyperactivity. If hyperactivity is not present then the disorder is usually called just Attention Deficit Disorder (ADD). Attention Deficit Disorder (ADD) or Attention Deficit Hyperactivity Disorder (ADHD) affects about 5% of school-aged children and it is possible that about 10% of children have a milder form of the disorder. Some children with ADD or ADHD may also have other difficulties such as specific learning difficulties, e.g. dyslexia. Boys are more likely to be affected than girls. ADD and ADHD are rarely diagnosed before the age of 6 years because many young children demonstrate the behaviours characteristic of this disorder as part of the usual sequence of development. From about 6 years old it is easier to assess whether the child's behaviour is *significantly* different from the expected norm. Most children with ADD or ADHD are formally identified between 5 and 9 years old.

Pupils with ADD are usually:

> ✫ *Inattentive* with a short attention span; unable to concentrate on tasks, easily distracted; they forget instructions due to poor short-term memory; they may seem distant or be prone to 'day dreaming'.

- ✭ *Lacking in co-ordination skills* and may have poor hand-eye co-ordination resulting in untidy written work; they may be accident prone.
- ✭ *Disorganised* and unable to structure their own time; unable to motivate themselves unless directed on a one-to-one basis; they may be very untidy.

In addition pupils with ADHD are usually:

- ✭ *Over-active* with high levels of activity and movement; restless and fiddle with objects.
- ✭ *Extremely impulsive* which may lead to accidents as they have no sense of danger; they often speak and act without thinking.
- ✭ *Lacking in social skills* as they do not know how to behave with others; very bossy and domineering; unable to make or keep friends; they may demonstrate inappropriate behaviour or misread social cues, e.g. treating complete strangers as close friends.
- ✭ *Changeable and unpredictable*, with severe, unexplained mood swings; short-tempered with frequent emotional or extremely aggressive outbursts.

The National Institute for Clinical Excellence recommends that 1% of children with severe ADHD (around 100,000) should receive medication such as methylphenidate (Ritalin). Methylphenidate is a stimulant which enhances brain function and has been very effective in children with severe ADHD. Such medication helps focus the child's attention, keeps them on task and allows the child to think before they act. Once the child's concentration and behaviour improves the dose can be decreased. With or without medication, it is important to have a consistent system for managing the child's behaviour within the childcare/education setting and at home.

In schools staff need to provide the following for pupils with ADD or ADHD: a quiet group/class with one or two adults who are firm but fair and can provide consistent care and education throughout the year; calmness and a clear routine; seating near a known adult away from distracting pupils; step-by-step instructions; constant feedback, praise and encouragement.

Strategies to support pupils with behavioural, social and emotional difficulties

Providing support for pupils with behavioural, social and emotional difficulties is one of the most challenging roles that teaching assistants may have to undertake. When supporting pupils with such difficulties you may sometimes feel hopeless, annoyed or helpless. However, working with pupils with additional behavioural, social and emotional needs can also be very rewarding, as by providing appropriate support, you are helping them to develop the life skills and coping strategies they need.

You can provide effective support through positive strategies and inclusion by:

- ✭ enhancing the pupil's self-esteem
- ✭ assisting the pupil to recognise the effect of the behaviour
- ✭ being constructive
- ✭ clearly explaining what constitutes unacceptable behaviour

☆ fostering and encouraging parental support where possible
☆ early identification of possible difficulties
☆ using rewards and sanctions that are fair, and consistently applied
☆ liaising with colleagues and other professionals.

Pupils with behavioural, social and emotional difficulties usually have an Individual Education Plan (IEP) and/or an Individual Behaviour Support Plan (BSP) or a Pastoral Support Plan (PSP) if they are at risk of being excluded from school. These plans will give you information about the support being provided to help the pupil and will often include details of your role and responsibilities in providing behaviour support. You may sometimes be involved in drawing up these plans, along with the teacher, the pupil and their parents or carers. (For detailed information see sections on promoting positive behaviour and managing pupils' challenging behaviour in Chapter 4. See also sections on encouraging positive social interactions in Chapter 5 and promoting children's social development in Chapter 3.)

 KEY TASK

Provide examples of how you have encouraged (or could encourage) a pupil with behavioural, social and emotional difficulties to participate in the full range of activities and experiences in your school, e.g. encouraging the pupil to participate effectively in learning activities; encouraging the pupil to behave in more acceptable ways by using appropriate rewards and sanctions; improving school attendance; helping the pupil to develop a positive self-image and self-esteem; providing opportunities for the pupil to express their feelings more appropriately such as discussion, storytime and play activities.

NVQ LINKS:

Level 2:
STL3.4 STL12.1 STL12.2

Level 3:
STL19.1 STL19.2 STL20.3
STL37.1 STL37.2 STL37.3
STL38.1 STL38.2 STL40.1
STL40.2 STL41.1 STL41.2
STL41.3 STL45.1 STL45.4
STL50.1 STL50.2 STL50.3
STL50.4 STL51.1 STL51.2

Supporting pupils with sensory and/or physical needs

Some pupils may require additional support in school due to sensory and/or physical needs such as hearing, visual and/or physical impairment. As pupils with sensory or physical impairments may be dependent on others for some of their needs, it is essential to provide opportunities for them to be as independent as possible. Give them every chance to join in, to express opinions and to interact with their peer group. Remember to focus on each child as a unique person with individual strengths rather than focusing on the child's particular disabilities, e.g. what they *can* do rather than what they cannot.

Supporting pupils with hearing impairment

Hearing loss may range from a slight impairment to profound deafness. One in four children under the age of seven experiences a hearing loss of some degree at some time. The loss may affect one or both ears at different levels. There are two types of hearing impairment:

1. **Conductive hearing loss** – involving the interference of the transmission of sound from the outer to the inner ear. This may be due to congestion or damage to the inner ear. The loss may be temporary or permanent; it makes sounds seem like the volume has been turned down. Hearing aids can be useful to amplify speech sounds, but unfortunately background noise is also increased. The most common form of conductive hearing loss in younger children is *glue ear*. This temporary condition is caused by the collection of fluid behind the ear drum triggered by congestion during an ear, nose or throat infection. Sometimes glue ear can cause language delay as it interferes with a young child's hearing at an important stage of speech development. Persistent or repetitive cases of glue ear may require a minor operation to drain the fluid and to insert a grommet or small tube into the ear drum to prevent further fluid build up (see below).

2. **Sensori-neural loss** is a rarer condition that is more likely to result in permanent hearing impairment. The damage to the inner ear results in distorted sounds where some sounds are heard but not others. *High frequency loss* affects the child's ability to hear consonants; *low frequency loss* is a less common condition. Hearing aids are not as

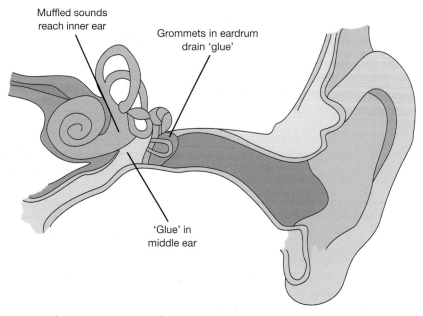

Muffled sounds reach inner ear

Grommets in eardrum drain 'glue'

'Glue' in middle ear

An ear with a grommet inserted

effective with this type of hearing impairment as the child will still be unable to hear the missing sounds. Children with sensori-neural loss therefore find it more difficult to develop speech and have a more significant language delay.

Identifying pupils with hearing impairment

Pupils with hearing impairment, especially those with conductive hearing loss, may be difficult to identify. However, even a slight hearing loss may affect a pupil's language development. Look out for these signs of possible hearing loss in pupils: slow reactions; delay in following instructions; constantly checking what to do; apparently day-dreaming or inattentive; over-anxiety; watching faces closely; turning head to one side to listen; asking to repeat what was said; difficulty regulating voice; poor language development; spoken work more difficult to do than written work; may have emotional or aggressive outbursts due to frustration; problems with social interaction.

Pupils with hearing loss will use lip-reading and non-verbal clues such as gesture and body language to work out what is being said. Some pupils will wear hearing aids to improve their hearing abilities. Cochlear implants are relatively new but are being used with more and more children. A prosthesis is worn partly inside the body and partly outside, and is used to aid hearing. Some schools may encourage the use of signing systems such as British Sign Language or Makaton and have specially trained staff to facilitate the use of sign language throughout the school.

Strategies to support pupils with hearing impairment

The following suggestions may help when working with pupils with hearing impairment:

* ✯ Reduce background noise, e.g. have carpets where possible.
* ✯ Ensure the pupil is near to you.
* ✯ Use facial expressions and gestures.
* ✯ Use visual aids, e.g. real objects, pictures, books, photos, etc.
* ✯ Keep your mouth visible.
* ✯ Do not shout but speak clearly and naturally.
* ✯ Check the pupil is paying attention.
* ✯ Develop listening skills through music and games.
* ✯ Include the pupil in group activities in sensitive manner.
* ✯ Get specialist advice and support, e.g. Royal National Institute for the Deaf (RNID); health visitor; special needs advisor; specialist teacher; speech and language therapist.

Supporting pupils with visual impairment

Visual impairment is a low incidence condition affecting approximately two children per thousand. There are many causes of blindness and partial sight and the effect of particular conditions is unique to the individual. The broadest definition is that vision can be considered to be impaired if, even with the use of contact lenses or glasses, a person's sight cannot be fully corrected (ATL, 2002).

Some pupils may wear glasses to correct short or long sight, but these pupils are not considered to be visually impaired. Pupils with normal vision in only one eye (monocular vision) are not considered to be visually impaired, because one eye enables them to see quite well for most activities. Pupils with monocular vision will have difficulties with 3D perception and judging distances. Remember pupils with a squint may be relying on the vision of the one 'good' eye. Some pupils may be 'colour blind' and have difficulty differentiating between certain colours, usually red and green. Again this is not a visual impairment, but may cause occasional difficulties in the setting, e.g. when doing activities involving colour recognition, colour mixing, etc. There is also a safety implication, e.g. red for danger/stop may be confused with green for go.

Identifying pupils with visual impairment

The majority of pupils with visual impairment will have been identified before they start school but there may be a few pupils who have not, particularly in the younger age range. Be aware of the following, a pupil who: blinks or rubs eyes a lot; has itchy, watery or inflamed eyes; frowns, squints or peers at work; closes/covers one eye when looking at books; bumps into people or furniture; has difficulty with physical games/appears clumsy; has difficulty forming letters and numbers; omits words or sentences when reading; says they cannot see the chalkboard or worksheet; suffers from frequent headaches; dislikes classroom/nursery lighting.

Strategies to support pupils with visual impairment

Vision is an essential component of learning in mainstream settings; visual impairment can affect language development in terms of written language and learning to read. It is essential to work with colleagues and parents to provide the best care and education for pupils with visual impairment. Specialist advice and equipment may be necessary depending on the extent of the visual impairment. The following strategies may help when supporting such pupils:

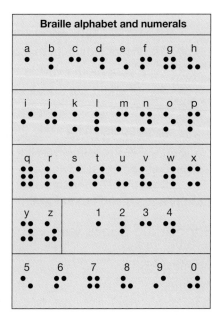

Braille alphabet and numerals

* ✩ Ensure the pupil is near to you.
* ✩ Make sure the pupil wears glasses if they are supposed to.
* ✩ Keep the room tidy and free from obstacles.
* ✩ Black writing on a matt white board is better than using a chalkboard.
* ✩ Make worksheets clear and bold.
* ✩ Allow time for writing when necessary.
* ✩ Keep writing to a minimum; use oral methods, e.g. tape recorder.

* Use word-processing where possible.
* Enlarge worksheets and books.
* Use other senses, e.g. touch and sound, to reinforce learning.
* Use visual aids such as a magnifier.
* Be aware of possible mobility problems during physical activities.
* Use talking books and story books with Braille on plastic inserts.
* Get specialist advice and support, e.g. Royal National Institute for the Blind (RNIB); health visitor; special needs advisor; specialist teacher.
* Provide pre-Braille and Braille activities after consulting a specialist advisor.

 KEY TASK

Provide examples of how you have encouraged (or could encourage) a pupil with hearing or visual impairment to participate in the full range of activities and experiences in your school.

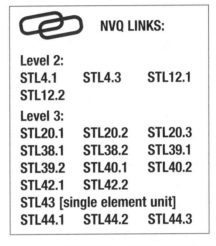

NVQ LINKS:

Level 2:
STL4.1   STL4.3   STL12.1
STL12.2

Level 3:
STL20.1   STL20.2   STL20.3
STL38.1   STL38.2   STL39.1
STL39.2   STL40.1   STL40.2
STL42.1   STL42.2
STL43 [single element unit]
STL44.1   STL44.2   STL44.3

Supporting pupils with physical disabilities

As part of your role you may be involved in supporting pupils with physical disabilities. Medical conditions may also affect children's stamina and their ability to participate fully in all areas of the school curriculum. Some physical disabilities have related medical conditions which require regular medication, sometimes to be taken during school hours. (For more detailed information see the sections on following the procedures for storing and administering medicines and supporting pupils with special medical needs in Chapter 2.)

Identifying pupils with physical disabilities

About 15% of children have some kind of physical disability: some children are severely disabled by physical difficulties due to damage to the neurological system which controls motor functions, e.g. cerebral palsy and spina bifida; some children have relatively minor difficulties such as dyspraxia.

Some children have multiple disabilities, affecting several physical functions, such as hearing or visual impairment combined with motor disorders. Some physical and medical problems are congenital; others emerge later on. Some children with a physical disability will be easily identifiable, but others less so if their condition can be effectively controlled. Schools need to know enough about children's medical conditions to help them access their educational entitlement (ATL, 2002: p.29).

Examples of physical disabilities and medical conditions that may affect pupils include:

- ✵ **Cystic fibrosis** – Cystic Fibrosis Trust: www.cftrust.org.uk
- ✵ **Muscular dystrophy** – Muscular Dystrophy Campaign: www.muscular-dystrophy.org
- ✵ **Haemophilia** – The Haemophilia Society: www.haemophilia.org.uk
- ✵ **Sickle cell anaemia** – The Sickle Cell Society: www.sicklecellsociety.org
- ✵ **Cerebral palsy** – Scope: www.scope.org.uk
- ✵ **Spina bifida and hydrocephalus** – ASBAH: www.asbah.org.

(For detailed information on asthma, diabetes, epilepsy and severe allergic reaction (anaphylaxis) see the section on supporting pupils with special medical needs in Chapter 2.)

Strategies for supporting pupils with physical disabilities

You need to develop skills and strategies to enable pupils with physical disabilities to participate in play and learning activities. When supporting the teacher in planning and implementing these, remember that some pupils with physical disabilities may not be able to make full use of materials and equipment. They may not be able to participate fully in some activities with other pupils and may need the understanding and sensitive support of other pupils and staff, as well as specially adapted play and learning equipment.

Working with the teacher, you need to ensure that the classroom, learning activities and equipment are adapted where necessary to enable pupils with physical disabilities to participate as fully as possible. If you are involved in planning how to adapt the setting for a pupil with a physical disability, consider the space needed for a wheelchair, frame or other walking aids, and also where ramps will be required instead of steps. Provide sufficient space between tables and chairs to allow a pupil with mobility aids to move freely without obstacles. If you work in a mainstream education setting you will need to consider the needs of *all* the pupils.

You should know how to help pupils with physical disabilities to participate in the full range of activities and experiences, e.g. adapting learning activities or using specialist equipment to enable the pupil's full participation (for more information see sections on promoting equality and inclusion in Chapter 5 and helping to organise the learning environment in Chapter 12).

Pupils should be encouraged to participate in a wide a range of play and learning activities as appropriate to their needs including their level of development, physical abilities/limitations. Modified or specialised equipment and learning materials should be used to meet the children's needs, allowing for maximum participation in play opportunities and learning activities. (For more information see sections on promoting equality and inclusion in Chapter 5 and promoting children's physical development in Chapter 3.) Work with the teacher to provide appropriate challenges for the pupils, whilst maintaining their health and safety (see section on maintaining pupil safety during play and learning activities in Chapter 2). You can support pupils with physical disabilities by:

- ✸ using learning activities that are self-correcting
- ✸ encouraging pupils to make choices, e.g. selecting materials for creative activities
- ✸ praising pupils for effort and small achievements
- ✸ having high but realistic expectations for their learning
- ✸ ensuring pupils are not ridiculed or bullied
- ✸ informing colleagues about pupil progress.

There are a number of agencies which offer specialist advice and support for children with physical disabilities, for example: advisory teacher; charities, e.g. SCOPE; health visitor; nursery provision for children with special needs; occupational therapist; physiotherapist; special needs assistant; speech and language therapist.

KEY TASK

Describe how you have encouraged (or could encourage) a pupil with a physical disability to positively participate in discussions and activities in your school, e.g. adapting learning activities or using specialist equipment to enable the pupil's full participation.

NVQ LINKS:

Level 2:

STL4.1	STL4.3	STL12.1	STL12.2
STL13.1	STL13.2	STL14.1	STL14.2
STL14.3			

Level 3:

STL20.1	STL20.2	STL20.3	STL38.1
STL38.2	STL39.1	STL39.2	STL40.1
STL40.2	STL42.1	STL42.2	
STL43 [single element unit]			STL44.1
STL44.2	STL44.3		

Further reading

Alcott, M. (2002) *An introduction to children with special needs.* Hodder Arnold.

ATL (2002) *Achievement for all: working with children with special educational needs in mainstream schools and colleges.* Association of Teachers and Lecturers. (Available free at www.atl.org.uk.)

Autism Working Group (2002) *Autistic spectrum disorders: good practice guidance.* DfES.

CWDC (2007) *Learning mentors practice guide.* Children's Workforce Development council. (Available free at www.cwdcouncil.org.uk.)

DfES (2001) *The special educational needs code of practice 2001.* HMSO.

DfES (2003) *Removing barriers to achievement: the government's strategy for SEN.* DfES.

Diaz, L. (2008) *The teaching assistant's guide to speech, language and communication needs.* Continuum International Publishing.

Distin, K. (ed.) *Gifted children: a guide for parents and professionals.* Jessica Kingsley Publishers.

Lee, C. (2007) *Resolving behaviour problems in your school: a practical guide for teachers and support staff.* Paul Chapman Educational Publishing.

Spohrer, K. (2007) *The teaching assistant's guide to ADHD.* Continuum International Publishing.

Spooner, W. (2006) *The SEN handbook for trainee teachers, NQTs and teaching Assistants.* Routledge.

(Note: DfES publications are available free at www.teachernet.gov.uk.)

12 Supporting the wider work of the school

Key points:

* Helping to organise the learning environment
* Organising classroom resources
* Organising displays
* Organising cover for absent colleagues
* Invigilating tests and examinations
* Maintaining pupil records
* Organising and supervising travel.

Helping to organise the learning environment

Central to creating an appropriate learning environment for all pupils in school is providing space, time and resources relevant to the needs of the pupils and the requirements of the National Curriculum. As well as provision for the National Curriculum subjects, there should be regular times for routines such as playtimes/breaks, lunchtime, etc. A daily routine provides stability and security for pupils. The class timetable should be clearly displayed in a manner appropriate to the ages of the pupils; older pupils should have their own copy of their weekly timetable. Flexibility is also important to allow for special events such as educational visits, swimming lessons or visitors to the school. In addition to knowing the timetable for the pupil and/or class you work with, you should have your own timetable showing where, what and with whom you are working throughout the school day.

> EXERCISE:
> 1. Outline the daily/weekly routine for the pupil and/or class whose learning you support.
> 2. Provide a copy of your own personal timetable.

The organisation of the learning environment

The precise way the learning environment is organised depends on: specific curriculum requirements; the resources for particular subject areas; the learning objectives for the pupils; individual teaching and learning styles; behaviour management strategies; the inclusion of pupils with special educational needs. Effective organisation is also influenced by the general quality of the learning environment. The learning environment should have the following:

1. **Adequate floor space for the age, size and needs of the pupils:** This means teaching space including space for teaching assistants to work with individuals or groups of pupils as needed. Pupils with physical disabilities may require additional floor space for wheelchairs and other specialised equipment or furniture. Pupils with emotional and/or behavioural difficulties may also benefit from adequate personal classroom space.

2. **Appropriate sources of heating, lighting and ventilation:** Pupils need to work in an environment that is neither too hot nor too cold as these can affect concentration levels. The heating source must be safe and fitted/maintained to the required legal standards. There should be good sources of both natural and artificial light.

3. **Appropriate acoustic conditions:** Needed to enable pupils to listen during essential discussions and to help reduce noise levels. Carpeted floor areas, sound absorbent screens, displays, drapes and curtains all help to absorb reverberation.

4. **Adequate storage space:** Required for the materials and equipment needed to meet the demands of the National Curriculum. There should also be space for computer workstations with access to mains power.

The classroom layout should be free from clutter and easily accessible to all pupils including those with physical disabilities or sensory impairment. The learning environment should also be welcoming and user-friendly. This includes taking account of cultural differences by providing displays and notices which reflect the cultural diversity of the school and local community.

As part of your role of assisting the teacher with the organisation of the learning environment, you may be responsible for:

☆ **a group of pupils** and be involved in setting out materials or helping the pupils to access them, explaining a task, maintaining their concentration and interest, asking and/or answering questions, helping pupils to clear away afterwards before moving on to support them with their next activity

☆ **a specific activity** with different groups of pupils throughout the day or week (e.g. supporting literacy, numeracy, science or ICT)

☆ **a pupil with special educational needs** and ensuring that they have the necessary materials and equipment to participate in the lesson including any specialist equipment.

KEY TASK

With the class teacher's permission, take a photograph of the classroom and comment on how the learning environment provides:

- adequate floor space for the age, size and needs of the children
- appropriate sources of heating, lighting and ventilation
- appropriate acoustic conditions
- adequate storage space for materials and equipment
- access for all pupils including those with physical disabilities or sensory impairment.

NVQ LINKS:

Level 2:
STL1.1 STL2.4 STL3.1

Level 3:
STL18.1 STL18.2 STL23.1
STL24.1 STL28.2 STL31.1
STL31.2 STL31.3 STL38.1
STL45.2

The location of safety equipment

You should know where the fire alarm points and fire exits are, the location of fire extinguishers and fire blankets and their use. There may be different types of extinguishers for use with different hazardous substances, e.g. in science laboratories and kitchens, water must not be used to put out oil or electrical fires as this can make the situation worse. Carbon dioxide extinguishers will be located in the necessary places.

You should also know the location of first-aid equipment/facilities. First-aid equipment must be clearly labelled and easily accessible. All first-aid containers must be marked with a white cross on a green background. There should be at least one fully stocked first-aid container for each building within the school with extra first-aid containers available on split-sites/levels, distant playing fields/playgrounds and any other high-risk areas (e.g. kitchens) and for outings or educational visits.

EXERCISE:
1. Where is the safety equipment located in your classroom?
2. Where is the nearest first-aid box?

Organising classroom resources

Every classroom is equipped with a basic set of resources and books appropriate to the age range. Care is taken to ensure that resources reflect the cultural and linguistic diversity of our society, and that all pupils have equality of access. Examples of **general classroom resources** include the following:

- ☆ Visual aids: wall displays including pupils' work, maps, posters, pictures and posters; interest tables with interesting objects related to topic work; 3D displays of pupils' work including construction models; videos;

computer graphics and books. Displays in the classroom reflect the linguistic and cultural diversity of the school.

An example of an effective learning environment

☆ Groups of tables for whole-class and group work including literacy and numeracy activities.

☆ Groups of tables for 'messy' practical activities (e.g. art and design, design technology) including storage for art/design materials and equipment, e.g. paint, paint pots, drying rack; sink for washing paint pots and brushes; basin for washing hands.

☆ Some computers and a printer with selection of appropriate software.

☆ Tape recorder/compact disc player with headphones with a selection of audiotapes/CDs.

☆ Book/story corner with appropriate range of fiction and non-fiction books including some dual language books.

☆ Storage units for specific curriculum areas.

☆ Whiteboard, over-head projector and teaching base including marker pens, transparencies, textbooks, teaching manuals and other resources needed by the teacher or teaching assistant on a regular basis.

☆ Writing and drawing materials including a variety of writing tools (crayons, pencils, pens, pastels, chalks); different shapes, sizes and types of paper (e.g. plain, coloured, graph).

☆ Children's work trays to store individual exercise books for literacy, numeracy and science; individual folders for topic work; individual reading books and reading logs; personal named pencils; individual crayon tins.

☆ Area with individual coat pegs for coats and PE bags.

The learning environment will also have **specialist resources** to support specific curriculum areas: English; mathematics; science; information and communication technology (ICT); art and design; design technology; food technology; physical education (PE); music; PSHE, citizenship, religious studies, geography and history. Specialist resources include: videos, maps, posters, pictures, artefacts, story and information books related to class topics or themes. Specialist resources should be stored in the appropriate curriculum resource cupboard or area, and be regularly audited by the curriculum subject co-ordinator. Staff may contact curriculum subject co-ordinators with suggestions for specialist materials that may need ordering. If you support pupils' learning in any of these areas then you need to be aware of the specific resources and any particular safety requirements.

EXERCISE:
1. What are general classroom resources?
2. What are specialist resources for specific curriculum areas? If possible, give examples from the resources you use on a regular basis.

Here are some general guidelines about organising resources and materials in the classroom:

- ☆ Fire exits must not be obstructed, locked or hidden from view.
- ☆ Chairs and tables need to be the correct size and height for the age and level of development of the children.
- ☆ Books, jigsaws, art/design materials and computers need to be used in areas with a good source of light, if possible near a source of natural light.
- ☆ Water, sand, art and design technology activities need to be provided in an area with an appropriate floor surface with washing facilities nearby.
- ☆ Ensure that activities requiring maximum concentration such as literacy or numeracy activities are not on the direct route to the hand-washing area or too close to messy/noisy activities or doorways.
- ☆ Any large or heavy equipment that has to be moved for use should be close to where it is stored.

Checking classroom resources

As part of your role you may need to make regular checks to ensure that essential materials or equipment are not running out. Clearing away equipment and materials provides you with a regular opportunity to check whether classroom supplies are running low. You may need to keep a weekly check on **consumable resources** such as art and craft materials, paper, cardboard and other stationery items. Items such as soap, paper towels and so on may need to be checked everyday. When the class teacher or teaching assistant requires resources, a stock requisition form should be completed and given to the person responsible for the storage area. **Non-consumable resources** are things like teaching packs, flashcards, posters and books. When you need to borrow non-consumable resources, it is necessary to sign them out. There should be a logbook in each storage area for this purpose. There will be an inventory or stock list for classroom resources that is checked on a regular basis. Larger items such as classroom furniture may be included on an inventory checked annually. There will be a school procedure for doing this.

KEY TASK

1. Outline your main role and responsibilities for helping to organise the learning environment.
2. What are the school's procedures for monitoring and maintaining the supply of classroom resources?
3. What is your role and responsibility in relation to these procedures? Include examples of different records you have used to monitor and maintain the supply of classroom resources, e.g. copies of stock requisition form, inventory or stock list.

NVQ LINKS:

Level 2:

STL1.1	STL2.4	STL3.1

Level 3:

STL18.1	STL18.2	STL23.1
STL24.1	STL28.2	STL31.1
STL31.2	STL31.3	STL38.1
STL45.1	STL45.2	STL45.3
STL47.1	STL52.1	STL52.2
STL56.1	STL56.2	

Encouraging pupils to help maintain their learning environment

The routine of getting out and putting away equipment is part of the learning experience for pupils. This routine helps younger pupils to develop mathematical concepts such as sorting and matching sets of objects and judging space, capacity and volume. It helps all pupils to develop a sense of responsibility for caring for their own learning environment. Pupils of all ages can also gain confidence and independence when involved in setting out and clearing away learning materials as appropriate to their age/level of development and any safety requirements. Materials and equipment should be stored and/or displayed in ways that will enable pupils to choose, use and return them easily. You must ensure that pupils only help in ways that are in line with the school's Health and Safety policy. Pupils must never have access to dangerous materials such as bleach or use very hot water for cleaning and they should not carry large, heavy or awkward objects due to the potential risks of serious injury. (Detailed information about health and safety is in Chapter 2.)

Organising displays

Part of your role may involve organising visual and tactile displays to stimulate the curiosity and involvement of pupils. When organising displays you need to consider these points:

1. *The purpose of the display*, e.g. to stimulate discussion and to consolidate learning.
2. *The choice of materials*, e.g. the colour and texture of backing paper; using drapes or boxes to create 3D effects; different ways to frame/mount 2D work to make it more eye-catching.
3. *The vocabulary and size of lettering*, e.g. use words and lettering appropriate to the children's ages and levels of development; remember

to use the school's preferred hand-writing style or word-process captions using an appropriate font.

4. *Use appropriate equipment*, e.g. paper trimmers, scissors, glue and staple gun.

You should display children's work in ways that encourage creativity and positive self-esteem. Focus on the creative process of children's pictures and writing, not the end product. Give children lots of praise for their attempts at creating pictures, models or written work and put their efforts on display. Do not worry that the finished results do not look neat, especially in the early years; it is having a go that is important. Where appropriate encourage the pupils to use their ICT skills to word-process their written work and/or to create captions for their pictures and models.

Displays should be appropriate to the work of the setting and the children's play and learning needs. Ensure that displays are updated or renewed on a regular basis. Displays in the setting should reflect the linguistic and cultural diversity of the setting and local community. The displays should reflect positive images of race, culture, gender and disability. Examples of displays include:

✵ *wall displays* to provide a stimulus for discussions and to consolidate learning including diagrams, maps, posters, pictures and children's work with appropriate labels or captions; alphabet and key words lists; number line and 100 square

✵ *tabletop displays* to stimulate discussion and further learning including interest tables with interesting artefacts to talk about, look at and explore linked to topics and themes such as colour, shape, sound, musical instruments, texture

✵ *displays of models made by the children* with captions in the form of questions to stimulate discussion, e.g. 'How many...?', 'What will happen if...?'

✵ *book displays* to promote children's interest in books, to develop their literacy skills and to extend learning including books relating to topics and themes.

Interactive display in a classroom

Your tutor/assessor should be able to give you guidance and practical tips on what to do when organising displays. You can also develop your display skills by looking at other people's displays (e.g. senior colleagues) and books about displays (see Further reading at the end of this chapter).

KEY TASK

Plan, organise and evaluate a display suitable for the pupils you work with. Include the following information: the type of display and how it supports learning; pupil contributions to the display (e.g. drawings, paintings, written work); how you made the display; the effectiveness of the finished display and any possible improvements; pupil and staff responses to the display; how the display promotes positive images. Include a photograph of the finished display.

NVQ LINKS:

Level 2:
STL1.1   STL2.4   STL3.1
STL16.1   STL16.2

Level 3:
STL16.1   STL16.2   STL18.1
STL18.2   STL23.1   STL24.1
STL28.2   STL31.1   STL31.2
STL31.3   STL38.1   STL45.2
STL46.1   STL46.2

Organising cover for absent colleagues

Part of your role may include organising cover for absent colleagues on a day-to-day basis. The cover will be short term and consistent with the policy, regulations and code of practice that apply to your own country and workplace. This may involve organising cover when a teacher or support staff colleague normally responsible for teaching or supporting a particular class is absent from the classroom during the time they have been timetabled to teach/support. This includes absence which is known in advance (e.g. where a colleague has a medical appointment or is undergoing professional development) and unexpected absence (e.g. absence due to illness) (TDA, 2007).

The people available to cover for absent colleagues will depend on the policy, regulations and code of practice that apply to your own country and workplace, and may include: cover staff employed by the school; support staff who provide cover supervision as part of a wider job role; supply staff; teaching staff (within agreed limits on providing cover for absent teachers).

Organising cover for absent colleagues may involve the following:

- ✯ Receiving telephone calls from absent staff and arranging cover for their lessons by: using cover supervisors; calling in supply teachers; using teaching staff within the school to cover for absent colleagues.
- ✯ Responding quickly when staff need to leave school at short notice, e.g. sudden illness or accident; family emergency.
- ✯ Monitoring the frequency of which teaching staff are used for cover; maintaining an equitable workload for all staff.
- ✯ Linking appropriate cover staff with particular teaching groups.
- ✯ Building appropriate relationships with outside agencies and supply teachers.
- ✯ Supporting cover staff with information.
- ✯ Ensuring the payment of supply staff.
- ✯ Liaising with the bursar on supply budget.

KEY TASK

Outline your role and responsibilities for organising cover for absent colleagues. Include information on the following: the policy, regulations and code of practice applicable to your school; how you arrange cover for absent colleagues; how you monitor and review cover arrangements.

NVQ LINKS:

Level 3:
STL57.1 STL57.2

Invigilating tests and examinations

Part of your role may include invigilating external or internal tests and examinations, including module tests, practical and oral examinations, under formal conditions. This involves running tests and examinations in the presence of candidates and includes: preparing the examination room and resources; bringing candidates into the room; running the test or examination session according to the centre's procedures; dealing with situations such as access arrangements, emergencies and suspicion of malpractice (e.g. cheating) (TDA, 2007). Invigilating tests and examinations may involve:

1. Assisting with making public examinations entries and receiving and processing results.
2. Assisting with the organisation of public examinations before, during and after each session.
3. Assisting with the administration of school examinations.
4. Ensuring the requirements for the conduct of tests and examinations are met, e.g. the required number and positioning of desks/work stations, display of notices, seating plan, clock, centre number, instructions for candidates and attendance register.
5. Considering health and safety arrangements and environmental conditions such as heating, lighting, ventilation and the level of outside noise.
6. Meeting specific requirements such as additional requirements in relation to further guidance, erratum notices, supervision of individual candidates between tests or examinations, and access arrangements for candidates with additional needs, e.g. reading assistance, scribe, sign interpreter.
7. Being responsible for the issue of certificates and archives.
8. Producing the school's examination statistics.

KEY TASK

Outline your role and responsibilities for invigilating tests and examinations. Include information on the following: the policy, procedures and regulations applicable to tests and examinations in your school; how you prepare to run tests and examinations; how you implement and maintain invigilation requirements.

NVQ LINKS:

Level 2 and Level 3:
STL17.1 STL17.2

Maintaining pupil records

As a teaching assistant, you will help with classroom records under the close supervision of the teacher responsible for maintaining them. This includes helping with the range of written records used within the school to monitor individual pupils, learning activities, classroom resources and requisitions.

The range of pupil records

All schools keep records of essential personal information for each pupil including: home address and telephone number; emergency information, e.g. names and contact telephone numbers for parents/guardians/carers, GP; medical history and conditions such as allergies; cultural or religious practices which may have implications for the care and education of the pupil such as special diets, exclusion from RE and assemblies; who collects the pupil (if applicable) including the transport arrangements (such as taxi or minibus) for a pupil with special educational needs. Schools also have records relating to administrative duties, for example, permission slips for educational visits, requisition forms for school supplies.

Schools also have education records relating to the assessment of pupil progress and their achievements within the National Curriculum framework. Formative assessments include: reading records; maths records; tick charts/lists; observation sheets; daily target records for pupils with Individual Education Plans. Summative assessments include: class teacher assessments; SATs results; pupils' annual school reports; reviews of pupils with SEN.

EXERCISE: What is the range of pupil records? If possible, give examples of the types of pupil records used for the pupils with whom you work.

Record-keeping systems and procedures

Record-keeping systems and procedures are essential to: monitor pupil progress; provide accurate and detailed information regarding pupils' learning and behaviour; determine the effectiveness of an activity or target; determine the effectiveness of adult support or intervention; give constructive feedback to the pupil; share information with the teacher, other professionals and parents; identify and plan for new learning objectives or behaviour targets.

The record-keeping systems and procedures you need to follow will depend on the planning and assessment requirements of the school, the class/subject teacher, SENCO and any other professionals involved in meeting the pupils' educational needs. It is important to update records on a regular basis; the frequency of updating depends on the different types of records that you make a contribution towards. Records that may indicate potential problems with individual pupils should be shown to the class teacher (e.g. observations of unacceptable behaviour; daily records which show poor performance).

EXERCISE: Find out about the record-keeping systems and procedures used within the school.

The roles and responsibilities for record-keeping

As a teaching assistant, most of your work with pupils will be planned by others – for example, by the class/subject teacher, SENCO or relevant specialists. They will need regular information about your work such as updates about a particular pupil's progress. Where, when and how to record pupil information should be as directed by the teacher. For example, when recording a pupil's behaviour using time or event sampling, you will need to agree on specific dates and times on which observations will take place. Some information may be given orally, for example outlining a pupil's progress on a particular activity or commenting on a pupil's behaviour.

Spoken information needs to be given in a professional manner, that is: to the appropriate person (class or subject teacher or SENCO); in the right place (not in a corridor where confidential information could be overheard); at the right time (urgent matters need to be discussed with the class or subject teacher immediately while others may wait until a team meeting).

Requests for records or reports should be dealt with professionally and handed in on time. This is particularly important if the information is needed for a meeting or review as any delay may stop others from performing their responsibilities effectively. Always remember to maintain confidentiality as appropriate to the school's requirements (see below).

● KEY TASK

1. Find out about the school's record-keeping policy. Highlight the responsibilities of the teaching assistant as set out in this policy.

2. What are your role and responsibilities in maintaining pupil records? With the teacher's permission include: copies of individual pupil records, e.g. literacy and numeracy records, Foundation Stage profile, Individual Education Plans (IEPs), behaviour support plans/logs and copies of school or class records, e.g. registers, educational visit documentation with your comments about your involvement.

 NVQ LINKS:

Level 2:

STL1.3	STL4.4	STL5.1
STL9.1	STL9.2	STL14.3

Level 3:

STL18.1	STL20.4	STL21.1
STL23.3	STL24.2	STL27.3
STL29.1	STL30.1	STL30.2
STL36.1	STL40.3	STL44.3
STL50.4	STL51.1	STL51.2
STL55.1	STL55.2	STL58.1
STL60.2	STL61.1	STL61.2
STL69.1	STL69.2	

Storing records

You need to know the exact policy and procedures for storing records in the school. You should also know what your own role and responsibilities are regarding the storage of records. Most pupil and staff records are stored and locked away in a central location such as the school office. Some formative records that need to be accessed or updated on a regular basis may be kept in the pupils' classrooms.

You must maintain the safe and secure storage of school records at all times. You should not leave important documents lying around; always put them back in storage after use. As well as the physical security of records, you need to be aware of the levels of staff access to information. You should never give out the passwords to school equipment (e.g. computers) unless you have permission from the member of staff responsible for the record-keeping systems.

EXERCISE: What is the school policy for the storage and security of pupil records?

Maintaining confidentiality

Confidentiality is important with regard to record-keeping and the storing of information; only the appropriate people should have access to confidential records. Except where a pupil is potentially at risk, information should not be given to other agencies unless previously agreed. Where the passing of confidential information is acceptable then it should be given in the agreed format. Always follow the school policy and procedures regarding confidentiality and the sharing of information; check with the teacher (or your line manager) if you have any concerns about these matters.

Legal implications and restrictions

You should be aware of any legal requirements with regard to record-keeping in the school. These include: Data Protection Act 1998; Children Act 1989; The Education Act 2002; Race Relations Act 1976; SEN Code of Practice 2001. In particular, you need to be aware of the basic legal requirements concerning the recording and filing of personal information under The Data Protection Act 1998 (see section on confidentiality matters in Chapter 5).

There are some circumstances where access to educational records may be restricted: *'The Secretary of State may by order exempt from the subject information provisions, or modify those provisions in relation to personal data in respect of which the data controller is the proprietor of, or a teacher at, a school, and which consist of information relating to persons who are or have been pupils at the school...'* (Section 30(2) Data Protection Act, 1998).

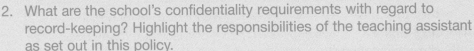

EXERCISE:
1. What are the basic legal requirements concerning the recording and filing of personal information under The Data Protection Act 1998?
2. What are the school's confidentiality requirements with regard to record-keeping? Highlight the responsibilities of the teaching assistant as set out in this policy.
3. Outline your main responsibilities for maintaining the confidentiality of pupil information.

Organising and supervising travel

Part of your role may include organising travel involving children and young people with adult supervision, e.g. for home-to-school travel, educational visits, field studies or sports fixtures. This may involve organising and supervising travel for children, young people and adults. Travel may be 'self-powered', e.g. on foot or by bicycle, in an owned or hired vehicle, or by public transport (TDA, 2007).

To ensure pupil safety you must follow the school's policy and procedures for organising and supervising travel including:

* ✩ collecting the relevant information for the pupils to be escorted
* ✩ ensuring the staff/pupil ratio meets organisational and legal requirements
* ✩ ensuring that everyone involved is aware of the travel arrangements
* ✩ ensuring that staff are at the meeting point at the agreed time
* ✩ escorting the pupils in a safe manner using the agreed route and mode of transport
* ✩ ensuring the pupils enter the setting in a safe manner
* ✩ carrying out the agreed procedures for pupils who are not at the meeting point.

KEY TASK

If applicable to your role, describe the policy and procedures for organising and supervising travel.

 NVQ LINKS:

Level 3:
STL3.1   **STL3.2**   **STL58.1**
STL58.2   **STL59.1**   **STL59.2**

Supervising pupils on educational trips and out-of-school activities

The health and safety of pupils on educational visits is part of the school's overall health and safety policy. The most senior member of staff on the educational visit will usually have overall responsibility and act as the group leader. Any other teachers present will also have responsibility for pupils on educational visits at all times. Teaching assistants on educational visits should be clear about their exact roles and responsibilities during any visit. Teaching assistants helping to supervise pupils on educational visits must:

* ✩ follow the instructions of the group leader and teacher supervisors
* ✩ not have sole charge of pupils (unless previously agreed as part of the risk assessment for the visit)
* ✩ help to maintain the health and safety of everyone on the visit
* ✩ help with the control and discipline of pupils to avoid potential dangers/accidents
* ✩ never be alone with a pupil wherever possible (this is for the protection of both the adult and the pupil)

☆ report any concerns about the health or safety of pupils to the group leader or teacher supervisors immediately.

(DfEE, 1998b)

Teaching assistants should be aware of pupils who might require closer supervision during educational visits (e.g. pupils with special educational needs or behavioural difficulties). Additional safety procedures to those used in school may be necessary to support pupils with medical needs during educational visits (e.g. arrangements for taking medication). Sometimes it might be appropriate to ask the parent or a care assistant to accompany the pupil to provide extra help and support during the visit.

Organising emergency procedures is a fundamental part of planning an educational visit. All participants, including staff, pupils and parents, should know who will take charge in an emergency during the educational visit and what their individual responsibilities are in the event of an emergency. The group leader would usually take charge in an emergency and must ensure that emergency procedures including back up cover have been arranged (see section in Chapter 2 on dealing with accidents and injuries).

Ten golden rules for maintaining pupil safety during educational visits

All outings with pupils should be both safe and enjoyable, so to make this possible you should work with the teacher and follow these ten golden rules:

1. Check the educational visit is suitable for the ages and levels of development of the pupils participating.

2. Obtain written permission from the children's parents.

3. Ensure the destination, leaving time and expected return times are written down.

4. Know how to get there, e.g. location, route and mode of transport.

5. Check the seasonal conditions, weather and time available.

6. Assess any potential dangers or risks, e.g. activities near water, suitability and safety of playground equipment.

7. Carry essential information/equipment such as identification, emergency contact numbers, mobile phone, first-aid, spare clothing, food, money, and any essential medication.

8. Make sure you and the pupils are suitably dressed for the occasion, e.g. sensible shoes or boots for walks; waterproof clothing for wet weather; sunhat and sun screen in hot weather; clean, tidy clothes for cinema, theatre, museum visits, etc.

9. Ensure the number of children is correct throughout the outing.

▶

10. All participants, including staff, children and parents, should know who will take charge in an emergency during the outing and what their individual responsibilities are in the event of an emergency.

KEY TASK

1. Outline your role and responsibilities with regard to maintaining pupil safety during educational visits and out-of-school activities.
2. Give a reflective account of your involvement on an educational visit.

 NVQ LINKS:

Level 3:
STL32.1   STL31.2   STL32.1
STL32.2   STL58.1   STL58.2

Further reading

DfEE (1998b) *Health and safety of pupils on educational visits: a good practice guide.* DfEE.

DfES (2000) *Working with teaching assistants: a good practice guide.* DfES.

DfES (2006) *Learning outside the classroom.* DfES.

Kerry, T. (2001) *Working with support staff: their roles and effective management in schools.* Pearson Education.

Seefeldt, C. (2002) *Creating rooms of wonder: valuing and displaying children's work to enhance the learning process.* Gryphon House.

Appendix: Record of key tasks

Key task	Date completed

Chapter 1: Supporting learning activities

- Describe two learning activities you have helped to plan, deliver and evaluate.

Chapter 2: Safeguarding children

- Find out about the statutory and regulatory requirements that apply to your school.
- Outline your school's policies and procedures relating to health and safety and maintaining pupil safety during play and learning activities.
- Find out about your school's procedures for dealing with accidents and injuries.
- What are your role and responsibilities for reporting information on possible abuse to a senior colleague?
- Think about the ways your setting helps children and young people to protect themselves.

Chapter 3: Supporting children's development

- Observe a pupil during a learning activity.
- Use your suggestions from your observation of a pupil during a learning activity to plan an activity to extend the pupil's skills in a specific area.
- Observe a group of pupils during a play activity or playing a game. Focus on one pupil's social development.
- Plan a play activity which encourages or extends a pupil's social development.
- Observe a pupil involved in a physical activity, e.g. using play equipment or PE apparatus.
- Plan an activity which encourages or extends a pupil's physical skills.
- Observe a pupil during a learning activity. Focus on the pupil's intellectual development.
- Plan a learning activity which encourages or extends a pupil's intellectual development.
- Observe a pupil involved in a conversation, discussion or circle time.
- Plan an activity which encourages or extends a pupil's language and communication skills.
- Observe a pupil during imaginative play or a creative activity.
- Plan an activity which encourages or extends a pupil's emotional development.

Appendix: Record of key tasks

Key task	Date completed

Chapter 4: Promoting positive pupil behaviour

- List examples of methods you have used to encourage children's positive behaviour.
- What sorts of behaviour patterns might indicate problems such as child abuse, substance abuse or bullying?
- Think about the goals and boundaries that might be appropriate to the pupil or pupils you work with in your school.
- Working with the teacher, set goals and boundaries for a pupil or group of pupils as part of a framework for positive behaviour.
- Observe a pupil who regularly demonstrates challenging or unwanted behaviour during group activities.
- Think about the basic principles of behaviour modification.
- Outline your school's anti-bullying policy and main strategies for dealing with bullying behaviour.

Chapter 5: Promoting positive working relationships

- Outline how you contribute to developing and promoting positive relationships with pupils in your school.
- Find out about your school's policies and practices for inclusion including equal opportunities and special educational needs.
- Compile a resource pack that promotes positive images.
- Listen to adults talking with children in a variety of situations.
- Outline your school's policy for dealing with a pupil's emotional outburst.
- Give examples of how your school shares information with parents.
- What are the policy and procedures regarding confidentiality in your school?
- Describe how you have responded (or would respond) to a disagreement or conflict situation with another adult in your school.

Chapter 6: Developing professional practice

- Participate in a team meeting relevant to your role in school.
- Describe how you have asked for help, information or support from your colleagues.
- Describe how you set and achieve team objectives in consultation with your team members.
- Give examples of effective planning and fair allocation of work within your area of responsibility.

Appendix: Record of key tasks

- Outline the methods you use to monitor the work of colleagues and provide feedback on their performance.
- Outline the methods you use to lead and motivate the work of volunteers.
- Outline the standards of professional practice expected from you and your colleagues.
- How do you monitor the processes, practices and outcomes from your work?
- Describe how you assess your personal development and training needs.
- Find out about the professional development and training opportunities for teaching assistants in your local area.
- Describe how you provide information and advice to aid the development of strategies, policies, practice and provision.
- Describe how you identify the learning needs of your colleagues.
- Which training programmes are available in your setting?
- Outline the methods you use to support competence achieved in the workplace.

Chapter 7: Promoting children's well-being and resilience

- Plan and implement an activity that encourages pupils to relate to others.
- Observe a pupil demonstrating self-help skills.
- How does your school involve children and young people in decision-making?
- Describe how you have helped pupils to develop emotional well-being and resilience.
- How does your setting support children and young people during transitions?
- Describe the procedures in your school for preparing pupils for transitions.

Chapter 8: Supporting children's play

- Give an example of a play opportunity.
- Collect information on the play needs and preferences.
- Give examples of your involvement in planning and creating play spaces.
- Describe how you have supported self-directed play.
- Outline your setting's policies and procedures that are relevant to managing risk during play activities.

Appendix: Record of key tasks

Chapter 9: Supporting curriculum delivery
- Provide examples of the planning you and the teacher(s) use within the curriculum framework applicable to the pupils in your school.
- What are the assessment requirements of the curriculum framework applicable to the pupils you work with in school?
- Observe a pupil during an activity involving the use of ICT skills.
- Plan an activity to encourage a pupil to work more independently using ICT skills.

Chapter 10: Supporting literacy and numeracy activities
- Observe a pupil during a literacy activity in Key Stage 1, 2, 3 or 4.
- Describe how you have helped pupils to develop their speaking and listening skills.
- Give examples of activities to help pupils develop their literacy skills.
- Give a detailed account of an activity to help pupils to develop their literacy skills.
- Describe how you have provided support for pupils with special language needs.
- Give examples of how your school promotes language diversity.
- Design a booklet about supporting pupils in bilingual or multilingual settings.
- Observe a pupil during a mathematics activity in Key Stage 1, 2, 3 or 4.
- Give examples of activities to help pupils to develop their mathematical skills.
- Give a detailed account of an activity to help pupils to develop their mathematical knowledge and skills.
- Describe how you have provided support for pupils with special numeracy needs.
- Describe how you have provided literacy and numeracy support to help pupils access different subjects within the curriculum.

Chapter 11: Supporting pupils with additional needs
- Outline your school's procedures for ensuring that Individual Education Plans for pupils are in place and regularly reviewed.
- Compile an information booklet suitable for new teaching assistants about SEN.
- Provide examples of how you have encouraged a pupil with additional communication and/or interaction needs to participate.

Appendix: Record of key tasks

Key task	Date completed

- Provide examples of how you have encouraged a pupil with general or specific learning difficulties to participate.
- Provide examples of how you have encouraged gifted or talented pupils to extend their learning.
- Provide examples of how you have encouraged a pupil with behavioural, social and emotional difficulties to participate.
- Provide examples of how you have encouraged a pupil with hearing or visual impairment to participate.
- Describe how you have encouraged a pupil with a physical disability to positively participate.

Chapter 12: Supporting the wider work of the school

- Take a photograph of the classroom. Comment on the learning environment.
- Outline your main role and responsibilities for helping to organise the learning environment.
- Plan, organise and evaluate a display suitable for the pupils you work with.
- Outline your role and responsibilities for organising cover for absent colleagues.
- Outline your role and responsibilities for invigilating tests and examinations.
- Find out about the school's record-keeping policy.
- Describe the policy and procedures for organising and supervising travel.
- Outline your role and responsibilities with regard to maintaining pupil safety during educational visits and out-of-school activities.

Glossary

active learning: learning by doing; participation in activities in meaningful situations.

activity: learning opportunity which involves active participation and discussion.

anti-discriminatory practice: taking positive action to counter discrimination and prejudice.

behaviour: a person's actions, reactions and treatment of others.

behaviour modification: using positive reinforcement to encourage acceptable behaviour.

carer: any person with responsibility for the care/education of a child during the parent's temporary or permanent absence.

cognitive: intellectual abilities involving processing information received through the senses.

community language: main language spoken in a child's home.

concepts: the ways people make sense of and organise information in the world around them.

conflict situation: verbal or physical disagreement, e.g. arguments, fighting, disputing rules.

curriculum: the course of study in a school.

discrimination: biased and unfair treatment based on inaccurate judgements (e.g. prejudice) about an individual or group of people due to their age, gender, race, culture or disability.

egocentric: pre-occupied with own needs; unable to see another person's viewpoint.

emotional outburst: uncontrolled expression of intense emotion, e.g. rage or frustration.

holistic approach: looking at the 'whole' child, e.g. *all* aspects of the child's development.

inclusion: the principle whereby all children with special educational needs should be included in mainstream settings where reasonably practicable.

inclusive practice: identifying barriers to participation and taking positive action to eliminate those barriers and encourage participation in the full range of activities provided by the setting.

intelligence quotient: a person's mental age in comparison to their chronological age.

key factor: an essential aspect affecting learning and development.

mediator: a person who acts as an intermediary between parties in a dispute.

milestones: significant skills which children develop in and around certain ages as part of the usual or expected pattern of development.

norm: the usual pattern or expected level of development/behaviour.

operations: the term used by Piaget to describe the way people use their cognitive abilities.

parent: person with parental responsibility for a child (as defined in The Children Act, 1989).

peers: children of similar age within the setting.

personality: distinctive and individual characteristics which affect each person's view of themselves, their needs, feelings and relationships with others.

prejudice: an opinion formed prematurely or without consideration of all the relevant information. Prejudice can arise due to ignorance about the differences (and similarities) between individuals and a lack of understanding or intolerance of other people's individual needs and preferences.

Glossary

problem-solving: activities which involve finding solutions to a difficulty or question.

rationale: the main reason for implementing a particular activity; the principle behind an idea or opportunity.

ratios: the numbers of adults in relation to children within a group setting, e.g. three adults with a group of 30 children would be shown as a ratio of 1:10.

regression: demonstrating behaviour characteristic of a previous level of development.

role model: significant person whose actions, speech or mannerisms are imitated by a child.

scaffolding: adult assistance given to support child's thinking and learning – as child develops competence the adult decreases support until child works independently.

schemas: term used mainly by Piaget and Froebel to describe internal thought processes.

SENCO (special educational needs co-ordinator): the teacher responsible for co-ordinating the support for pupils with special educational needs in a school.

sensory: relating to the senses; sensory experiences enable children to *make sense* of their environment.

sequence: development following the same basic pattern but not necessarily at fixed ages.

social constructivism: the viewpoint that *all* learning takes place within a social and cultural context.

social context: *any* situation or environment where social interaction occurs, e.g. home, nursery, school, local community.

social interaction: *any* contact with other people including actions and reactions, e.g. play, verbal and non-verbal communication.

special educational needs: all children have *individual* needs, but some children may have *additional* needs due to physical disability, sensory impairment, learning difficulty or emotional/behavioural difficulty.

specialist: person with specific training/ additional qualifications in a particular area of development, e.g. speech and language therapist, educational psychologist.

stages: development which occurs at fixed ages.

stereotype: simplistic characterisation or expectation of a person based on perceived differences or prejudices relating to their race, culture, gender, disability or age.

teaching assistant: an adult whose main role is to assist the teacher in supporting the development and learning of pupils in a primary, secondary or special school.

temperament: person's disposition or personality, especially their emotional responses.

time in: giving children special individual attention to reinforce positive behaviour, e.g. adult discussing positive aspects of the day with a child.

time out: a short break or suspension of an activity which allows a cooling-off period for all involved but which especially gives the child a chance to calm down.

zone of proximal development: Vygotsky's description for a child's next area of development where adult assistance is required only until the child has developed the skill and can do it independently.

Bibliography

ATL (2000) 'ATL guide to children's attitudes' in *Report*. June/July issue. London: Association of Teachers and Lecturers.

ATL (2002) *Achievement for all: working with children with special educational needs in mainstream schools and colleges*. London: Association of Teachers and Lecturers.

Ball, C. (1994) *Start right: the importance of early learning*. London: RSA.

Balshaw, M. and Farrell, P. (2002) *Teaching assistants: practical strategies for effective classroom support*. London: David Fulton Publishers.

Bartholomew, L. and Bruce, T. (1993) *Getting to know you: a guide to record-keeping in early childhood education and care*. London: Hodder Arnold.

BDA (1997) 'Dyslexia: an introduction for parents and teachers and others with an interest in dyslexia'. London: British Dyslexia Association.

Becta (2004) *Data protection and security – a summary for schools*. British Educational Communications and Technology Agency.

Becta (2006) British Educational Communications and Technology Agency website: www.becta.org.uk.

Booth, T. and Coulby, D. (eds) (1987) *Producing and reducing disaffection*. Milton Keynes: Open University Press.

Booth, T. *et al*. (ed.) (1987) *Preventing difficulties in learning*. Oxford: Blackwell/Open University Press.

Booth, T. and Swann, W. (eds) (1987) *Including pupils with disabilities*. Milton Keynes: Open University Press.

Bostock, L. (2004) *Promoting resilience in fostered children and young people*. London: Social Care Institute for Excellence.

Brennan, W. K. (1987) *Changing special education now*. Milton Keynes: Open University Press.

Bruce, T. and Meggitt, C. (2006) *Child care and education*. 4th edition. London: Hodder Arnold.

Burton, G. and Dimbleby, R. (1995) *Between ourselves: an introduction to interpersonal communication*. Revised edition. London: Hodder Arnold.

CAPT [Child Accident Prevention Trust] (2002) *Taking chances: the lifestyles and leisure risks of young people*. London: Child Accident Prevention Trust.

CAPT (2004a) *Factsheet: children and accidents*. London: Child Accident Prevention Trust.

CAPT (2004b) *Factsheet: home accidents*. London: Child Accident Prevention Trust.

CAPT (2004c) *Factsheet: playground accidents*. London: Child Accident Prevention Trust.

Clay, M. (1992) *Becoming literate*. London: Heinemann.

CRE (December 1989) *From cradle to school: a practical guide to race equality and childcare*. London: Commission for Racial Equality.

Cunningham, B. (1993) *Child development*. London: HarperCollins.

CYPU [Children and Young People's Unit] (2001) *Learning to listen: core principles for the involvement of children and young people*. London: DfES.

Davie, R. (1984) 'Social development and social behaviour' (see Fontana, D.).

DES (1978a) *Special educational needs* (The Warnock Report). London. HMSO.

DCMS (2004) *Getting serious about play: a review of children's play*. London: Department for Culture, Media & Sport.

Dessent, T. (1987) *Making the ordinary school special*. London: The Falmer Press.

DfEE (1998a) *Guidance on first-aid for schools: a good practice guide*. London: Department for Education and Employment.

DfEE (1998b) *Health and safety of pupils on educational visits: a good practice guide*. London: DfEE.

Bibliography

DfEE (1998c) *Meeting special educational needs: a programme of action.* London: DfEE.

DfEE (2000a) *Learning journey* [3–7 and 7–11]. London: DfEE.

DfEE (2000b) *Learning journey* [11–16]. London: DfEE.

DfEE (2001) *The national literacy strategy: developing early writing.* London: DfEE.

DfES (1998) *The national literacy strategy – framework for teaching YR to Y6.* London: DfES.

DfES (1999) *The national numeracy strategy – framework for teaching mathematics from reception to Y6.* London: DfES.

DfES (2000a) *Bullying: don't suffer in silence – an anti-bullying pack for schools.* London: DfES.

DfES (2000b) *Working with teaching assistants: a good practice guide.* London: DfES.

DfES (2001a) *The Key Stage 3 national strategy – framework for teaching English: Years 7, 8 and 9.* London: DfES.

DfES (2001b) *The Key Stage 3 national strategy – framework for teaching mathematics: Years 7, 8 and 9.* London: DfES.

DfES (2001c) *The Special Educational Needs Code of Practice 2001.* London: HMSO.

DfES (2002) *Further literacy support: resource pack.* London: DfES.

DfES (2003a) *Electronic adult numeracy core curriculum with access for all.* London: DfES.

DfES (2003b) *Key Stage 3 national strategy: advice on whole school behaviour and attendance policy.* London: HMSO.

DfES (2003c) *Primary national strategy – speaking, listening, learning: working with children in Key Stages 1 and 2 handbook.* London: DfES.

DfES (2004) *Every child matters: change for children.* London: DfES.

DfES (2005) *Primary national strategy: KEEP – key elements of effective practice.* London: DfES.

DfES (2006a) *Information sharing: practitioners' guide.* London: DfES.

DfES (2006b) *Primary framework for literacy and mathematics.* London: DfES.

DfES/DH (2005) *Managing medicines in schools and early years settings.* London: DfES/Department of Health.

DfES/QCA (1999) *The National Curriculum: handbook for primary teachers in England and Wales.* London: DfES.

DfES/QCA (1999) *The National Curriculum: handbook for secondary teachers in England and Wales.* London: DfES.

DH [Department of Health] (1991) *The Children Act 1989 guidance and regulations – volume 2: family support, day care and educational provision for young children.* London: HMSO.

DH (1999) *Working together to safeguard children.* London: HMSO.

DH (2000) *Assessing children in need and their families: practice guidance.* London: TSO.

DH (2003) *What to do if you're worried a child is being abused.* London: HMSO.

Donaldson, M. (1978) *Children's minds.* London: Fontana.

Drummond, M. *et al.* (1994) *Making assessment work.* Swindon: NFER Nelson.

Fontana, D. (1984) 'Personality and personal development' in D. Fontana (ed.) *The education of the young child.* Oxford: Blackwell.

Foster-Cohen, S. (1999) *Introduction to child language development.* Harlow: Longman.

Fox, G. (1998) *A handbook for learning support assistants.* London: David Fulton Publishers.

Gatiss, S. (1991) '5. Parents as Partners' in *Signposts to special needs: An information pack on meeting special educational needs in the mainstream classroom.* London: National Children's Bureau and NES Arnold.

Goleman, D. (1996) *Emotional intelligence.* London: Bloomsbury.

Green, C. and Chee, K. (1995) *Understanding ADD.* London: Vermilion.

Bibliography

Harding, J. and **Meldon-Smith**, L. (2001) *How to make observations and assessments.* 2nd edition. London: Hodder Arnold.

HM Government (2006) *Working together to safeguard children: a guide to inter-agency working to safeguard and promote the welfare of children.* London: TSO.

Houghton, D. and **McColgan**, M. (1995) *Working with children.* London: Collins Educational.

HSE (2004) *Getting to grips with manual handling: a short guide.* Leaflet INDG143 (rev2). London: Health and Safety Executive Books.

Hutchcroft, D. (1981) *Making language work.* London: McGraw-Hill.

ILAM (1999) *Indoor play areas: guidance on safe practice.* Reading: Institute of Leisure and Amenity Management.

Kamen, T. (2000) *Psychology for childhood studies.* London: Hodder Arnold.

Kamen, T. (2005) *The playworker's handbook.* Hodder Arnold.

Kay, J. (2002) *Teaching assistant's handbook.* London: Continuum.

Laing, A. and **Chazan**, M. (1984) 'Young children with special educational needs' (see **Fontana**, D.).

Leach, P. (1994) *Children first.* London: Penguin.

Lee, V. and **Das Gupta**, P. (eds) (1995) *Children's cognitive and language development.* Oxford: Blackwell.

Light, P. *et al.* (ed.) (1991) *Learning to think.* London: Routledge.

Lindenfield, G. (1995) *Self esteem.* London: Thorsons.

Lindon (2002) *What is play?* Children's Play Information Service factsheet. London: National Children's Bureau.

Masheder, M. (1989a) *Let's co-operate.* London: Peace Education Project.

Masheder, M. (1989b) *Let's play together.* London: Green Print.

Matterson, E. (1989) *Play with a purpose for the under-sevens.* London: Penguin.

Matthews, G. (1984) 'Learning and teaching mathematical skills' (see **Fontana**, D.).

Meadows, S. (1993) *Child as thinker: the development of cognition in childhood.* London: Routledge.

Modgil, C. and **Modgil**, S. (1984) 'The development of thinking and reasoning' (see **Fontana**, D.).

Moon, A. (1992) 'Take care of yourself' in *Child education*, February issue. Leamington Spa: Scholastic.

Morris, J. and **Mort**, J. (1997) *Bright ideas for the early years: learning through play.* Leamington Spa: Scholastic.

Moyle, D. (1976) *The teaching of reading.* London: Ward Lock Educational.

Mulvaney, A. (1995) *Talking with kids.* Sydney: Simon & Schuster.

Munn, P. *et al.* (1992) *Effective discipline in secondary schools and classrooms.* London: Paul Chapman Publishing Ltd.

NAGC (2007) *Factsheet: able children's needs.* Milton Keynes: National Association for Gifted Children.

National Commission on Education (1993) *Learning to succeed.* London: Heinemann.

NDNA (2004) *National occupational standards in children's care, learning and development.* Brighouse: NDNA.

Neaum, S. and **Tallack**, J. (1997) *Good practice in implementing the pre-school curriculum.* Cheltenham: Stanley Thornes.

NPFA *et al.* (2000) *Best play: what play provision should do for children.* London: National Playing Fields Association.

O'Hagan, M. and **Smith**, M. (1994) *Special issues in child care.* London: Bailliere Tindall.

Parsloe, E. (1999) *The manager as coach and mentor.* London: Chartered Institute of Personnel & Development.

Petrie, P. (1989) *Communication with children and adults.* London: Edward Arnold.

Bibliography

Prisk, T. (1987) 'Letting them get on with it: a study of unsupervised group talk in an infant school' in A. Pollard (ed.) *Children and their primary schools.* London: Falmer Press.

QCA (2000) *Curriculum guidance for the foundation stage.* London: Qualifications and Curriculum Authority.

QCA (2001a) *Planning for learning in the foundation stage.* London: QCA.

QCA (2001b) *Planning, teaching and assessing the curriculum for pupils with learning difficulties.* London: QCA.

QCA (2003) *Foundation stage profile handbook.* London: QCA.

QCA (2005) *ICT in the foundation stage.* London: QCA.

QCA/DfES (2002) *Assessment and reporting arrangements 2003.* London: QCA.

RoSPA (2004a) *Play safety information sheet: information sheet number 16 – legal aspects of safety on children's play areas.* Birmingham: Royal Society for the Prevention of Accidents.

RoSPA (2004b) *Play safety information sheet: information sheet number 25 – risk assessment of children's play areas.* Birmingham: Royal Society for the Prevention of Accidents.

Rutter, M. (1991) *Maternal deprivation reassessed.* London: Penguin.

Sameroff, A. (1991) 'The social context of development' in M. Woodhead *et al.* (eds) *Becoming a person.* London: Routledge.

SkillsActive (2004) *National occupational standards NVQ/SVQ level 3 in playwork.* London: SkillsActive.

Smart, C. (2001) *Special educational needs policy.* Abbots Bromley: Special Needs Information Press.

Street, C. (2002) *The benefits of play.* Highlight No.195. London: National Children's Bureau.

Taylor, J. (1973) *Reading and writing in the first school.* London: George Allen and Unwin.

TDA (2007) *National occupational standards for supporting teaching and learning in schools.* Training and Development Agency for Schools.

Tharp, R. and Gallimore, R. (1991) 'A theory of teaching as assisted performance' (see Light, P.).

Tizard, B. (1991) 'Working mothers and the care of young children' (see Woodhead, M.).

Tobias, C. (1996) *The way they learn.* Colorado Springs: Focus on the Family Publishing.

Tough, J. (1976) *Listening to children talking.* London: Ward Lock Educational.

Tough, J. (1984) 'How young children develop and use language' (see Fontana, D.).

Train, A. (1996) *ADHD: How to deal with very difficult children.* London: Souvenir Press.

Wandsworth EYDCP (2001) *The business of childcare.* London: Wandsworth Early Years Development and Childcare Partnership.

Watkinson, A. (2003) *The essential guide for competent teaching assistants.* London: David Fulton Publishers.

Whitehead, M. (1996) *The development of language and literacy.* London: Hodder Arnold.

Wing, L. (2003) *The autistic spectrum: a guide for parents and professionals.* Revised Edition. Constable and Robinson.

Wood, D. (1988) *How children think and learn.* Oxford: Blackwell.

Wood, D. (1991) 'Aspects of teaching and learning' (see Light, P.).

Woodhead, M. (1991) 'Psychology and the cultural construction of children's needs' in M. Woodhead *et al.* (ed.) (1991) *Growing up in a changing society.* London: Routledge.

Woolfson, R. (1989) *Understanding your child: a parents' guide to child psychology.* London: Faber & Faber.

Woolfson, R. (1991) *Children with special needs: a guide for parents and carers.* London: Faber & Faber.

Yardley, A. (1984) 'Understanding and encouraging children's play' (see Fontana, D.).

Index

absence, staff cover 290
abuse 38–47
accidents 25, 28–30
accommodation (information) 198, *199*
achievement records 213
active learning 202
active listening 124
activities
    competitive 164
    for emotional expression 127
    for ICT 219–20
    implementation and evaluation 57
    for intellectual development 73
    learning activities 6–15, *11*
    for literacy 230–1
    for numeracy 245–7
    observation 50–1
    participation by adults 73, 187
    participation by children 11–12, 84
    for physical development 67
    planning 6–8, 55–7, 193
    play 188–9, 189–90, 190–1
    to promote positive attitudes 120
    safety 21
    for social development 62
adaptation (information) 198, *199*
ADD/ADHD 94, 273–4
adrenaline, for anaphylaxis 36
AIDS 36
allergic reactions 36
analytic learners 203
anaphylaxis 36
answering questions 124–5
anti-bullying policies 109
anti-discriminatory practice 118–21
    see also equal opportunities
apprenticeship reading approach 228
arrival at school 23
Asperger syndrome 263
assertive behaviour 142
assessment 49, 52, 54, 211–14
assimilation (information) 198, *199*
assisted learning 200
asthma 34
'at-risk' children 42, 45, 135
attachment 80, 161
attainment targets 207
Attention Deficit Disorder (ADD) 94,
    273–4
Attention Deficit Hyperactivity Disorder
    (ADHD) 273–4
attention-seeking behaviour 90–1, 103
auditory learners 203
autistic spectrum disorders 94, 263
autocratic leadership 145

babies, attachment 80
backgrounds, awareness of 51, 91, 231

ball games 188
behaviour management 84, 86–107,
    126–7, 140
behaviour modification 104–5, *105*
behaviour patterns 94–5
Behaviour Support Plans 106–7, 275
behavioural problems 89, 93–4, 101–4,
    106–7, 272–5
bilingualism 237–40
blindness 277–9
blood 28, 37
blood sugar levels 35
body fluids 28, 37
boundaries 62, 91, 97–8, *98*, 102
Braille *278*
Bruner, J. 200–1
BSPs 106–7, 275
building maintenance 18
bullying 107–9

carers 131, 132–3
    see also parents
carrying pupils 19
challenging behaviour 101–4, 107
    see also behaviour management;
        negative behaviour
chickenpox *33*
child abuse 38–47
child development 52, 59–84, 182
child protection 40–7, *43*
Childcare Act (2006) 205
childhood illnesses 30–7, *33*
Children Acts 38, 40, 101, 115–16
children in difficulties 47
children's rights 101, 113–17, 167
classroom organisation 232, 284–8
    see also learning environment
cleft lip/palate 262
closed questions 124
co-operation 62, 84, 164
co-ordination 63, 229–30
codes of conduct 96–7
cognitive development *see* intellectual
        development; learning difficulties
colds 31
collage 189
colleagues 131, 134, 138–44, 140–1, 144,
    156–60, 260
colour blindness 278
colouring activities 189
communication
    with children 79, 123–5
    with colleagues 140–1, 260–1
    with parents 132, 188, 259–60
communication difficulties 261–4
communication skills 74–6, 123–4, 132
competitive activities 164
concentration 68–9, 73

conditioning 104–5
conductive hearing loss 276
confidentiality
    child protection issues 41, 45–6
    of information 37, 51, 134–5, 294
conflict resolution
    between adults 135–6
    between children 129–30
consent, for observation 52
consistency, in managing behaviour 84,
    100, 102
continuing professional development
    155–6, 157–8
cooking 21, 189
corporal punishment 101
cultural diversity 51, 119–21, 233
curriculum 4, 92, 204–10, 212, 222–6,
    253
curriculum plans 207–10
curriculum support 5

daily mathematics lessons 240–1
daily routines 283, 288
Data Protection Act (1998) 45, 134–5,
    294
deafness 276–7
decision-making, encouraging 84, 167
delayed language development 262
delegation 148–9
democratic leadership 145
departure procedures 23
development *see* child development
diabetes 34–5
differentiation, in assessment 212
disability 119, 121, 279–81
    see also special educational needs
Disability Discrimination Acts 117
disaffected pupils 273
discipline 84, 126
    see also rewards; sanctions
disclosure of abuse 43–4
discrimination, legislation 117–18
disordered language development 262
displays 230, 233, 288–9
diversionary tactics 102
doll play 191
drawing 189
dressing-up 190
dyscalculia 268–9
dysfluency 262
dyslexia 267

EAL 238, 252
Early Years Foundation Stage 204–6, 211
Early Years of School Action/Plus 256
Education Act (1993) 121
Education (School Premises) Regulations
    (1999) 18

Index

educational trips 295–7
effective practice 152–3
emergency procedures 19, 26–7, 296
emotional abuse 38–9, 39–40
emotional development 80–4
emotional difficulties 272–3
emotional intelligence 172–3
emotional needs 114
emotional outbursts 128–9
emotional well-being
   children 80, 161–79
   teaching assistants 143
emotions 103, 127
encouragement 67, 83, 103, 125, 266
   see also praise
English, National Curriculum 222–5
English as an additional language (EAL)
   238, 252
epilepsy 35
equal opportunities 84, 117–21
equipment
   fire extinguishers 27, 285
   first aid 30
   getting out/putting away 288
   for play 188–9, 189–90, 191, 191–2
   safety 18, 19–20, 21, 25, 67, 214, 215
   see also learning resources
evacuation procedures 26–7
evaluation
   learning activities 14–15
   policies and practices 156–7
Every Child Matters: Change for
   Children 116–17, 205
examinations, invigilation 291
exploratory play 187, 189–90

feedback 8, 9, 13–14
   see also praise
feelings *see* emotional; emotions
fifth disease *33*
fire extinguishers 27, 285
first-aid 28, 30, 285
floor space 284
floors, safety 23
flu 31
formative assessments 211
Framework for the Assessment of
   Children in Need and their
   Families 41
Framework for teaching mathematics:
   Years 7, 8 and 9 241

gender, attitudes towards 119–21
general learning difficulties 265–6
German measles *33*
gifted children 270–1, 273
global learners 203
glue ear 276

goals 62, 91, 97–8, *98*
groups 162–3

headteachers, roles 1, 2
health care plans 37
health and safety
   accidents/emergencies 26–30
   illness 30–7
   learning environment 19–25
   legislation 17–19, 20, 28
   see also safety
Health and Safety at Work Act (1974) 18,
   20
hearing impairment 276–7
heating 284
HIV 36–7
holistic approach 51, 56
home-school agreement 126–7
human immunodeficiency virus 36–7
hygiene 22, 28
hypo/hypoglycaemia 35

ICT 214–20, 231
identifying children with problems
   from behaviour 94
   communication difficulties 262–3
   learning difficulties 265–6, 267, 268, 269
   sensory impairment 277, 278
illness 30–7, *33*
imaginative play 188, 190–1
immunisations 30
incentives 90, 98, 99–100, *99*, 103
inclusive practice 117–21, 187
independence, encouraging 62, 67
independent learning 12–13, 219–20
independent play 192–5
Individual Education Plans (IEPs) 256–7,
   258, 275
individual support 3, 104, 128, 248,
   256–7, 275
   see also special educational needs
information
   for colleagues 134, 293
   sharing with carers 132–3
   to support policies 156–7
   for teaching assistants 3
information and communication
   technology 214–20, 231
information processing styles 203
information sharing 132–4, 293
injuries 28–30
intellectual development 68–73,
   197–201
inter-personal skills 123–4
internal assessments 213
intranets 216
inventories 287

jealousy 128
job descriptions 5

KEEP framework 152
keeping calm 91, 129
Key Elements of Effective Practice
   (KEEP) 152
Key Stages 206–7, 217–18, 224, 225,
   241–2
kinesthetic learners 203

labelling of pupils, avoiding 84, 103
laissez-faire leadership 145
language
   in behaviour management 126
   in cognitive development 68, 182, 201
   communicating with adults 131
   communicating with children 79
   see also literacy
language development 74–9, 262
language difficulties 236
language of learning 124
law *see* legislation
leadership 145–6
learning activities 6–15, *11*, 73
learning difficulties 13–14, 235–6, 250–3,
   265–9
learning environment 17–25, 103, 143,
   204, 280, 283–8
   see also classroom organisation; safety
learning mentors 259
learning needs 114
learning pathways 201–2
learning resources 10–11, 214–15,
   232–3, 247–8, 285–6
   see also equipment
learning styles 203
legal duties 45, 95
legislation
   children 38, 40–1, 45, 101, 115–17, 205
   data protection 45, 134–5, 294
   education 91, 117, 121–2
   equality 117–18
   health and safety 17–19, 20, 28
lesson plans 9–10
lifting pupils 19
lighting 284, 287
lisping 262
listening skills 226
literacy hour 223–4
literacy skills 225–31, 234
look and say approach 228

Management of Health and Safety at
   Work Regulations (1999) 18–19
management skills 146
Manual Handling Operations Regulations
   (1992) 19

Index

mathematics, National Curriculum 223, 240–2
measles 33
media, influence 88
medical needs 34–7
medication 32, 36, 274
memory 68, 73
menstruation 22
mentoring 158–9, 259
miniature worlds 191
missing pupils 27
models 189, 289
modes of language 74, 75
monitoring
  children see assessment; observation
  policies and practices 156–7
  teamwork 149
motor skills 63, 67
movement of pupils, safety 22–3
multilingualism 237–40
mumps 33
music making 190

name calling 108
National Curriculum 206–7, 212, 222–6
needs, children's 113–14, 162, 168, 183–4
negative behaviour 89, 93–4
  see also behaviour management;
    challenging behaviour
neglect 39, 40
new settings 174–9
noise levels 284
numeracy skills 243–7, 249

observation of pupils 14, 49–55, 50, 53
open questions 124
out-of-school activities 295–7
outcomes framework 116–17
outdoor play 188
outings 295–7

painting 189
parents 87, 131, 132–3, 188, 259–60
partial sight 277–9
participation in activities
  by adults 73, 187
  by children 11–12, 84
partnerships with teachers 9
parvovirus 33
Pastoral Support Plans 275
Pavlov, I., conditioning 104
peer pressure, influence of 88
personal development 154–6
phonics 228
physical abuse 38, 39
physical development 63–7
physical disabilities 279–81

physical play 187, 188–9
physical punishment 101
Piaget, J., cognitive theories 197–9
planning
  activities 6–8, 55–7, 193
  for curriculum 207–10
  play spaces 186–92
  school 147–8
  for transitions 175–7
planning cycle 56–7, 56
planning meetings 7–8, 139–40
play 181–95, 202
play areas, safety 20–1, 25
play cues 194
play cycle 194
play equipment 188–9, 189–90, 191, 191–2
play frames 194–5
play objectives 184–5
play resources 191–2
play spaces 186–92
portfolios
  professional 154
  on pupils 52
positive attitudes 51, 103, 119–21
positive behaviour 86, 89–91
praise 67, 83, 103, 125, 170, 266, 289
PRAISE (mnemonic) 105
preparation for activities 9–10, 57, 90
pretend play 190, 191, 232
Primary Framework for literacy and mathematics 222–4, 240–1
problems see identifying children with problems
professional development 155–6, 157–8
Protection of Children Act (1999) 41
PSPs 275
psychosis 93
punishments 103
  see also sanctions
pupil records 15, 112, 292–4
pupil support 3, 5
puppet play 191

qualifications 156
questions, asking and answering 124–5

race see cultural diversity
Race Relations Acts 117–18
reading skills 227–9
record keeping 9
  accidents and injuries 28, 29
  activities 57–8
  child protection issues 41, 44
  illness 32
  learning difficulties 14
  observations and assessments 54, 54
  pupil records 15, 112, 213, 292–4
  volunteer meetings 150

records, storage 293–4
reflective practice 152–5
relationships
  between children 126–30, 161–4
  promoting well-being 161–4
  with pupils 111–12
  working with adults 130–6, 159, 260–1
reporting concerns 95
Reporting of Injuries, Diseases and Dangerous Occurrences Regulations (1985) 28
resilience 172–4
resources see equipment; learning resources
responsibilities (teaching assistants) 4–6, 147–8
  behaviour management 106–7
  for child protection 42–3, 45–6
  for health and safety 24–5
  in learning environment 192, 284
  in mentoring 159
  see also role
rewards 90, 98, 99–100, 99, 103
rights 101, 113–17, 167
risk assessment, learning environment 23
risk management, in play 195–6
risk-taking, by children 47
Ritalin 274
role (teaching assistants) 2–4
  in behaviour management 90–1, 92–3, 95–6, 97–8, 101–4, 106–7, 126, 274–5
  with bullied pupils 109
  in child protection 39, 46–7
  in emergencies 26–7, 28
  emotional support 112, 127–8, 166, 173–4, 274–5
  with gifted/talented pupils 271
  in inclusive practice 118–21
  invigilation 291
  learning support 7–16, 193, 267–8, 268–9
  literacy support 230–1, 233–5, 239–40
  maintaining hygiene 22, 28
  in mentoring 159
  numeracy support 245–7, 248–50
  observation of pupils 52–4
  with physically disabled pupils 277, 278–9, 280–1
  promoting child development 59, 63, 68, 73, 79, 83–4
  promoting independence 12–13, 219
  record keeping 293
  responding to illness 31–2, 37
  special educational needs 122–3, 257–8, 259–61, 263–4, 266–7, 267–8

Index

staff absence 290
travel and school trips 295–6
see also responsibilities
role models 88
role play 190
routines 283, 288
rubella *33*
rules 84, 90, 91, 103

safety
from abuse 46–7
learning environment 17–25, 67,
214–15, 288
medicines 32
of pupils 23, 216, 296–7
safety equipment 19, 285
sanctions 100–1
see also punishments
sand play 190
SATs 212
scaffolding 200
schemas 198
schemes of work 210
school policies 41–2, 87, 91–2, 100, 109
school reports 213–14
School Standards and Framework Act
(1998) 91
school trips 295–7
secondary school transitions 179
secure attachments 80, 161
security
of pupils 23, 216, 296–7
of records 294
seizures (epilepsy) 35
selective mutism 262–3
self-directed play 192–5
self-esteem
children 168, 169, 170–1, 266
teaching assistants 142, 170
self-evaluation 153
self-image 169–70, 171
self-reliance 165–6
SENCOs 140, 258
sensory impairments 275–9
Sex Discrimination Act (1875) 117
sexual abuse 39, 40
sharing 62, 79, 164
shouting, to maintain discipline 101
signs
of abuse 39–40
of attention deficit 273–4
of bullying 108
of illness 31–2
of learning difficulties 267, 268, 269
of sensory impairment 277, 278
of talent and giftedness 270
Skinner, B.F., conditioning 105
slapped cheek disease *33*

slow learners 265–6
smacking 101
SMART objectives 154
social constructivism 199
social development 59–62, 182–3
social and emotional difficulties 272–5
social needs 114
social play 62, 103, 182–3
social skills 59
speaking and listening skills 226
special educational needs 27, 114,
255–61
behaviour problems 106-7
legislation 121-2
literacy 230, 231, 235-6
numeracy 251–2
and relationships 161–2
and school trips 296
special educational needs co-ordinators
(SENCOs) 140, 258
*Special Educational Needs Code of
Practice* 121–2
Special Educational Needs and Disability
Act (2001) 117, 121
special medical needs 34–7, 296
specific learning difficulties 267–9
speech disorders 262–3
staff
allegations of abuse 44–5
communication with 140–1
cover in absence 290
monitoring 149
relationships with 9, 131
roles and responsibilities 1–6, 258–9
see also responsibilities; role
staff appraisals 149, 154
staff development 155–6, 157–8
staff meetings 141, 147
staff training 155–6, 157–60
stage theory, cognitive development 198
stammering 262
statutory assessment 212, 256
storage 20, 284, 288
medicines 32
records 293–4
strategies
for challenging behaviour 107, 274–5
for encouraging self-esteem 171
for gifted/talented pupils 271
learning support 11–12
for literacy/numeracy 234
medical needs support 37
for physical disabilities 277, 278–9,
280–1
for special educational needs 263–4,
266, 267–8, 268–9
supporting transitions 177
success 172, *172*

summative assessments 211
supervision, for safety 24–5
support
for children in difficulty 47
by teaching assistants *see* role
(teaching assistants)
swimming 189
symptoms, illness 31–2
see also signs

taking turns 62, 79, 164
talented children 270–1, 273
tasks (teaching assistant) 4, 6
see also role
teacher assessments 213
teachers
partnership with 9
roles 1, 2, 258–9
support by teaching assistants 3, 5,
6–15
teamwork 138–40, 145–51
temper tantrums 128–9
tests 212, 291
time management 143
timetables 283
toilet facilities 22
topic webs 208, *209*
toy safety 20
training 155–6, 157–60
transitions 174–9
travel arrangements 295–7
turn-taking 62, 79, 164

UN Convention on the Rights of the
Child 101, 113, 115, 167

vaccinations 30
visitors 27
visual aids 233, 285, 286
visual impairment 277–9
visual learners 203
VITAL play opportunities 185
volunteers 150–1
Vygotsky, L.S. 200

washing facilities 22
water play 190
well-being *see* emotional well-being
whole word approach 228
whooping cough *33*
work surfaces 20
*Working Together to Safeguard Children
2006* 40, 41
Workplace (Health, Safety and Welfare)
Regulations (1992) 18
writing skills 229–31

zone of proximal development 200